Sports fitness
and sports injuries

SPORTS FITNESS AND SPORTS INJURIES

Edited by

THOMAS REILLY

BA, DPE, MSc, PhD, MIBiol

Principal Lecturer in Sports Science, Liverpool Polytechnic
and a British Amateur Athletic Board Senior Coach

With a Foreword by

DICK JEEPS CBE

Chairman, The Sports Council

Wolfe Publishing Ltd

Published by
Wolfe Publishing Ltd
Brook House
2–16 Torrington Place
London WC1E 7LT

Reprinted 1992, by Richard Clay Ltd, Bungay, Suffolk

First published in 1981 by Faber and Faber Limited. Reprinted
1984 and 1985.

ISBN 0 7234 1830 6

For full details of all Wolfe titles please write to Wolfe Publishing
Ltd, Brook House, 2–16 Torrington Place, London WC1E 7LT,
England.

British Library Cataloging in Publication Data

Sports fitness and sports injuries.
1. Sports – Accidents and injuries
I. Reilly, Thomas
617'.1027   RD97

ISBN 0 7234 1830 6

Contents

Section 3
INJURIES IN TEAM GAMES

Section 4
INJURIES IN SELECTED INDIVIDUAL SPORTS

Section 5
ORTHOPAEDIC ASPECTS OF SPORTS INJURIES

Section 6
CONSIDERATIONS AFTER INJURY: TREATMENT

Foreword

Injuries to sportspeople are frequent, and often particularly sad leading to the disappearance from the scene of several bright stars who bring pleasure to millions and prestige to the country. Very often the trained medical expert can work wonders, as indeed can those near magicians sometimes unfairly called 'quacks'.

As a former rugger player and now a golfer, I know exactly what back pain can do to someone who, like myself, enjoys an active life. A book aimed at medical and paramedical practitioners is therefore an important aid and one to be welcomed in an age when increasing numbers of people are accepting responsibility for their own health and fitness and often doing good work at home, with weights and exercise.

All too often, however, these Do-it-Yourself exercise types can and do overdo the training bit. Hanging on doors can be good for some, as back straightening, I've no doubt, but it can complicate the physical condition of the human body. We read about contra-exercises for athletes constantly putting a strain on themselves but few of us can really rate our own fitness level.

Sport and the world of medicine go hand-in-hand and this is right. A book like this, which gathers together experts in the field, is valuable indeed, particularly at a time when drug abuse throughout the world is so prevalent.

After years of preaching the benefits of good health in sport, I'm particularly distressed to see younger people using more and more drugs in almost every area of sport. These people do not realise the damage they are inflicting on themselves as they regard anabolic steroids in the same way as we used to think of boiled sweets.

It's true that the reckless use of drugs in sport has indeed revolutionised many sports during the past fifteen years and those in the business know full well that the fantastic records being set up, often leaping away from the previous non-dope records, have been achieved at the expense of someone's future. Doctors have seen the effect and I think more publicity should be given to the consequences.

As chairman of the Sports Council I am delighted to introduce this book to its responsible readers who, we hope, will have great influence in sport. No matter what the game, we depend on the world of medicine to enable us to continue, and on the best advice from world-wide leaders in this vital field.

DICK JEEPS CBE
Chairman of the Sports Council
1981

Preface

Rather than being regarded as a specialist clinical text on sports injuries, this book is designed to be of use to a variety of practitioners, including general practitioners, physiotherapists, remedial gymnasts, students of medicine and sports science, physical educationists, coaches and physical trainers. The background sporting environment, the mechanism of injury occurrence in sports, the trauma induced and the methods of treatment are spotlighted so that a greater understanding of the problems peculiar to the injured athlete will result.

The subject area is necessarily diverse and starts with a consideration of the human factors which are associated with fitness, freedom from injury and risk probability. The nature and role of physical training occupies the second section with emphasis being placed on the safe development of specific aspects of fitness. The core of the book focuses on how injuries occur in different sports and attention is directed to strategies for their prevention and for safety in performance. As individual sports vary in nature and generate specific hazards as a consequence, these differences are reflected in the various approaches and stances assumed by the respective authors. Similarly, approaches between chapters in the clinical section reflect differences in the complexity of the joints discussed and their susceptibility to sports injuries. The final section concentrates on post-injury phases, methods of treatment and the return to play.

The text is the culmination of a sustained effort to bring together contributions from different disciplines and professions which are concerned with fitness and sports injuries. These include psychology, physiology, orthopaedic surgery, physiotherapy and coaching. Much of the material was presented initially at a series of seminars organised at Liverpool Polytechnic in collaboration with the Association of Chartered Physiotherapists in Sports Medicine. These presentations have been extended and expanded to give the text an overall balance and to embrace the majority of the popular sports. It is hoped that an understanding of the basic problems confronted by the practitioner in dealing with sports injuries is promoted and the highlighting of precursors of injury will encourage preventive practices.

THOMAS REILLY,
Liverpool Polytechnic
1981

Acknowledgements

A number of people have been concerned with the emergence of this book. Vaughan Thomas and Grant Smith were the sowers of the original seed; they promoted the annual series of interdisciplinary meetings which considered the many aspects of sports injuries and from which this text has sprung. All the contributors have made the compilation of the material the easier by their enthusiasm and diligence. Many thanks must be extended to my colleagues at Liverpool Polytechnic for reading selected manuscripts. Without the encouragement of Patricia Downie FCSP, the publisher's editor, a shadow would have fallen between the conception and the creation of this text.

The majority of the line drawings have been produced by Audrey Besterman to whom I extend sincere thanks. I also thank the following for help with illustration: David Bryce for those in Chapter 21; the England Basketball Association for those in Chapter 13; John Shore and Gerry Bishop for Figure 19/2 and John Court for Figure 19/3. Many thanks also to Keith Wilkinson for help with other photographs.

The contribution of the many typists whose hands made the work lighter is recognised as invaluable.

Contributors

I. D. Adams MD
Consultant Physician, Accident and Emergency
  Department
St James' Hospital, Leeds LS9 7TF

J. A. Fowler BA, MCSP, DipTP, SRP, MBIM
Principal, The School of Physiotherapy
The Royal Liverpool Hospital College
Liverpool L7 8XN

Norman Fox MEd, DASE, DPE
Department of Sport and Recreation Studies
Faculty of Science, Liverpool Polytechnic
Liverpool L3 3AF

R. J. Hardiker BSc
Department of Sport and Recreation Studies
Faculty of Science, Liverpool Polytechnic
Liverpool L3 3AF

Warren J. Huffman BA, MA, EdM, EdD
Professor of Health and Safety; Coordinator,
  University of Tennessee Safety Centre
School of Health, Physical Education and Recreation
University of Tennessee, Knoxville,
  Tennessee 37916
Professor Emeritus, Health Education
University of Illinois
Urbana-Champaign, Illinois 61820
United States of America

Bernard I. Loft HSD
Professor of Health and Safety Education *and*
  Director, Centre for Safety Studies
School of Health, Physical Education and Recreation
Indiana University, Bloomington, Indiana 47405
United States of America

Barry T. Maddox BA, MCSP, SRP
Edgbaston Health Clinic
24 Somerset Road, Edgbaston
Birmingham B15 2QD

D. E. Markham FRCS
Consultant Orthopaedic Surgeon
Manchester Royal Infirmary
Manchester M13 9WL

R. J. Maughan BSc, PhD
Department of Surgery, University Medical School
Foresterhill
Aberdeen AB9 2XS

M. McDermott MB, BCh, BAO
Department of Rheumatology
Mater Misericordiae Hospital
Dublin, Ireland

G. R. McLatchie MB, ChB, FRCS, CPSG
Institute of Neurological Sciences, Southern General
  Hospital
Glasgow G51 4TF
and
Medical Adviser, Martial Arts Commission
Medical Officer, Scottish Karate Board of Control

Surgeon Rear-Admiral Stanley Miles CB, MSc,
  MD, FRCP, FRCS
Pear Tree Cottage, Nomansland
Salisbury SP5 2BN
Formerly: Postgraduate Dean, Faculty of Medicine,
  University of Manchester

W. Moore BSc
Department of Sport and Recreation Studies
Faculty of Science, Liverpool Polytechnic
Liverpool L3 3AF
and
National Coach, British Cycling Federation

W. J. Murphy MEd, DPE, DAE
Department of Sport and Recreation Studies
Faculty of Science, Liverpool Polytechnic
Liverpool L3 3AF

Tony O'Neill BSc, MB, BCh, BAO
Medical Officer, Football League of Ireland
Dublin, Ireland

T. Reilly BA, DPE, MSc, PhD, MIBiol
Department of Sport and Recreation Studies
Faculty of Science, Liverpool Polytechnic
Liverpool L3 3AF

J. N. Rimmer MChOrth, FRCS
Accident and Emergency Department
Newsham General Hospital
Liverpool L6 4AF

F. H. Sanderson DCC, BEd, MA, PhD
Department of Sport and Recreation Studies
Faculty of Science, Liverpool Polytechnic
Liverpool L3 3AF

J. J. Shuttleworth DLC, BA, MA, PhD
Department of Sport and Recreation Studies
Faculty of Science, Liverpool Polytechnic
Liverpool L3 3AF

Valerie Steele MCSP, SRP
Physiotherapy Department
St James' Hospital, Leeds LS9 7TF

Vaughan Thomas DLC, MSc, PhD, DMS,
    AMBIM, FPEA
Department of Sport and Recreation Studies
Faculty of Science, Liverpool Polytechnic
Liverpool L3 3AF

Lisle Thompson TD, MChOrth, FRCS
Consultant Orthopaedic Surgeon
Fazakerley Hospital
Liverpool L9 7AL

J. D. G. Troup PhD, MRCS, LRCP
University Department of Orthopaedic and Accident
    Surgery
Royal Liverpool Hospital
Liverpool L7 8XP

Leon Walkden MRCS, LRCP
Honorary Medical Officer, Rugby Football Union
Twickenham, Middlesex

W. H. George Wilkinson DMS, MPhil
Course Leader, BA Sport Studies,
Newcastle upon Tyne Polytechnic
Newcastle upon Tyne NE1 8ST

Dennis Wright MCSP, DipTP, SRP
Area Superintendent Physiotherapist, Rochdale Area
    Health Authority
The Infirmary, Rochdale OL12 0NB
and
Physiotherapist, Great Britain Rugby League

SECTION 1

Fitness and sports injuries: the human factor

CHAPTER 1

Fitness within sport

VAUGHAN THOMAS DLC, MSc, PhD, DMS, AMBIM, FPEA

The generally held view of fitness for sport includes concepts such as the ability to reach high levels of performance, and the ability to withstand the stresses imposed on the sportsman by his participation. These two concepts are closely linked, but do lead to contextual applications which may generate conflicting aims and objectives in the minds of those who are concerned with the acquisition of fitness by sportsmen. In particular, increasing levels of performance are accompanied frequently by increasing levels of stress on the performer. If fitness to perform is improved without a simultaneous enhancement of fitness to withstand competition stress, the performer is prone to become overstressed. In other words, the result is that the individual is strained or injured.

Clearly therefore, the development of sport fitness in training must include injury preventive elements, since the occurrence of injuries is counter-productive in performance terms. The fitness status at which training is initiated may lie anywhere along the continuum of fitness, and is often temporarily depressed by injury. Rehabilitation from a sports injury is a special example of fitness training, but is still subject to the same criteria and principles as normal fitness training.

TOTAL FITNESS

The majority of those who participate in sport, whether as trainers, players, spectators or others, have an imperfect and narrow view of what constitutes total fitness in sport. Most of those who participate actively, that is the trainers and players, are not educated in the theory of sport, and are unqualified in a formal sense for the task of achieving optimal fitness. The professional preparation even of qualified coaches and trainers, in this country and many others, is sadly deficient in the general theory of sport fitness and methods of achieving fitness. National governing bodies of sport tend to concentrate on sport techniques and tactics in the training of coaches, and make little provision for the education of players. Attempts are currently being made to rectify this situation by the introduction of diploma and postgraduate degree courses in coaching theory and practice.

The major parameters of fitness in a modern performance context are:

strength – the ability to exert force.
speed – the ability to react and/or move quickly. This includes an optimal degree of joint mobility.
stamina – the ability to maintain function over time.
skill – the ability to select and execute effective and efficient methods of achieving sporting objectives.
spirit – the ability to optimally motivate performance.
sports medicine – the avoidance or minimising of injurious effects of competition and training stress.

While identifying these parameters separately, it is quite apparent that they are integrated completely in the sport performance. Strength cannot be viewed in isolation in a sport context. It must manifest itself for example in movement, e.g. speed; in isometric positions, e.g. stamina; in extreme positions, e.g. suppleness; in difficult manoeuvres, e.g. skill; with explosive determination, e.g. spirit; and without or despite injury, e.g. sports medicine. Similar links can be established between all the parameters, and fitness training programmes must reflect the concept of integration between them. The achievement of this integration is an extremely complex matter, involving constant optimisation of interaction between training elements, and frequent assessment of comparative priorities of different parameters.

Of particular importance in the sports injury context is the part played by stamina. It should be appreciated that the capacity of a given function to cope with stress fluctuates during the competitive event. Particularly during phases of fatigue, there will be a diminishing of functional capacity which may fall below the level required to avoid strain. This phenomenon occurs during both local (or specific) fatigue and general fatigue. Local and general stamina (or endurance) training is an essential element of training for all sports, even those which would not be classed as endurance sports. In the latter case, the training routines for short duration sports may constitute a considerable test of endurance – quite apart from the endurance demands of repeated performances of a short duration activity during a competition. For example, a weightlifter's activity is of very short duration, but the training sessions demand considerable endurance – as also does a competition, where the warm-up and series of competitive lifts generate significant levels of local fatigue.

TRAINING

An effective total fitness training programme should include elements catering for all fitness parameters. The prevention of, or rehabilitation from, sports injuries includes a large element of what may be termed 'physical medicine'. The aims of physical medicine in this context may be in terms of strength, speed, stamina, skill and spirit. The physical medicine component of sports medicine is allied with other components, for example prophylactic, psychiatric, pharmaceutical. The total sports medical package should be thoughtfully integrated and the most desirable approach to the sports fitness/injury prevention may be achieved by the team approach (Fig. 1/1).

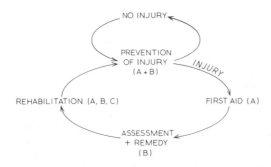

Fig. 1/1 The team approach to sports injuries
A=Coach: B=Sports medical specialist:
C=Physiotherapist

Figure 1/1 illustrates the basic concept of the preventive measures of sports medicine leading to the non-occurrence of injury. The responsibility for prevention is shared between the coach and the doctor. Despite insightful prevention, injury may occur. First aid in the great majority of cases is undertaken by the players and/or the coach. This first aid is largely unqualified, usually idiosyncratic and superstitious, and frequently harmful. A fundamental necessity in the process of achieving and maintaining sporting fitness is proper sports first aid personnel. In most cases, the coach is the most feasible person to be trained to provide effective first aid.

The assessment of an injury and the prescription of immediate and successive remedy should be, in all except trivial cases, the business of a sports medical specialist. These specialists can be distinguished by their great scarcity, and by their difficulty of access to sportsmen. It ought to be the practice of all sports organisations to institute systems of immediate access to specialist medical attention. In very few instances is this practice a reality.

The rehabilitation of the injured sportsman must be a concerted effort involving the coach and doctor, and on many occasions the exercise therapist – either physiotherapist or remedial gymnast. There should be communication between these, and agreement on the aim of sport rehabilitation – which is to facilitate the return of the player to training and competition at as high a standard and in as short a time as the specific priorities of each player determine. It is perhaps superfluous to comment that this team-work in sports medicine generally, and rehabilitation particularly, is almost always distinguishably absent.

NORMAL STRESS

The stresses which, by virtue of being more powerful than the ability of the sportsman to withstand them, cause injuries may be classified into normal and abnormal. These apply both to acute and chronic stresses. Normal stresses may be defined as those which have a significant probability of occurrence during sporting activities. As usual in medical statistics, the level of significance will be determined by the critical nature of the injury which may be caused by the stress. If partial rupture of the hamstrings is sufficiently common in sprint running, and is such a critical injury as to prevent further competition for such a period of time as is likely to upset the competitive programme of the runner, then the causative stresses of hamstring rupture may be defined as 'normal' in sprinting. At the other extreme, peripheral soft tissue injuries suffered by professional soccer players who become the targets of missiles thrown by irate supporters are so infrequent, and of such little disabling effect, that they would fall outside the definition of 'normal' in a soccer context.

The implication of this classification for the fitness training of sportsmen is clear. Trainers should have clearly defined objectives which are stated in terms of the normal stresses of the sport, embracing both the achievement of excellent performance and the avoidance of injury. The training programme should be designed to equip the sportsman to deal successfully with these stresses. By definition, the training programme does not need to include elements which cater for abnormal stresses, except for a general training described later.

The relationship between the two training elements of performance and stress is not always obvious to the trainer. Some stresses are inherent in the performance itself, and are proportional to the level of performance. Of these some are exacerbated by the increased intensity of performance without the increased fitness operating as a preventive; for example, the degenerative effects of deep squat heavy weightlifting on the articular cartilage of the knee are proportionate to the amount and intensity of such lifting performed. On the other hand, others are prevented by the increasing fitness generated by the increased activity. An example of this phenomenon is the effect of increasing levels of performance on the ability of the cardiac muscle and circulation to cope with the increased stress.

Other stresses are not inherent in the performance itself, but are the product of a breakdown in performance caused either by a lack of fitness or by external forces which are not anticipated. The first of these present the trainer with the problem of developing the fitness of the performer in advance of the demands of competition, that is, to give the performer a level of fitness which is greater than that required for even maximal competition and thereby provide a margin of safety. Since all competitive performance involves an integration of many performance elements, it is very rare for any single element to operate at maximum even though the integration may be maximal. By carefully structuring training programmes, it is possible to isolate each major element of the performance, and stress it maximally by controlled overload. In many instances training is harder than competition.

Competitive strain from abnormal, unanticipated stresses is by definition impossible to plan for in training. If the stress is unanticipated its prediction cannot form the basis of a training plan. On the other hand, a 'general avoidance skill' can be developed in training. Such skill involves the development of awareness to danger, practice of avoidance manoeuvres, and effective use of stress absorption techniques. The Brazilian national football team includes training in gymnastic manoeuvres for this purpose. Figure 1/2 shows the subdivisions of stress.

The competitive requirements of sportsmen need to be analysed carefully from a stress viewpoint so that training programmes can be devised which will cater specifically for each of the categories of stress. Just as a failure to achieve high levels of performance may be viewed as a defect in an athlete's potential or in his training, so may the occurrence of a sports injury be seen as a defect in an athlete's basic medical integrity or in his training.

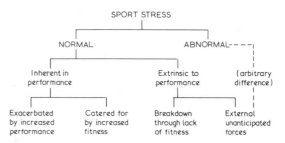

Fig. 1/2 Major subdivisions of sport stress as injury causation

MOTIVATION

Sportsmen may compete for a variety of reasons, ranging from intense aggression and ambition to mild socialisation and well-being. Their motivation for competing may vary, therefore, both in intensity and in kind. When recuperating from an injury the treatment that a sportsman receives must be responsive to his personal motivations. Two extreme examples of this moderation of rehabilitation may be considered.

The first example would be a middle-aged sedentary person participating in sport mainly as a means of developing positive health. If such a sportsman suffered an acute injury to the Achilles tendon, the treatment should be conservative and accompanied by a lengthy period of rest in order to avoid the development of a chronic tendinitis since that would be counter-productive in health terms.

The second example would be a mature world class runner suffering a similar injury a few weeks before his last Olympic Games prior to retirement – with a significant chance of winning a gold medal. In that case many an athlete would choose to receive the most radical treatment, with no break in training, even if he realised that there was a high probability of incurring a severe chronic tendinitis which might necessitate a subsequent tendon strip.

Sports medicine, or rather the medical treatment of sportsmen, is bedevilled by an unsympathetic and unenlightened attitude from many practitioners. They should point out the risks of radical treatment to the intensely motivated sportsman, but should allow the sportsman to decide whether the risk is compatible with the rewards he seeks.

Such intense motivation on the part of a rehabilitating sportsman not only modifies the normal safety margins of conservative treatment, but also may affect significantly the normal recovery time from injuries. Particularly in cases where recovery is dependent upon initial fitness status, and upon the degree of effort in rehabilitation by the patient, sportsmen may decimate the normal recuperative period.

It has long been a medical precept that it is the patient who should be treated rather than the disease. Patients are individuals. In the case of fitness for sport, both preventive and remedial medical practice should be based on an enlightened attitude to the needs of competitors (of their specific sports and their specific personae), and an understanding of the place of medical treatment within the training programmes of sportsmen. This can only be achieved by a conscious and concerted effort by competitors, trainers/coaches, administrators, doctors and paramedical practitioners to inform and learn from one another. All must realise that fitness for sport and the training programmes which develop fitness, involve not only the concept of 'capacity for activity', but also the concept of 'freedom from injury'.

CHAPTER 2

A formula for health

STANLEY MILES CB, MSc, MD, FRCP, FRCS

HEALTH

Health can be defined as 'the ability of an individual to mobilise his resources, physical, mental and spiritual, to the preservation and advantage of himself, his dependants and the society to which he belongs'. Health is thus a state of preparedness for activity to ensure personal survival and achievement while at the same time safeguarding human relationships, especially in the family.

The way in which a person uses this ability is not necessarily one which will be beneficial and is of course influenced by many personal and environmental factors. However, such is man's 'make up' that continuing misuse of resources will result in their deterioration with failing health and ultimate destruction.

The ability to mobilise resources advantageously is therefore dependent upon the extent and quality of those resources which accordingly reflect the degree of 'health'. Where resources are inadequate they cannot be successfully mobilised and ill-health results.

Resources

Resources are either inherited or acquired. At conception the fertilised ovum is provided with a genetic blueprint for its development embodying characteristic trends from both parents and their ancestors. The fertilised ovum is thus the investment for the survival of the species and a manifestation of the immortality of protoplasm.

The genetic blueprint, it must be emphasised, is designed for living in a wholly natural environment in which survival is largely dependent on physical strength and swift reactions. Physical resources, providing adequate nutrition is available, are programmed for activity. Without activity atrophy is inevitable. Thus, in an affluent society, where there is a lessening demand for physical effort, the built-in drive, designed to maintain an adequate muscular growth, must, unless met by satisfying planned activity such as sport, lead to aggression and violence. Life itself is the ongoing manifestation of the continuing inflow of energy from the sun to the earth in biological evolution. Man

absorbs an almost measurable amount of energy from food and oxygen whose intake is somewhat automatic. His metabolism demands the expenditure in positive activity of sufficient energy to balance the equation. Man's physical resources thus provide an extensive and highly efficient locomotor system with groups of muscles in a highly mobile skeletal system crying out for regular and coordinated usage under the strict control of an equally advanced nervous system both reflex and conscious. Much activity is provided in everyday contact with the environment though this may be less demanding with mechanical alternatives to human effort. Thus if the physical resources are to be maintained at an optimal standard their continuing exercise must be assured.

Unfortunately, health has been regarded as synonymous with physical or muscular development; 'physical fitness' being the key to good health. Equally important, however, are the sensory organs of the body whose care and exercise is essential to ensure the smooth and continuing acceptance of a summated sensory intake from the environment. Such a sensory input is necessary for the efficient working of both the mental and spiritual resources.

Similarly, mental resources are programmed in the genetic blueprint for survival of the individual, to assess the promises and threats of the sensory intake, to secure food and shelter, to find a mate and to provide for children. Experience from generations of trial and error and an ability to cooperate with other members of the species have produced exceptional development of mental resources. This has enabled man to exploit for his advantage the extensive potential of the natural environment. Storage and re-call of information, memory, is one of man's greatest assets enabling him to accumulate knowledge and use it in coordinating incoming data with outgoing motor activity. Muscular response, vocal communication, the use of equipment and technology are the direct results of mobilising his advanced mental resources.

Mental resources are today becoming of greater personal importance than the physical ones. If the human race is to survive it must ensure that a reasoned use of motor energy is maintained by controlled activity to avoid outbursts of violence. Mental and physical resources are entirely complementary and must be exercised together. To maintain health each must be exposed to a minimum standard of usage.

Finally the third resource, 'spiritual', is the most difficult to define and yet the most important. However much mental resources may develop, each person maintains a unique individuality. To what extent spiritual resources are influenced by the genetic blueprint is not known but curiosity most certainly is an inherited human trait.

The spiritual aspect of life is found in attachment to a creed or code of practice, in beliefs which are stepping stones to truth, and a faith that there is some finite purpose in living. It is manifest in motivation and maturity, in affectionate regard for others, and an appreciation of the responsibility to use the more tangible resources not only for self-preservation but for the advantage of dependants and fellow human beings. It is a commitment to competitive and abundant living sometimes described by sportsmen as 'heart'.

In an age where man is caught up in the turbulent wake of advancing technology he becomes increasingly dependent on the strength and integrity of his spiritual resources.

The assessment of health

Medicine has been more concerned with the treatment of the sick than the care of the healthy and the assessment of health has been more concerned with physical examination for fitness for specific activities, e.g. service in the Forces, strenuous games, hazardous occupations, routine examinations for life insurance. More recently regular screening for specific illness such as cancer and heart disease has gained popularity with executive personnel in industry and others with specific responsibility.

In the field of sport, particularly the professional, assessment is important both in the maintenance of an ongoing standard of health and as a check on fitness immediately before competition. Boxing provides us with a good example.

Today, there is an increasing need for a wide acceptance and availability of health assessment, a need to divert some proportion of medical expertise away from the sick to the healthy as a more positive approach to preventive medicine. Any examination however will only reveal the health at the moment of investigation and follow-up is essential, i.e. assessment followed by regular monitoring. Screening, if presented as the sole object, may produce hypochondriacs. It should be no more than a bonus of the assessment and monitoring programme ensuring that where necessary a small proportion of those examined would be referred to conventional medicine for investigation and any necessary treatment.

Full health evaluation must include a wide range of physical tests for all systems, motor, sensory, metabolic and coordination with considerable aptitude testing, i.e. practical tests of the ability to mobilise resources for a variety of realistic tasks. Biochemical, haematological, radiological and other laboratory procedures are available to assist the examiner. Complete examination of the nervous system must be supplemented with investigations of mental aptitude, memory and decision making. Psychological probing can be valuable and revealing, particularly with a confident and confidential person-to-person session.

Finally, the spiritual resources must be considered with a frank assessment of the quality of life; affectionate regard for others; status, wealth, possessions and achievement; skill and knowledge, motivation and morale; attitudes to work, rest and recreation, and above all faith and philosophy. A simple scoring system could be adopted for the whole investigation and all the results used to form a basic profile for subsequent monitoring. Correlation can frequently be found and maintained between the profile and the continuing life style.

ILL-HEALTH

When resources cannot be mobilised to maintain survival and they themselves deteriorate or are damaged, ill-health is assumed. Without therapeutic intervention this state will progressively worsen.

The resources are, however, interdependent and failure in one area can be compensated by increased support from elsewhere. For example, gross physical deformities can be overcome by mental re-adjustment and spiritual strength so that a handicapped person can maintain good health. Man's diseases can similarly be compensated for, and life enjoyed with advantage.

The maintenance of health throughout the normal life span can only be impaired by birth deformities, malnutrition, ageing, illness and injury. In the developing and productive years of life it is illness and injury which are largely responsible for ill-health and death. Prevention is therefore closely associated with health assessment and medical services might well re-orientate their activities to health maintenance with facilities for active intervention when things go wrong, i.e. a new and positive dimension in health care.

For practical purposes illness and injury can be considered together. Each may produce distress, pain, disability and tissue damage. Each involves the whole person and each demands assessment, therapeutic intervention and appropriate rehabilitation. Each involves personal and environmental factors and the influence of chance. Each invites an epidemiological approach to control and elimination.

If man is to enjoy the health which gives him, his dependants and society continuing advantage he must find a compromise to his dual role. On the one hand he is a very private and unique individual with innate urges of aggressive selfishness seeking advantage for himself. On the other hand he is a member of a constantly changing and often hazardous environment of which his fellow men are also active participants. His health thus depends on the sympathetic interplay of three forces (Fig. 2/1). This gives the pattern for

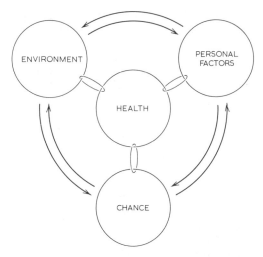

Fig. 2/1 Interplay of forces determining health

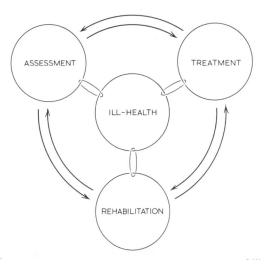

Fig. 2/2 Interplay of action in the management of ill-health

epidemiological investigation, with the maintenance of health in mind, of illness or injury.

Similarly, taking the individual as the starting point for management of illness or injury, i.e. ill-health, a similar pattern emerges (Fig. 2/2).

THE ACCIDENT (INJURY OR ILLNESS) EQUATION

The use of the word 'accident' ('an untoward event without apparent cause') is perhaps unfortunate but it is nevertheless generally accepted as involving injury. In the sporting world 'injury' is a more formal and acceptable term as indeed it would be in any epidemiological investigation. The formula, equally applicable to injury and illness is:

$$I = CE \frac{p\,r\,f}{t\,m\,s}$$

where 'I' represents the incident, injury, illness or even accident; 'C' represents chance and 'E' the environment, both of which may be favourable or unfavourable as far as the cause of the incident is concerned.

Factors which are known to be contributory are **p, r** and **f** which respectively represent accident proneness, risk acceptance and personal failings which are usually temporary.

Lessening the impact of the situation and helping towards prevention are **t, m** and **s**, signifying training, maturity and safety precautions. These like **p, r** and **f** are the personal factors represented in Figure 2/1.

This equation is more symbolic than mathematical but it can be modified to allow a scoring procedure for an incident research programme. The interpretation is made on the following lines and is particularly applicable to sporting activities.

Chance
Chance is the random coincidence of time and place. It plays a vital part in both physical and biological evolution and adds much to the interest and excitement of sport and recreation. Experience can help estimate the probability of events but the purely random factors cannot be forecast. If they could, life and evolution would come to a grinding halt!

As far as injury is concerned in the United Kingdom the average person has, in any week, an 8 000 to 1 chance against being seriously injured. Injury however gives no protection as far as chance is concerned and the odds remain the same for the survivor in subsequent weeks.

Environment
The environment is natural or man made. The former includes all the hazards of land, sea, air and outer

space. Some areas may not even sustain life. Animal and vegetable life is also an essential part of the natural environment and includes man himself.

The man-made environment is of great significance including shelter, work place, sports arena and the many agents associated with modern life, weapons, vehicles, machines, clothing and so on. Man may come to terms with his environment and use its properties for safety and survival or on the other hand he may be caught by its hazards and succumb to injury or disaster. He may create a personal environment or 'with-around' of protective clothing and life-support systems to improve his chances of survival. In sport the breathing apparatus and suit of the underwater swimmer is a good example.

Personal factors

Accident proneness ($\mathbf{p}$) is currently a reality. Increased vulnerability to accident and injury (and indeed illness) is common in a society where the pace of life leads to frustration, anxiety, and instability.

The normal reaction of a healthy man to an emergency, sudden threat or crisis is a natural call on reserves with adrenaline output, increase in heart rate and respiration, improved muscle tone and sensory awareness, i.e. an increased state of readiness with anxiousness and anticipation, which returns to normal after the crisis has passed. However, in conditions of continuing stress and harassment the reserves are already in demand. When the further crisis occurs there is little left to call upon and in extreme cases the result is panic, a common prelude to accident and injury.

The acceptance of risk ($\mathbf{r}$) is a natural human characteristic. In the crudest situation, risks are taken for survival, to obtain food, and for mating. In a more rational society they are taken for personal gain, for praise and adulation or simply for the thrill and enjoyment of the experience, i.e. for fortune, fame or fun.

Risk taking is a very personal factor influenced largely by local opportunities and responsibilities. In sport it is available at all levels from gentle activities to dangerous highly competitive events such as car and motor-bike racing. High risk sports attract high rewards, glamour and real excitement. The dangers are accepted but codes of practice offer some protection.

Many other human factors or personal failings ($\mathbf{f}$) increase vulnerability to injury. Most of these are temporary, such as illness, the incubation or post-febrile state of an infection, alcohol, drugs, hangover, hunger, fatigue, anger and the day-to-day physical and emotional upsets which are so common. The performance of a sportsman can be greatly reduced by such occurrences and the likelihood of injury increased.

Training ($\mathbf{t}$) is fundamental to any human activity and is possibly the most important single factor. It is closely associated with health. A person in good health is able to be trained for almost any activity. In the wide variety of sports, training may demand attention to selected muscle groups and reflexes but at all times this must be supported by a high standard of efficiency in all physical, mental and spiritual systems to achieve the best results.

Maturity ($\mathbf{m}$) is not just the experience gained with age but a state of high motivation and understanding which ensures a coordinated and productive use of resources. Economy of effort aids endurance and emotional stability ensures success. Skills are more flexible and adapt with ease to changing circumstances and demands. In sport, maturity may follow the physical triumphs of youthful endeavour to give help and example to the less experienced.

Finally, the safety precautions ($\mathbf{s}$) or codes of practice are at the end of the list. Though essential for the protection of learners, the young and the elderly, they must be applied with care lest they interfere with production and enjoyment. All too often in a highly competitive commercial world they are used in place of training. Employers may also be pressed to take excessive precautions for fear of litigation. In sport a compromise is needed and usually achieved by introducing rules which give equal opportunity to all competitors, fair play and a degree of personal safety to encourage adequate participation.

Safety precautions are but one area in a wide range of personal, environmental and chance factors. In the investigation of injuries in sport and elsewhere there is invariably evidence of the summation of many predisposing factors with one being responsible for the final nudge into catastrophe. Unfortunately many investigations seek to apportion blame and fail to look beyond the immediate cause to the background of events which gradually build up to the final critical pattern.

A FORMULA FOR HEALTH

Life is an ongoing positive experience and too much attention to illness, injury and prevention may detract from enjoyment and achievement. In seeking better health and quality of life it is possible to apply the same factors with advantage. Only the simplest change in the formula is needed thus – with 'H' for health substituted for 'I':

$$H = CE \frac{t \, m \, s}{p \, r \, f}$$

The formula is applicable to any human activity and ideal for sporting and recreational occupations.

If man's genetic blueprint demands a continuing

state of good health, all systems – physical, mental and spiritual – must be exercised in harmony. Where much of the physical activity associated with productive work is being replaced by machines and technology, rewarding alternatives must be found. Sport, recreation and adventure activities will be increasingly necessary to ensure the well-being and quality of life for the human race.

The maintenance of health is essential. It can and must be given absolute priority.

CHAPTER 3

The aetiology of injury

D. E. MARKHAM FRCS

A clear appreciation of the manner in which a disease or condition develops is of paramount importance in its diagnosis. While this is true of all conditions it is particularly important in the diagnosis and management of sporting injuries where a detailed and accurate understanding of the aetiology of a particular injury forms the corner-stone of its diagnosis and subsequent management. In order to facilitate this understanding it is important that anyone involved in the management of sporting injuries should have an appreciation of the activities undertaken by individual sportsmen in different fields at relatively close quarters. This should involve an understanding of the athlete's training as well as his performance. It is fortunate that most athletes and sportsmen have a far greater proprioceptive awareness than other individuals, which can be invaluable in attempting to evaluate the complexity of individual injuries.

There are three basic categories of sporting activity, each of which has its own different and unique medical problems.

PHYSICAL CONTACT SPORTS

These require an understanding of the various injuries which can be sustained by physical contact as well as a detailed awareness of the individual function of a player within a team. This is well illustrated in the game of soccer where defensive players 'attack the attacker' while attacking players 'attack the ball'. This must be partly responsible for the greater preponderance of injuries sustained by attacking and mid-field players noted in recent surveys of injuries sustained in this particular sport.

INDIVIDUAL PERFORMANCE ACTIVITIES

These demand a performance from the musculo-skeletal system approaching the point of biochemical, physiological and mechanical fatigue. The point of fatigue is undoubtedly related to training schedules prior to competition but when the individual athlete demands a performance beyond the physiological or mechanical limit of an individual muscle or muscle group he is likely to sustain an injury in that area which is entirely related to those self-induced and excessive demands.

REPETITIVE TRAINING INJURIES

These are common to all athletes and have the tendency to be chronic in nature. They may be related to badly designed training schedules, unsatisfactory equipment used during training (this is particularly pertinent in terms of footwear used during training) and pursuing long training schedules in an environment which is not conducive to such activity. Inflammation around the Achilles tendon is a common problem which is invariably related to badly organised training schedules in sportsmen who wear unsatisfactory footwear and who run for long distances on hard surfaces to which they are not accustomed.

INJURIES RELATED TO TYPE OF ACTIVITY

In general terms, sportsmen involved in physical contact sports tend to suffer fractures, acute ligament injuries and massive haematomata in skeletal muscle, all of which are common sequelae of violent contact between competitors or result from subsequent falls. In contrast, individual performers suffer from acute muscle strains and sprains caused by competitive performances which drive individual muscles or muscle groups beyond the point of physiological and mechanical fatigue. Training injuries usually take the form of chronic tendinitis and are often precipitated by a change in training regime or develop during early training sessions at the beginning of a sporting season where the schedules are too demanding for the individual's overall state of fitness at the time. This is particularly true in the pre-season fitness training of soccer and rugby players who are often invited to undertake sprinting activities on hard, unyielding grounds or tracks and who subsequently develop chronic tenosynovitis around the ankles and feet.

ASSESSMENT

A fair understanding of the sportsman's normal training and competitive activities is of invaluable assistance in assessing the aetiology of an individual sporting injury.

A particular injury should be assessed in terms of the athlete's activity in three phases surrounding the injury itself. His activity immediately before the injury must be analysed in detail. In addition to his physical activity, this must also include a psychological assessment noting the degree of competition, aggression, fear or other emotion which the individual felt just before the injury happened. An understanding of the individual's mental attitude is important, since this can have a profound influence on the musculo-skeletal system and the way in which it responds subconsciously to potential impact or sudden excessive demands upon it. In assessing this phase of activity, it is useful to ask specific questions notably about the individual's control with reference to his balance and foothold. He should also be questioned about his relationship with other competitors and their combined activity immediately before his injury. Was he wholly committed to a particular course of action before the injury or did he have an opportunity to opt out and avoid potential harm? To what extent was he competing in this phase, since it is well recognised that intense competition often overrides physical ability and can strain the physical resources of an athlete to the point of injury?

A detailed analysis of the events happening at the precise moment of injury should then be attempted. This must include the spacial relationships of his limbs in relation to other competitors or in relation to any apparatus which he or she is using at the time. He should then be questioned about the presence or absence of acute pain at the time of injury and whether or not he experienced any mechanical interference with his performance. Did he feel a tearing sensation in his muscles? Did the torn meniscus within his knee joint prevent free movement of the joint? Was there any loss of sensation in the limb?

This middle phase merges almost imperceptibly with the third phase of activity which is that immediately following injury. He must be questioned about the degree and distribution of pain, his inability to continue the pre-injury activity, the development of any swelling or bruising and whether his symptoms in this third phase became more or less severe with continued involvement. It must be remembered that continuing sporting commitment in the presence of aggression, achievement and spectator involvement can often lead to a lack of appreciation of severe injury by the athlete until after the game. Conversely, relatively trivial training injuries can impinge upon conscious pain thresholds when such psychological stimulants are absent.

Consideration of symptoms immediately after the injury usually involves a recognition by the athlete that all is not well. This is very much related to an appreciation of pain and limitation of activity. It must be appreciated that pain is a warning that 'all is not well' and that there is no excuse for the old and dangerous phrases such as 'it is only pain'. Pain is a symptom, a warning and should be respected and investigated. It is essential that an accurate second by second assessment of the three phases of activity surrounding and including an injury should be made in order to reach an accurate diagnosis. It is often necessary to re-appraise these phases of activity on several occasions with the individual athlete before a clear understanding of the problem is reached. Without this understanding coupled with detailed physical examination, dangerous or ineffective management may be instituted.

PRE-REQUISITES FOR MANAGEMENT OF INJURY

The accurate and expeditious treatment of sporting injuries depends upon an equally accurate diagnosis which can only be made by a detailed appreciation of the aetiology of a specific injury. This has an essential bearing on its eventual successful management. Sporting activity is often complex and is a combination of controlled, often complex, physical and psychological activities. It is only by detailed appreciation of the complexities of individual sporting activity, coupled with a detailed understanding of factors leading up to an individual injury, that one can arrive at a correct diagnosis which in turn is vital to expeditious treatment and restoration of full function.

It should be possible for a physiotherapist or doctor with a knowledge of musculo-skeletal anatomy and physiology coupled with an appreciation of sporting activities to be able to make an accurate assessment of a particular injury through a knowledge of its aetiology combined with physical examination of the patient. Many errors in management of sporting injuries are made by failing to take a detailed and accurate history of the development of the individual problem before physical examination is undertaken. This is particularly unfortunate since expeditious management of sporting injuries is important not only in terms of the individual's desire to regain full fitness, but mainly because musculo-skeletal injuries are often most successfully treated when they are in the acute phase. Expeditious treatment, however, should always be directed towards the individual's well-being and not towards ambition or commercial considerations.

An accurate assessment of the aetiology of sporting injuries demands an appreciation of the individual athlete's sporting category, notably whether this involves physical contact or individual competition since these involve specific types of injury.

An accurate detailed history should be taken of the individual's activity immediately before, during and immediately after the injury was sustained. This history should embody an enquiry into the athlete's physical control, relationship with other competitors and the degree of psychological commitment coupled with the presence or absence of pain and the degree of mechanical interference with mobility at the time of injury.

There should be no commitment to continued activity in the presence of pain since this is an indication of dysfunction, nor should there be any attempt to treat the injury until an accurate diagnosis based upon the aetiology of the injury coupled with physical examination has been made. An accurate appreciation of the aetiology of an injury is an aid to its early diagnosis and expeditious treatment.

CHAPTER 4

The psychology of the injury-prone athlete

F. H. SANDERSON DCC, BEd, MA, PhD

Detailed appraisal of the literature on injury-proneness reveals that the syndrome has a multitude of possible causes which can also interact in complex ways. The concern here is primarily with those sports' participants who are injury-prone partly or largely because of the effect of psychological influences. Even then this does not represent a homogeneous group, as the psychological variables operating are both numerous and complex, and can have many different repercussions.

Initially, the experimental evidence about the psychological antecedents of real injury will be discussed. In the second section the role of unconscious motives which can underlie real and imagined injury is examined.

EXPERIMENTAL APPROACHES TO INJURY-PRONENESS

Experimental attempts to identify the correlates of injury-proneness did not begin until the 1960s. One of the earliest studies by Goven and Koppenhaver (1965) concentrated on psychological factors and found that neurotic college athletes were no more injury-prone than those without this tendency.

Kraus and Gullen (1969) conducted a large-scale epidemiological investigation of predictor variables associated with intramural touch football injuries. Age, kind of job (active or sedentary) and history of injury were identified as significant predictors but personality traits were not found to be related to injury susceptibility. Similarly, Brown (1971) was unable to discriminate between injured and non-injured athletes on the basis of trait scores on the California Personality Inventory.

More recent investigations however have suggested that personality factors may be related to injury-proneness. Jackson et al (1978), after finding no relationship between joint flexibility and joint injuries among various groups of athletes, examined the potential of the Cattell 16PF for predicting football injuries. Non-injured and injured players could be differentiated on Factor I, tender-minded players being more likely to be injured. These investigators acknowledged that frequency of play was not controlled in the non-injured group and that tender-minded players are intrinsically more likely to seek medical attention for injury. Reilly (1975) also used the Cattell 16PF but with professional soccer players, and found a relationship between Factor O (apprehensiveness) and the number of joint injuries sustained in a season. These findings seem to be complementary and post hoc explanations might well converge on the association of anxiety-based indecisiveness and injury susceptibility. Jackson et al (1978) also found that Cattell's Factor A was related to severity of injury, in that those players who were the most reserved and detached tended to have the most severe injury.

These trait investigations have been complemented by the study of Bramwell et al (1975) into the effect of psychological states on injury-proneness. Specifically, they examined the relationship between athletic injuries and experience of stressful life events as identified by the Social and Athletic Readjustment Rating Scale. A sample of 82 American football players indicated the incidence and kind of life events which demanded coping behaviour in the two-year period prior to the season under study. An individual accumulated Life Change Units (LCU) based on an estimate of how stressful were the events (death in the family, troubles with the head coach, etc) he had experienced. At the end of the playing season, players were divided into non-injured and injured groups. The results of the analysis are presented in Table 1 (see page 32).

It is clear that the injured players had accumulated significantly more LCU in both the one-year and two-year periods prior to the season. When the players were categorised into low, moderate and high-risk groups according to LCU magnitude, it was found that 30 per cent of low risk, 50 per cent of moderate risk, and 73 per cent of high risk players experienced significant time-loss through injury. As to why these relationships exist, Bramwell et al (1975) suggested that preoccupation with life change might affect concentration on the game and enhance the likelihood of injury. Also, they argued that life change stress could lead to a blocking of adaptive responses in potentially dangerous game situations.

It is generally accepted that many injuries could be

Table 1 Mean Life Change Units of injured and non-injured groups (Bramwell et al, 1975; reproduced from *Journal of Human Stress*, **1**, 6–20, by permission of the editor)

	1 Year score	2 Year score
Injured (N=36)	632 (range 142–2 260)	1 008 (range 299–3 900)
Non-injured (N=46)	494 (range 150–1 552)	797 (range 296–1 972)
Mean difference	138 (p ⪅ 0.05)*	211 (p ⪅ 0.05)*

* Student's t-test

avoided if participants were more perceptually aware and able to recognise and negotiate these potentially dangerous situations. Presumably with this in mind, Pargman and his associates have examined the relationships between perceptual style and injury in groups of American football players. Pargman (1976), using the Group Hidden Figures Test (GHFT), found that a non-injured group of players had a significantly greater visual disembedding ability than a group of injured players. Pargman et al (1976) however, found no relationship between incidence of injury in football and field dependence-independence as measured by the Rod and Frame Test. The fact that the GHFT and the Rod and Frame Test are measuring different aspects of perceptual style may account for the apparently contradictory results. It should also be noted that Pargman's (1976) results were obtained from a relatively small sample.

Several authors have offered reasons why the results of experimental investigations of injury-predictor variables have been equivocal. Haddon (1966) and Jackson et al (1978) noted that injury is a result of a complex interaction of many variables such as type of sport, level of competition, equipment used, experience, coaching technique, playing conditions, and the athlete's physical and personality characteristics. Taerk (1977) also mentioned degree of 'exposure', characteristics of the opponent and psychosocial factors, as relevant parameters. Jackson et al (1978) suggested that 'lack of awareness of surroundings' and pain threshold/tolerance should be considered. No study to date has attempted to monitor all these variables, or to control them.

Taerk (1977) and Jackson et al (1978) observed that groups of athletes being investigated are of necessity biased samples in that many injury-prone individuals have already been selected out. This restriction in range can cause radical reductions in the correlations between injury and the predictor variables.

Realistically, it must be acknowledged that if progress is to be made, then the research methodology employed must be considerably refined. Taerk (1977) concluded that maximum control can be exerted over extraneous variables only if a captive (college student) sample, involved in a non-contact indoor sport, for example, volleyball or swimming, is monitored on a wide range of variables over a period of years. The implication is that most of the previous data, usually gained from American football squads, is seriously contaminated by nuisance variables such as weather conditions and differential exposure to situations in which injury could occur. Consequently, many findings may be spurious or, even if legitimate, are not able to be reliably generalised. Further, the element of chance will always figure prominently in injury statistics which means that the most sophisticated battery of predictive indices will never account for anywhere near the total amount of variance. Individuals with low risk quotients will continue to be injured and many with high risk quotients will remain injury free. This fact alone caused Bramwell et al (1975) to have ethical reservations about the identification of predictor variables in the sense that 'high risk' athletes might be needlessly screened out of participation. This is a particular problem when prediction is based on global analysis of groups rather than a consideration of the unique circumstances of the individual. It is likely that advances in understanding of the psychologically injury-prone can be made in the context of the effect of unconscious motives and forces on the behaviour of the individual.

DYNAMIC APPROACHES TO THE SYNDROME OF INJURY-PRONENESS

Dynamic theories of personality are often used, in a case-study context, to explain the maladaptive behaviour of individuals with psychological problems. A recurring tenet of these theories is that abnormal behaviour results from the individual's unconscious attempts to cope with anxiety reactions.

In Freudian terms, an important cause of anxiety is the subject's ambivalence about the commission of aggression. It is instinctual and yet the process of social and moral education determines that by adulthood, we are conditioned to channel our aggressive impulses into generally acceptable avenues – what Moore (1967) described as a useful assertiveness in life. The ambivalence is generated by the existence in society of two areas of conduct in which direct physical aggression is encouraged – war and competitive sports. This, for many, will induce a classic conflict situation of the 'approach-avoidance' type (Dollard and Miller, 1950). On the one hand the athlete wishes to approach the contest because there are rewards, such as victory and prestige to be had. On the other hand, however, he wishes to avoid the game as it offers repulsive aggression and punishment, maybe in the form of injury. The anxiety and tension which is associated with such conflict can seriously affect performance and increase the likelihood of real or imagined injury, as an unconscious means of reducing tension.

Anxiety reactions are universal, and to counteract their effect, to reduce tension and maintain psychological equilibrium, the individual usually has recourse to quite effective coping mechanisms. These serve to reduce transient tension and the individual is more or less aware of their value in this respect. On the other hand there are defence mechanisms which, although reducing psychological tension, usually involve some distortion of reality. An example of a defence mechanism in operation would be the manifestly anxious athlete at physiological boiling point who sincerely believes that he is not anxious. This reaction represents denial in psychoanalytic terms. The anxiety-prone athlete is more likely to employ defence mechanisms to maintain equilibrium. He is further identified by his emotional vulnerability, easy loss of composure, negative thinking, underlain by various kinds of exaggerated fears or phobias. Such individuals often display a recurring sense of guilt which they attempt to reduce by self-imposed suffering and punishment (Alexander, 1949). Their self-destructive tendencies include the elements of aggression, punition and propitiation (Menninger, 1936). The previously discussed evidence of Reilly (1975) and Jackson et al (1978) suggests that the anxiety-prone athlete is also a loser in the sense of being more injury-prone. Their results can be tentatively interpreted as evidence of the desirability of decisiveness and commitment in the sports arena rather than the hesitancy and half-heartedness to be expected from an anxiety-prone athlete. However, further evidence is necessary before firm conclusions can be drawn.

Although anxiety can be seen as the main psychological factor underlying psychological injury-proneness, the associated explanations of behaviour can vary markedly. Various types of injury-prone athlete can be delineated. Recognition of them in the clinical situation may well influence the kind of treatment administered.

Injury resulting from counter-phobia

Most sportsmen become injured at some stage in their careers and as a result they become a little wiser and are able to avoid situations in which injury is likely. Some, however, never learn from mistakes and this does not appear to be a function of intelligence (Ogilvie and Tutko, 1971). Typical of this type is the individual who finds the aggressive atmosphere of competitive sport very anxiety-inducing and he attempts to counteract the anxiety by meeting it head-on, by being overtly aggressive and fearless. It involves what Horney (1937) has described as the 'process of ruthlessly marching over an anxiety'. He repeatedly tempts fate by testing his indestructibility, a course of action which markedly increases the likelihood of injury. Moore (1960) maintained that this kind of individual is attracted to high risk sports such as downhill skiing, boxing, rugby or motor racing.

Moore (1967) reported the case of an ice hockey goalkeeper who had the puck smashed into his face many times. Yet in hospital for minor surgery after a car crash, he was terrified of allowing the surgeons to touch him. His counter-phobia was geared to the planned danger of ice hockey but his real fear of injury was revealed in the unplanned situation of the hospital ward.

Injury as a sign of masculinity

A type who may have counter-phobic tendencies is the athlete who uses injuries as a mark of his courage and masculinity. He lacks real confidence, needing the visible scars of battle to confirm his manhood. An indication of the pervasiveness of this feeling of enhanced masculinity can be gained by most sportsmen simply by reference to their own history of injury. Who at some stage has not felt a certain pride and satisfaction when carrying the visible scars of contest – the marks of distinction and toughness?

Expression of masculinity is one of the motivating forces which produce the injury-prone hero. He takes a martyr's role by continuing to play despite his illness or injury. His sacrifice is accompanied by obvious signs of distress and pain. This serves the dual function of securing admiration for his courage and also giving himself a ready-made excuse in case he performs badly.

Injury resulting from masochism

The risk-taker may be what Menninger has termed 'chronically suicidal'. He is possessed of masochistic tendencies as a result of inward-directed hostility and he achieves satisfaction in injury. The hostility may be the result of obsessively seeking after athletic standards which he sets unrealistically high. The pain and injury are the punishment which relieves the feelings of guilt over his inevitable inability to meet the standards.

The inwardly directed hostility may alternatively be

the athlete's atonement for the injury he has caused another. The fact that he has injured another, or even contemplated it, indicates his aggressiveness, a picture of himself which he finds unacceptable.

Injury as a weapon

Conversely, there is another kind of athlete who uses injury as a means of punishing another or others in an indirect way. Ogilvie and Tutko (1971) gave the example of the reluctant athlete forced to play because of an athletically-frustrated father. By being injured, he can accomplish several objectives: he can make his father feel guilty for pressurising him; he can frustrate his father's displaced aspirations; and he can avoid the undesired competition.

Injury as an escape

There is the athlete who fears competition so much that he virtually needs to be injured. An example is the 'training-room athlete' who gets injured in practice, thereby avoiding competition (Ogilvie and Tutko, 1971). He has strong feelings of inferiority but cannot straightforwardly opt out because of his fear of isolation and rejection. With injury, whether real or imagined, he can avoid the feared competition, remain a member of the squad, and keep his ego intact because he can always tell himself that had he not suffered so much injury, he would have been an outstanding athlete. His disability can be used by his team mates as a rationalisation of their failure. A related type is the compulsive failure-seeker who sees an injury-full life as the best means of maintaining the illusion of his great potential had he not suffered so much injury.

Ryde (1965) described the case of a top female athlete who had a leg injury which did not respond to treatment over a period of months. It transpired that the injury represented a form of escapism. It enabled her to avoid her dominant father-figure coach who, she felt, would strongly disapprove of her impending engagement.

Psychosomatic injury

Unconscious psychological forces can be so great as to precipitate psychosomatic injury. The athlete frequently complains of injury and yet no organic reasons can be obtained to substantiate the claim. A coach faced with this situation may feel that the complaint has been assessed incorrectly as his attempts to help are frustrated. The athlete does not respond to conventional treatment. This athlete is also likely to be unreliable in that injury is possible at any time. He might be dismissed as not too much of a problem if his ability is low but it is extremely frustrating to all concerned if he is a talented sportsman. If he is the latter, then a

build-up of resentment in the team will enlarge his psychological problems.

With this kind of athlete it is possible that a Freudian defence mechanism entitled somatisation is involved. Somatisation is occurring when emotional disturbance is reflected in physical symptoms. Freud referred to this syndrome as conversion hysteria and specifically investigated several cases of blindness and paralysis of limbs which were primarily emotional in origin. These are extreme examples, but it is not uncommon for individuals, including sportsmen under stress, to develop physical symptoms which at once protect them from anxiety and provide them with an excuse for withdrawing from the stressful situation. The physical symptoms may well disappear when the emotional problem is solved.

Injury as a concoction

Another type of athlete whose injuries cannot be substantiated physically is the malingerer, i.e. the athlete who concocts injuries for his own ends (Ogilvie and Tutko, 1971). He is given to ostentatious demonstrations of pain and injury, and displays a large discrepancy between his stated intentions and his actual performance. The reasons underlying this behaviour vary both between and within individuals:

1. He may seek to avoid training, which is seen as irksome and not strictly necessary.
2. He fears actual injury if he participates.
3. He wishes to cause difficulties for the team and/or the coach because of real or imagined grievances – a particularly effective technique when the player is valuable. He lacks courage for a confrontation, so he reacts in this indirect but effective way.
4. He wants to avoid unfavourable comparison with others, which might occur if he practises and competes.
5. He may not even like the sport, having been coerced into it because of his physical talents or he may have been attracted by the financial prospects.

IMPLICATIONS

As for recognising and treating the various kinds of injury-prone athlete it is important that all personnel concerned with ensuring the athlete's complete recovery should have access to as much information about the individual as possible. Ideally, medical, physical and psychological records should be available to be used by, say, the physiotherapist, to enrich his interaction with the athlete during the treatment phase. If he can establish that he is dealing with a particular kind of injury-prone athlete, then there will be much he can do in terms of lessening the likelihood of future injuries, by encouraging caution, instilling confidence, recommending psychotherapy or advising the athlete's doctor of his suspicions. The causes of the underlying anxiety would have to be identified to enhance the prospects of complete recovery.

Several authors have emphasised the need for cooperation among players, coaches, physical educators, trainers, physiotherapists, psychologists and physicians (e.g. Ryde, 1971; Godshall, 1975; Jackson et al, 1978). Vulnerability profiles could be established on the basis of epidemiological data. Any athlete could then be checked to assess his degree of vulnerability to injury or illness, thus allowing the possibility of positive injury prevention. Moore (1967) listed several conditions which might identify the psychologically vulnerable athlete:

1. Discrepancy between ability and aggressiveness.
2. Discrepancy between father and son in ability/aggressiveness.
3. Uninhibited aggressiveness and/or feelings of invulnerability.
4. Excessive fear of injury.
5. Extensive history of injuries.
6. Concealment or exaggeration of injuries.
7. Success phobia.

What is certain is that there is no one way of handling injury-prone athletes and even sympathy would not be recommended universally. With the malingerer or some of the psychologically injured athletes, sympathy would tend to reinforce the undesirable behaviour patterns. Concern for an athlete's well-being can lead to anxiety in the coach and anxious coaches tend to produce anxious athletes.

For progress to be made in the investigation of the phenomenon of injury occurrence and its prevention, systematic research is needed. It should embrace a wide variety of hypothetically important factors in a well-controlled context. However, much useful information could be gained without sophisticated experimental techniques. For example, the perceptive coach with comprehensive records of the athlete under his control could produce evidence meriting more detailed investigation. He may find that the lack of confidence displayed by a particular injury-prone athlete is a product of nothing more complex than a lack of fitness, induced by inadequate training per se, or by training constraints imposed by previous injury. It is obvious that any individual competing in sports where physical demands are high and injuries are common should be exceptionally fit. It is equally obvious that the physiotherapist and trainer have an essential role to play in preparing the injured athlete's path to maximum

fitness. Confidence, one of the keys to success, can only be enhanced by supreme fitness.

The highly motivated athlete presents a special problem in that complete physical fitness is essential if he is to avoid injuries. Any lack of fitness and his high competitiveness will lead him to push beyond a safety margin, and as a result incur injury. Such athletes are prone to becoming permanently weakened, both physically and psychologically.

Physical fitness together with psychological fitness has a liberating effect on the athlete. One often hears the remark that an athlete should know his limitations. It is suggested that the greatest athletes are those who do not know their limitations, but who have the confidence to explore their potential and push back the limits, a confidence born of supreme physical and psychological fitness.

REFERENCES

Alexander, F. (1949). The accident-prone individual. *Public Health Report*, **64**, 357–362.

Bramwell, S. T., Masuda, M., Wagner, N. N. and Holmes, T. H. (1975). Psychosocial factors in athletic injuries: development and application of the social and athletic readjustment rating scale (SARRS). *Journal of Human Stress*, **1**, 6–20.

Brown, R. B. (1971). Personality characteristics related to injury in football. *Research Quarterly*, **42**, 133–138.

Dollard, J. and Miller, N. E. (1950). *Personality and psychotherapy*. McGraw-Hill, New York.

Godshall, R. W. (1975). The predictability of athletic injuries: an eight-year study. *Journal of Sports Medicine*, **3**, 50–54.

Goven, J. W. and Koppenhaver, R. (1965). Attempt to predict athletic injuries. *Medical Times*, **93**, 421–422.

Haddon, W. (1966). Principles in research on the effects of sports on health. *Journal of the American Medical Association*, **197**, 885–889.

Horney, K. (1937). *The neurotic personality of our time*. Norton, New York.

Jackson, D. W., Jarrett, H., Bailey, D., Kausek, J., Swanson, J. and Powell, J. W. (1978). Injury prediction in the young athlete: a preliminary report. *American Journal of Sports Medicine*, **6**, 6–14.

Kraus, J. F. and Gullen, W. H. (1969). An epidemiologic investigation of predictor variables associated with intramural touch football injuries. *American Journal of Public Health*, **59**, 2144–2156.

Menninger, K. A. (1936). Purposive accidents as an expression of self-destructive tendencies. *International Journal of Psychoanalysis*, **17**, 6–16.

Moore, R. A. (1960). Psychological factors in athletic injuries. *Journal of the Michigan State Medical Society*, **59**, 1805–1808.

Moore, R. A. (1967). *Injury in athletics*. In R. Slovenko and J. A. Knight (eds). *Motivations in play, games and sports*. Charles C. Thomas, Springfield, Illinois.

Ogilvie, B. and Tutko, T. A. (1971). *Problem athletes and how to handle them*. Pelham Books, London.

Pargman, D. (1976). Visual disembedding and injury in college football players. *Perceptual and Motor Skills*, **42**, 762.

Pargman, D., Sachs, M. and Deshaies, P. (1976). Field dependence-independence and injury in college football players. *American Corrective Therapy Journal*, **3**, 174–176.

Reilly, T. (1975). *An ergonomic evaluation of occupational stress in professional football*. Unpublished Doctoral Thesis, Liverpool Polytechnic.

Ryde, D. (1965). The role of the physician in sports injury prevention: some psychological factors in sports injuries. *Journal of Sports Medicine and Physical Fitness*, **5**, 152–155.

Ryde, D. (1971). The athlete's 'nerves'. *Journal of the Royal College of General Practitioners*, **21**, 161–163.

Taerk, G. S. (1977). The injury-prone athlete: a psychosocial approach. *Journal of Sports Medicine and Physical Fitness*, **17**, 187–194.

CHAPTER 5

The psychological implications of injury

F. H. SANDERSON DCC, BEd, MA, PhD

The psychological factors which would render an individual more susceptible to injury have been discussed in Chapter 4. The present chapter is concerned with the psychological problems that can ensue from injury and that could prevent or delay recovery. This is seen as a problem because there are no straightforward relationships existing between the severity of an injury and the intensity of the psychological reactions. Of course many sportsmen have few psychological problems stemming from injury. If the injury is incapacitating, the sportsman convalesces for a while, possibly seeks the help of a physiotherapist or doctor, undergoes therapy and eventually resumes playing without any appreciable psychological side-effects. There are, however, many individuals whose injuries precipitate inappropriate psychological reactions which in turn lead to recurrent injury problems, inadequate recovery period or extended rehabilitation. The intensity of these psychological reactions is governed by several interacting factors.

FACTORS AFFECTING PSYCHOLOGICAL REACTION TO INJURY

The individual's history of injury
If the injury background is extensive then psychologically negative reactions are likely to be more intense; frustration, anger, resignation and despair may be intensely felt, creating an apathetic attitude during the recovery phase. In this kind of psychological state, the recovery phase is likely to be seriously extended and the chances of re-injury enhanced.

The nature of the injury
Other things being equal, the psychological trauma will tend to increase as a function of the severity of the injury, but only to the extent that the individual is aware of the severity. As Stein (1962) has noted, it is often the case that the more grave the injury, the fewer are the emotional complaints. This is partly because of immediate post-trauma shock which can leave a player amnestic and anaesthetised against feelings of pain. When full awareness returns, the process of rationalisation has already begun. Additionally there is a finality

about the severe injury which, in a sense, can lessen or eliminate the feelings of anger and irritation which normally accompany the injury. Thus the immediate psychological reactions may be minimal in contrast with the sometimes profound long-term reactions to severe injury. These reactions are influenced by the degree of disability and how apparent it is to others. The sportsman in particular tends to have a sophisticated body image based on an awareness of the beauty and integrity of his body. If he is physically damaged, his body image, an integral part of his ego, may be threatened to an intolerable degree. The psychological implications can be extensive.

The nature of the sport
Few participants in sport fully expect to be injured but it is clear that the likelihood of injury varies markedly across sports. For example, MacIntosh et al (1972) found that injury in golf was a rare event, whereas Mongillo (1968) reported Tabrah's calculation that the risk of disabling injury in high school (American) football was 13 666 times higher than in underground mining. It seems reasonable to hypothesise that the psychological trauma associated with particular injury will be a decreasing function of the general level of risk entailed in the sport. All else being equal, a particular sports injury will generate more emotional trauma in a low-injury risk golfer than in the high-injury risk football player. This tendency is enhanced by the stereotyped reactions of peers in the sense that the injured footballer may gain much sympathy and experience heightened feelings of masculinity. The injured male golfer is more likely to have his masculinity under threat.

The nature of the injury interacting with the nature of the sport
The interaction is important in that, for example, the psychological effect of a cut eye would be greater for a boxer than, say, for a free-style wrestler. Although both sports here are contact sports in which injury risk is relatively high, the nature of boxing ensures that a cut eye is a particularly devastating injury, encouraging greater psychological repercussions.

The level of competition in which the injury has occurred

The casual tennis player who plays a few times every summer and who sprains his wrist is unlikely to find the experience as traumatic as the tournament player who earns his living from the game. The implication of this is that the psychological effects of injury are only worthy of serious study in relation to what might be termed 'serious' sport. The holiday skier who fractures his leg may suffer considerable personal trauma but it is of no general significance. Physical fitness is also important; the sportsman who is physically fit, having become adapted to fairly severe physical stresses before injury, can more easily adapt to the demands of a physical rehabilitation programme – he is less likely to 'acquiesce' to the disability (Bender et al, 1971).

PERSONALITY AS A FACTOR AFFECTING REACTION TO INJURY

Eysenck's two-factor theory

The importance of personality in reaction to injury can be demonstrated by making reference to the theories of Eysenck who has studied the structure of personality. Eysenck (1957) delineated two major orthogonal dimensions along which the personality of individuals can vary, extroversion-introversion and neuroticism-stability.

Extroversion (E) is a commonly observed trait among sportsmen, and the typical extrovert is sociable, outgoing, carefree, changeable, assertive, physically active and optimistic. The typical introvert is hesitating, cautious, reflective, and pessimistic.

Those high on neuroticism tend to be nervous, anxious, depressive, moody and emotionally volatile. They are liable to neurotic breakdown under stress. Stable individuals, on the contrary, are even-tempered, calm and emotionally stable.

Eysenck's inhibition hypothesis associated with extroversion-introversion is of particular relevance – cortical inhibition is higher in extroverts, making them less sensitive and less able to tolerate tasks of a routine nature. Inhibition accumulates to a greater extent in the central nervous system (CNS). The relative insensitivity means that they have strong nervous systems and the effort to reduce cortical inhibition makes them crave for excitement. Eysenck (1967) reported that extroverts have higher pain thresholds and Lynn and Eysenck (1961) found a highly significant correlation between extroversion and pain tolerance.

A picture is emerging then of two extreme personality types which would produce quite different reactions to similar injuries. On the one hand there is the impulsive, optimistic, changeable extrovert. His general insensitivity to pain and need for excitement make him impatient to return to competition. Consequently, he is likely to under-react to the injury in the immediate post-trauma phase. Subsequently he may be unable to accept the routine and discipline of the treatment phase. Therefore, the need for caution must be impressed upon him by those interested in his full recovery. On the other hand, there is the hesitating, restrained, pessimistic introvert for whom the physical trauma has more psychological impact. He has low tolerance for pain and will have a tendency to over-react, making an injury appear more serious than it really is. This individual will need encouragement and reassurance during rehabilitation.

The difference between these extremes is well illustrated by the kind of question they might ask after severe sports injury. The extrovert asks, 'when can I play again?' In contrast the introvert asks 'can I play again?'

The tendencies outlined in relation to extroversion-introversion could be reinforced or diminished depending upon the degree of neuroticism of the individual. The individual's weightings on E and N will determine the kind and degree of psychological handicap he suffers (Fig. 5/1). Obviously both the stable extrovert and stable introvert will be least problematical, unless of course they suffer severe physical trauma associated with discouraging prognosis. In such circumstances even the most stable of individuals can develop severe psychological problems.

With reference to the interaction between E and N, Eysenck (1963) has suggested that phobias, anxiety states and similar phenomena are more likely to develop in the introvert, who seems to turn his neurosis in on himself. He is beset by psychological conflicts on which his anxiety feeds (Sanderson, 1977). Hence the trauma of sports injury is likely to be most severe in the neurotic introvert. Not only is it likely that his psychological state will have the effect of delaying his recovery – loss of function could partly be a result of anxiety – but on return to competition, apprehension is likely to remain. He may distort reality to the extent of being irrational about the possibilities of re-injury, e.g. the soccer player injured in a 50/50 tackle who subsequently avoids such situations at all costs. The irony is that the behaviour adopted to avoid anticipated injury could well lead to a greater probability of the player being injured again, as suggested by Reilly's (1975) findings. In the light of this, perhaps it is as well that evidence suggests that introverts, particularly neurotic introverts, constitute only a small minority of competitive sportsmen.

Self-concept or self-esteem is high in the extrovert and when he tends towards instability, the self-concept

Fig. 5/1 Extroversion/neuroticism and reaction
to injury

INTROVERT
(Low pain tolerance)

	Apprehensive
	Uncertain
	Pessimistic
	Tendency to
	over-react
	Injury possibly not as
	severe as it seems
	Lengthy
Post-trauma medical	rehabilitation
decisions	

STABLE ——————————————— NEUROTIC

relatively	
straightforward	Reckless
	Impatient
	Unreliable
	Optimistic
	Tendency to
	under-react
	Injury possibly more
	severe than it
	seems
	Inadequate
	rehabilitation
	enhances likelihood
	of re-injury

EXTROVERT
(High pain tolerance)

may be perceived as being threatened. The self-concept may be highly dependent on both physical appearance and physical function – and both may be impaired by injury, resulting in emotional stress associated with loss of self-esteem.

If the injury is not severe, such an individual may 'play through it' rather than suffer the indignity of succumbing to it. He represses the unwanted facts about the injury, using the Freudian defence mechanism of denial. If the injury is incapacitating, his neurotic recklessness may be exhibited in unwillingness to accept treatment and returning too early to competition. He lays the groundwork for re-injury maybe of a more serious nature and increases the likelihood of the development of chronic injury-proneness.

Injury and neurotic breakdown

Little (1969) found a relationship between injury and neurotic breakdown in individuals with so-called 'athletic' personalities. In his examination of patients with neurotic illness, he noticed that they could all be reliably categorised in terms of their athleticism (Table 1). He compared the distribution of athleticism in his male neurotic patients with that of a control group of 'normals' and found marked significant differences between them, i.e. a much greater tendency for neurotic males to be either extremely non-athletic or extremely athletic. He found clear aetiological differences between these extremes. The athletic neurotic was much more likely to have had his breakdown generated by a threat to his physical well-being, often in the form of injury. It was found that those with athletic personalities developed neurotic symptoms in their mid-thirties compared with the late-twenties for the other group. It appears that the 'athletes' became particularly vulnerable at a time when their over-valued physical abilities were declining. They were found to be relatively insensitive to other kinds of stressor. Several other points emerged from this study:

Table 1 Athleticism (After Little, 1969)

Grade +2	Grades +1, 0, −1	Grade −2
Extremely athletic attitudes and practices	'Normal' athletic attitudes and practices	Completely non-athletic attitudes and practices

Inter-observer reliability, r=0.93

1. Neurotic symptoms developed in the great majority of cases almost immediately following injury and often on the same day.

2. The trauma was generally mild, which encouraged the conclusion that level of vulnerability rather than severity of injury was the major factor precipitating neurotic breakdown.

3. The athletic neurotics did not have histories of neurotic illness and tended to be highly extroverted and of previous sound health.

Little concluded:

'Like exclusive and excessive emotional dependence on work, on key family relationship bonds, intellectual pursuits, physical beauty, sexual prowess or any other over-valued attribute or activity, athleticism can place the subject in a vulnerable pre-neurotic state leading to manifest neurotic illness in the event of an appropriate threat, or actual enforced deprivation, especially if abrupt and unexpected.'

Individual differences in reaction to pain

As mentioned earlier, personality is also an important factor in the perception of and tolerance to pain (Fig. 5/1). Historically, a stimulus-response (S–R) model of injury and pain was accepted, i.e. the behaviouristic idea of a linear relationship between severity of injury and intensity of pain (Fig. 5/2). But modern psychology postulates an S–O–R model which recognises that many variables other than severity of injury determine the reaction to pain (Fig. 5/3).

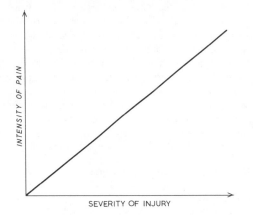

Fig. 5/2 The S–R model of pain experience

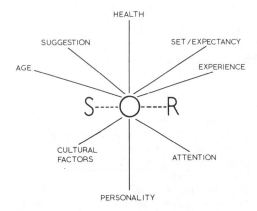

Fig. 5/3 A cognitive model of pain experience

For instance, there are cultural and ethnic differences in the reaction to pain; peoples of Mediterranean origin tend to complain and seek sympathy more readily for a level of pain to which North Europeans would register no reaction.

The 'meaning of the situation' is also an important factor, as evidenced by Beecher's (1959) observation that wounded soldiers requested morphine much less

frequently than similarly wounded civilians. Far from experiencing pain, the soldiers' reaction might well be that of relief at being removed from the arena of battle. In sport, the athlete who wishes to compete because of the potential glory but who finds the competitive situation anxiety-inducing, may well experience immediate psychological relief. Those in attendance immediately post-trauma, risk being misled as to the seriousness of the injury. Treatment of such an athlete may be made more difficult because of this feeling of relief; indeed, recovery might be delayed because of his, maybe unconscious, vested interest in maintaining his injured state. Anxiety at the prospect of recovery and return to the conflict situation can be converted into unconsciously sustained muscle tension, which delays the recovery.

Another example of reaction to injury being influenced by the meaning of the situation concerns the documented reaction of a Football League goalkeeper. In gathering a ball, a dog collided with him, damaging his cruciate ligaments so badly that he had to retire. However, he continued with the game, determined not to suffer the indignity of being removed from the game by a dog (Harris and Varney, 1977)! We can assume that his insistence on continuing the game affected the judgement of those tending his injury.

The amount of attention concentrated on stimuli contributes to the intensity of pain experience. The soccer player, for example, may well be unaware of a severe kick on the shin during the excitement of the contest. Melzack (1973) noted that many stimuli outside the focus of attention would be unnoticed, 'including wounds that would cause considerable suffering under normal circumstances'.

Even if the injury requires immediate treatment, there may often be sufficient reverberating central nervous system (CNS) activity to mask pain perception. Superficial observation of a player's psychological reactions might encourage the view that the injury is not severe and that the player can continue.

Pain therefore should be seen as a complex reaction to a wide range of interacting variables. Extreme reactions to injury in terms of pain perception and tolerance are as much a function of the psychological state of the person as they are of severity of injury. Those tending to the injured athlete must err on the side of caution and are not likely to ignore manifestations of extreme pain. However, a lack of such overt symptoms cannot automatically be interpreted as a sign of only mild trauma.

REACTION TO CONCUSSION

One physical reason for the absence of pain experience is concussion, a common injury in contact sports. The reactions which accompany concussion have implications for immediate post-trauma treatment. Yarnell and Lynch (1970, 1973), in documenting reactions to concussion in American football players, noticed that retrograde amnesia was a common phenomenon. Specifically, they found individuals who had intact memory of the pre-trauma play and the impact itself for several minutes post-trauma. As little as three minutes later, when retested, they had developed irretrievable memory loss of the impact and its antecedent events. They suggested that the concussive injury prevents short-term memory consolidation with consequent rapid decay of information. An obvious implication is that speedy examination and assessment is necessary in order to utilise information from the victim on what happened, how it feels, and so on, while he is still in possession of all his faculties. This is especially important if concussion is accompanied by other injuries.

In the conditions just described, the psychological trauma resulting from injury vary markedly. The common element is that emotional factors outweigh cognitive or intellectual factors.

Those attending to the needs of the injured athlete should be aware that his personality make-up may be a major factor in his behavioural reactions to the situation. Hence, general perceptiveness and, ideally, specific knowledge of the individual's psychological profile would be desirable. The efficacy of the treatment is likely to be enhanced if there is an awareness of the physiological and psychological determinants of pain. Treatment can then be based on a more precise assessment of the specific interaction of personality, pain, and injury.

During the rehabilitation phase, the sportsman should be given a realistic appreciation of the prognosis of the injury in order that the development or persistence of counter-productive emotions can be inhibited. In the more extreme cases, it would be an obvious advantage to the injured sportsman if all those with a vested interest in his complete recovery cooperated and pooled information in order to make the treatment phase more effective. At the least, this will be to the long-term benefit of the reckless and the over-cautious sportsman.

REFERENCES

Beecher, H. K. (1959). *Measurement of subjective responses*. Oxford University Press.

Bender, J. A., Renzaglia, G. A. and Kaplan, H. M. (1971). *Reaction to injury*. In L. A. Larson (ed). *Encyclopedia of sports sciences and medicine*. Macmillan, New York.

Eysenck, H. J. (1957). *The dynamics of anxiety and hysteria*. Routledge and Kegan Paul, London.

Eysenck, H. J. (1963). *Experiments with drugs*. Pergamon, New York.

Eysenck, H. J. (1967). *The biological basis of personality*. C. C. Thomas, Springfield, Illinois.

Harris, H. and Varney, M. (1977). *The treatment of football injuries*. MacDonald James, London.

Little, J. C. (1969). The athletes neurosis – a deprivation crisis. *Acta Psychiatrica Scandinavica*, **45**, 187–197.

Lynn, R. and Eysenck, H. J. (1961). Tolerance for pain, extroversion, and neuroticism. *Perceptual and Motor Skills*, **12**, 161–162.

MacIntosh, D. L., Skrien, I. and Shephard, R. J. (1972). Physical activity and injury: a study of sports injuries at the University of Toronto. 1951–1968. *Journal of Sports Medicine and Physical Fitness*, **12**, 224–237.

Melzack, R. (1973). *The puzzle of pain*. Penguin, Harmondsworth.

Mongillo, B. B. (1968). Psychological aspects in sports and psychosomatic problems in the athlete. *Rhode Island Medical Journal*, **51**, 339–343.

Reilly, T. (1975). *An ergonomic evaluation of occupational stress in professional football*. Unpublished Doctoral Thesis, Liverpool Polytechnic.

Sanderson, F. H. (1977). The psychology of the injury-prone athlete. *British Journal of Sports Medicine*, **11**, 56–57.

Stein, C. (1962). Psychological implications of personal injuries. *Medical Trial Technique Quarterly*, 17–28.

Yarnell, P. R. and Lynch, S. (1970). Retrograde memory immediately after concussion. *Lancet*, April 25, 863–864.

Yarnell, P. R. and Lynch, S. (1973). The 'ding': amnestic states in football trauma. *Neurology*, **23**, 196–197.

CHAPTER 6

Engineering human factors in sport

T. REILLY BA, DPE, MSc, PhD, MIBiol

Human factors engineering, known in Europe as ergonomics, gained initial impetus from sophisticated developments in military technology which presented unfamiliar problems to operators. Solutions required team-work involving specialists in human characteristics – anatomists, physiologists and psychologists – and engineers to make the man-machine combination an effective unit. Success of this inter-disciplinary approach led to its later extension to industrial and non-vocational contexts, inevitably embracing sport and recreation. Many examples are provided in McCormick's (1976) elaborate textbook.

Ergonomists systematically apply relevant information about human characteristics and behaviour in the design of objects, facilities and environments people use in the various aspects of their lives. (Useful source texts include Murrell, 1965; Kraiss and Moraal, 1976.) The focus is on the individual upon whom the task and environment are seen to impose specific physical, physiological and mental loading. The common strategy is to analyse human responses to these loads so that efficiency, comfort, safety or well-being is increased. Compared with industrial employees, athletes operate mostly close to maximal levels since competition is inherent in sport which usually involves heavy work: both, however, desire a working environment conducive to safe and efficient performance.

As the scope of ergonomics is extensive (in terms of its body of knowledge, problems tackled and methodologies available), detailed treatment is impractical here. The following sections attempt to highlight the more dominant general approaches and themes in human factors engineering. Specific environmental and interface aspects are considered briefly in the latter part of the chapter.

CLASSICAL ERGONOMICS

A recurrent theme in ergonomics is the concept of limited human capacity. This applies to such aspects as aerobic power and physical working capacity, anaerobic power, strength, reactions, stress tolerance, information processing and so on. The implication is

that a ceiling is placed on current functional ability. The individual will be unsuccessful, perhaps suffering injury, if task demands outstrip the capacity to meet them. Grandjean's (1969) text entitled 'fitting the task to the man' is representative of the classical approach.

In games, demands may be distributed unevenly as shown by the work rate of top soccer players expressed as distance covered per match (Fig. 6/1). The underlying pattern is that endurance is demanded most of midfielders while anaerobic power is emphasised in centre-backs. Without the specific requirements for these positions the individual is forced to play at an inferior level, to attempt to alter his capacity by appropriate training or to switch to a position more compatible with his current capabilities. Tailoring task demands to the individual has been a special hallmark of classical ergonomics. If in sport the individual and his task are poorly matched the outcome may be gross under-achievement or alternatively breakdown through injury.

The classical approach suggests implications for training and selection of athletes and for injury prevention. Analysis of competition demands, provides the framework on which training regimes can be devised and helps locate where competitors are particularly

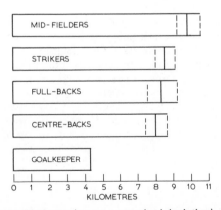

Fig. 6/1 Work rate (mean ± standard deviation) per game according to positional role in soccer (Reilly and Thomas, 1976)

liable to incur injury. Fitness testing helps evaluate preparedness for competition on a scientific basis and can assist in team selection as well as indicate specific individual weaknesses which appropriate training can then remedy. This is the broad rationale behind the testing of élite athletes in 'centres of excellence' in various countries. Monitoring fitness status throughout pre-season and competitive periods is advocated, as specific fitness parameters fluctuate. Time of day of performance is also relevant since many human functions show a circadian variation. As fitness has many facets, an inter-disciplinary approach is usually most effective. Psychological, anthropometric and physiological tests should be incorporated into a multivariate battery to provide a comprehensive profile since there are personality and temperament as well as biological and physical determinants of athletic success (see Vanek and Cratty, 1970).

Fitness testing helps also to determine the effectiveness of training programmes. The quest for an optimum regime based on sound scientific principles has attracted numerous researchers. Beneficiaries would include the habitually sedentary undertaking physical training for positive health and athletes undertaking severe conditioning schedules. The aim of training is to fit the individual to the task and allow realisation of potential. The degree to which even an optimal training stimulus can increase current capacity is itself limited and varies with the individual, the initial fitness level and the biological system being conditioned. As differences among individuals are generally greater than the maximal training effect, genetic factors are obviously important for a good performance potential. Greater attention to selection than training may be more attractive to coaches where the task is relatively inflexible. For team games a compromise is usual, preparation consisting of harmoniously fitting each individual for his job and fitting the job to the individual by appropriate training, selection and team tactics.

STRESS AND STRAIN

The concept of stress
Objectives of human factors engineering include the maintenance or enhancement of certain human values such as health, safety, satisfaction and well-being. Essentially this amounts to avoiding the adverse effects of stress which is often blamed as the main source of many malaises. Stress is a difficult concept to pin down since the meaning assigned to it varies with the individual discussing or investigating it. It has been the subject of study in medicine, psychiatry and sociology as well as in the scientific disciplines contributing to

sports ergonomics. Ramifications of the concept and its relationship to mental and physical loadings are treated in detail by Singleton et al (1971).

Disillusion may be expressed with the concept of stress often presented. Some clarification is obtained by adopting the engineering convention of using stress in the sense of a deforming force or stressor, and strain for the resultant deformation. The reaction can be monitored using psychological, physiological or biomechanical techniques. This viewpoint has proved consistently rewarding in analyses of occupational stress by highlighting sources of emotional strain, peak physiological loading and imperfect working postures. These avenues can equally be explored in sporting contexts where most suitable techniques tend often to be non-invasive. Assessment of physiological strain may involve measurement of the oxygen consumption level, heart rate, body temperature, or electromyogram, for example. Physical strain is often only manifested when injury is apparent: analysis of injury records may be sometimes a useful starting point for investigation. Psychological strain too may be camouflaged and difficult to uncover. It may be either transient pre-competition or a more persistent emotional burden.

Emotional strain
Imminent competition usually brings transient emotional strain. The nervous system prepares the individual for the forthcoming contest with elevated anticipatory responses. Methodologies for examining pre-competition stress are summarised in Table 1 and include behavioural and physiological measures.

Table 1 Summary of emotional strain measures in human factors research

Behavioural	Physiological
Hand tremor	Muscle tone
	Skin conductance
	Blood content
Behaviour observation	Urine content
Subjective scales	Blood pressure
	Heart rate

Emotional tachycardia has been used to indicate the pre-event stress in various sports. Figure 6/2 shows the extremely stressful nature of motor-racing and ski-jumping, quite apart from the stresses in actual performance. It is conceivable that the thrill of courting danger provides part of the attraction to participants and spectators in these sports. Individuals can

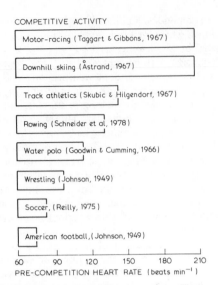

COMPETITIVE ACTIVITY

Motor-racing (Taggart & Gibbons, 1967)

Downhill skiing (Åstrand, 1967)

Track athletics (Skubic & Hilgendorf, 1967)

Rowing (Schneider et al, 1978)

Water polo (Goodwin & Cumming, 1966)

Wrestling (Johnson, 1949)

Soccer, (Reilly, 1975)

American football,(Johnson, 1949)

60   90   120   150   180   210
PRE-COMPETITION HEART RATE (beats min⁻¹)

Fig. 6/2 Pre-competition heart rate according to competitive activity reported by various investigators

habituate to stress while top athletes manage to harness it successfully for their benefit.

A certain amount of stress is desirable for the athlete to be optimally aroused to perform while performance deteriorates with over-arousal. The inverted U-shaped curve in Figure 6/3 shows the relationship between stress and performance in its simplest form and is implicated in many research findings. Psychological states indicating emotional vigour have been shown to correlate with performance in cross-country running (Reilly, 1977). The finding of a relationship between injuries and anxiety in soccer (Thomas and Reilly, 1975) suggested psychological reactions beyond an

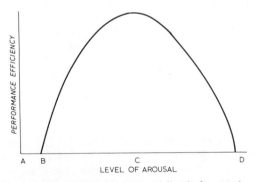

Fig. 6/3 The relationship between level of arousal and performance efficiency. AB indicates the sub-threshold level; BC the sub-maximal level; C the optimal arousal and CD the over arousal

optimal level. Though such results are understandable in hindsight, prediction of performance or injury from stress indices is fraught with difficulty (see Chapter 4).

Psychological strain may manifest itself during competition in errors in performance. These signal the start of a train of events which may lead to an accident and possible ensuing injury. Unforced errors and critical incidents where accidents nearly happen merit close attention in sports accident analyses which tend to be investigated retrospectively. Study of errors also provides valuable information for the coach. Eliminating precursors of errors, whether they are related to psychological or fitness factors or extraneous to the individual in origin, is immensely useful in reducing the incidence of injury. Intracompetition stress may also be reflected in increased aggressiveness and readiness to engage in conflicts. Since dangerous play could be promoted as a consequence, remedial coaching may be necessary.

Emotional strain may also exert itself in insidious adverse changes in morale. This will be especially relevant where competition is over an extended period with chronic emotional strain a possible outcome. Long-term subjection to intense competition may bring its own specific psychological wear and tear, a lot depending on the extent to which enjoyment and success can be preserved. Unfavourable changes include deterioration in vegetative functioning with poor appetite and sleep, and ultimately impairment in coordination and fine motor skills. A drawback of success in prolonged knock-out competitions is the more cluttered fixture list with reduced recovery between matches that results. Playing four soccer matches within ten days was reported to cause hyperfunction and enlargement of the thyroid which could lead to aggressive behaviour under the tension of competition (Andrejevic, 1973). Elevated levels of stress hormones in the urine of players were also found. In this sport goalkeepers show the greatest susceptibility to stress-induced ulcers because of the responsibilities of this role, while the highest incidences among players and coaches coincide with the season's peak period. Psychosomatic effects are described in detail in the general adaptation syndrome of Selye (1956). Dietary, pharmacological and physiotherapeutic methods have been suggested as remedies as well as varied regimes of training and relaxation. It should be conceded, however, that some players thrive on frequent competition so that it is imperative for the coach or trainer to know each individual well.

Group factors are evident in that stability of team composition is an important element in the development of sustained success in games. Individuals get to know each other's play intimately, team spirit is reinforced and tactical efficiency improves with familiarity. Frequent changes in personnel clearly militate against group morale and competence. A consistent line-up assumes absence of injuries so their avoidance is an important contribution towards victories achieved. Psychological counselling is often used at international playing level to maintain group cohesion, as poor individual morale can easily affect the whole team. Though harmony between members is undoubtedly associated with team success, it is not easily established whether it is the result or the determinant of that success.

THE SYSTEMS APPROACH

Many human factors problems, especially when associated with technology, are tackled by systems analysis. A system is defined as an assemblage of functional units with a common overall purpose and forming a connected whole. It can apply equally to a sports medical unit, a football team, a water-skier in tow or a biological system. The systems approach implies knowledge of the objectives, the input and output, while various aspects of system behaviour may be considered. (For further discussion the reader is referred to Singleton, 1974.) Discrepancies between input and output are especially relevant to accident analysis.

The ergonomist is particularly concerned with how the human harmonises with the other system elements. In operational systems, control is implemented by means of various control devices such as the pedals and handlebars of a bicycle or the joystick and steering wheel of a power boat. Frequently, computer assistance is enlisted as in regulating ski-resort usage for avoiding congestion and reducing accidents on the slopes. Whatever the system the fundamental human functions relate to information input, information processing, decision making and action or response. In serial tasks involving continuous control there is always some form of feedback to the operator: this allows frequent error correction and helps prevent accidents occurring.

Man-powered flight provides an example of problems related to control devices in a man-machine system. Conventional designers concentrated on the operator as an aero-engine and ignored the mental loading induced by having to guide the aircraft while simultaneously producing high power output. Since the crafts have large wing spans and operate best close to ground, the margin for error is considerably less than for gliding or normal flying. The type of movement optimising control of pitch, roll and yaw can be determined on a rig comprising an electronically controlled tracking task fitted onto a bicycle ergometer

(Evans and Reilly, 1979). Since field studies are impractical because of the high frequency of crashes the simulator described is useful for training potential man-powered craft pilots.

Simulation consists of reproducing or representing an actual or conceptual object, system, process or theoretical construct. It is used in ergonomics research where carrying out the investigation in real life circumstances is impractical or dangerous. It provides an opportunity to test the reactivity of a number of variables in advance without committing resources or operators to risk. Mechanical models may be used in accident simulation to investigate impact stresses in various sports and evaluate equipment designed to protect against injury. Variations in environmental temperature, humidity and pressure can be simulated in an environmental chamber and investigated without recourse to the cost and inconvenience of travelling to their locations. The dynamics of the cardiovascular responses can be studied by computer simply by altering electrical voltages.

The systems approach has stimulated much detailed study of human movement. Insight into the processes of skills acquisition, motor learning and proprioception has followed from inspired applications of control theory. Uses in sport of biofeedback, the presentation of biological signals to the individual generating them, have systematically unfolded. These include applications in reducing anxiety, neuromuscular training in rehabilitation and assisting skill acquisition.

ENVIRONMENT

Engineering the environment

Much attention in industrial ergonomics has been given to environmental factors. It is important to consider also the physical environment in which training or competition takes place. This is often the source of various stressors whether thermal, barometric, noise or pollution. Though much is known about the effects of discrete environmental stressors there is still a lot to be learned on how they interact when in combination. In outdoor sports the environment to be experienced can sometimes be foreseen and protected against. In man-built arenas it can be engineered so that human efficiency and comfort are promoted.

The essence of the schematic work station analysis in Figure 6/4 is that the design process starts by concentrating on the human and works outwards. The task and interface are then considered in turn. The workspace is constructed around these before factors in the physical environment complete the projection. Ergonomics is here an assistant technology to architecture and engineering and can save the embarrassment

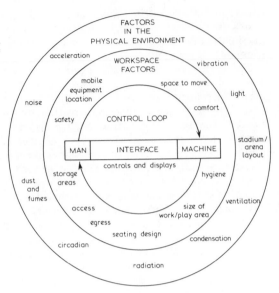

Fig. 6/4 Schematic work station analysis map for engineering the total working environment

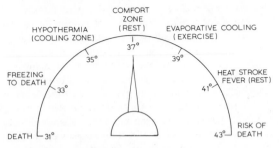

Fig. 6/5 Zones of thermal responses and mechanisms of heat exchange.

Heat Production (Gain)	Heat loss
Convection (C)	Evaporation (E)
Radiation (R)	Convection (C)
Conduction (K)	Radiation (R)
Activity	Conduction (K)
Shivering	
Increased basal metabolism	
Basal metabolism	

$M - S = E \pm C \pm R \pm K$
(M = metabolic heat production
S = storage)

of forced re-design from mistakes appearing after construction.

Thermal stress

Problems associated with heat injury and heat disorders have generated much research attention and medical concern. Heat injury is discussed separately elsewhere (see Chapter 17). Many equations have been derived as heat stress indices to express the total thermal load. Typically these include composites of environmental measures such as the WBGT Index (incorporating wet, dry bulb and globe temperatures), or predicted physiological responses from combinations of such measures as in the Predicted 4h Sweat Rate (P4SR) devised by McArdle et al (1947). In strenuous exercise, heat loss is mainly by evaporation of sweat from the skin (Fig. 6/5) and this avenue of loss is impaired in humid conditions, while cooling is assisted with increased air velocity. Most heat stress indices are, however, not entirely satisfactory for application to sports.

Athletes must often take preparatory rather than avoidance measures since the timing and location of competition are outside their control. Training in the heat allows circulatory and sweating mechanisms to respond by adapting within limits to heat stress. The stress is alleviated by sensible organisation if competitive events likely to produce heat injury are timetabled for the cooler part of the day.

In the case of indoor sports facilities, the environment can be engineered with human comfort as a major criterion. Thermal comfort is determined by air temperature, mean radiant temperature, relative air velocity, humidity, activity level, thermal resistance of clothing, all of which must be considered in deriving a thermal comfort equation (Fanger, 1973). This will help designers of indoor recreation centres, particularly in installing their heating and ventilation systems. Comfort needs of spectators and competitors may conflict as for example in competitive swimming arenas. Environmental engineering can provide acceptable compromises when the total areas and complete workspace are taken into account.

The wind-chill index (Siple and Passel, 1945) has long been used for assessment of extreme cold weather experienced by mountaineers, skiers and sailors. Wet-cold conditions must be safeguarded against by using suitably insulated and waterproof clothing. Garments can easily incorporate synthetic layers and buoyancy provision where water immersion is possible. After accidental immersion, heat loss is accelerated by the convective currents created in swimming so that imminent rescue is best awaited. Effective protective clothing for all cold conditions must secure the microclimate to which the skin is immediately exposed.

Neuromuscular function deteriorates with lowered temperatures so that accidents are promoted by declining motor performance. The hands cool especially rapidly and some strength as well as dexterity is lost. Frostbite is caused by ice crystals forming in the tissues and occurs first on the fingers, toes, nose and ears. Ulcers result in the affected areas which are slow to heal. Chilblains, which are chronic inflammatory swellings, can develop in the extremities from repeated exposures to cold insufficient to cause frostbite. Shivering represents an autonomic attempt to generate heat by involuntary muscle activity and wards off hypothermia. When the body's core temperature reaches about 32 °C (89.6 °F), shivering is replaced by permanent muscular rigidity and consciousness is gradually lost. This temperature is usually taken as the critical level of hypothermia though it is subject to controversy.

There is still much wanting in the design of clothing for a variety of outdoor winter sports that will afford protection against the weather and provide the mobility needed for unhampered activity. Products can be validated using physiological criteria in rain-sheds or environmental chambers and in the field, while mobility and durability are further requirements.

Pressure

Hypoxia or lack of oxygen is associated with sport performance at altitude. Discomfort on exposure can lead to 'mountain sickness' with symptoms including nausea, dizziness, headaches and sleeplessness. The main cause is hyperventilation which washes CO_2 out of the blood, disturbing its acid-base balance. Effects of visiting high altitudes have been observed in balloonists and parachutists, and in climbers attempting to scale the Himalayan peaks. Highly trained individuals tend to suffer less and acclimatise more quickly than those who are untrained. Strenuous activity can cause respiratory distress at moderate altitudes in sedentary individuals, a risk often ignored by unfit American adults flying to the Colorado mountains for skiing without prior conditioning.

With increasing altitude, atmospheric pressure falls causing a reduction in alveolar oxygen tension and in the oxygen saturation of the blood. Endurance performance deteriorates in consequence. Arterial oxygen saturation does not decrease at the same rate as alveolar partial pressure but does decline fairly rapidly after 3 000m. Olympic performances at 2 240m in Mexico 1968 were evidence of the adverse effects on endurance. The value of acclimatisation was demonstrated in that all gold medallists in running events at 1 500m and upwards were trained or living at altitude. In sprint events, which are not dependent on oxygen supply to the tissues, performances are actually assisted by the reduced air density.

Normally at 8 000 to 9 000m oxygen saturation falls to a point where the brain is inadequately provided with oxygen and unconsciousness usually follows. Humans can, however, acclimatise to these altitudes when sufficient and proper training procedures are used. The successful Everest ascent (8 848m) in 1978 unsupported by oxygen equipment is evidence of this. Mount Nuptse (7 833m) in the Himalayas was climbed without fixed camps or oxygen by a British group a year later.

Training resorts have been established in various countries with high plateaux so that athletes can acquire the physiological benefits associated with respiratory and circulatory adaptation to altitude for improving sea-level performances. As responses are individualistic their use may be unsuitable for many athletes, and sea-level results can be adversely affected by previous exposure to altitude. Some may be more vulnerable than others to effects of moderate and high altitude and require longer periods of adjustment. For those who might benefit the altitude, duration and frequency of exposure, and the timing of the return to sea-level before competing are critical. Where competition is at altitude, natives are endowed with a physiological headstart.

Conversely pressure increases the greater the depth underwater. Risks to which divers are exposed in this hyperbaric environment are discussed in Chapter 20. Though the underwater habitat is alien to man, Scuba and wet-suits make prolonged submersion possible. The pleasurable feelings associated with nitrogen narcosis known as 'raptures of the deep' illustrate that pleasant sensations are not necessarily conducive to optimal performance. At a simulated dive of 46m increased feelings of well-being have been found to accompany deteriorating performances (Thomas and Reilly, 1974). Because of these mental states divers tend to over-estimate their information processing capacity and commit errors of judgement.

Noise and lighting

The ears and eyes are delicate sensory mechanisms so the level of noise and lighting are important environmental aspects. Attention to acoustical features can appreciably benefit the comfort of indoor arenas. Surprisingly high noise levels are sometimes found in poorly designed pools when heavily crowded with young swimmers. Motor-racing and motor-cycling constitute hearing hazards for spectators close to the embankments. Ear protectors are essential for mechanics working in proximity to these sports vehicles for long periods. Shooters are subjected to high values of impulsive sound and significant noise doses in the range of 130 to 160 dB. Other potential sources of noise hazard include snowmobiling and careless use of starting pistols. Athletes subject to noise stress at work or to frequently standing close to amplified disco music are also vulnerable.

Middle ear deafness is usually caused by a stiffening and damping of the ossicles through which sound waves are transmitted to the inner ear. Alternatively there may be an infection in the middle ear, obstruction of the Eustachian tube or perforation of the ear drum causing hearing loss. Medical treatment or amplification by means of a hearing aid can be successful as long as the inner ear is intact. If the special receptor cells in the inner ear or the nerve trunks leading to the hearing centre in the brain are damaged amplification is ineffective. Nerve deafness may be due to severe head injuries, infections or exposure to high noise levels. The only way of avoiding risk of ear damage is by wearing protective devices, the fluid seal type of ear muff offering the best security.

Indoor sports facilities require artificial illumination which must meet the various sports association's standards: in ball games the faster the activity the more vital is the need for good lighting. Glare often disturbs performers, usually emanating from polished floors or adjacent glass panelling. Contrasting background may be important against which to judge the flight of, say, a badminton shuttle or squash ball. Attention to these features is often neglected in the design of sports facilities, including floodlit outdoor areas.

THE IMMEDIATE INTERFACE

Equipment
Equipment design can prevent injuries in three main ways. Firstly, quality control in production ensures injury is not encouraged by provision of faulty equipment. Secondly, strain is avoided if equipment matches individual needs and characteristics: the designer is referred initially to manuals such as Woodson and Conover (1966). Compatibility may necessitate a range of fabrications within the limits of current governing body standards. Controls, displays and workspace may be embraced as in the design of powered sea or terrestrial vehicles. The physical properties of the equipment, ease of operation, anthropometry and subjective responses of users are consistently relevant. Thirdly, effective and comfortable protective equipment can be provided to cushion individuals against harmful impact or environmental influences.

Sports equipment covers all aspects of interfacing the performer with the environment and includes clothing, footwear, implements, rackets and sports machines. Historically, man contrived equipment to extend his power and mobility: evolution of implemental, racket and machine sports is the direct result of this enhanced capability. Technological innovations, such as use of fibre-glass materials in sports, aid performance but in some cases require modification of existing competition rules before improvement can be realised. Often games skills need altering for a smooth changeover.

Footwear has tended to be more a matter of fashion and market forces, and so is often implicated in sports injuries. Ideally, shoes should be designed for specific sports and surface qualities. Biomechanical analysis and development of techniques such as pedobarography provide methodologies for validating current and new products which the customer could only benefit from. Swimfins assist movement underwater but their surface area and flexibility determine to what extent. The type of ski-binding, particularly the mode of release in falling, affects the type and frequency of injury (Shealy et al, 1974). The current international standard for setting ski-bindings has been shown by Pope et al (1976) to be invalid.

Special effort has been devoted to protecting the head in sport. This appears related to three factors – skull deformation, intracranial pressure and rotational motion. (Dynamic impact tests are preferable in determining the stiffness of materials for use as helmet liners.) Helmets are worn in a variety of activities from skateboarding to tobogganing. Effective headgear reduces the acceleration of the head when it is hit as well as attenuates compression forces. Mouthguards constructed over an accurate model of the wearers' teeth similarly lower the intracranial pressure from a blow on the chin. Special helmets with ear holes have been developed for hang-gliding so the pilot can sense air flow for a more accurate adjustment of his speed. In games the helmet may be used illegally as a weapon to butt opponents. In many sports the problem of protection is of such a magnitude that a helmet alone cannot supply total protection and additional modifications to the playing environment must be undertaken.

Surfaces
Interface also involves characteristics of the playing surface. Determination of the best flooring material for the various activities conducted in multi-purpose facilities is an area where the materials scientist, architect and human scientist can usefully cooperate. In multi-purpose sports halls the floor should be reasonably resilient, non-slip, non-reflective, should give a true bounce and roll, have good background colour, easy maintenance, be resistant to all types of footwear used and be non-abrasive. Special flooring considerations obtain for certain activities; squash courts should be capable of absorbing sweat falling from players while floors in weight-training areas must withstand possible damage from heavy pieces of equipment.

Synthetic turf for outdoor games must be waterproof, resistant to ultra-violet degradation and permit ball and play behaviour similar to natural turf. The development of synthetic indoor and outdoor surfaces has been due to their economic and organisational advantages. Artificial surfaces are often blamed for injuries and are rarely laid with human characteristics foremost in mind. The indoor running track at Harvard, with a surface polyurethane cover on a substrate consisting primarily of wood, provides an exception. The compliance of the track was set specifically to match the stiffness of human muscle determined after detailed experiments. Improved performances and reduced injury rates were reported to result (McMahon and Greene, 1978).

The majority of tests currently employed for artificial turf and synthetic surfaces are related to materials science more than human factors criteria. Those used invariably include durability, spike penetrability, crumb retention, inflammability, abrasive wear criteria, for example. Resistance, stiffness and friction tests should be added as a matter of course for more effective shoe/surface interface. For outdoor games surfaces, soil penetrability tests would provide a more objective means for choice of footwear and studs than the arbitrary heel plant into the ground usually employed pre-match.

Mismatch between the sportsman, his task and the performance environment can leave the individual at risk. An understanding of the effects of stressors can help to prepare the individual to meet them or eliminate environmental influences that are possibly damaging. In many cases an intuitive adaptation occurs in top performers, skills and work rate being altered to suit the conditions.

The craving continually to improve existing records leads to a search for better equipment as well as training methods. Frequently, safety is sacrificed for efficiency, a concession unacceptable to those concerned with sports accidents and injuries. Attention to ergonomic or human factors aspects at the design stage can encourage acceptable compromises.

REFERENCES

Andrejevic, M. (1973). *Sports medicine in football.* In Proceedings of international symposium on the medical aspects of soccer (football). CONCACAF, Toronto.

Åstrand, P. O. (1967). Physical activity and cardiovascular health: commentary. *Canadian Medical Association Journal*, **96**, 760.

Evans, A. D. B. and Reilly, T. (1979). *Design of a simulator for investigation of control functions in man-powered flight.* Paper presented at the Society of Sports Sciences Conference (Leeds).

Fanger, P. O. (1973). *Thermal comfort.* McGraw-Hill, New York.

Goodwin, A. B. and Cumming, G. R. (1966). Radio telemetry of the electrocardiogram, fitness tests and oxygen uptake of water polo players. *Canadian Medical Association Journal*, **95**, 402–406.

Grandjean, E. (1969). *Fitting the task to the man.* Taylor-Francis, London.

Johnson, W. R. (1949). A study of emotion revealed in two types of athletic sports contest. *Research Quarterly*, **20**, 72–79.

Kraiss, K. F. and Moraal, J. (1976). *An introduction to human engineering.* Verlag TUV Rheinland Gmbh, Köln.

McArdle, B., Dunham, W., Hollong, H. E., Ladell, W. S. S., Scott, J. W., Thomson, M. L. and Weiner, J. S. (1947). *The prediction of the physiological effects of warm and hot environments.* Medical Research Council Report No. RNP 47/391, London.

McCormick, E. J. (1976). *Human factors engineering and design.* McGraw-Hill, New York.

McMahon, T. A. and Greene, P. R. (1978). Fast running tracks. *Scientific American*, **239**, 112–121.

Murrell, K. F. H. (1965). *Ergonomics.* Chapman and Hall, London.

Pope, M. H., Johnson, R. H. and Ettlinger, C. F. (1976). Ski binding settings based on anthropometric and biomechanical data. *Human Factors*, **18**, 27–32.

Reilly, T. (1975). *An ergonomic evaluation of occupational stress in professional football.* Unpublished PhD Thesis, Liverpool Polytechnic.

Reilly, T. (1977). Pre-start moods of cross-country runners and their relationships to performance. *International Journal of Sports Psychology*, **8**, 210–217.

Reilly, T. and Thomas, V. (1976). A motion analysis of work-rate in different positional roles in professional football match-play. *Journal of Human Movement Studies*, **2**, 87–97.

Schneider, E., Angst, F. and Brandt, J. D. (1978). *Biomechanics in rowing.* In E. Asmussen and K. Jorgensen (eds). *Biomechanics VI-B.* University Park Press, Baltimore.

Selye, H. (1956). *The stress of life.* McGraw-Hill, New York.

Shealy, J. E., Geyer, L. H. and Hayden, R. (1974). Epidemiology of ski injuries: effects of skill acquisition and release-binding on accident rates. *Human Factors*, **16**, 459–473.

Singleton, W. T. (1974). *Man-machine systems*. Penguin Books, Harmondsworth.

Singleton, W. T., Fox, J. J. and Whitfield, D. (1971). *Measurement of man at work*. Taylor-Francis, London.

Siple, P. A. and Passel, C. F. (1945). Measurement of dry atmospheric cooling in subfreezing temperatures. *Proceedings of American Physiology Society*, **89**, 177–199.

Skubic, V. and Hilgendorf, J. (1964). Anticipatory exercise and recovery heart rate of girls as affected by four running events. *Journal of Applied Physiology*, **19**, 853–856.

Taggart, P. and Gibbons, D. (1967). Motor car driving and the heart rate. *British Medical Journal*, i, 411–412.

Thomas, V. and Reilly, T. (1974). Effects of compression on human performance and affective states. *British Journal of Sports Medicine*, **8**, 188–190.

Thomas, V. and Reilly, T. (1975). The relationship between anxiety variables and injuries in top-class soccer. *Proceedings European Sports Psychology Conference (Edinburgh)*.

Vanek, M. and Cratty, B. J. (1970). *The psychology of the superior athlete*. Macmillan, London.

Woodson, W. E. and Conover, D. W. (1966). *Human engineering guide for equipment design*. University of California Press, Los Angeles.

SECTION 2

Training

CHAPTER 7

Observations on weight training

T. REILLY BA, DPE, MSc, PhD, MIBiol

The use of weights to improve the functional efficiency of the human is probably as old as sport itself. The celebrated Milo of Croton is reputed to have started his athletic training by raising a new-born calf over his head and continuing the practice daily, he grew in strength until the animal reached maturity. He provides a good illustration of the use of progressive resistance exercise. In subsequent centuries man has continued to search for ingenious methods of resisting muscle action to enhance his function as well as derive a variety of lifting and throwing competitions. This chapter outlines some common uses of weight training and suggests ways that injuries associated with the practice may be avoided.

It is first necessary to distinguish between weightlifting and weight training. Weightlifting is a competitive sport contested in the Olympic Games whereas weight training describes the employment of weights in the training regimes of non-athletes as well as athletes. The two Olympic lifts most commonly demonstrated to illustrate the sport are the snatch and the clean and jerk. These are known as the quick lifts because of the agility and coordination required for their execution. The rules for each event determine how the lift is performed.

THE SNATCH

In the snatch, the weight must be brought from the floor to a position overhead without interruption. This action involves pulling the weight as high as possible, then splitting the legs apart in the sagittal plane to nip underneath as it ascends. The arms must lock straight promptly as the weight reaches the peak of its ascent. The lifter must then stand upright with the weight held overhead.

THE CLEAN AND JERK

This is performed in two phases. The clean requires that the weight be pulled to the chest in an uninterrupted motion. This has some similarity with the snatch though heavier loads can be lifted. Preparatory to the next phase the lifter stands with the load at his chest. He flexes his knees, then jumps upwards with

the weight, throwing it to an overhead position as he again parts his legs to get underneath the ascending weight. Here also the upright position must be assumed with the weight held overhead to achieve a valid lift.

There are a few observations about weightlifting that also help to illuminate the field of weight training. Weightlifting is a heavy resistance weight-bearing action, necessitating great explosive power and the ability to hold great weights momentarily under control. The lifter uses maximal efforts against extremely heavy loads in training and in competition. It is at these intensities that stresses on the articulo-skeletal system are greatest. The lifts are rapidly executed, taking in toto less than six seconds per lift. Studies of weightlifters show that over a two-hour training session they may be actually working for only two to six minutes, though this work will be extremely strenuous. It is essential that correct techniques be applied to reduce the strain at body sites of greatest vulnerability – the knee, the back and the wrist.

The knee joint is particularly vulnerable at the initiation of the lift before the quadriceps contract powerfully. The back experiences high levels of strain, the force acting on a lumbo-sacral disc being calculated to exceed 1 000kg in the study of Morris and co-workers (1961). The load on the spine is to an extent alleviated by the intra-abdominal pressure induced. For these reasons it is essential that the lift be carried out in a manner that minimises mechanical strain on the spine. Frequently the annulus fibrosus cartilage is strained. Efficient lifting actions should be practised, imperfections being corrected during the early stages of learning the techniques. Deterioration at the wrist may occur due to hyperextension associated with repetitive lifting and holding weights overhead. Fractures of the distal radial epiphysis have been reported in adolescent weightlifters executing the military press (Ryan and Salciccioli, 1976). Rowe (1979) reported a comminuted fracture of the distal end of the radius and fracture of the ulnar styloid process on sudden hyperextension of the wrist on losing control of the weight. Finally, it is important not to suspend breathing during the moment of extreme exertion. With the breath held and the epiglottis closed the chest is compressed and intrathoracic pressure builds up. This precipitates the Valsalva manoeuvre, resulting in a reduced venous return to the heart and consequent rapid drop in blood pressure with possible loss of consciousness. International weightlifters have fainted during competition as a result of failure to time their breathing correctly.

CONVENTIONAL WEIGHT TRAINING EXERCISES

Quite apart from the Olympic lifts used at the International Weightlifting Federation's competitions, the British Amateur Weightlifters' Association recognises 31 lifts. From this battery a number have been adopted over the last two decades or so by athletes for use in general conditioning. In most cases the lifts have been modified to provide an action compatible with the athlete's specific requirements. A typical sample of such exercises, which can also be used by sedentary individuals for positive health purposes follows. These exercises are divided according to the degree of skeletal muscle involvement into light muscle group (for example arm and shoulder) or large muscle group (thigh or trunk) work. Emphasis is placed on the correct execution of the routines since injury frequently results from using a faulty technique.

Arm and shoulder work

BENCH PRESS

The athlete lies supine on the bench with feet apart and supported on the ground on either side. Two spotters are used for precautionary reasons. The bar is taken from supporting stands by the spotters and handed to the athlete on his upper chest. The posture of the performer is shown in Figure 7/1.

Taking the bar in too high near the throat is to be avoided on safety considerations. Normally a wide knuckles-up grip is taken. A wider hand hold is used to handle greater weights, though this defeats the purpose of imposing greatest resistance on pectorales majores, anterior deltoids and triceps. However, care must be taken that the grip is sufficiently wide not to jeopardise security and continual concentration is required of the spotters as 40kg is sufficient to lacerate the facial bones from a fall of half a metre. The weight is pushed vertically from the chest. Prior to the movement it is necessary to have the chest full of air to provide a rigid base from which the weight is moved. The performer exhales after the weight ascends. The bar should be lowered slowly so as to permit complete control of the weight throughout. Altering the hand spacing affects the pattern of muscular involvement. Dumb-bells may be used to replace the barbell and, though this invariably means a lower resistance, it allows movement through a greater range.

An alternative procedure is to have the assistants lift the barbell, the athlete's task being to control its lowering by eccentric muscle contractions. This overcomes the limitation of performing only uni-directional work. Heavier loads can be handled than in concentric work. The benefits of the training programme are enhanced when both concentric and eccentric actions are employed.

Bench pressing is ubiquitous in the weight-training programmes of sportsmen. It has been widely accepted by runners, jumpers and games players. It would seem

Fig. 7/1 Spotters overseeing performance of bench press

particularly beneficial to rugby-forwards, swimmers and weight-throwers.

OVERHEAD PRESS

Overhead press can be performed standing upright or sitting on a bench. The starting position can be from the chest but usually the weight is pressed vertically from behind the neck until the arms are at full stretch overhead, an inflated chest acting as a platform from which the action takes place. In the standing posture heavy weights may produce compensating movements in the legs or trunk to allow the action to be completed. In younger individuals acquiring the technique, an assistant can apply light pressure at the scapulae to prevent swaying (Fig. 7/2).

Fig. 7/2 Supervision of overhead press

Alternatively, it may help if the action is performed with immediate visual feedback from a mirror. If dumb-bells are used the line of action of the specific competitive performance can be employed. Shot putters, for example, may use one or both arms alternately or simultaneously at an angle of release in the sagittal plane of approximately 45°.

ROWING

Rowing may be performed from an upright or a bent-forward posture. The action should be restricted to the arms and shoulders, with careful attention given to the exclusion of the back and trunk. In both forms, the downward movement of the bar should be controlled. An observer can ensure the posture does not get progressively higher with each succeeding effort in bent-forward rowing. This can indicate the performer is tiring and it is when fatigued that he is most likely to handle weights incorrectly. Again, the use of a mirror in learning the technique is recommended. A partner may be used to exert light pressure on the upper back to prevent accentuation of the lordotic curve. If performed in a quick jerky manner with the knees locked, damage to the intervertebral discs can occur with pressure on the disc forcing its fluid-like centre, the nucleus pulposus, to project posteriorly causing medical complications. This can be avoided either by resting the forehead on a padded table while the lift is performed or bending the knees to about 15° flexion. This releases tension from the muscles of the posterior thigh and back and allows the lumbar spine to retain a normal curvature. The muscles isolated in this exercise are the latissimus dorsi, teres major and rhomboids.

In upright rowing a narrow grip is used with the elbows pointing upwards. In bent-forward rowing the elbows assume a more lateral orientation. Both procedures are widely used by individuals seeking an increase in upper body strength.

OVERARM-PULLS

This exercise may be performed with the athlete lying supine on a bench and feet supported on the ground. The arms may be held straight or flexed. A mild flexion is recommended to reduce strain on the shoulder joint. The weights lifted should not be unduly heavy, otherwise they will be difficult to control at the outer ranges of movement. The barbell may be taken from a position on the ground in a circular motion forward to a position over the chest or continued further to rest on the thighs. Endurance athletes can usefully employ this exercise because the serratus anterior is stretched as the weight is lowered to recommence the movement. Correct timing of breathing is important, inhalation occurring as the weight descends towards the ground and exhalation as the load is taken back up.

CURLS

Curls implicate elbow flexion and may be performed with barbells or with one or two dumb-bells. It is difficult to operate at maximal loads in standing without other muscle groups being introduced to assist fatiguing elbow flexors. Again, care should be taken so that with heavy loads the lordotic curve is not over-emphasised. Isolation of elbow flexion is facilitated by conducting the exercise with the limb supported at the elbow on a bench or table. Attention should also be given to elbow extension work to avoid imbalanced arm strength development.

Large muscle-group work

SIT-UPS (TRUNK CURLS)

The resistance is normally provided by approximately half the body mass which the abdominal muscles must move against gravity. The load on the abdominals in a sit-up action from supine lying can be increased by holding a loaded barbell on the chest (Fig. 7/3). This is preferable on comfort criteria alone to holding a disc behind the neck. An assistant is needed to hold the ankles of the athlete to facilitate the action. Another variation is to sit-up with a twist, arms behind the head, to touch each knee alternately with contra-lateral elbows.

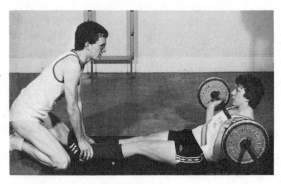

Fig. 7/3 Sit-ups against a load

SQUATS

A loaded barbell is supported on the back of the neck. Sometimes a piece of foam rubber or a towel is used to alleviate pressure on the cervical vertebrae. The body is lowered from standing to a squat position, from which its weight plus the loaded barbell must be lifted by powerful contraction of the knee extensors. This exercise has come in for much criticism because of the risk of knee joint degeneration from strain on the patellar bursae (Reilly, 1977). During deep knee bending without attendant weights the patello-tendon force has been calculated by Reilly and Martens (1972) to reach 7.6 times bodyweight.

In the full squat position with posterior aspects of thigh and calf in contact, the knee ligaments are overstretched and long-term ligamentous damage may be caused (Klein, 1962). In this position the lateral meniscus may also suffer from being caught between the

femoral condyle and the tibial plateau (O'Donoghue, 1970). For these reasons performance of partial squats is advised, though full squats may be permitted at much less frequent intervals to provide maximum overload and maintain the joint's range of movement.

Maintenance of stability may present a problem during this exercise. Initially the athlete assumes a starting position with feet apart underneath the hips to best support the bodyweight. Stability is achieved by keeping the line of gravity within the base of support. This is effected by pushing the hips back slowly as the bodyweight is lowered. By retaining heel contact with the ground the base of support is kept relatively large and stability facilitated.

One manoeuvre to assist balance is to elevate the heels by means of an inclined board or to perform the exercise with a board placed underneath the heels. A more satisfactory procedure is to use a steel rack which arrests movement of the bar in the fore and aft direction and which incorporates obvious additional safety factors. These racks are installed in all well-equipped gymnasia.

Since greater weights can be lowered than lifted, a useful modification of the half-squat is to overload the individual beyond his lifting capacity and allow him to slowly lower the weight under eccentric muscular control. A weight about 120 per cent of lifting capacity can easily be handled for six repetitions (Johnson et al, 1976). If the stretching force is 130 to 140 per cent of one concentric repetition maximum (1RM), it is not possible to slow the lowering sufficiently in a free movement resisting gravity to permit involved muscles to develop maximal tension. For safety the load must be supported by pins at the end of the eccentric movement.

POWER CLEANS

This exercise involves approximately the same energy demands as a full squat (Reilly, 1971). The weight is lifted from the floor to above head height in one complete movement. Special attention to technique is needed in the initial lifting movement. There has been considerable discussion for many years of the relative demerits of the back-lift with knees straight (the derrick lift) and with the trunk erect and knees flexed (the knee action) in various industrial contexts. Whitney (1962), for example, compared the strength of the lifting action in both types of lift. The knee lift is preferable, with the back straight to prevent the turning of the spine into a cantilever with consequent spinal strain. Correct placement of the feet is essential prior to attempting the lift. The athlete should become accustomed to performing the action with the head erect and

looking directly ahead and so avoid the natural temptation to look down at the weight as he attempts to
overcome its inertia. As the forces on the spine are a
function of the distance the weight is away from it, it is
recommended to keep the weight close to the body as it
is being lifted.

HIGH PULLS

This involves basically the same gross muscular action
and equivalent energy expenditure as power cleans
(Reilly, 1979). The barbell is taken from the floor to a
height roughly in line with the clavicles. The athlete
may increase the work done by coming up on to his toes
to complete the lift, good coordination being
demanded for this. The elbows are raised above the bar
at its high-point, which does not go overhead. Again it
is important to keep the back straight during the lift as
jerking into back extension, particularly during the
early phase of the action, can be damaging.

SQUAT JUMPS

Here the athlete jumps high into the air from a squat or
partial squat position with a loaded barbell supported
on his shoulders. Good coordination is essential to
prevent overbalancing on landing. Frequently a towel
is used underneath the bar to cushion its jarring effect.
When ascending it is necessary to pull down hard on
the bar to avoid its bouncing against the back of the
neck (Fig. 7/4). It is particularly beneficial to athletes
who during performance move the body explosively
against gravity.

BENCH STEP-UPS

Bodyweight plus a weighted barbell provide the resistance as the athlete steps repeatedly on to a bench with
load supported on the shoulders (Fig. 7/5). Ideally the
bench height should be matched to the stature of the
individual, otherwise quadriceps tear is a risk where
the smaller athletes operate with a high bench. With
too heavy weights the rhythm of stepping may be disrupted with consequent danger of overbalancing and
injury.

ACCOMMODATING RESISTANCE MODES

Isokinetics

Isokinetics describes the form of exercise permitted by
machinery with the facility to adapt resistance to the
force exerted. Normally when weights are lifted
through a range of movement the maximum load is
limited to that sustainable by the muscles involved at
the weakest point in the range. Consequently other
points within the range undergo sub-maximal training

*Fig. 7/4
Squat
jumps*

*Fig. 7/5
Bench
stepping
with load*

stimuli. With isokinetic machines this problem is overcome as the speed of contraction is pre-set, a speed governor in the apparatus allowing the resistance to adapt to the force applied. In this way, the greater the effort exerted the greater is the resistance, and maximal effort can be performed throughout the complete range of movement. Where comparisons have been made, training programmes using isokinetic machines have proved superior to isometric and typical progressive resistance programmes with high speeds producing best results (Thistle et al, 1967; Pipes and Wilmore, 1975).

Using Mini-Gym, Lumex or Cybex isokinetic apparatus, the weight-thrower can go through the pattern of shoulder and arm motion of his competitive event, so getting a training effect suitable for his specific purpose. Accessory equipment can be attached to the machine to accommodate specificity training for a range of sports.

A limitation of isokinetic exercise is that it may interfere with the natural pattern of acceleration employed in the competitive action. Additionally it provides opportunity for just concentric work. However, muscle soreness from eccentric action is avoided as recovery is passive (Talag, 1973). It is likely specially to benefit swimmers since they contract their arm muscles more or less isokinetically when pulling through water.

Nautilus equipment

An alternative form of accommodating resistance is provided by Nautilus equipment. This is not isokinetic machinery since the speed of contraction may vary. The apparatus provides stretching the involved muscle group in the starting position and resistance throughout the range of movement correlated to the force exerted. A specially shaped cam compensates for the variations in force by changing the moment arm and the resistance is increased or decreased even though the machine loading remains constant. The machinery allows a rotary movement in 17 different stations for various exercises. The cams for each machine are designed according to the strength curves of the different muscle groups with varying angles. As a result the resistance is lowest at the joint's weakest position and greatest in its peak strength position.

USES OF WEIGHT TRAINING

Weight training can be exploited to achieve different results. Since the classic report of De Lorme (1945) it has been known that few repetitions of high intensity work produce a strength training stimulus while many repetitions at low or moderate intensity improve local endurance. Skeletal muscle is an extremely adaptable

tissue and exercise of an endurance nature, although it produces biochemical changes leading to greater oxidative capacity, leaves the size of the musculature relatively unchanged. Maximal intensity of relatively short duration tends to promote growth in skeletal muscle, its connective tissue and tendonous attachment. The important ultra-structural change in muscle hypertrophy is increase in the myofibril content of the cell.

It appears that an important factor determining the extent of hypertrophy is the speed of contraction as well as the work intensity. There is, as yet, no exact demarcation in physiological terms between a strength training stimulus and a power training stimulus. In studies of women throwers, appreciable gains in strength using maximal resistance are found without evidence of the muscle hypertrophy that might be unwanted in females for social reasons (Brown and Wilmore, 1974). There is ample evidence that weight training can improve speed of limb movement and muscular coordination in addition to strength (Jensen and Fisher, 1972) and enhances conventional conditioning programmes (Clarke, 1973). Masley et al (1953) showed that performance in fencing could be improved by engaging in specific weight training exercises. Undoubtedly weight training aptly used can have manifold benefits beyond the seasoning of muscular strength.

Caution is needed in the early stages of a weight training programme. At first the athlete starts off with modest loads during familiarisation with the exercises. Then the principle of progressive resistance is applied to scheduling the programme. The load is gradually increased as the individual adapts to meet the demands the schedule imposes. To improve further a higher load is needed. This procedure is continuously applied as strength develops. Normally the athlete will perform, say, six repetitions at high intensity, rest completely and repeat a few times before progressing to another exercise. An alternative is the pyramid system where after the first six repetitions or first set, the load is actually increased. This necessarily reduces the number of repetitions the athlete can perform. The load is progressively increased until it is too heavy to be overcome. Equipment for leg pressing provides an ideal set-up for most athletes working on a pyramid system to improve leg strength – even when the load cannot be moved an isometric contraction can be held for a fixed period to terminate the sets.

Another use of weight training is its incorporation in circuit-training for the purpose of conditioning the circulatory system. Circuit-training designed by Morgan and Adamson (1962) is so called because a series of separate exercises is organised for performance in a circle. Individuals rotate around the circle as they progress through the training session. The circuit should allow variation of muscle-groups involved between work stations to avoid cessation of work due to local muscular fatigue. In theory this method is ideal for team training provided the number in the group does not exceed the number of work stations laid out. In practice group organisation invariably presents some problems as do inter-individual differences. Where weight training is included in the circuit, a fixed load may not be suitable for all or many of the group while altering the loads slows up the performance and allows untimely recovery. Ideally a homogeneous group, a thoroughly well organised routine and repetition of the circuit or supplementary training are necessary to achieve objectives.

Multi-station exercise machines overcome the organisational problems of circuit-training and the injury risks of weight training using traditional resistance modes. The machine illustrated in Figure 7/6 was designed on ergonomic principles to provide the training stimulus requirements for strength, power, local and general endurance. Resistance is alternately supplied by bodyweight, weighted stacks and isokinetic machines. Muscle groups change from station to station and use of the machine involves abdominals, leg, shoulder, arm, and back muscle work. Physiological studies have shown the training stimulus to the circulatory system is significantly greater than conventional circuit-training routines (Reilly and Thomas, 1978). However, as delay in altering loads at any one station is minimal the circuit of 12 stations can be repeated to perform two or more sets in a training session.

Safety factors are inherent in the design of each station which accommodates a wide range of physiques and capacities. Over a lengthy validation period no accidents or injuries were found with extensive use of the machine. Additionally individual stations provide the facility for training of specific muscle groups. This type of equipment is in use in many professional sports clubs and sport centre complexes.

The use of heavy weights in resistance training emphasises the need for teaching lifting techniques correctly. Most injuries occur when heavy weights are lifted and most back injuries occur when spinal flexion is permitted. This is manifested in the relatively much larger proportion of injuries in male than in female athletes using weight training, females tending to operate at intensities permitting greater safety margins. Special care should be given to young athletes to prevent undue over-exertion in lifting weights. This should be an important consideration before the epiphyses of the long bones close as further growth might be affected.

Safety considerations should override all others where large groups are involved. This may require more careful programming of the gymnasium timetable. Spotters and weight-racks should be used where appropriate. Use of commercially available chalk blocks can ensure a continuing good grip on the bar once the palms commence to sweat. In addition a suitable surface is needed, most lifting exercises being conducted from rubber mats. Appropriate footwear is required to provide sufficient frictional contact with the floor, in most cases the orthodox multi-purpose

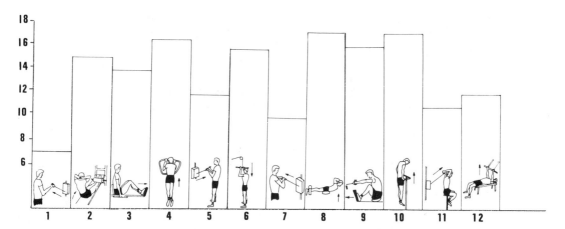

Fig. 7/6 Typical exercises in multi-station apparatus. The bars show the rating of perceived exertion at each station indicating the circulatory strain involved (Reproduced from *Applied Ergonomics*, **9**, 201–206, by permission of the editor)

gymnasium shoe is inadequate. Collars must be used to firmly fix the discs to the bar as many injuries arise from insecurely attached equipment falling on the feet. Weights should be returned to place after exercise to avoid tripping other users.

Frequently athletes do not continue their weight training once the competitive season has commenced. This is an oversight, as the principle of reversibility implies. The training effect obtained from strength training gradually disappears if the training is terminated and the muscles atrophy. In general the loss depends on the rate of acquisition. The gain may be retained by exercising at a frequency much less than when strength was being developed.

REFERENCES

Brown, C. H. and Wilmore, J. H. (1974). The effects of maximal resistance training on the strength and body composition of women athletes. *Medicine and Science in Sports*, **6**, 174–177.

Clarke, D. H. (1973). *Adaptations in strength and muscular endurance*. In J. H. Wilmore (ed). *Exercise and sport sciences reviews*. Volume 1. Academic Press, New York.

De Lorme, T. L. (1945). Restoration of muscle power by heavy resistance exercises. *Journal of Bone and Joint Surgery*, **27**, 645–667.

Hettinger, T. (1971). *Physiology of strength*. Charles C. Thomas, Springfield, Illinois.

Jensen, C. R. and Fisher, A. G. (1972). *Scientific basis of athletic conditioning*. Lea and Febiger, Philadelphia.

Johnson, B. L., Adamszyk, J. W., Tennøe, K. O. and Strømme, S. B. (1976). A comparison of concentric and eccentric muscle training. *Medicine and Science in Sports*, **8**, 35–38.

Klein, K. K. (1962). The knee and its ligaments. *Journal of Bone and Joint Surgery*, **44A**, 1191–1193.

Masley, J. W., Harabedian, A. and Donaldson, D. N. (1953). Weight training in relation to strength, speed and coordination. *Research Quarterly*, **24**, 308–315.

Morgan, R. E. and Adamson, G. T. (1962). *Circuit training*. Bell, London.

Morris, J. M., Lucos, D. R. and Bresslet, B. (1961). Role of the trunk in stability of the spine. *Journal of Bone and Joint Surgery*, **43**, 327–351.

O'Donoghue, D. H. (1970). *Treatment of injuries to athletes*. W. B. Saunders, Philadelphia.

Pipes, T. V. and Wilmore, J. H. (1975). Isokinetics vs isotonic strength training in adults. *Medicine and Science in Sports*, **7**, 262–274.

Reilly, D. T. and Martens, M. (1972). Experimental analysis of the quadriceps muscle force and patello-femoral joint reaction force for various activities. *Acta Orthopaedica Scandinavica*, **43**, 126–137.

Reilly, T. (1971). *An ergonomics study of a gymnasium exercise regime*. Unpublished M.Sc. Thesis, University of London.

Reilly, T. (1977). Some risk factors in selected track and field events. *British Journal of Sports Medicine*, **11**, 53–56.

Reilly, T. (1979). The mechanical efficiency of weight training. *Proceedings VII International Congress of Biomechanics (Warsaw)*.

Reilly, T. and Thomas, V. (1978). Multi-station equipment for physical training: design and validation of a prototype. *Applied Ergonomics*, **9**, 201–206.

Rowe, P. H. (1979). Colles fracture due to weight-lifting. *British Journal of Sports Medicine*, **13**, 130–131.

Ryan, J. R. and Salciccioli, G. G. (1976). Fractures of the distal radial epiphysis in adolescent weight-lifters. *American Journal of Sports Medicine*, **4**, 26–27.

Talag, T. S. (1973). Residual muscle soreness as influenced by concentric, eccentric and static contractions. *Research Quarterly*, **44**, 458–469.

Thistle, H. G., Hislop, H. J., Moffroid, M. and Lowman, E. W. (1967). Isokinetic contraction: a new concept of resistance exercise. *Archives of Physical Medicine and Rehabilitation*, **48**, 279–282.

Whitney, R. J. (1958). The strength of the lifting action in man. *Ergonomics*, **1**, 101–128.

CHAPTER 8

The concept, measurement and development of flexibility

T. REILLY BA, DPE, MSc, PhD, MIBiol

THE CONCEPT OF FLEXIBILITY

Flexibility, mobility and suppleness tend to signify the same fundamental faculty. Each denotes amplitude of joint movement and absence of stiffness. The vocabulary is further extended when calisthenics, mobilising or stretching exercises describe training procedures. Two attributes have been distinguished – extent (or static) and dynamic flexibility (Fleishman, 1964). Extent flexibility refers to the range of movement possible at a particular joint or series of joints in functional combination. Dynamic flexibility describes the ability to move part or parts of the body quickly or make rapid and repeated movements involving muscle flexibility. The concern is with stiffness or the forces opposing movement over any range rather than the magnitude of the motion. It is manifested in such actions as squat-thrusts and is likely to be important in speed and power events.

It is misleading to regard extent flexibility as a general factor since it is largely joint specific (Harris, 1969). Good flexibility in a particular joint does not guarantee better than average values elsewhere. Different sport events have specialised forms of action that in turn produce particular changes in the range of motion so that specific patterns of flexibility are found in selected sports. Hurdlers and karate competitors, for example, need great hip abduction while gymnasts and soccer goalkeepers need good lateral flexion of the spine. Javelin throwers and shot putters tend to have outstanding wrist flexibility, while tennis players are mobile in the shoulder. Weightlifters excel in trunk, gymnasts in hip and swimmers in ankle extent flexibility, reflecting particular requirements for those sports (Leighton, 1957a; 1957b).

Dynamic flexibility has been called 'agility that does not involve running' (McCloy and Young, 1954). It is clearly distinct from agility which is defined as the ability to change direction of the body or its parts rapidly and is usually measured by standardised run tests (Cureton, 1970). Agility depends on a number of underlying abilities such as muscular power, reaction time, coordination, dynamic flexibility and at least a normal amount of extent flexibility. Agility can be paramount in avoiding hazards that present themselves without warning in field games especially.

Flexibility exercises are used in warming-up for training and competition and for more permanent effects as a component of the training programme. Justification for their practice is based on a number of counts.

Firstly, suppling exercises are employed in warming-up as a precaution against injury in the more strenuous exercise to follow. There is an immediate beneficial effect on flexibility so that muscles are less tight when competition starts (Atha and Wheatley, 1976a). Consequently they are better able to survive a sudden stretch intact. Performance is also likely to be assisted by the elevation in muscle temperature produced. Though there is no conclusive evidence that preliminary flexibility exercises substantially reduce the risk of injury, their practice is uniformly supported as sound by practitioners. Muscle soreness from succeeding activity is known to be reduced (De Vries, 1959), and stretching exercises the day after strenuous competition help to ameliorate sore muscles (De Vries, 1961; 1962).

Secondly, improvement in extent flexibility is likely to assist performance by allowing a more efficient posture to be assumed. The butterfly swimmer, for example, can more easily get into a flat streamlined position and still recover his arms over water. Increased flexibility in specific regions is likely to improve technique in hurdling, diving, gymnastics and ballet, all of which require extremes of particular movements. Greater flexibility also allows application of force over a wider distance. Increased hyperextension of the shoulder permits the javelin thrower to exert force on the implement over a longer distance before release. This should increase the acceleration and assist the throw.

Thirdly, improved flexibility reduces the susceptibility to injury since the joint has greater margin to yield under strain. Liemohn (1978) presented evidence that inflexibility in the hip predisposes towards hamstring strains. Alternatively, hypermobility can be disadvantageous in that the individual may adopt extreme positions where the joint is unstable and unable to withstand the mechanical strain imposed on it. For this reason extreme flexibility measures have been proposed as a screening tool for contact sports (Mathews and Fox, 1976).

Finally, adaptive shortening of connective tissue resulting from inactivity and resisting movement can be reversed by flexibility routines. Though extremes of flexibility are of little value in normal activity, inactive individuals tend to be inflexible (McCue, 1953) and lack adequate range of motion for many day-to-day activities. Attention to restoring extensibility applies to athletes returning to training after enforced inaction through injury as well as to the habitually sedentary embarking on an exercise regimen.

THE MEASUREMENT OF FLEXIBILITY

A variety of instruments have been devised for measurement of flexibility and procedures standardised for extent flexibility measurement (Billig and Loewendahl, 1949; Cureton, 1947).

Goniometry

The goniometer consists of a 180° protractor constructed of plexiglass, wood or stainless steel. It may have two extended arms, one fixed at the zero line and one mobile, or just one mobile arm which can be locked in any position (Fig. 8/1). The centre point of the protractor is aligned with the centre of the joint being measured and readings taken in extreme flexion and extension.

Flexometry

The flexometer designed by Leighton (1955) overcomes the disadvantage of the goniometer in that no decision is required as to what constitutes the axis of a bony lever. The device contains a rotating circular dial marked off in degrees and a pointer counter-balanced to ensure it always points vertically (Fig. 8/1). It is strapped on to the appropriate body segment and the range of motion determined in respect to this perpendicular.

Electrogoniometry (elgon)

The universal electrogoniometer designed by Karpovich and Karpovich (1959) consists of two brass shafts attached to the knob and housing of a potentiometer. The shafts are secured by snap fasteners to a chassis strapped to a body segment, the length of the chassis and shafts depending on the joint studied. Displacement and velocity are continuously recorded during motion so that changes in joint angles throughout a movement are monitored. According to Adrian (1973) over a dozen types of elgons have been designed since the original. Currently miniature potentiometers and lightweight plastics are employed so movement is not inhibited and concomitant emg analysis permitted.

Photography

Photographic techniques reported by Hunnebelle et al (1972) are useful for measuring flexibility in body segments difficult to stabilise, notably the hips and trunk.

Fig. 8/1
Stainless steel goniometer and flexometer

Maximal flexion and extension movements are held for one to two seconds while photographs are taken. Amplitude of each movement is determined from the photographs after drawing the direction of the body segments and measurement of appropriate angles.

Performance tests

Flexibility has been measured with different forms of a general test incorporating hip and back flexion. Three practical tests are more commonly used.

SCOTT AND FRENCH (1950) BOBBING TEST

A 20 inch (50cm) scale marked in half-inch (1cm) units is attached to a stable bench, the middle of the scale being level with the bench top. Standing with toes even with the front edge of the bench, the subject bobs downwards forcefully four times reaching equally with fingers of both hands while keeping the knees fully extended. The score is the lowest point reached in the series or attained and held for two to three seconds. This test has been modified for non-athletes to permit mild knee flexion and requires slow rather than bobbing movements to avoid possible hamstring strain (Reilly, 1971).

KRAUS AND HIRSCHLAND (1954) FLOOR-TOUCH TEST

This consists of attempting to touch the floor from standing, keeping the knees extended and holding the end position for three seconds. The test originated in a posture clinic for treatment of patients with low back pain as it was maintained that a certain degree of flexibility in the back and hamstrings is essential for preventing low back disorders. It was included with five other items in a battery of minimum muscular fitness tests which have been extensively applied to children, the flexibility test typically producing the highest failure rate.

WELLS AND DILLON (1952) SIT AND REACH TEST

The subject assumes a long-sitting position and slides both hands forward on a suitably placed low table as far as possible. A marked scale is incorporated on the table with the zero line directly over his feet which in turn are firmly pressed against a cross-board. The score is the distance reached by the finger-tips.

Arthrography

Methods have been designed to measure the torque needed to move a joint through various ranges of motion at varying speeds (Wright and Johns, 1960). The apparatus of Goddard et al (1969), for measuring the passive resistance of the human knee joint to an applied force, used a strain gauge torque plate and an angular displacement transducer. The contribution of a simple frictional component proportional to the normal force between the joint surfaces, a viscous component due to the shear of the synovial fluid film between the articulating surfaces as well as an elastic component can be extracted. Results can be expressed in dissipative stiffness, representing the resistive torque exerted by the articular surfaces and their lubrication, and elastic stiffness due to the soft tissue around the joint. Arthrography has, as yet, been applied more to study diseased conditions such as rheumatoid arthritis and osteoarthrosis than to physical performance.

LIMITATIONS TO MOVEMENT

Limitations to movement vary with the type of joint and the soft tissue around it. Hinge joints for example may be limited in the extreme position by adjacent bony surfaces as occur in elbow and knee extension. This factor is unlikely to alter once epiphyseal growth plates have closed. The long bones are especially more pliable during growth and hence their joints can be affected by hard training in the developmental years. Ballet dancers as well as gymnasts commence training at an early age and have a significantly higher incidence of hypermobility in many joints (Grahame, 1971). Extreme hypermobility may be due to osteogenesis imperfecta (McKusick, 1966) or to intense training prior to calcification of the growth plates (Fig. 8/2).

Inextensibility of soft tissue may be the factor limiting movement as occurs in shoulder or hip flexion and extension at the ankle joint. By far the greater flexibility in flexion and extension is found in the shoulder joint being approximately 260° compared with 65° at the ankle and hip or 75° at the trunk in normal individuals (Leighton, 1957a; 1957b). The greater flexibility is at the expense of stability and arises from the

Fig. 8/2 Extreme mobility in a gymnast

shallow insertion of the humeral head into the glenoid cavity, security being attained by the surrounding ligaments and muscles. Lax ligaments may in some cases cause hypermobility and can be due to pathological conditions whereas excessively tight ligaments may restrict limbs from moving to extreme positions. Prevalence of ligamentous laxity due to a process of natural selection and heredity has been put forward to partially account for the hypermobility in ballet students (Grahame and Jenkins, 1972). The restraint on movement imposed by ligaments may at many points be reinforced by muscular tension which may actually check movement before the ligaments are fully stretched. This effect is called passive insufficiency or the ligamentous action of muscle. Tension in the hamstrings, for example, while the knee is fully extended, limits hip flexion.

Dynamic flexibility may be restricted by the resistance of soft tissue. Data obtained by Johns and Wright (1962) indicate that the largest contribution to stiffness in the mid-range of free movement is from the joint capsule (47 per cent), secondly muscles and their fascial sheaths (41 per cent) and thirdly tendon (10 per cent), while skin contributes minimally (2 per cent). At extremes of motion, tendons have a more limiting effect while excess subcutaneous fat deposits may impede mobility particularly in the hip/trunk region. Hypertrophied muscle, as could occur with highly developed biceps, deltoid or hamstrings, might impair flexibility. The contractile elements of muscle comprising the acto-myosin complex are mainly affected by strength training while the elastic components, consisting of the fascia and connective tissue surrounding the fibres and to some extent the Z discs linking successive sarcomeres, are provoked in stretching exercises. Consequently it is recommended that muscle extensibility should not be neglected when intensive strength training programmes are followed.

Movement may also be limited by neuromuscular factors. As actions proceed, sensory information about movement and limb positions is provided by proprioception. The muscle spindle is activated when a muscle is passively stretched and evokes reflex contraction in the muscle being stretched. This is called the myotatic or stretch reflex. It serves to facilitate the contraction of the muscle stretched but has also a protective function in securing appropriate postural adjustments or withdrawal from extreme positions. Golgi tendon organs, found mainly in musculotendonous junctions, are deformed whether the muscle is shortening or being stretched. This effect is inhibitory and functions to protect the entire operating muscle group by damping moto-neuronal discharges. Pacinian corpuscles, located in joints and in sheaths of muscle

and tendon, sense pressure and along with the free nerve endings are involved in pain tolerance at extreme positions. The condition of peripheral nerve trunks may also limit movement. Hip flexion, for example, may be limited by irritability of the sciatic nerve as well as tight hamstrings.

Flexibility seems to be independent of physique (Laubach and McConville, 1966) and largely unrelated to anthropometric variations (Mathews et al, 1957). Only extremely disproportionate body builds were found by Broer and Galles (1958) to have any advantage in a toe touch test. There is a circadian variation in joint stiffness with lowest levels in the morning and late evening (Wright et al, 1969). Since stiffness increases with decreased temperature the proximity of the curve to the circadian rhythm of body temperature is not surprising. A similar circadian variation has been found for hip/trunk flexibility (Stockton et al, 1978). Preliminary stretching exercises are especially advisable for those athletes engaged in early morning training.

It is well established that girls of most ages have greater hip/trunk flexibility than boys (Phillips, 1955). It seems this superiority exists at all ages and persists through adult life. Boys lose flexibility as they enter adolescence from 10 to 12 years of age, then improve until late teens without regaining the early childhood levels. Girls increase in flexibility from 6 to 12 years of age and then gradually deteriorate (Hupprich and Sigerseth, 1950).

In normal individuals, dynamic flexibility appears to grow steadily poorer from childhood onwards though this is largely due to low habitual activity levels rather than an innate early ageing effect.

TRAINING FLEXIBILITY
Training effects
Training effects on flexibility are observed within a single session as a warm-up result and this persists for more than one day (Atha and Wheatley, 1976a). Persistent effects are found after three to four weeks of regular training and may be attributable to various causes.

Firstly, structural changes in the mechanical realignment of the network of tissues crossing the joint or lengthening of semi-plastic elements in those tissues may occur. This results from moving a joint beyond the normal end position to the point of real discomfort. The principle is that the rate of increase of flexibility depends on the magnitude of the imposed stretch.

Secondly, greater relaxation is found in the antagonist which permits further movement without producing tension to oppose it. This is achieved by proprioceptive neuromuscular facilitation. Increased flexibility follows the reflex inhibition of muscles resisting movement in the limiting position.

Thirdly, tolerance to pain induced by maximum stretching of the tissues crossing the joint improves. Alterations occur in receptor bias which change the strength of the stimulus needed to exceed the pain threshold of a limiting position.

Overload to which restricting tissues adapt is presented by stretching them to the point of discomfort. If this stimulus is discarded the training effect reverses as the joint gradually loses flexibility. It is important to maintain flexibility exercises in training routines through the competitive season. The exercises should be conducted before exhausting strength or endurance training so that they can more easily be executed properly. Stretching exercises are particularly important for injured muscle as scar tissue forms so that repair in a shortened position must be avoided. During recovery, exercises can be worked out which contract the antagonist to the injured muscle which is itself stretched in consequence.

Training methods

ACTIVE EXERCISES

In active flexibility movement is carried to the end position. An example is lateral flexion of the spine performed while standing where the trunk is bent as far as possible alternately to left and right sides. Movements may be carried out slowly or in a jerking ballistic action. Both methods achieve similar results, the slow stretching being preferable for its reduced injury risk as pain can be felt before any tissue damage occurs. Active exercises are suitable in a general warm-up where all major joint complexes can be systematically mobilised. A sound strategy is to start with neck rotation and progress downwards to end with ankle exercises.

STATIC STRETCHING

In static stretching the limiting position is actively held for a period or body segments to be extended are locked in position at their greatest possible range. This is exemplified in the achievement of certain positions in Hatha Yoga postures (Fig. 8/3).

PASSIVE EXERCISES

In passive exercises the limb is moved to its end position and held there by external resistance. This method can be useful to the physiotherapist in restoring normal joint function to an injured limb. It must be applied cautiously even by experienced coaches and it is essential that the athlete relaxes completely during the exercises. Typical examples using partners or manipulation by a trainer are shown in Figure 8/4. The theoretical advantage of this technique is that the normal limb rebound in active exercises due to the stretch reflex is prevented. Passive flexibility work should be followed up by active exercises which allow the agonist to contract so that the increased flexibility is accompanied by increased strength to enhance stability in the newly acquired range. This passive lift to the limit can also be followed by a maximum isometric contraction for about six seconds against the manual resistance provided, and repeated five or six times.

PASSIVE MOBILISING METHODS

Short-term improvements in flexibility have been found with heat treatment and cycloid vibration massage. Diathermy has long been known to allow

Fig. 8/3
Static stretching postures

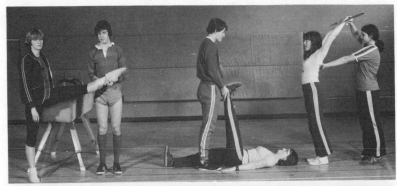

Fig. 8/4 Passive flexibility routines

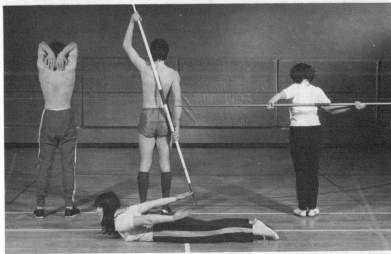

Fig. 8/5 Flexibility exercises for the shoulder

Fig. 8/6 Quadriceps exercises for flexibility

Fig. 8/7 Hip flexibility exercises

greater mobility in stiff joints (Benson, 1930). Dynamic flexibility is improved 20 per cent by local warming of a joint to 45 °C and is decreased 10 to 20 per cent by cooling to 18 °C (De Vries, 1977). Local application for 15 minutes of cycloid vibration of low amplitude and frequency can be equally as effective as a programme of flexibility exercise of similar duration (Atha and Wheatley, 1976b). These changes occur as a result of improved muscle relaxation (Bierman, 1960). In practice exercise-induced flexibility is preferred because of its known long-term effects and additional concomitant benefits.

FLEXIBILITY EXERCISES

An almost endless number of exercises can be devised for flexibility. These will depend on the degrees of freedom of movement at the particular joint and the needs of the athlete. Particular sports call for their own special emphasis. Considerable variety can be achieved on any one exercise simply by changing posture. Lateral flexion of the spine can be conducted either by slowly reaching down the side of the leg on each side successively while standing, or from a supine position parting the legs, and attempting to touch the ankle first on the left then the right while keeping legs and shoulders in contact with the floor. A further example is the performance of hamstring stretching either by high kicks from a standing position or by raising one leg at a time from a supine posture. A selection of typical exercises for the major complexes of the body is now described.

Shoulder exercises
Ballistic exercises include arm circling singly or together in as wide an arc as possible and repeatedly shaking hands behind the back with an imaginary person, the shoulder hyperextended. Elbows may be taken overhead and the fingers attempt to crawl down the back to the inferior angle of the scapulae. From a kneeling position with the back parallel to the ground, the hands supporting well in front, the armpits are forced towards the floor. Lying prone with the arms outstretched to form a cross, the arms are raised as high as possible. Additional exercises used with top sportsmen are demonstrated in Figure 8/5.

Trunk exercises
Active exercises should include lateral flexion, rotation and twisting of the trunk as well as spinal flexion and extension. Trunk twisting can be combined with hamstring exercises in touching alternate toes with feet wide apart and knees extended from a standing or sitting position. Spinal flexion can be improved by attempting, from a sitting posture and legs outstretched in front, to bend forward and take the chin between both knees. Spinal extension can be performed while kneeling by pushing the hips forward and attempting to look overhead to see the floor directly behind. It can also be improved by holding an arch to crab position for 20 seconds or so, or with less flexible individuals holding an arch supported by the shoulders at the scapulae rather than the palmar surface of the hand. Another exercise is to repeatedly raise the legs, head and outstretched arms from a prone posture and hold this for about 15 seconds at a time.

Hip exercises
A wide variety of exercises are possible because of the freedom of movement at this joint. Hamstring exercises should be counter-balanced by quadriceps stretching routines (Fig. 8/6). A suitable advanced exercise for the hamstrings is to slowly move the feet forward from a press-up position until they are in line with the hands keeping the palms on the floor and the knees extended. Basic exercises involve attempting to touch the toes keeping the knees as straight as possible. With top athletes the leg may be retained for about 20 seconds in a high kick position by the experienced coach or at its end position when raised from supine for a similar period. With less flexible individuals it may be retained after a kick forward to rest on a chair top.

In most sports, considerable attention is needed to improve the ability to achieve a wide split between the legs in the sagittal and frontal planes. Long jumpers, decathletes, sprinters and fencers particularly need great fore-and-aft flexibility while outdoor games and racket players, gymnasts and combat sports competitors need great flexibility in the frontal plane to avoid adductor strains. Many athletes including hurdlers, skiers and gymnasts need both. Starting with the lotus position, appropriate split positions can be held while sitting. A lateral split can be facilitated by putting both feet against a wall while sitting, slowly moving the hips as close to the wall as possible by edging the feet further and further apart. A selection of additional exercises for hip flexibility is shown in Figure 8/7.

Flexibility training should be regarded as having an important role in the preparation of athletes for competition. It should help to reduce the risk of injury and facilitate optimum performance production. Special emphasis must be placed on the individual's needs and bilateral flexibility development encouraged. Controlled active stretching is recommended for safety and good results. Passive manipulation at the limiting position should be conducted only with top athletes and under expert supervision. Communication between subject and partner helps to avoid any unnecessary strain. Stretching exercises are advised in the warm-up prior to competition and on the day following to eliminate stiffness.

REFERENCES

Adrian, M. (1973) *Cinematographic, electromyographic, and electrogoniometric techniques for analysing human movements*. In J. H. Wilmore (ed). *Exercise and sports science reviews*. Volume 1. Academic Press, New York.

Atha, J. and Wheatley, D. W. (1976a). The mobilising effects of repeated measurement of hip flexion. *British Journal of Sports Medicine*, **10**, 22–25.

Atha, J. and Wheatley, D. W. (1976b). Joint mobility changes due to low frequency vibration and stretching exercise. *British Journal of Sports Medicine*, **10**, 26–34.

Benson, S. (1930). Relative influences of diathermy and other physical therapy measures on stiffened joints. *Research Quarterly*, **1**, 57–73.

Bierman, W. (1960). Influence of cycloid vibration massage on trunk flexion. *American Journal of Physical Medicine*, **39**, 219–224.

Billig, H. and Loewendahl, E. (1949). *Mobilisation of the human body*. Stanford University Press, Palo Alto, California.

Broer, M. L. and Galles, N. R. G. (1958). Importance of relationships between various body measurements in performance of the toe touch test. *Research Quarterly*, **29**, 253–263.

Cureton, T. K. (1947). *Physical fitness, appraisal and guidance*. C. V. Mosby, St Louis.

Cureton, T. K. 1970. *Illinois agility run*. In *Physical fitness workbook for adults*. Stipes Publishing Company, Champaign, Illinois.

De Vries, H. A. (1959). Effects of various warm-up procedures on 100 yards times of competitive swimmers. *Research Quarterly*, **30**, 11–20.

De Vries, H. A. (1961). Prevention of muscular distress after exercise. *Research Quarterly*, **32**, 468–479.

De Vries, H. A. (1962). Evaluation of static stretching procedures for improvement of flexibility. *Research Quarterly*, **33**, 222–229.

De Vries, H. A. (1977). *Physiology of exercise for physical education and athletics*. Wm C. Brown Company, Dubuque, Iowa.

Fleishman, E. A. (1964). *The structure and measurement of physical fitness*. Prentice-Hall, Englewood Clifts.

Goddard, R., Dawson, D., Longfield, M. D. and Wright, V. (1969). The measurement of stiffness in human joints. *Acta Rheologica*, **8**, 229–234.

Grahame, R. (1971). Joint hypermobility – clinical aspects. *Proceedings of the Royal Society of Medicine*, **64**, 692–694.

Grahame, R. and Jenkins, J. M. (1972). Joint hypermobility – asset or liability. *Annals of the Rheumatic Diseases*, **31**, 109–111.

Harris, M. L. (1969). A factor analytic study of flexibility. *Research Quarterly*, **90**, 62–70.

Hunnebelle, G., Marechal, J. P. and Falize, J. (1972). *Relationships between amplitude of hip movements and jumping performances*. In A. W. Taylor (ed). *Training: scientific basis and application*. C.C. Thomas. Springfield, Illinois.

Hupprich, F. L. and Sigerseth, P. O. (1950). The specificity of flexibility in girls. *Research Quarterly*, **21**, 25–33.

Johns, R. J. and Wright, V. (1962). Relative importance of various tissues on joint stiffness. *Journal of Applied Physiology*, **17**, 824–828.

Karpovich, P. V. and Karpovich, G. P. (1959). Electrogoniometer: a new device for study of joints in action. *Federation Proceedings*, **18**, 79.

Kraus, H. and Hirschland, R. P. (1954). Minimum muscular fitness tests in school children. *Research Quarterly*, **25**, 178–188.

Laubach, L. L. and McConville, J. T. (1966). Relationships between flexibility, anthropometry and the somatotype of college men. *Research Quarterly*, **37**, 241–251.

Leighton, J. (1955). Instrument and technic for measurement of range in joint motion. *Archives of Physical Medicine and Rehabilitation*, **36**, 571–578.

Leighton, J. (1957a). Flexibility characteristics of four specialised skill groups of college athletes. *Archives of Physical Medicine and Rehabilitation*, **38**, 24–28.

Leighton, J. (1957b). Flexibility characteristics of three specialised skill groups of champion athletes. *Archives of Physical Medicine and Rehabilitation*, **38**, 580–583.

Liemohn, W. (1978). Factors related to hamstring strains. *Journal of Sports Medicine and Physical Fitness*, **18**, 71–76.

Mathews, D. K., Shaw, V. and Bohnen, M. (1957). Hip flexibility of college women as related to length of body segments. *Research Quarterly*, **28**, 352–356.

Mathews, D. K. and Fox, E. L. (1976). *The physiological basis of physical education and athletics*. W. B. Saunders, Philadelphia.

McCloy, C. H. and Young, N. D. (1954) *Tests and measurements in health and physical education*. Appleton-Century-Crofts, New York.

McCue, B. F. (1953). Flexibility of college women. *Research Quarterly*, **24**, 316–318.

McKusick, V. A. (1966). *Heritable disorders of connective tissue*. C. V. Mosby, St Louis.

Phillips, M. (1955). Analysis of results from the Kraus-Weber test of minimum muscular fitness in children. *Research Quarterly*, **26**, 314–323.

Reilly, T. (1971). *An ergonomics study of a gymnasium exercise regime*. Unpublished M.Sc. Thesis, University of London.

Scott, M. G. and French, E. (1950). *Evaluation in physical education*. C. V. Mosby, St Louis.

Stockton, I. D., Reilly, T., Sanderson, F. H. and Walsh, T. J. (1978). *Investigations of circadian rhythm in selected components of sports performance*. Paper presented at the Society of Sports Sciences Conference (Crewe and Alsager).

Wells, K. and Dillon, E. (1952). The sit and reach – a test of back and leg flexibility. *Research Quarterly*, **23**, 115–118.

Wright, V. and Johns, R. J. (1960). Physical factors concerned with the stiffness of normal and diseased joints. *Johns Hopkins Hospital Bulletin*, **106**, 215–231.

Wright, V., Dowson, D. and Longfield, M. D. (1969). Joint stiffness – its characterisation and significance. *Bio-Medical Engineering*, **4**, 8–14.

CHAPTER 9

Strength training for injury prevention

T. REILLY BA, DPE, MSc, PhD, MIBiol

STRENGTH

Strength reflects the ability to apply force and overcome resistance. It is a function of the neuro-musculo-skeletal system and closely related to muscle cross-sectional area. Its development is indispensable for success in sports performed against high resistance including combat sports, rock-climbing and rowing. It is a pre-requisite for activities with high power demands as shown by the muscular physique in top throwers, jumpers, sprinters and gymnasts. Muscularity and strength also favour performance in contact sports where the rigours of competition are more easily endured without injury. Manifestation of strength is found under various conditions.

Isometric strength

Maximum isometric strength is defined operationally as the force of reaction achieved when the greatest possible effort is intentionally brought to bear in a static muscle contraction from two to six seconds duration. The muscle length stays constant and no movement occurs. Isometric strength is important when allied to the requisite sport skills where performance is periodically under static conditions or movement initiated by overcoming large resistances. This applies in rugby scrummaging, tug-of-war, weightlifting and wrestling, for example. The hammer thrower needs to counter great centrifugal forces as he rotates and the soccer player balances statically on one leg while place-kicking.

Explosive strength

Explosive strength as defined by Fleishman (1964) denotes the ability to expend energy in one explosive act, as in jumping or projecting some object as far as possible. The force generated may be sub-maximal since force and velocity are interrelated. Muscle shortening velocity is greatest when externally unloaded while force is maximal at zero velocity or isometric conditions. In rapid contractions there is limited time for liberation of chemical energy and interconnections of myofibrilar filaments. Forces developed in eccentric contractions are greater at all velocities than those of concentric work. Power output and mechanical efficiency are improved if muscle is pre-stretched allowing storage of elastic energy for immediate utilisation in concentric action (Thys et al, 1972). This is achieved in appropriate leg musculature by sinking the hips prior to jumping and in arm muscles by winding up before bowling. As explosive strength is applied rapidly under dynamic conditions it is imperative that technique is perfected to avoid injury. Absolute strength provides inadequate compensation for poor coordination when muscle or articulo-skeletal damage is promoted. In team games explosive strength must be allied to good timing. The rugby forward must strive to outjump his line-out opponent, win ball possession and avoid collisions at the same time.

Dynamic strength

The strength of the limb muscles applied to moving or supporting body mass repeatedly over a given period of time was known as dynamic strength by Fleishman (1964). It reflects the strength endurance of the organism or its ability to withstand fatigue under sustained strength expenditure exemplified in performing press-ups (or holding maximum isometric tension to exhaustion). Dynamic strength is especially important in maximal efforts of half-minute to three minutes duration. It is distinct from muscle endurance which indicates the ability of a muscle group to contract continually against a light load and which depends on the circulation. When muscle repeatedly contracts in a vigorous fashion fatigue is shown by its inability to continue delivering the same mechanical work. Maximal power output declines more rapidly due to a shift in the substrate subserving contraction. Highest power is produced in the first few seconds of activity, values up to six horse power being found (Davies, 1971). Fuel here is furnished by intramuscular phosphagens. When all-out effort is extended beyond these first seconds energy is supplied from glycogen within muscle anaerobically. This store increases the work capacity at a reduced power production. Eventually maximal effort is limited within a minute or so of onset by accumulation of metabolites and lowered pH within muscle, or lack of metabolic substrate due to retarded adenosine triphosphate (ATP) synthesis (Gollnick and Hermansen, 1973). Under such fatigued conditions skill may become disjoined, judgement impaired and injury promoted. Even in sustained activities where the organism operates with almost limitless though subdued power supply through oxidative phosphorylation, added strength facilitates both performance and individual safety since the relative strain on working muscles imposed by a fixed work load is now reduced. The poor strength and muscularity of endurance competitors leaves them vulnerable when responding to spurts from opponents or encountering steep uphill gradients.

Strength and muscle size

In general the larger the muscle the greater its strength, though the relationship has qualifications. Differences between muscles in strength capability arise from their pennation or manner of tendonous attachment. Muscles with parallel fibres, e.g. sartorius, have poor force production but great mobility compared to muscles whose fibres converge obliquely on the tendon. Surface area of contact is increased where muscle fibres approach the tendon from one side, e.g. soleus, both sides, e.g. rectus femoris, or multi-pennately, e.g. deltoid, rather than the end. Distributions of fibre types similarly account for variability between muscles and between individuals. Thigh and calf muscles of top sprinters are endowed with high proportions of white or fast-twitch fibres compared with the abundance of red or slow-twitch fibres in endurance athletes. Responses of muscles and individuals to work-induced hypertrophy may vary because of differences in fibre-type distributions. Finally, endurance training may reduce muscle size by decreasing intramuscular lipids or temporarily increase muscle diameter by combining exhaustive training and diet to boost muscular glycogen stores as done by marathon runners the week before racing.

STRENGTH FOR INJURY PREVENTION

Muscles act as agonists, antagonists and synergists to cause, permit and assist movement. Unwanted actions are prevented by muscles acting as stabilisers. The orderliness of patterned muscular involvement is regulated by the nervous system. Greater strength in stabilising musculature improves individual tolerance to those external exigencies promoting imbalance in various sports. The gymnast needs great leg strength to control landing from a vault as well as for the more explosive operations. In field-invasive games, greater leg strength assists the manifold manoeuvres such as

turning, accelerating, decelerating, tackling and avoiding tackles without injury. In contact games great roborisation is needed and players with poor strength have greater difficulty in surviving prolonged competitive periods without being injured (Reilly, 1975; Reilly and Thomas, 1977). Cahill and Griffith (1978) showed that pre-season total body conditioning significantly reduces the frequency and severity of knee injuries in American university footballers.

Imperfect strength development in particular muscle groups may predispose to local injury. This is because muscles may secure the integrity of joints by crossing the joint or having their tendons inserted around the capsule. Knee stability, for example, is considerably enhanced by strengthening the quadriceps which safeguard the joint in conjunction with the cruciate and collateral ligaments. Quadriceps exercises are especially recommended in rehabilitation of knee injuries as the joint is further unstable if their strength subsides. Return to contact games should be delayed until adequate knee strength is restored. Quadriceps development can allow professional athletes to mask ligament or meniscus damage and osteoarthrosis (Smillie, 1970). Similarly, shoulder stability is enhanced by training surrounding musculature and many back problems are avoided by developing the erector spinae. Improving the strength of abdominal and back muscles not only helps prevent lumbar pain but serves also to remedy low back pain conditions (Corbin, 1971). Bodnar (1977) reported a relationship between the incidence of shoulder and neck injuries and weakness of the cervical muscles in American college footballers and recommended strengthening cervical and trunk muscles as protective measures.

Uneven distribution of strength is likely to predispose to injury. This may be manifested in disproportionate development in one of the agonist/antagonist pair. The hamstrings, antagonists to the quadriceps during the first 160 to 165° of leg extension, must equally be considered when devising training programmes for quadriceps. A greater susceptibility to hamstring strains is found when individuals have an inappropriate flexor-extensor strength ratio (Burkett, 1970). The hamstring/quadriceps strength ratio recommended by Klein and Allman (1969) is 0.60.

Uneven distribution is also evident in contra-lateral differences in strength acquisition. This inequality is seen in the girth of the serving arm in top tennis players compared with the non-playing limb and is a logical outcome of repetitive practice in throwing events and racket sports which impose unilateral demands. Imbalance can have serious consequences in the lower extremities as it is then likely to prompt asymmetrical locomotion. Liemohn (1978) found that all hamstring injuries in a group of track and field athletes were to the non-dominant leg, substantiating that the weaker side is the more susceptible. Though specific unilateral demands are imposed in certain athletic performances, preparation should still involve bilateral strength training to avoid uneven gains. Some contra-lateral effects do occur in the non-exercised limb but are of insufficient magnitude to excuse not training both. Cross-training effects can however be exploited to reduce muscle atrophy and for reconditioning after immobilisation. Isotonic exercise has been found preferable to isometric for producing cross-training (Clarke, 1973) though both methods have shown equal effectiveness when equated for load and duration (Coleman, 1969). Action potentials occur in contralateral musculature, demonstrating the irradiation of nerve impulses to extremities other than those directly engaged in activity (Bowers, 1966). Seemingly, innervation of descending pyramidal fibres that cross sides before supplying muscles overflows to the smaller number of uncrossed fibres, so that movement occurs in an activated muscle and isometric contractions in its symmetrical partner. Sufficient overflow occurs only under strong volition so high intensity is desirable for cross-education (De Vries, 1977). The effect is supported by histological findings (Reitsma, 1969) and underlines nervous system involvement in force application.

Neural control of maximal voluntary effort results in a strength reserve not normally expressed. This reservoir may amount to 25 per cent and is released in exceptional circumstances and emergencies. It serves normally to protect the muscle, its tendon and bony attachment from over-exertion. This inhibition is eliminated under extreme motivational conditions (Ikai and Steinhaus, 1961). The effect is attributed to adrenalin release and reduced nervous inhibition which permit greater motor unit recruitment. This safety reserve is harnessed under strong motivation by athletes prior to strength events. It may also be tapped in training muscle by electrical stimulation though attendant risks make it inadvisable. Electrotherapy is valuable in rehabilitation to stimulate muscle which has temporarily lost its effective innervation since the motor pathways are minimally involved in electrical training. Strength training reduces the effect of the inhibitory mechanism and permits greater tension to occur. This may be due to greater antagonist relaxation as the movement proceeds or to increased shielding of Golgi sensory organs by muscle connective tissue thickened from training, allowing innervation of the muscles to progress further uninhibited.

A basic programme of general muscle conditioning is advocated to avoid leaving local weaknesses in the ath-

lete's make-up. A broad basis of general strength sets a foundation on which specific strength can be safely developed. Improved arm and back strength allows the legs to be overloaded in power cleans and half-squats when leg strength is being specifically developed. An outstanding single benefit to a strengthened muscle is that greater stresses can be borne without tearing. Developed muscle also provides a fleshy shield to cushion the effect of blows on bone or abdominal organs, thereby affording some protection in combat sports.

STRENGTH TRAINING
Law of use and disuse
The organism habituates to the load placed on it indicating that structure is modified by function. Connective tissue and bone adapt as well as skeletal muscle. The muscle fibre and its surrounding sarcolemma thicken and the connective tissue of the muscle broadens and toughens. Primary cellular multiplication occurs in ligaments and tendons which grow and increase in tensile strength. Bones adapt to suit stresses and strains within their tolerance by forming new supportive trabeculae. Calcium phosphate and calcium carbonate in bone increase in response to training providing greater sturdiness. Severe repetitive strain may result in inflammation and osteoporosis as occurs in stress fractures. With prolonged rest, bones demineralise and weaken and muscles atrophy. The trainer's quandary is the recognition of the thin line separating harmful overload from the maximal stimulant for physiological accommodation. The triple principles of overload, reversibility and specificity contain a framework for regulating training regimes to permit continuous adaptation.

Principle of overload
The principle of overload indicates that physiological systems improve in function when challenged to work at supra-normal levels. Muscle hypertrophies only when forced to operate beyond customary intensities. The stimulus threshold represents the work intensity below which no effect accrues. The ability to train muscle is greatest when strength training begins though some muscles may be in poorer condition than others and respond more readily. The load must be progressively increased to elicit further adaptive reactions as training develops and the training stimulus gradually raised. Gains become increasingly difficult to obtain as the muscle approaches its theoretical potential.

Overload is accomplished by emphasising the duration or intensity of exercise. Many repetitions of low intensity work improve muscular endurance while few repetitions at high intensity develop strength. High intensity work at speed promotes muscular power as well as strength. Many sportsmen wish to develop strength without accompanying hypertrophy. Boxers, wrestlers and oarsmen want to avoid excessive increases in muscle bulk which necessitate moving to a higher competitive weight category. Belated attempts to shed weight by dehydration are counter-productive since strength abates with fluid loss. Hurdlers and jumpers whose extra muscle constitutes an additional load to be lifted against gravity similarly seek to avoid undue weight gains. Alternatively throwers and rugby forwards can utilise beneficially the extra mass acquired. Though the demarcation line for non-hypertrophy is unclear, speed of contraction appears important in reducing the extent of hypertrophy. Experience suggests that repeated sets of four to six repetitions at maximal intensity invokes hypertrophy while fewer sets of six to ten repetitions short of maximal effort promotes strength without concomitant muscle growth. Maximum can be conveniently determined by De Lorme's (1945) repetition maximum (RM) criterion which indicates the maximum load that can be lifted a given number of repetitions and varies with the number attempted. MacQueen (1954) reported that when body builders employed less than RM intensity for considerably more than 10 repetitions and more than four or five sets hypertrophy did not result. Hypertrophy is regulated largely by testosterone which explains why pronounced muscle growth is not found when female athletes undertake severe strength training regimes (Brown and Wilmore, 1974). Hypertrophy is observed when training is supplemented by synthetic sex hormones or anabolic steroids.

Bouts of progressive exercise overload should be interspersed by regular rest periods to allow recovery. The common practice of weight training three or four times a week seems reasonable to avoid overuse but a minimum of twice-weekly strength sessions is recommended to provide adequate training stimulus. Ryan (1968) acknowledged insufficient rest as a factor contributing to injury and intermittent illness. De Lorme and Watkins (1948) found that five days per week was usually the heaviest schedule that could be employed without developing serious signs of delayed recovery. Clarke (1973) concluded that training at 6RM for three sets, three times a week seemed an optimal combination. Progression involves an evolving upward spiral of overload-fatigue-recovery, with recovery improving as the individual gets fitter. Frequency and intensity may be reduced during the peak of the competitive season when the objective is to maintain the strength level already acquired and concentrate on speed and skill.

The principle of reversibility

Reversibility indicates that a training effect subsides if training is discontinued. Strength gains are lost at about one-third their rate of acquisition (Jensen and Fisher, 1972). Athletes who abruptly terminate a crash course of pre-season strength training are likely to lose form in mid-season due to the relatively rapid strength loss. Isotonic training leads to greater retention than isometric (Rasch and Morehouse, 1957). Strength loss after daily isometric training equalled the rate at which it was acquired in Müller's (1959) investigations. Hettinger (1961) and Morehouse (1967) claimed that strength gained can be retained with one high intensity session every two weeks. At least a weekly work-out seems preferable for retention in top athletes through the competitive period though fortnightly sessions probably serve to retard strength loss. Strength gained is not entirely lost, a portion of it remaining indefinitely (McMorris and Elkins, 1954). Retraining, when commenced, is also considerably easier than initially (Waldeman and Stull, 1959). Special care is needed during the early weeks of retraining to avoid muscle pulls as athletes are often reluctant to accept their diminished function through inactivity.

The principle of specificity

Specificity suggests that strength training effects may be limited to the pattern of muscular involvement in the conditioning exercise. Different types of motor units exist within muscle so that a given type of exercise recruits a specific combination of motor units best adapted to that demand. It is desirable that strength training routines should simulate closely the motor programme of the event and employ the specific muscle groups involved. This invites preliminary analysis of competitive skills. Specificity is also shown in isometric exercise in that strength gains may be restricted to the angle at which training occurred (Belka, 1968), so that isometrics should be undertaken at a series of joint angles. Where great strength is needed only at the beginning of the movement, as in ballistic actions, exercises in that range may suffice. Specificity is further corroborated in that isometric programmes increase isometric strength more than they do isotonic strength, the reverse being also true (Berger, 1962).

A strength training schedule should evidently be planned to suit individual needs. This must vary with the sport and be adjusted for age and sex. The curves showing average strength values in relation to age and sex (Fig. 9/1) can be altered by training which not only arrests the normal gradual decline after mid-20s but brings further improvement for another 10 to 15 years. Though the difference between the sexes varies with muscle groups, it is common after adolescence to

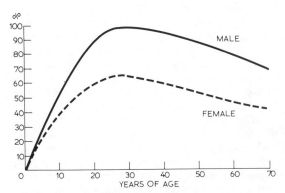

Fig. 9/1 Average strength values in relation to age and sex

expect two-thirds of male strength in females. The difference is largely attributable to men's greater muscle mass though on average their bones, tendons and ligaments are also more robustly constructed. Female athletes are often unwilling to undertake strength regimes for social reasons and in consequence suffer more injuries in sports requiring explosive efforts (Klaus, 1964).

Evaluation and measurement
Regular strength testing provides an objective basis for rescheduling regimes to apply progressive resistance. It serves also to evaluate the conditioning programme and give valuable feedback on the athlete's progress. It helps to identify weaknesses and devise individual schedules.

Performance tests provide convenient criteria for strength measurement. Selected weight lifts can be used for 1RM, 6RM or 10RM. Tests involving moving a heavy load to exhaustion are also employed since muscular strength and absolute endurance are highly correlated (Baumgartner and Jackson, 1975). Strength measurement has typically employed instruments capable of recording the maximum force of an isometric contraction. These include cable tensiometers, dynamometers, spring balances and electrical strain gauges (Clarke, 1967) and administration is hardly feasible outside a sports science laboratory. Peak force during dynamic movements may be recorded using isokinetic machinery. Static and dynamic measurement of rotational movements can be achieved by a dynamometer based on a rotary torque activator (Jensen, 1976).

The vertical and standing broad jumps conveniently indicate explosive strength and leg power. The softball throw or shot putt for distance have been used as

indicants of muscle power in arm work. As power is a function of the rate of force application, strength is a major component. A power lever, based on a wheel and axle lever system (Glencross, 1966), permits direct measurement of the horsepower in a single explosive movement. The stair run test of Margaria et al (1966) was designed to indicate the horsepower output of the phosphagens or maximum alactic anaerobic power. A comparable test for the bicycle ergometer has also been designed (Pirnay and Crielaard, 1978). Though these tests may be used for monitoring conditioning progress, the ultimate test of the validity of the training is the competitive performance.

STRENGTH TRAINING METHODS
Isometrics
Isometrics implicate muscular tension without corresponding limb movement. Body segments or external objects may provide the resistance. Special isometric racks have been designed for use in diverse fashions in gymnasia. The scrummaging rack used by rugby forwards in training outdoors affords another example.

Isometric programmes gained widespread appeal from the pioneer studies of Müller (1957). The magnitude of the training effects reported initially were not replicated in later studies of fitter subjects. For these the work load had to be substantially elevated beyond the advocated daily contraction held for six seconds at 66 per cent of maximal isometric capacity to get similar results. Consequently the claims attributed earlier to isometrics were considerably qualified. Furthermore improvement may be restricted to the angle at which the contraction is held and this may not appreciably assist dynamic performance. Thirdly, the concomitant compression of the vascular bed with occlusion of blood supply to the muscles under tension and the rise in blood pressure this precipitates make isometrics unsuitable for sedentary individuals undergoing exercise for prevention of coronary heart disease, particularly if they already possess predisposing factors.

Isometric training is recommended where competition places specific demands for isometric strength. It may be especially valuable to athletes desiring increased muscle strength without corresponding hypertrophy since isometrics do not provoke muscle growth (Falls et al, 1970). For the majority, isometrics can be judiciously incorporated into a broader conditioning programme.

Mechanical and physical resistances
Weight training presents a convenient method of overloading muscle and is commonly employed in conditioning for competition. Loads are provided by

dumb-bells or weighted barbells and are easily adjustable for progressive resistance. Eccentric work can be incorporated by weight lowering in addition to the more usual lifting exercises so elastic as well as contractile elements in muscle are trained. Spring loaded devices allow eccentric arm work though they do not have inherent progressive resistance.

Pulley systems permit alteration of the direction of force application and are frequently employed in land conditioning of swimmers. Hydraulics have been effectively incorporated in the design of rowing machines. Isokinetic equipment allows constant speed of contraction and maximal force exertion throughout the complete range of movement. Multi-station apparatus affords an opportunity of training various muscle groups and engaging a squad of players on a single machine.

Strength training can employ partner work if equipment is unavailable. Routines may involve pushing against an opponent's shoulder who reciprocates or performing half-squats with partner supported supine on the back. A whole team can be occupied in relay races, each member carrying a colleague on his back during his effort, adding variety to training. Resistance work using a partner is useful in sports where a partner or opponent is actually supported during performance as in ice-skating or wrestling. Where facilities are impoverished, a bench, box or chair is still easily obtained for step-ups. This can be useful where different strength requirements are juxtaposed. The long jumper, for instance, who needs great leg strength for take off and isometric back strength to stabilise his upper body in flight, can train both simultaneously by holding a medicine ball while stepping-up.

Bench stepping has long been used for fitness testing as well as training as it permits calculation of mechanical work done. Other ergometric modes present suitable strength training methods under precisely controlled conditions. Cyclists might use friction braked bicycles which are also valuable in rehabilitation since bodyweight is not supported. Whole body and rowing ergometers are useful in conditioning oarsmen while motor driven treadmills can be modified for skiers. Flumes could be used for preparation of swimmers, canoeists and rowers under exact control. These facilities are expensive and could reasonably be made available only to the élite at centres of sporting excellence.

Natural resistance

Muscles may be overloaded in working against supranormal resistance by carefully exploiting natural conditions. Running up sand dunes was vindicated in the performances of Australian middle-distance runners in the early 1960s. Flat soled shoes are recommended as barefoot athletes may tread on broken glass concealed in the sand. Weekly sessions are sufficient in incorporating sandhill training into the overall schedule in the early phase to avoid Achilles tendon trouble. Running along a flat beach or soft sand is another form of resistance training. In inland areas grassy hills provide a satisfactory alternative to sand dunes (Fig. 9/2).

Fig. 9/2 Hilly ground provides a good opportunity for strengthening leg muscles

Running on soft ground is also recommended provided conditions are not so slippery that hamstring tears are possible. All these methods are eminently suitable for training dynamic strength. Other variations depending on climate and location include running on snow or ankle deep in water, as long as the normal running motion is not severely altered. Work in water may be especially useful for rehabilitation of leg muscles as the strain from lifting bodyweight against gravity is absent. Cyclists may take advantage of otherwise inclement windy conditions by repetitive short sprints against the wind.

Man built environments may similarly be exploited. If conditions are too difficult for outdoor work, suitable indoor staircases can substitute for uphill gradients. Stadium terrace steps are frequently used by football coaches in the training of players.

Functional overload

Strength can be improved by overloading the individual in practices closely related to competition requirements. Running in heavy boots, jumping with ankle weights or jackets weighted with lead are examples. The obvious advantage of this approach is the high likelihood of strength transfer to the event trained for.

Functional overload can be applied to runners either by attachment of a harness held by a trainer at its ends

Fig. 9/3 Functional overload using a running harness

(Fig. 9/3), or drawing a sled. The vigorous running action needed should not be greatly modified from normal for optimal effects. Wrist weights used by gymnasts are another example while weight throwers use excessively heavy implements or attempt explosive release of medicine balls.

Various forms of rebounding and plyometric drills fall within this category. These emphasise elastic properties of muscle in their execution and tend to develop explosive strength. Drills include repetitive hopping on both legs together or separately, jumping decathlons or exaggerated bounding strides. In hopping, the hips should not sink below the level where the femur is parallel to the floor to safeguard the knee joint. Depth jumping drills (Fig. 9/4) involve explosive elevation onto or over a bench or box top on descent from a greater height. The quadriceps are stretched in lowering bodyweight prior to contracting powerfully and by storing elastic energy in the process increase the tension developed in positive work (Cavagna et al, 1968). Since the shock on landing is absorbed largely by the knee joints the complete drill must be smoothly controlled to avoid injury.

Fig. 9/4 Examples of drills for training explosive leg strength

Strength training is considered an indispensable part of preparation for athletic competition and injury prevention. The programme should be geared to the individual's specific needs and be based on progressive resistance. General and specific conditioning should be developed and uneven strength gains avoided. Retraining during rehabilitation is important before returning to competition. Testing provides a sound basis for monitoring progress and evaluating the programme. Strength training may be tapered during the competitive season in many sports to retain the capacity already developed so as to allow greater emphasis on technique and tactical aspects.

REFERENCES

Baumgartner, T. A. and Jackson, A. S. (1975). *Measurement for evaluation in physical education.* Houghton Mifflin, Boston.

Belka, D. (1968). Comparison of dynamic, static and combination training on dominant wrist flexor muscles. *Research Quarterly*, **39**, 244–250.

Berger, R. (1962). Comparison of static and dynamic strength increases. *Research Quarterly*, **33**, 329–333.

Bodnar, L. A. (1977). Sports medicine with reference to back and neck injuries. *Current Practice in Orthopaedic Surgery*, **7**, 116–153.

Bowers, L. (1966). Effect of autosuggested muscle contraction on muscular size and strength. *Research Quarterly*, **37**, 302–312.

Brown, C. H. and Wilmore, J. H. (1974). The effects of maximal resistance training on the strength and body composition of women athletes. *Medicine and Science in Sports*, **6**, 174–177.

Burkett, L. N. (1970). Causative factors in hamstring strains. *Medicine and Science in Sports*, **2**, 39–42.

Cahill, B. R. and Griffith, E. H. (1978). Effect of preseason conditioning on the incidence and severity of high school football knee injuries. *American Journal of Sports Medicine*, **6**, 180–184.

Cavagna, G. A., Dusman, B. and Margaria, R. (1968). Positive work done by a previously stretched muscle. *Journal of Applied Physiology*, **24**, 21–32.

Clarke, D. H. (1973). *Adaptations in strength and muscle endurance.* In J. H. Wilmore (ed). *Exercise and sport sciences reviews.* Volume 1. Academic Press, New York.

Clarke, H. H. (1967). *Application of measurement to health and physical education.* Prentice-Hall, New Jersey.

Coleman, A. E. (1968). Effect of unilateral isometric and isotonic contraction on the strength of the contralateral limb. *Research Quarterly*, **40**, 490–495.

Corbin, C. B. (1971). *Overload.* In L. A. Larson (ed). *Encyclopedia of sports sciences and medicine.* Macmillan, New York.

Davies, C. T. M. (1971). Human power output in exercise of short duration in relation to body size and composition. *Ergonomics*, **14**, 245–256.

De Lorme, T. L. (1945). Restoration of muscle power by heavy resistance exercises. *Journal of Bone and Joint Surgery*, **27**, 645–667.

De Lorme, T. L. and Watkins, A. (1948). Techniques of progressive resistance exercise. *Archives of Physical Medicine and Rehabilitation*, **29**, 263–273.

De Vries, H. A. (1977). *Physiology of exercise for physical education and athletics.* Wm C. Brown Company, Dubuque, Iowa.

Falls, H. B., Wallis, E. L. and Logan, G. A. (1970). *Foundations of conditioning.* Academic Press, New York.

Fleishman, E. A. (1964). *The structure and measurement of physical fitness.* Prentice-Hall, Englewood Cliffs.

Glencross, D. J. (1966). The power lever: an instrument for measuring muscle power. *Research Quarterly*, **37**, 202–210.

Gollnick, P. D. and Hermansen, L. (1973). *Biochemical adaptations to exercise: anaerobic metabolism.* In J. H. Wilmore (ed). *Exercise and sport sciences reviews.* Volume 1. New York. Academic Press.

Hettinger, T. (1961). *Physiology of strength.* C. C. Thomas, Springfield, Illinois.

Ikai, M. and Steinhaus, A. (1961). Some factors modifying the expression of human strength. *Journal of Applied Physiology*, **16**, 157–163.

Jensen, C. R. and Fisher, A. G. (1972). *Scientific basis of athletic conditioning.* Lea and Febiger, Philadelphia.

Jensen, R. K. (1976). Dynamometer for static and dynamic measurements of rotational movement. *Research Quarterly*, **47**, 56–61.

Klaus, E. J. (1964). *The athletic status of women.* In E. Jokl and E. Simon (eds). *International research in sports and physical education.* C. C. Thomas, Springfield, Illinois.

Klein, K. K. and Allman, F. L. (1969). *The knee in sports.* Pemberton Press, New York.

Liemohn, W. (1978). Factors related to hamstring strains. *Journal of Sports Medicine and Physical Fitness*, **18**, 71–76.

Margaria, R., Aghemo, P. and Rovelli, E. (1966). Measurement of muscular power (anaerobic) in man. *Journal of Applied Physiology*, **21**, 1661–1664.

McMorris, R. O. and Elkins, E. C. (1954). A study of production and evaluation of muscular hypertrophy. *Archives of Physical Medicine and Rehabilitation*, **35**, 420–426.

MacQueen, I. J. (1954). Recent advances in the technique of progressive resistance exercise. *British Medical Journal*, **2**, 1193–1198.

Morehouse, C. A. (1967). Development and maintenance of isometric strength of subjects with diverse initial strengths. *Research Quarterly*, **38**, 449–456.

Müller, E. A. (1957). The regulation of muscular strength. *Journal of the Association of Physical Medicine and Rehabilitation*, **112**, 41–47.

Müller, E. A. (1959). Training muscle strength. *Ergonomics*, **2**, 216–222.

Pirnay, F. and Crielaard, J. M. (1978). *Anaerobic power of top athletes in relation to maximal oxygen uptake.* Paper presented at the IInd International Seminar on Kinanthropometry (Leuven, Belgium).

Rasch, P. J. and Morehouse, L. E. (1957). Effect of static and dynamic exercises on muscular strength and hypertrophy. *Journal of Applied Physiology*, **11**, 29–34.

Reilly, T. (1975). *An ergonomic evaluation of occupational stress in professional football.* Unpublished PhD thesis, Liverpool Polytechnic.

Reilly, T. and Thomas, V. (1977). Applications of multivariate analysis to the fitness assessment of soccer players. *British Journal of Sports Medicine*, **11**, 183–184.

Reitsma, W. (1969). Skeletal muscle hypertrophy after heavy exercise in rats with surgically reduced muscle function. *American Journal of Physical Medicine*, **48**, 237–258.

Ryan, A. J. (1968). *The physician and exercise physiology.* In H. B. Falls (ed). *Exercise physiology.* Academic Press, New York.

Smillie, I. S. (1970). *Injuries to the knee joint.* Churchill Livingstone, Edinburgh.

Thys, H., Faraggiana, T. and Margaria, R. (1972). Utilisation of muscle elasticity in exercise. *Journal of Applied Physiology*, **32**, 491–494.

Waldeman, R. and Stull, G. A. (1967). Effects of various periods of inactivity on retention of newly acquired levels of muscular endurance. *Research Quarterly*, **40**, 396–401.

CHAPTER 10

Considerations in endurance training

T. REILLY BA, DPE, MSc, PhD, MIBiol

The athlete who is physically ill-prepared for endurance activities is at least as likely to suffer adversely in participation as his counterpart in power events. Analysis of time of injuries in major team games indicates that injuries predominate towards the end of the contest. At this time, fatigue prevails in the poorly conditioned athlete with errors creeping increasingly into play which in turn promote injury. Lack of fitness also shows after competition in that recovery takes longer.

Endurance fitness or stamina has local and general aspects. Local or muscular endurance expresses the ability of a muscle group to continue working over a prolonged period without performance impairment. Activity may be cyclical as in the repetitive stride of the distance runner or pedalling of the stage cyclist; it is acyclical in the arm and shoulder muscle involvement of the tennis player over five sets or the basketballer's jump endurance requirement. These are specific in that local endurance is needed in the muscle group emphasised and training sessions must be designed accordingly. Endurance is promoted by many repetitions at moderate intensity and does not result in muscle hypertrophy. General endurance is manifested in an efficient oxygen transport system by means of which inhaled oxygen is carried in the blood for tissue respiration. In exercise the oxygen required for sustained contractions is offered to working muscles by the cardiovascular system, the portion extracted as it passes through the muscle being indicated by the arterio-venous O_2 difference. Endurance exercise elicits both central and peripheral adaptive responses which will to a large degree be specific to the training mode.

PHYSIOLOGICAL BACKGROUND

Energetics

Contraction results from the splitting of adenosine triphosphate (ATP), the only molecule the muscle can use directly. This is supplied by alactacid, lactacid and oxidative mechanisms. As exercise commences, energy is immediately furnishable from intramuscular ATP and creatine phosphate (CP) collectively known as the phosphagens. This constitutes the powerful alactacid mechanism whose capacity is limited to 20 to 30 kJ (5 to 7 kcal). Glycogen stored within muscle may be broken down anaerobically (without oxygen) with resultant lactate formation. This lactacid mechanism extends maximal performance for about 30 seconds. In aerobic glycolysis pyruvic acid, the precursor of lactate, is diverted into the aerobic pathway after ATP formation. Here glucose is further broken down to CO_2 and water with additional ATP simultaneously produced. The lactacid mechanism uses only carbohydrates as its fuel and produces relatively few ATP molecules whereas the aerobic system can use fats, proteins and carbohydrates and yields relatively large amounts of ATP.

Apart from the oxygen bound to myoglobin within the muscle, which may provide limited energy in the acute response to exercise, the aerobic mechanism depends on O_2 supply and CO_2 removal through the ventilatory and cardiovascular systems. In the short term an oxygen deficit develops because of the lag in the system's responses while anaerobic metabolism is utilised in the meantime before a steady state is attained. The fitter the athlete the sooner this is reached for a given work intensity, allowing the more highly trained to settle earlier to the competitive pace. The more prolonged the work period the smaller is the proportionate involvement of anaerobic processes until it is almost insubstantial in long-term contests. The relative contribution of aerobic and anaerobic mechanisms to energy provision for maximal exercise of various durations is shown in Table 1. This provides a key for determining the relative emphasis in training for continuous exercise competitions such as running or swimming. These mechanisms obviously interact in a number of endurance sports, many games requiring intermittent acyclical short bursts of intense action depending on lactate producing anaerobic metabolism superimposed on the continuous endurance need. In the intervening periods of cruising, the oxygen debt is mostly repaid and the majority of the lactate removed and recycled or oxidised directly. The ability to tolerate high metabolite levels and quickly recover from anaerobiosis during ongoing performance needs to be developed in training for these events.

Table 1 Relative contributions of anaerobic and aerobic processes to total energy output, during maximal exercise of different duration (based on Gollnick and Hermansen, 1973 and reproduced from *Exercise and sport sciences reviews*, Volume 1, by permission of the publishers, Academic Press, New York)

Energy Output (kJ)				Relative contribution (%)	
Work time maximal exercise	Anaerobic processes	Aerobic processes	Total	Anaerobic processes	Aerobic processes
10s	84	16	100	83	17
1min	126	84	210	60	40
2min	126	189	315	40	60
5min	126	504	630	20	80
10min	105	1 025	1 130	9	91
30min	84	2 825	2 909	3	97
60min	63	5 023	5 086	1	99

Energy sources

Foodstuffs provide fuel sources in the form of protein, fat and carbohydrates. Normal fat and protein stores in a well-fed adult are relatively inexhaustible while survival time is limited if dependent on carbohydrate reserves. Protein is, however, not concerned with energy production during exercise. Normally, fat depots exceed 200MJ (50 000kcal) and carbohydrate stores approximate 7.5MJ (1 800kcal).

Carbohydrates are stored in the muscles or liver as glycogen. The total glycogen stored by a 70 kg sportsman is about 460 g, 15 per cent held in the liver of which only half is made available. Liver glycogen is mobilised as blood glucose: blood sugar normally totals less than 6 g, 60 per cent of which serves the brain. If blood glucose levels fall appreciably hypoglycaemia develops and both mental concentration and continuing hard exercise are soon impossible. Ingestion of liquid glucose can prevent this condition or provide relief. Fats mobilised from adipose tissue depots provide an alternative substrate to glucose and ensure that glucose supply to the central nervous system is not compromised.

Individuals with diabetes mellitus, a condition that involves fluctuating blood sugar levels, need not be excluded from endurance events where good control of the condition is maintained by medication and preparation made to treat hypoglycaemic shock if necessary. Adequate feeding before training or competition is advised while symptoms including difficulties in concentration, focusing and coordination should be taken as warnings.

Much attention has been focused on the significance of initial muscle glycogen stores for endurance performance, particularly as the development of the muscle biopsy technique made successive sampling of muscle tissue during prolonged exertion possible. Saltin (1973) reported a correlation between starting muscle glycogen stores and ability to maintain working at 75 per cent of maximal oxygen uptake ($\dot{V}O_2$ max). Besides, Swedish soccer players with the lowest glycogen content in their thigh muscle before play were found to cover 25 per cent less distance in the second half of the game than the others. An even more marked difference was observed for running speed. Clearly where muscle glycogen stores are near depletion the pace of work must be reduced or exhaustion follows.

The maximal work load at which an individual can perform sustained exercise is determined by the local capacity to oxidise pyruvate in the working muscles. Local glycogen stores are critical for performance between 65 to 89% $\dot{V}O_2$ max (Hultman, 1971). These stores can be dramatically augmented by an astute combination of training and diet. After glycogen depletion by exhaustive training re-synthesis overshoots to double initial concentrations. The final levels can be boosted further if carbohydrates are avoided for a few days after glycogen depletion. The optimal routine first described by Saltin and Hermansen (1967) is undertaken throughout the week before competition starting with an exhaustive training session. This is followed by three days on a carbohydrate-free diet during which training continues. Then follow a further three days on a carbohydrate enriched diet, in the last two of which training is very light to avoid any reduction of the replenished stores. This procedure is commonly used by marathon runners in the week before racing but is impractical for many sports because of the greater frequency of competition. It is unlikely to be of benefit where competitions are less than one hour in duration.

The relative contribution of fats and carbohydrates depends on the exercise intensity and is modified according to the duration of activity while the type of work, fitness and prior diet affect the proportions of each source used. Carbohydrate metabolism increases with work intensity while fat involvement is greater as exercise is prolonged. Indeed one advantage of prolonged training is the improvement produced in fat mobilisation and utilisation. At the same relative work load, endurance trained athletes derive a greater percentage of their energy from oxidation of fatty acids and less from carbohydrates than do untrained subjects. Though mechanical efficiency is lower when fat is the source of fuel, when the individual case is considered, the greater fat involvement ensures that glycogen is spared so that depletion occurs later, if at all. As caffeine stimulates free fatty acid mobilisation and subsequent oxidation, its ingestion in the hour before endurance work has been advocated by Costill et al (1978). A practical disadvantage is its diuretic effect. The influence of the type of work on choice of substrate is seen in the higher carbohydrate participation during arm work than during leg work at a given level of oxygen uptake. Additionally intermittent work or changes of pace make disproportionate demands on carbohydrate reserves. An inconsistent pace at the commencement of a distance race may contribute towards an increasingly early decrement in performance.

The benefits of a carbohydrate-rich diet for athletic performance are well established. Bergstrom and colleagues (1967) showed that subjects on a diet heavily loaded with carbohydrates could continue at a fixed work load for 189 minutes compared with 126 minutes for subjects on a normal mixed diet and 59 minutes for those on a fat plus protein diet. Broader aspects of diet and nutrition are now considered.

Nutrition

Endurance athletes in hard training tend to expend supra-normal amounts of energy. Finnish distance runners, for example, increased daily energy transformations from 12.56 to 14.65MJ (3 000 to 4 000kcal) to 20.93 to 25.12MJ (5 000 to 6 000kcal) between 1968 and 1972 with an increase in training distance covered from 70 to 300 km/week (Kvanta, 1972). The balance of dietary foodstuffs is normally 10 to 15 per cent protein, 35 to 40 per cent fat and 50 per cent carbohydrate. This balance can be retained during hard training simply by eating more of the same, though a further bias towards carbohydrate rather than protein more readily provides the energy for arduous physical effort. A large protein intake does not improve endurance performance and is disproportionate to the athlete's needs.

With athletes training twice or three times and consuming over 21MJ (5 000kcal) daily, eating is best distributed over five to six separate meals rather than the conventional three. This could involve three major meals and three snacks conveniently placed according to the timing of training sessions. This would avoid overloading the digestive system and permit adequate pre-activity nourishment. Meals before competition should be light, preferably mainly carbohydrate and at least three hours beforehand to allow time for digestion. In many sports a liquid pre-game meal has proved effective. Eating too near vigorous exercise may be a cause of stitch, usually felt as a sharp pain in the upper abdomen. Stopping briefly may relieve the condition as can abdominal breathing with exhalation against resistance, while modifying pre-start eating can help prevent it.

Endurance athletes are extremely susceptible to suggestions of magical diets. Vitamin and mineral supplements tend to be readily accepted on presentation of flimsy evidence of any benefit. In the vast majority of cases a well balanced diet is all that is necessary. Fat soluble vitamins – A, D, E, and K – are stored in the body and can be toxic in excess. Water soluble vitamins are rapidly excreted in excess and supplementation leaves the athlete with the doubtful privilege of producing expensive urine. Physical performance is however decreased with deficiencies in B-complex or C vitamins, both involved in energy metabolism, while vitamin E deficiency causes muscle degeneration. Deficiency in B-complex and E vitamins is rare since they are widely distributed in foods. Much vitamin C is lost in processing and cooking foods so some fresh fruit can be a desirable inclusion in the athlete's diet.

Minerals, like vitamins, are important dietary substances being needed for cell structure and metabolism. Mineral deficiencies can reduce performance proficiency especially in hot conditions where sweating reduces sodium and chloride stores. Exercise can also alter the body's balance for potassium, calcium, magnesium and phosphorus. A generous salting of food or the taking of a commercially available electrolyte solution should adequately maintain sodium and chloride levels in hard training sessions. Excessive salt intake can however lead to unwanted potassium loss and water retention. Potassium deficiency is inimical to efficient muscle function as well as to storage and synthesis of glycogen and can develop during training in very hot conditions (Knochel, 1977). In stressful training in hot climates limited potassium supplementation may be desirable. Many of the foods rich in potassium also contain magnesium which, too, is lost in sweat: these include fruit juices, cabbage, carrots and nuts. Milk, cheese and fish in the diet ensure against any possible calcium and phosphate lack. Iron which is the active constituent of haemoglobin is the most common of mineral deficiencies particularly in females. Anaemic individuals may also contract zinc shortage, a mineral constituent of some enzymes involved in muscle metabolism. Other trace elements essential for prevention of anaemia include copper and cobalt, a constituent of vitamin B_{12}. The general symptoms of fatigue associated with anaemia should be heeded by undergoing a blood test and can be prevented by the inclusion of meat, liver and greens in the diet.

Whatever conclusions are drawn by the scientific community about diet for endurance specialists they are unlikely to be hailed universally by sports practitioners. Scientific knowledge is probably insufficient at present to set out guidelines in detail for optimal nutrition during hard training. Authorities agree that the secret to successful attainment of potential lies in training rather than elusively in the contents of a pill or bottle. A varied natural diet consisting of grains, fresh vegetables, fruits, berries, milk and eggs, supplemented if so desired by fish and lean meat provides all the fats, carbohydrates, essential proteins, minerals and vitamins needed.

ENDURANCE CAPACITY

Aerobic capacity

The maximal oxygen uptake ($\dot{V}O_2$ max) of the individual is generally accepted to be the best overall physiological measure of aerobic power and hence endurance capacity. It indicates the maximal rate at which oxygen can be consumed per minute or the power of the aerobic system. In sports without weight categories where body mass is not repetitively lifted against gravity, the absolute value is important. In long-distance running the relative value expressed per kg bodyweight is more crucial. Both absolute and relative values may be relevant as, for example, in cross-country skiing where the mass on the skis is helpful going downhill and the relative value significant in level or uphill work. Figures for $\dot{V}O_2$ max of international representatives are shown in Figure 10/1. It will be seen that the values for various sports closely correspond with the severity of activity indicated by the energy expenditure data in Table 2. The most arduous sports include cross-country skiing, distance running and rowing, while elite competitors in these sports have high values for $\dot{V}O_2$ max.

Measurement of $\dot{V}O_2$ max requires laboratory facilities for collection of expired air and analysis of its volume, O_2 and CO_2 content (Fig. 10/2). Repeated measurements allow monitoring of individual response to endurance training as well as evaluation of the regime employed. The $\dot{V}O_2$ max does not provide the complete answer to the determination of endurance performance though it is highly correlated with proficiency in stamina events, including for example cross-country running (Costill, 1967) and work-rate in soccer (Thomas and Reilly, 1976). An important consideration is the percentage of the aerobic power that can be utilised throughout the contest. Costill (1972) showed that top marathon runners were not necessarily those with the highest $\dot{V}O_2$ max figures but rather those that could work at a high fraction of it for the complete race.

The $\dot{V}O_2$ max presents an overall picture of the functional integration of the lungs, heart, blood and active muscles in aerobic work. Ventilatory capacity does not normally limit endurance performance except at altitude though pulmonary dimensions may show chronic adaptive changes, especially if hard training is undertaken in adolescence. In swimming events, apart from the backstroke, the respiratory rate is tied to the stroke rhythm and must be entrained to it. The ability of the heart to cope with the needs of working muscles for a greater supply of oxygenated blood is normally a more likely limitation of performance.

The volume of blood pumped from the heart per minute is known as the cardiac output. Its increase is much more pronounced than that in arterio-venous O_2 difference in the acute response to exercise. Although considerable variability in chronic response exists among individuals, on average the maximum cardiac output and the extraction of O_2 by the active muscles appear to account equally for the rise in $\dot{V}O_2$ max with training (Holloszy, 1978). The determinants of the oxidative capacity of the muscles are probably more important during prolonged sub-maximal work when a relatively small muscle mass is involved (Rusko, 1976). The greater cardiac output with training is attributable to a larger stroke volume or amount pumped out per heart beat. This itself is the result of cardiac muscle hypertrophy, a more powerful pumping action and an enlarged chamber size. The low resting pulse rates of endurance athletes are an obvious training effect. Those changes have long been known but were once thought to be pathological. There is no evidence that the normal healthy heart can be damaged by hard exercise. Myocarditis or inflammation of the heart muscle is possible if exercising severely while suffering viral illness. Caution is needed in returning to hard training or competition after influenzal infection.

The blood pumped from the left ventricle of the heart carries oxygen bound to haemoglobin for distribution to the various regions of the body. The total body haemoglobin (TBH) is higher than normal in top athletes and is significantly correlated with $\dot{V}O_2$ max.

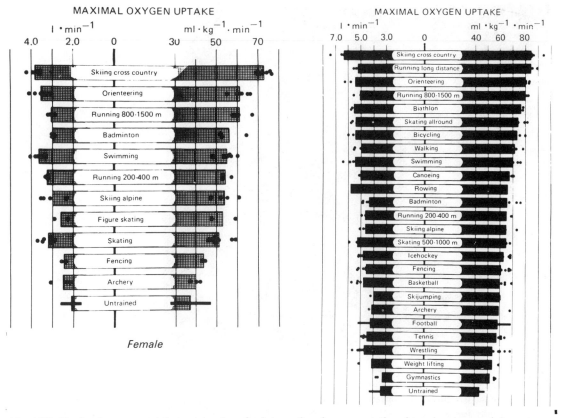

Fig. 10/1 Maximal oxygen uptake mean values for international representatives in various sports (after Åstrand and Rodahl, 1977; reproduced from their *Textbook of work physiology*, by permission of the publishers, McGraw Hill, New York)

Table 2. Severity of selected sports based on typical gross energy costs collected from various sources for male subjects. These values may underestimate the energy expended in top-flight competition in some cases

Light (kJ min⁻¹)		Moderate (kJ min⁻¹)		Heavy (kJ min⁻¹)		Very heavy (kJ min⁻¹)	
Archery	13–24	Badminton	26	American football	30–43	Cross-country running (16–17 km h⁻¹)	63–67
Billiards	11	Baseball	20–27	Basketball	38–46	Cross-country skiing	41–78
Bowls	17	Cricket	21–33	Boxing	38–60	Cycling (>21km h⁻¹)	46–84
				Handball	46	Rowing	59
Fencing	21	Gymnastics	10–50	Hockey	36	Professional soccer	50–69
Golf	20	Horse riding	13–42	Lawn tennis	29–46	Squash	42–76
Table tennis	15–22	Volleyball	24–27	Rugby	33–60		
		Water-skiing	29				

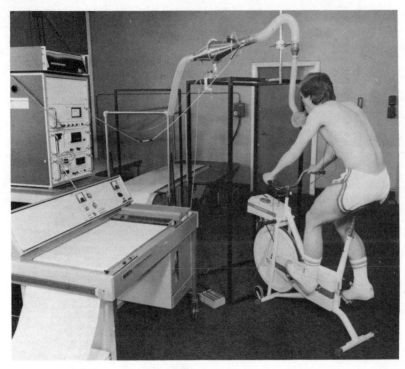

Fig. 10/2 Subject is shown undergoing V̇O₂max test on a bicycle ergometer. Heart rate is being monitored by electrocardiography

The high TBH values are explained by a greater blood volume so that haemoglobin concentrations may be normal. Brotherhood et al (1975) found that athletes taking iron and folate supplements were no different in haematological status than others: this observation casts doubt on a widespread practice among endurance athletes, with the exception of females and cases of anaemia. Additionally, 2, 3-diphosphoglycerate (2–3 DPG), an intermediate involved in red blood cell metabolism, was found to be higher in athletes than non-athletes, which would provide them with an advantage in liberating O_2 to the tissues. Athletes who donate blood are likely to have reduced endurance performance for two to three weeks afterwards due to the lowered oxygen carrying capacity until the red cell production in bone marrow compensates for the loss. Altruistic athletes feeling an obligation to donate blood will suffer only minimal disruption if they do so during the off-season.

Substantial improvements in oxygen transport capacity and endurance performance have been reported by Ekblom et al (1972) for blood doping. This refers to acutely expanding blood volume (hypervolaemia) and the number of red cells (polycythaemia). Elsewhere, Williams (1978) cast doubt on the effects of blood withdrawal and re-infusion as an ergogenic aid, whether it be whole blood, plasma or packed red cells.

It is likely that the quality of storage of blood withdrawn, the timing of the injection and the quantity involved may be critical for achieving any effects. Though banning blood doping is futile because of difficulties of detection, its practice contravenes normal medical and sporting ethics.

At tissue level highly trained athletes are capable of extracting a greater proportion of the oxygen offered for a number of reasons. Oxidative enzymes, which provide for the conversion of fuel into energy through the aerobic resynthesis of ATP, increase with training thereby facilitating aerobic metabolism. Proteins, particularly cytochrome C, involved in aerobic metabolism and located in the mitochondria, increase. Secondly, the number and size of mitochondria, the sites of aerobic metabolism, increase providing a greater surface area for oxygen utilisation. Thirdly, endurance training provokes increased capillarisation within muscle which assists in oxygen supply. Myoglobin content in skeletal muscle increases following training, aiding the diffusion of oxygen from the cell membrane to the mitochondria where it is consumed.

A long-term effect of endurance training is the better mechanical efficiency that is achieved. This means that greater external work is possible for a similar outlay of oxygen consumption. The improvements reflect the more skilful execution of performance, a better coordination of muscles for the task in hand and optimal use of the oxygen delivered to them. The degree of improvement is variable being greater for running than cycling and greater still for swimming with its larger muscle mass involvement.

Heritability and trainability

Inevitably the question arises as to the relative contributions of nature and nurture in the emergence of an endurance athlete. It is generally considered that champions are born more so than made and Åstrand (1967) concluded 'I am convinced that anyone interested in winning Olympic gold medals must select his or her parents very carefully'. Other authorities might even extend the choice to include grandparents. The variance between individuals in $\dot{V}O_2$ max is considerably greater than the 20 to 25 per cent generally regarded as a good training effect. However, improvements approaching 45 per cent have been found when intensive training programmes are conducted for longer than the customary experimental periods of investigation (Hickson et al, 1977; Holloszy, 1973). The predominance of endowment over environment in determining the maximal aerobic power was substantiated by Klissouras (1971) in investigations of intra-pair differences in identical and non-identical twins. In his study the variation observed in maximal aerobic power was 93 per cent genetically determined. However, it

should be realised that such figures might be misleading when considering top athletes since nature and nurture are intertwined so that an organic attribute cannot develop without both a hereditary basis and an appropriate environment.

Genetic factors may also be exemplified in the distribution of different types of skeletal muscle fibres. Two contrasting general fibre types have been distinguished, fast twitch (FT) or white, and slow twitch (ST) or red. The characteristics of the two types are summarised in Table 3, a high proportion and surface area

Table 3 Characteristics of fast twitch and slow twitch skeletal muscle fibres. These are sometimes referred to as Type 11b and Type 1 respectively. Type 11a refers to the fast red type described in the text

Fast twitch (White)	Slow twitch (Red)
Rich in glycolytic enzymes	High concentrations of myoglobin and respiratory enzymes
Few mitochondria (Containing enzymes needed for O_2 use)	Many mitochondria
Work largely anaerobically	Capable of prolonged oxidative processes (% ST fibres is correlated with $\dot{V}O_2$ max)
Possess large cross-sectional area	Smaller cross-section
Supplied by neurons of large size	Supplied by neurons of smaller size and having lower thresholds
Operate at high work intensities	Operate at low and moderate intensities
Have fast contraction rate	Slower contraction rate
High percentage found in weightlifters, sprinters, etc	High percentage in distance-runners, cross-country skiers, etc
High percentage in phasic muscles (e.g. gastrocnemius)	High percentage in tonic muscles (e.g. soleus)

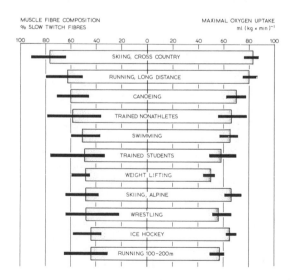

Fig. 10/3 Percentage slow twitch fibres (left part) and maximal oxygen uptake (right part) in athletes representing different sports. The horizontal bars denote the range (after Bergh et al, 1978; reproduced from *Medicine and Science in Sports*, **10**, 151–154, by permission of the editor)

of ST fibres facilitating endurance, while a predominance of FT fibres promotes strength and power. The percentage ST fibres in specific muscles of various sports groups and corresponding $\dot{V}O_2$ max figures are shown in Figure 10/3. Each type is selectively recruited according to the task required: one type cannot be altered to the other except by transplanting their nerve supply. A subdivision of FT fibres is described as fast red or fast oxidative glycolytic (FOG). This has a rich vascularisation, high myoglobin and mitochondrial content and so a high capacity for oxidative as well as anaerobic metabolism. Though the muscle machinery is the same for the different fibre types, the myosin in FT and FOG contains a high level of myosin ATPase, the specialised section of the muscle protein controlling the rate at which ATP is split, compared with lower levels in ST fibres. These levels are increased in ST fibres and decreased in FOG fibres with no changes in the fast white type since they are not recruited in endurance training except intermittently during games. It seems the fast red type tends to take on more characteristics of the ST fibres. Efforts such as repeated 400m runs increase the capacity of the anaerobic system in ST fibres but have no effect on the fast-contracting types. Ingjer (1979), using a refined ATPase method for sub-dividing FT fibres into four groups, found evidence of changes in these subtypes with endurance training. All fibre types showed a transition towards more mitochondria-rich fibres in the training period. Consequently it seems the biochemical characteristics of muscle fibres can be selectively manipulated to an extent by training though the distribution of fibre types between ST and FT is completely determined by genotype.

Body build is also largely the result of endowment and can be a significant factor in determining athletic success. There is a tendency at top level sport for individuals to gravitate towards the task they are anthropometrically best suited to. This is manifested in terms of body size, proportions, shape and composition. Runners, for example, are on average smaller, leaner and less muscular as the competitive distance increases. The greater surface area relative to mass gives the smaller individual an advantage in heat dissipation. However, this can obviously be outweighed by compensating factors since some very good marathon runners are tall. Walkers tend to have more body fat than runners of corresponding distances and since body mass is not lifted vertically to the same extent they are not appreciably disadvantaged by the excess dead weight (Reilly et al, 1979). Apart from diet the total energy expended in training is the predominant factor in assisting weight control so that once the training severity exceeds the stimulus threshold, prolonged work periods are recommended for losing weight.

Distance runners also have less muscle mass than their middle-distance counterparts and, since strength tends to be correlated with muscular endurance, could benefit from greater attention to strength training. This conceivably would provide some protection against injury, especially if the tibial, quadriceps and abdominal groups are developed to counter-balance the anticipated training in the calf, hamstrings and iliopsoas from repetitive locomotion. Games players tend to have impressive muscular development to fit them for the rigours of match play.

Somatotype describes physique in the three dimensions of endomorphy (fatness), mesomorphy (muscularity) and ectomorphy (linearty). The somatotype is mainly inherited but is to a much lesser degree affected by environmental factors including nutrition and training. The method has been used widely in describing the physiques of athletes. Figure 10/4 summarises the distribution found for top competitors in various sports. The majority of Olympic champions appear in the northern section of the somatochart while participants in particular sports tend to cluster together with minor ethnic variations. Endurance athletes are easily separated from specialists in anaerobic power events while specific requirements of the various endurance games are also implicated. It is possible that individuals could flounder indefinitely in an activity for which they are physically ill-equipped by nature, though it is likely that a subtle process of self-selection usually applies.

TYPES OF TRAINING

Long slow distance (LSD)

Long slow distance (LSD) training implies continuous low-intensity activity of an extended duration. This approach has been attributed to the German coach and physician Van Aaken in the 1960s. It was also included about the same time in the background preparation of New Zealand runners coached by Lydiard who advocated high mileage easy runs in the off-season. Applied to other sports it places emphasis on prolonged uninterrupted work-outs eliciting heart rates 60 to 80 per cent of maximal. This roughly corresponds to running speeds of 16 to 14kmh^{-1}. Indeed it is probably effective once the training stimulus threshold is exceeded. This can be calculated according to Karvonen's (1957) formula using the heart rate (fH):

$$\text{Training } fH = 0.60 \, (fH_{max} - fH \text{ rest}) + fH \text{ rest}$$

An individual with a maximal heart rate of 180 beats min^{-1} and a resting heart rate of 60 beats min^{-1}, will have a training target heart rate of 132 beats min^{-1}. The formula is frequently used in evaluation of jogging regimes.

The extreme durations in LSD work can lead to significant muscle and joint discomfort and real injury. Training sessions should be progressively lengthened as fitness develops and long work-outs should not be attempted without a gradual build-up.

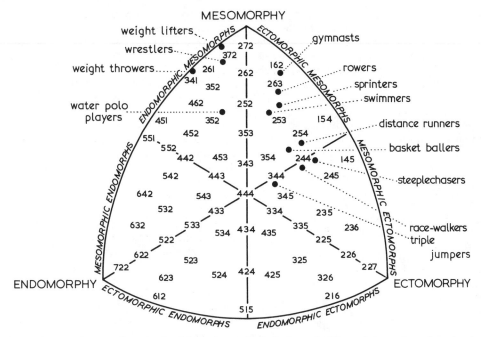

Fig. 10/4 Mean somatotype of top male athletes in a selection of sports. The points are based on the data of De Garay et al (1973), Reilly et al (1979) and Tanner (1964)

As the cardiovascular and respiratory systems are not distressed by LSD the more pronounced effects are likely to be peripheral. The respiratory capacity of muscle fibres is related to their habitual contractile activity so that in broad generalisation the greater the number of contractions, the greater the improvement (Holloszy et al, 1977). Considerable increases are found in muscle mitochondrial content and oxidation of fats and carbohydrates improves. Enhanced mechanical efficiency represents an overall training effect.

Tempolauf

Tempo training emphasises high intensity efforts equalling or approaching competitive stress. Its basis is to accustom the performer to the tempo of competition. It may take the form of continuous or intermittent work as in time trials or brief repetitions of the competitive distance with adequate intervening rest periods. It should be used guardedly for time-trial purposes.

The demands of this type of training are harsh, especially if frequently employed. Slower-paced variations should be used in conjunction with tempolauf to allow days of relative relief from the exhaustive high intensity work. Apart from its physiological effects it is likely to assist pace judgement and condition the athlete to the pain of competition.

Fartlek

Fartlek or speed-play is a form of continuous exercise fluctuating in intensity providing welcome variety to the normal routine. It originated in Sweden during the 1940s, being particularly suited to the Scandinavian forest paths but is also compatible with parklands or hilly countryside. Work intensity is varied spontaneously from fast bursts to jogging according to the terrain and the athlete's current disposition. The relative freedom from time and distance considerations make it immensely enjoyable. It is claimed to develop aerobic and anaerobic endurance equally with some effect also on speed (Wilt, 1968). Though originally devised for runners it is immediately applicable in principle to the training of other sports such as cross-country skiing, cycling, orienteering and race-walking.

Pyramid training

Pyramid training provides a formal method of varying the duration and intensity of work bouts and the recovery intervals. It was incorporated in training programmes of the Russian distance runners Bolotnikov and Kuts. Sessions may involve, for example, precise interval accelerations of 100, 200, 400, 800 and 1 200m. A complete work-out for a distance runner is shown in Table 4. This approach is appropriate also to water sports such as canoeing and swimming. It ensures that speed and speed-endurance are not neglected in the quest for greater endurance.

Table 4 Example of a pyramid training session of a middle or long-distance runner

Jog	2km	warm-up,	Run	1.5km	steady;
Jog	1km	recovery,	Run	1km	hard;
Jog	600m	recovery,	Run	600m	hard;
Jog	400m	recovery,	Run	400m	hard;
Jog	200m	recovery,	Run	200m	hard;
Jog	100m	recovery,	Run	100m	all-out;
Jog	100m	recovery,	Run	100m	all-out;
Jog	2km	recovery,	Run	1.5km	steady;
Jog	1km	recovery,	Run	1km	hard;
Jog	600m	recovery,	Run	600m	hard;
Jog	400m	recovery,	Run	400m	hard;
Jog	200m	recovery,	Run	200m	hard;
Jog	100m	recovery,	Run	100m	all-out;
Jog	100m	recovery,	Run	100m	all-out;
Jog	2km	warm-down			

Interval training

Classical interval training was developed in Germany in the 1930s and in its various forms has been the basis of training of numerous world and Olympic champions in running, cycling, rowing, swimming and other sports. It involves alternating short periods of hard work with brief periods of rest or reduced activity. The work periods may vary from 0.5 to 5 minutes while recovery varies in duration from that of the work bout to approximately double it. The complete work-out is fairly tightly structured and monitored by stop-watch.

The variables associated with interval training include the number of repetitions, the duration of effort, work intensity and duration of recovery. Altering the duration of effort between days introduces variety into the programme. The number of repetitions can be systematically increased as conditioning develops, while the pace can then be accelerated. Finally, the recovery periods can be shortened: where these are inadequate to allow recovery, anaerobic endurance is also stressed. Light activity rather than complete rest in the intermission speeds lactate removal from the active muscles.

In the original form pioneered by Gerschler and Reindall the optimum work intensity was considered to be that which elicited heart rates of about 180 beats min^{-1} while recovery was terminated when the rate

dropped to around 120 beats min^{-1}. These rates were considered to provide the optimum stimulus for the heart to expand and pronounced hypertrophy was found to result. The work speed can however be varied to put more or less emphasis on anaerobic endurance as peripheral, as well as central factors, respond to this type of training.

Parlauf

Parlauf or continuous relays can be introduced periodically into training routines especially for stimulation of club morale. It can employ two, three or four members per team for a period pre-determined by the coach. In the two-per-team format, rest periods do not allow complete recovery so that performance inevitably drops off. This type of regime is particularly suited for swimming and middle-distance running but can also be incorporated into the fitness training of games players.

Circuit training

Circuit training provides a good method of general conditioning. The individual rotates around a series of exercises laid out in a circle, usually 8 to 12 separate exercises being involved. Muscle groups are varied between work stations so that local fatigue is avoided while stress is maintained on the cardiovascular system. This method lends itself to group involvement and so is frequently used for squad training.

As fitness develops the number of sets can be increased and the pace accelerated. As progress is readily apparent the athlete is easily motivated by this form of training. It is particularly popular in pre-season conditioning of games players.

Combination methods

It might be thought that the ideal endurance training programme is a combination of the best features of various specific methods so as to secure the best of all possible worlds. However, there is no guarantee that the benefits are in any way additive and indeed the different regimes overlap to a great degree in their physiological effects. Besides there is unlikely to be one perfect schedule which will be applicable to all as each individual athlete is unique with special strengths and weaknesses. Experience indicates that athletes do employ admixtures of different approaches according to what seems to work for them. An example of a combined approach is given in Table 5 which shows the schedule of John Treacy, world cross-country champion.

Experimentally it is difficult to unravel the complex ways in which the different elements of fitness in a combined programme interact. It is known that aerobic training leads to a fall in muscle glycolytic

Table 5 Typical schedule of élite young distance runners. The example provided is of world cross-country champion John Treacy as a junior (aged 17). The schedule includes combinations of different training methods outlined in the text and presents some indication of the training loads in developmental years of top runners. All track sessions were conducted on grass, preceded by a 4 to 5km warm-up jog and followed by a warm-down of 5 to 7km

	Winter	Pre-track season	Summer
Monday	18km road run	18km road run	10 × 400m (track)
Tuesday	18km road run	8 × 600m (track)	21km run
Wednesday	8 × 600m (track)	20km run	3 × 8 × 150m (anaerobic endurance)
Thursday	16km hard run	12 × 400m (track)	16 × 200m (track)
Friday	20km easy run	20km run	23km run
Saturday	Fartlek – 60min or Cross-country RACE	6 × 800m (track)	12 × 300m (track) or Track RACE
Sunday	24km run	24km run	27km easy run

enzymes (Sjodin et al, 1976). This has been substantiated in the fall in strength and anaerobic power of soccer players after a pre-season programme of aerobic conditioning (Reilly and Thomas, 1978). For this reason some speed-endurance work should be included in endurance training programmes. Conditioning the cardiovascular system should be given priority in the early build-up to the competitive season. Specificity of training ensures that local effects are achieved. During the competitive season more emphasis may be placed on the speed of work. Competitive performance will provide invaluable feedback as to ongoing modifications. These subtle adjustments in programming training are, however, currently as much an art as a science.

Training and competing in endurance sports make enormous claims on personal time and effort. It is important for individual peace of mind that work-outs be organised so that a regular habitual pattern is established: soon training sessions are felt to be an integral part of the daily routine. Rapid results should not be expected as improvement tends to be gradual. The training load should be elevated in sensible increments to avoid injury from excessive overload. It is also sound to intersperse easy and hard days work particularly during periods of heavy competition. A circumspect approach to conditioning should enable the body's

tremendous adaptive potential to be realised without interruption from trauma.

REFERENCES

Åstrand, P. O. (1967). Physical activity and cardiovascular health: commentary. *Canadian Medical Association Journal*, **96**, 730.

Åstrand, P. O. and Rodahl, K. (1977). *Textbook of work physiology*. McGraw Hill, New York.

Bergh, U., Thorstensson, A., Sjodin, B., Hulten, B., Piehl, K. and Karlsson, J. (1978). Maximal oxygen uptake and muscle fibre types in trained and untrained humans. *Medicine and Science in Sports*, **10**, 151–154.

Bergstrom, J., Hermansen, L., Hultman, E. and Saltin, B. (1967). Diet, muscle glycogen and physical performance. *Acta Physiologica Scandinavica*, **71**, 140–150.

Brotherhood, J., Brozovic, B. and Pugh, L. G. C. (1975). Haematological status of middle- and long-distance runners. *Clinical Science and Molecular Medicine*, **48**, 139–145.

Costill, D. L. (1967). The relationship between selected physiological variables and distance running performance. *Journal of Sports Medicine and Physical Fitness*, **7**, 61–66.

Costill, D. L. (1972). Physiology of marathon running. *Journal of the American Medical Association*, **221**, 1024–1029.

Costill, D. L., Dalsky, G. P. and Fink, W. J. (1978). Effects of caffeine ingestion on metabolism and exercise performance. *Medicine and Science in Sports*, **10**, 155–158.

De Garay, A. L., Levine, L. and Carter, J. E. L. (1974). *Genetic and anthropological studies of Olympic athletes*. Academic Press, New York.

Ekblom, B., Goldberg, A. N. and Gullbring, B. (1972). Response to exercise after blood loss and reinfusion. *Journal of Applied Physiology*, **33**, 175–180.

Gollnick, P. D. and Hermansen, L. (1973). *Biochemical adaptations to exercise: anaerobic metabolism*. In J. H. Wilmore (ed). *Exercise and sport sciences reviews*. Volume 1. Academic Press, New York.

Hickson, R. C., Bomze, H. A. and Holloszy, J. O. (1977). Linear increase in aerobic power induced by a strenuous programme of endurance exercise. *Journal of Applied Physiology*, **42**, 372–376.

Holloszy, J. O. (1973). *Biochemical adaptations to exercise: aerobic metabolism*. In J. H. Wilmore (ed). *Exercise and sport sciences reviews*. Volume 1. Academic Press, New York.

Holloszy, J. O. (1978). *Adaptations of skeletal muscle to endurance exercise*. In P. E. Allsen (ed). *Conditioning and physical fitness*. Wm C. Brown Company, Dubuque, Iowa.

Holloszy, J. O., Rennie, M. J., Hickson, R. C., Conlee, R. K. and Hagberg, J. M. (1977). *Physiological consequences of the biochemical adaptations to endurance exercise*. In P. Milvy (ed). *The marathon: physiological, medical, epidemiological and psychological studies*. New York Academy of Sciences, New York.

Hultman, E. (1971). *Muscle glycogen stores and prolonged exercise*. In R. J. Shephard (ed). *Frontiers of fitness*. C. C. Thomas, Springfield, Illinois.

Ingjer, F. (1979). Effects of endurance training on muscle fibre ATP-ase activity, capillary supply and mitochondrial content in man. *Journal of Physiology*, **294**, 419–432.

Karvonen, M., Kentala, E. and Mustala, O. (1957). The effects of training on heart rate. *Annales Medicinnae Experimentalis et Biologiae Fenniae*, **35**, 307–315.

Klissouris, V. (1971). Heritability of adaptive variation. *Journal of Applied Physiology*, **31**, 338–344.

Knochel, J. P. (1977). *Potassium deficiency during training in the heat*. In P. Milvy (ed). *The marathon: physiological, medical, epidemiological and psychological studies*. New York Academy of Sciences, New York.

Kvanta, E. (1972). *Symposium on nutritional physiology, summary*. In E. Kvanta (ed). Proceedings of symposium on the effect of nutritive supplement on athletes (Helsingborg).

Reilly, T. and Thomas, V. (1978). *The stability of fitness factors over a season of professional soccer as indicated by serial factor analyses*. Proceedings IInd International Seminar on Kinanthropometry (Leuven).

Reilly, T., Hopkins, J. and Howlett, N. (1979). Fitness test profiles and training intensities in skilled race-walkers. *British Journal of Sports Medicine*, **13**, 70–76.

Rusko, H. (1976). *Physical performance characteristics in Finnish athletes*. Studies in sport, physical education and health, 8. (University of Jyvaskyla.)

Saltin, B. (1973). Metabolic fundamentals in exercise. *Medicine and Science in Sports*, **5**, 136–146.

Saltin, B. and Hermansen, L. (1967). *Glycogen stores and prolonged severe exercise*. In G. Blix (ed). *Nutrition and physical activity*. Almqvist and Wiksell, Uppsala.

Sjodin, B., Thorstensson, A., Frith, K. and Karlsson, J. (1976). Effects of physical training on LDH activity and LDH isozyme pattern in human skeletal muscle. *Acta Physiologica Scandinavica*, **97**, 150–57.

Tanner, J. M. (1964). *The physique of the Olympic athlete*. George Allen and Unwin, London.

Thomas, V. and Reilly, T. (1976). *Application of motion analysis to assess performance in competitive football*. Paper presented at the Ergonomics Society Conference (Edinburgh).

Williams, M. H. (1978). *Blood doping – does it really help athletes?* In P. E. Allsen (ed). *Conditioning and physical fitness*. Wm C. Brown Company, Dubuque, Iowa.

Wilt, F. (1968). *Training for competitive running*. In H. B. Falls (ed). *Exercise physiology*. Academic Press, New York.

SECTION 3

Injuries in team games

CHAPTER 11

Injuries and their prevention in American football

BERNARD I. LOFT HSD

CHALLENGING ASPECTS IN THE PREVENTION OF AMERICAN FOOTBALL INJURIES

Competitive American football continues to expand with an ever increasing popularity particularly throughout the United States of America. The adventurous and challenging nature of this sport attracts participants from a young age in the elementary schools through the higher levels of tertiary education. There is an indication that in excess of 15 000 public and private secondary schools in the USA enter the sponsor organised competitive football programmes during the autumn with approximately 1.2 million young people partaking. Participation at the college or university level has proved to be popular for some 1.2 million spread throughout the nation. There is also substantial evidence that communities contribute to an estimated 200 000 boys supported by various social agencies that have a particular interest in wholesome athletic competitive youth programmes. Additional consideration for football participation on sandlots on a semi-organised basis would probably contribute to a total in the vicinity of two million participants in the USA alone. The game is also significantly popular in Canada and Japan as well as being played in some South American countries.

There is an indication by the medical profession that at least 50 per cent of the football participants are subjected to injuries of a low grade of severity each year. Obviously, this outcome presents a health problem resulting from competition generated in football participation. In recognition of this exposure to potential injury, the health problem is of significant magnitude to concern school administrators, athletic directors, coaches, team physicians, physical educators, athletic trainers, and, most certainly, parents of the athletes.

A description of football immediately identifies a contact sport that may also be categorised as a collision sport (Fig. 11/1). Observations have revealed that the athlete with a larger body type who has the ability to move more rapidly will activate increased energy and therefore establish contact with a greater degree of force. This form of movement has a potential for

Fig. 11/1 Dispersal of players of opposing teams

inflicting injury either to a lesser or greater degree of severity. The innovative developments in coaching technology continue to produce an improved athlete with more speed and force to the extent that certain types of football injuries have increased in both frequency and severity. With the inclusion of specific rules to protect the participant, the prevalance of other forms of injury indicates a reduction in the injury rate. A major concern of all football enthusiasts is to control the sport to the extent that injuries will be reduced to a minimum without detracting from the gratification derived from participation.

The availability of valid and reliable statistics will be valuable for a variety of purposes. At the secondary school level, statistics can be of inestimable value in evaluating and analysing the contributory factors in injury causation. When the indirect and direct causes of athletic injury become apparent, the possibility exists for creating corrective and remedial controls for the prevention and reduction of similar injuries in the future. The National Federation of State High School Athletic Associations has been actively involved in the formulation of significant data to assist in a scholarly understanding of injury control in competitive football. Frequently many injuries in football are not reported. How to determine the extent and significance of an injury presents variable factors to compound the problem of data considered to be valid and reliable with nation-wide implications.

When considering the movement and exposure in football there is a general acceptance that it is inevitable that injuries will result from participation in the sport. In a game requiring direct bodily contact in a designated area for 48 to 60 minutes in playing time, it is easy to understand that a potential for injury most certainly exists. This is not to infer that injuries cannot be controlled, prevented and reduced to a minimum. The following sections present in some detail the considerations that will contribute to a reduction in football injuries.

The coach

From the standpoint of priority, the selection of a competent coach is of paramount importance. An efficiently qualified coach is an essential prerequisite in the prevention of injuries which may be incurred through participation in football. Coaching responsibilities require an individual with a variety of capabilities and characteristics that will ultimately contribute to success both for his players and for himself. The coach initially should possess excellent teaching and leadership qualities. Emotional stability and sound moral character are exceedingly important traits. A firm dedication in applying conditioning and training methods must be stressed by the coach in enhancing skill and motivating the control of athletic injuries. This will be of concern to individual needs and team play involving all personnel on the squad.

The coach must be certain that all participants have the proper personal protective equipment in quality and fit and a knowledge of how to use the equipment according to designated standards. A coach has the responsibility of instilling in athletes a sensitivity and awareness for accident prevention and injury control. Any movements or contact that may inflict injury must be eliminated without reservation. The coach as an administrator and organiser should arrange planned practice sessions of desirable time periods as a means of eliminating and reducing injuries that may result from fatigue. A fatigued athlete is more susceptible to the possibility of injury to himself and other participants.

Effective coaching methods necessitate the teaching of skills and imparting player knowledge that will be instrumental in injury control. Desirable attitudes and behaviour need to be developed for competitive sport participation and must be emphasised in all practice sessions and game conditions. A desire to win must never take place at the sacrifice of players being unnecessarily injured to achieve victory. A successful coach and football programme will always be in rela-

tionship to the highest level of efficiency that can be applied in the process.

Personal health of the athlete

In the secondary school this is essentially the responsibility of the coach or team physician with assistance from either a professional or student trainer. At the college level this is usually the task of a team physician who is qualified in sports medicine and a professionally qualified athletic trainer. A coach needs to understand and apply the many ramifications of health care to assure that his athletes receive the proper attention for their well-being on and off the athletic field. All ultimate medical decisions become the responsibility of a team physician. By the application of appropriate health practices there should be a reduction of the injuries that take place in football. The medical and athletic training professions continue to make a commendatory contribution in this sport that has a significant place particularly in American society.

CONTRIBUTIONS OF THE ALLIED HEALTH PROFESSIONS

Numerous scientific and professional individuals are applying themselves diligently to research and study in approaching solutions to the prevention of injuries in football. In addition to the medical profession, there are exercise physiologists, psychologists, engineers, sports sociologists and members of other related professions applying themselves to the problems of sports injuries. A variety of professional organisations such as the American College of Sports Medicine, the Committee on the Medical Aspects of Sports of the American Medical Association, the American Academy of Orthopaedic Surgeons, the National Athletic Trainers Association, and State and County Medical Societies continue to provide valuable assistance in health care and injury prevention in sports participation. Comparable national organisations elsewhere include the British Association of Sport and Medicine, the Society of Sports Sciences (in Great Britain), the Canadian Association of Sports Sciences, the Japanese Society of Sports Medicine, the Japan Union of Sports Sciences, the Australian Association of Sports Medicine and the New Zealand Association of Sports Medicine. International bodies concerned include ICSPE, ICHPER and FIMS.

PROTECTIVE FOOTBALL EQUIPMENT

Standards

The selection and proper fit of football protective equipment are essential factors in the control of football injuries. When proper decisions are made in outfitting participants with adaptable protective equipment, the health and welfare of the athlete is receiving a type of consideration that is of primary importance.

The concern for standards related to the design and manufacture of protective equipment has been receiving consideration by various professional individuals and organisations. Standards devoted to material durability, manufacture of equipment through mass production, establishing standards and scientific testing procedures require deliberation and study by appropriately qualified authorities. The requirements for the proper use of protective equipment are being defined through application of rules and regulations governing the sport at various levels of participation. There is also concern that equipment designed for the protection of an athlete may be used against an opponent.

There is also a need for formulating standards in the conditioning and rehabilitation of athletes and when to dispose of protective equipment. The practice of utilising worn out university equipment for the reserves and players with fewer skills will frequently add to the injury and risk syndrome. While appearance, colour, and style will sometimes be a concern of coaches, the most important aspect is the adaptability of equipment in the prevention of injury.

Guidelines for purchase of protective equipment

In purchasing football protective equipment, the following suggestions are intended to serve as a guide to prospective purchasers for varying age levels of football participants:

1. The sporting goods manufacturer should have a reputation for quality merchandise, and warranty is favourably recognised by the coaching profession.
2. The very best equipment meeting the highest level of quality standards should be purchased.
3. All equipment for the football participant should be properly fitted to meet the individual's needs.
4. Equipment should be specifically designed to provide protection against hazards, by establishing a buffer between the hazard and the participant.
5. No new hazards should be created from the use of protective equipment.
6. Without exception the use of protective equipment as set forth in the rules, regulations and existing standards of governing organisations, should be insisted upon.

FOOTBALL HELMETS AND FACE BAR (Fig. 11/2a, b, c)

As an integral aspect of protective equipment the football helmet deserves maximum deliberation. Many different types of helmets are being used in a variety of football programmes. For the most part, helmets will be placed in three essential categories, i.e. padded, air, or fluid and suspension. A combination of all three is also available. There should be conformity to the following fit standards and specifications:

1. The base of the skull should be adequately covered.
2. There should be no shifting of the helmet when manual pressure is applied.

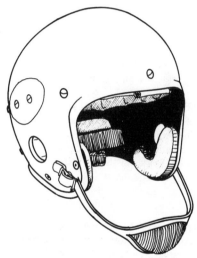

Fig. 11/2a Football helmet with strap suspension and padding

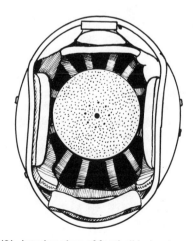

Fig. 11/2b Interior view of football helmet

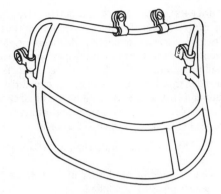

Fig. 11/2c Football face guard. Note the four points for attachment to the helmet

3. The helmet should not come down and impair visibility.
4. There should be no recoil upon impact.
5. The ear, the ear cut-out should match and be in proper alignment.
6. The shell of the helmet's front edge should fit 1.9cm (¾ inch) above a player's eyebrows.
7. The chin strap should be equally distant from the midpoint of the helmet. Equal tension is required on both sides of the chin strap.
8. Jaw pads should fit against the sides of the face without any space in between. This should prevent any movement in the form of lateral rocking.

The purpose of the face-bar (Fig. 11/2c) is to provide the maximum of protection from either soft tissue injury or fractures to the facial bone structure. The prevention of injuries to the teeth has been reduced through proper use of the face-bar. There has been criticism on occasion that the face-bar impairs vision and has been used by tacklers as a handle for stopping the forward progress of a runner. Apparently, injuries of low severity to severe neck injuries have taken place from this practice. However, the protection afforded to the facial area outweighs the potentiality for injuries with varying degrees of severity. Face-bars can be either the 'bird-cage' type used essentially by linemen or the double-bar type assigned predominantly to ball handlers. Most important is that a good face-bar should extend forward for more than 7.6cm (3in). Under no circumstances should face protection be less than two bars properly fitted to the helmet with approved mountings.

ADHERENCE TO RULES AND REGULATIONS

Exceedingly important in the prevention of football

injuries is the promulgation and enforcement of well-designed rules and regulations. Unnecessary injuries may be experienced from an ineffective rule; no rule to apply in a particular situation; or failure to enforce existing rules. Football officials with concern for the participants can be instrumental in reducing injuries. Athletic administrators should exert a concentrated effort in obtaining only competent officials with an established competency record. Coaches have a significant responsibility in instructing their athletes to participate within the confines of established rules and not abuse regulations by the use of unauthorised and dangerous manoeuvres employed in practice sessions or actual game conditions. Representative athletic authorities from higher education institutions and secondary schools meet annually to motivate research as a means of determining the contributory factors and causation of football injuries. A significantly important consideration is the responsibility placed on officials for rule enforcement and, through the various state and national organisations, for a continuous evaluation concerning applicability and effectiveness of the rules. Coaching technique and strategy must always be directed to complete compliance with the established rules.

PREVENTION OF SPORTS INJURIES THROUGH PHYSICAL CONDITIONING

The need for conditioning

Coaches and athletic trainers are convinced without question that an absence of proper physical conditioning is a major contributory cause related to athletic injuries. Lack of the appropriate coordination, reflex action, muscular imbalance, neuromuscular deficiencies, low grade ligamentous or tendonous strength and insufficient muscle bulk represent some of the contributory aspects in accident causation resulting from improper and insufficient physical conditioning. Nutritional requirements and psychological preparedness are also of concern in the preparation of athletes for sports participation.

Pre-season and in-season conditioning

The quantity of time allocated to pre-season and in-season conditioning is dependent upon both the type of activity and the status of the athlete's physical fitness at the inception of the conditioning activities. In applying this concept to the football athlete who, at the beginning of the practice sessions, reports in an overweight flabby condition, there will be a need for a more comprehensive schedule over an extended period of time as compared to the athlete who has maintained a desirable condition of fitness applicable to participation in football. Obviously, the latter will not require the same programme of physical conditioning.

Warm-up procedures

Precautions must be applied by the athlete who should undertake the appropriate warm-up activity to eliminate possibility of strains or muscle injuries. Deep body temperature and muscle thermal conditions must be at their most desirable levels. For effective motor performance, neuromuscular skills need to be developed to include both speed and endurance. The athlete who is slow, easily fatigued, or awkward will be more susceptible to injury.

Weight training for football

The footballer should adhere to an approved general weight training programme as a means of acquiring a high level of overall development. Punters and place kickers can use weighted shoes in the practice of the high kick. This should contribute to desirable results in skill development. A weighted ball can be of assistance for passing, punting and centring, in that certain muscles that have a relationship to these skills are developed. For construction, merely stuff a ball with preferably sponge rubber scraps to a weight of approximately 1.36kg (3lb). A lineman can advantageously use a press bar for increased effort with the shoulder shrug and leg lift. This should be performed both isotonically and isometrically. An effective activity for the lineman is to execute the wrestler's bridge and pivot while supporting on the chest a weight of 9 to 18kg (20 to 40lb).

GUIDELINES FOR THE PREVENTION OF INJURIES IN TACKLING SKILLS

Maintain good physical condition throughout the year

An efficient football player maintains a desirable physical condition throughout the entire year. Endurance, stamina, reflexes, and strength should be kept up to standard on a daily basis. The trainer can be of assistance relative to weight training and isometric exercises.

Spring or summer training programmes

In the spring and summer workouts the use of heavy gear should be eliminated. Football gear should include helmets and lightweight shirts and shorts should be used during these practices. Running will prove to be of inestimable value but running on hard surfaces should be omitted. The use of turf is desirable and the use of tennis or gym shoes will contribute to foot comfort. Endeavour to stretch all muscles, with particular emphasis on the thighs.

Avoid head injuries

Be certain to check all protective equipment and have the manager or trainer immediately inspect any deficient equipment. Always wear a mouthguard for practice and games. The proper development of neck muscles will aid in the prevention of head and neck injuries. When tackling, keep the eyes wide open and set your vision on the ball handler. In making contact, keep the chin elevated and both feet firmly on the ground when making contact. Avoid diving tackles and straight-on tackles.

Never totally leave the ground when tackling

One foot should be maintained on the ground at all times when executing a tackle. This will assist in controlling body momentum in the desired direction. The bodyweight should be maintained in a forward thrust position. Maintaining control will contribute in preventing back, shoulder, arm, neck and leg injuries.

Follow-through

In the approach to contact, *don't* pause; impetus is an injury prevention technique. Use body momentum to the best possible advantage. Endeavour to stay on top when executing a head-and-shoulder tackle. When contact has been established and the tackle completed do not permit your legs to drag. This can be accomplished by drawing the knees in close to the body. Figure 11/3, p. 98, shows a shoulder pad which also offers protection for the chest, ribs and back.

Early season tackling

Tackling techniques in early season drills can be efficiently performed on the tackling dummies prior to working with human targets (Fig. 11/4, p. 98).

BODY-ACROSS TACKLE

Endeavour to use your full weight and make contact at chest height by grasping the ball handler with your arms.

DO NOT RELAX WHEN EXECUTING A TACKLE

Muscular and tendon tension should be maintained throughout the tackling procedure. Avoid a driving tackle with the use of one arm or leg. Contact should be made with the shoulder or hip padding.

Complete and efficient equipment is essential; participation in football necessitates every item of protective equipment as stipulated by the regulations and policies set forth by the coaching staff.

The prevention of football injuries can be achieved by

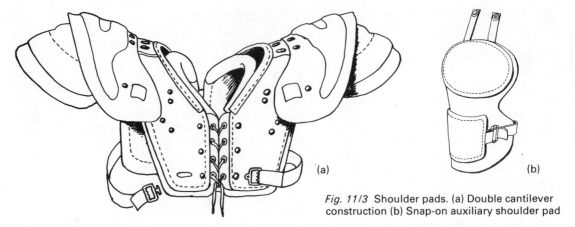

(a)

(b)

Fig. 11/3 Shoulder pads. (a) Double cantilever construction (b) Snap-on auxiliary shoulder pad

Fig. 11/4 A practice tackling dummy

placing a continued emphasis on having professionally trained athletic leadership, desirable facilities in compliance with acceptable standards and equipment that is designed with safety receiving the highest priority of consideration.

BIBLIOGRAPHY

American Alliance for Health, Physical Education, and Recreation, C. P. Yost (ed) (1971). *Sports safety.* AAHPER Publication-Sales, Washington, DC.

American School and Community Safety Association, D. A. Morehouse (ed) (1977). *Sports safety II.* AAHPER Publication-Sales, Washington, DC.

Cerney, J. V. (1976). *The prevent-system for football injuries.* Prentice-Hall, Englewood Cliffs.

Klafs, C. E. and Arnheim, D. D. (1977). *Modern principles of athletic training*, 4th edition. C. V. Mosby, Saint Louis.

Olson, O. C. (1971). *Prevention of football injuries.* Lea and Febiger, Philadelphia.

CHAPTER 12

Injuries in baseball

WARREN J. HUFFMAN BA, MA, EdM, EdD

THE GAME

The origin of the American game of baseball is uncertain. There are those who insist that it is of purely American origin, but some historians contend that it had its roots in the old English game of rounders. Regardless of its origin, the game has been very popular for at least 150 years and it continues to be one of the most popular sports in America and in the Far East, particularly Japan.

Originally, baseball was a warm, fair weather game played outdoors on natural grass and dirt under daylight conditions. For the most part this is still true, although, thanks to technological developments, some changes have taken place. Since 1930, many fields have been artificially lit, thus allowing games to be played outdoors after dark. In recent years several large arenas have been built which allow for play indoors under any weather conditions and at any time of the day or night. Because of the failure of grass to grow inside the arenas,

synthetic surfaces have been developed and even some outdoor stadia now have synthetic surfaces, particularly those that also stage football.

Playing area

Baseball is played on a large field consisting of an infield and an outfield. The infield is laid out to exact measurements and in such a manner that the batters will not have the sun in their eyes when they face the pitcher. The infield is a 90-foot (27.4m) square (60-foot (18.3cm) for younger players). The corners are known as home plate and in a counterclockwise direction first, second, and third bases. The pitching mound (where the pitcher stands to throw the ball) is equidistant from third to first bases on the line from home plate (where the batter stands to hit the ball) to second base but slightly closer to home plate.

The outfield is the area beyond the infield between the foul lines formed by extending the two sides of the square from home plate past first and third bases to the end of the field. Everywhere within the boundaries

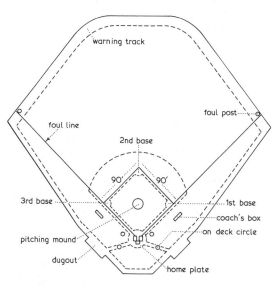
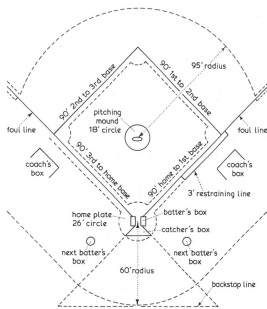

Fig. 12/1a&b The layout and critical dimensions of the playing field (12/1a) and the diamond (12/1b)

formed by these two lines is known as fair territory. It is recommended that the outfield should be enclosed by a fence. Except for a minimum requirement of 250 feet (76.2m) from home plate to the nearest obstruction in fair territory, there are no specific requirements for placement of the fence, even though greater distances are recommended. The required distance for younger players is less than 250 feet (Figs. 12/1a and 1b).

Equipment

There are numerous specifications for equipment, but only the specifications for the ball and the bat are covered here. Specifications for the baseball were determined in 1872 and still apply. The ball is a sphere weighing not less than 5 nor more than $5\frac{1}{4}$oz (142–149g), and measures not less than 9 nor more than $9\frac{1}{4}$in (22.9–23.5cm) in circumference. It is formed by yarn wound around a small core of rubber, cork, or combination of both, and covered by two pieces of white horsehide or cowhide tightly stitched together (until several years ago only horsehide was allowed).

Specifications for the bat were determined in 1876 and still apply. The bat must not exceed 42in (107cm) in length nor be over $2\frac{3}{4}$in (7cm) in diameter at its thickest part. Until recently all bats were constructed of solid wood; for games, other than professional, laminated wood or aluminium bats are now allowed.

DESCRIPTION OF THE GAME

Baseball competition requires two teams of nine players each. However, teams carry additional players for substitution purposes. Unlike some other games, a player cannot return to play, after he has been removed from the line up.

The team at bat is known as the offensive team and its objective is to have its batters score runs. The batter stands along either side of the home plate in a designated marked-out area 6×4ft (1.83×1.22m) called the batter's box. It is the aim of the batter to hit the ball thrown by the pitcher and drive it into fair territory. The batter then becomes a baserunner, and his objective is to reach each base safely, and to proceed on a tour of the bases: from home to first, from first to second, from second to third, and from third to home in that order. If he does this legally before the third man is put out, he scores a run.

Batters may start their journey around the bases in a variety of ways: (1) hitting safely; (2) being hit by a pitched ball while in the batter's box; (3) being given first base on balls (that is, the pitcher fails to throw the ball over the plate on four pitches before the batter hits the ball or strikes out); and (4) on a defensive player's error. They may advance by stealing bases, on hits,

errors, passed balls and in other ways.

The team in the field is known as the defensive team and its objective is to prevent offensive players from becoming base runners and to prevent their advance around the bases. When three offensive players are legally put out, the teams change positions.

The pitcher and catcher form what is known as the battery. The pitcher must throw from the designated spot in the infield to the catcher whose position is back of home plate. The infield is composed of a first baseman, second baseman, third baseman, and a short stop who is stationed between second and third bases. There are three outfielders who play in left, centre, and right fields. None of the players is stationary; they all move about as the situation warrants, taking in as much territory as their abilities permit in fielding the ball and covering the bases.

A batsman or a base runner may be put out in a number of ways (only five are listed here): (1) he may strike out (swing and miss the ball three times); (2) he may hit a ball in the air that is caught by a defensive player before it touches the ground; (3) he may hit a ground ball in fair territory and be thrown out, the first baseman getting the ball and touching the base before the runner gets there; (4) a defensive player touching a base with the ball in his possession before the runner arrives at that base; or (5) by touching the runner with the ball when the runner is not touching the base.

When each team has a turn at bat (offense) that is known as an inning. The usual number of innings is nine; for the younger players a game is usually shorter than nine innings. If the game is tied at the end of the designated number of innings, the game continues with equal turns at bat until one team has scored one more run than the other.

INJURIES

While few deaths to either players or spectators have resulted directly from the American game of baseball, serious and minor injuries occur each year to thousands of players. Injuries curtail the sports careers of baseball players from the little league to the major professional league (Owen, 1974).

The hazards of the game can be divided into five groups: (1) running; (2) body contact; (3) risk from both the bat and the ball; (4) the barriers which enclose the field; and (5) hard throwing and swinging motions (Ryan, 1962).

In his survey of professional and college baseball injuries, Polk (1968) noted that 82.5 per cent of all injuries may be attributed to five types: (1) sprains, 27.3 per cent; (2) strains, 18.7 per cent; (3) contusions, 16.9 per cent; (4) pulled muscles, 11.3 per cent, and (5) fractures, 8.3 per cent. Polk found that sliding and running between bases were the primary causes of sprains. Strains were predominantly caused by throwing, followed by running between bases. Contusions were caused by the batter being hit by a pitched ball, followed closely by collisions between players. Pulled muscles occurred primarily running between bases, followed by throwing the baseball. Fractures were caused equally by sliding, and the batter being hit by a pitched ball.

Catcher

The catcher is the most likely player to be injured because of his position immediately behind the batter. Hazards include the pounding of the hand by the pitched ball, the jolt of foul balls (tips), home plate collisions, and bruised throwing arms. It is the task of the catcher to catch all the throws of the pitcher not hit by the batter. When many pitchers throw the baseball with a velocity of 80 to 100mph (130–160kmh^{-1}), the possibility of injury is obvious. This velocity is greatly accelerated when the batter barely touches the ball with the bat. The resulting foul ball or tips are a major cause of injuries. The catcher wears protective equipment for the face, chest, shins, and one hand, but it is impossible to completely protect the body. The bare hand is the most vulnerable.

A play that causes injury to the catcher occurs at home plate when the runner tries to score and the ball is thrown to the catcher who tries to tag the runner with the ball which may be in his gloved hand before the runner touches home plate. Frequently the catcher, depending upon his added protective equipment, will block the plate trying to keep the runner from scoring. The oncoming runner knocks the catcher down with possible injury to either the catcher or runner or both.

Pitcher

The pitcher is the key person in the game. Most of the game action is initiated when he throws the ball towards home plate. Injuries happen to pitchers while throwing the ball and attempting to catch or stop the batted ball. Arm and shoulder injuries are the most common, because the overhand motion is an unnatural motor movement. These problems can result from: (1) throwing pitches or using styles of delivery which puts a great deal of strain on the arm or shoulder; (2) a lack of conditioning; or (3) throwing too hard for a long period of time or throwing too many pitches.

Regardless of the level of the sport, the pitcher is in the most vulnerable position for being hit by the batted ball. The pitcher is only 60½ft (18.4m) (45ft (13.7m) for younger players) from the batter. Contusions and even fractures may result from extremely hard hit balls.

Infielders

The majority of injuries occur in the tagging or forcing out of a base runner. Infielders suffer spike wounds of varying severity on plays where an opposing runner slides, feet first and spikes high, into the base the infielder is attempting to cover.

Infielders are subject to contusions and even fractures, because the batted ground ball sometimes hops badly and hits the fielder on some part of the body other than the gloved hand. Because of errant throws from the other players, the first baseman is especially vulnerable to injury from collision when he is forced to move into the path of the player running from home plate to first base in order to catch the thrown ball.

Outfielders

Usually an outfielder must run a greater distance to catch the ball. As a result, the major danger of playing the outfield is that of collision with the fence, with other outfielders, or with infielders. Because of the layout of the field, on sunny days one or more of the outfielders must face into the sun. There is a possibility of being hit by the ball after losing sight of it against the sun. Because of the distance from the batter, outfielders have fewer chances of throwing the ball than infielders. When they do, they must make long hard throws to get the runner. As a result, sore arms are a common occurrence among outfielders.

Batter

The greatest risk of injury to the batter comes from being hit by the ball. The batter may be hit by a ball thrown by the pitcher, or from his fouling the ball off his shin or foot. Contusions and occasionally fractures result from being hit by the ball. Pulled or strained muscles can result if the batter does not warm up properly before attempting to take strong swings in batting practice or in the game.

Base runner

Quick starting, speed in running the bases, and the ability to slide properly are fundamental skills for the base runner. The player must be properly conditioned in order not to pull muscles through quick starts. Sliding (where the runner hooks the base with a foot or hand to avoid being tagged by the defensive player) is one of the most common causes of injury to the base runner. Many injuries occur when the runner changes his mind while in the act of sliding. Litwhiler (1967) concluded that more sprained ankles, broken legs, and other injuries are inflicted on base runners by this mental lapse than by any other playing action.

INJURY PREVENTION

Hein (1963) listed five general underlying principles for injury prevention in sports. These principles fall under the following headings: (1) developing skills; (2) conditioning of participants; (3) supervising play; (4) providing equipment and facilities; and (5) assuring health care. Each of these principles plays an important role.

McConnell (1960) stressed the importance of skills:

'It is possible to perfect baseball skills and at the same time to avoid injury. In fact the possession of skills helps to prevent accidents. Very seldom do we hear of a player who executes a play properly being injured. The man who knows how to throw, and uses this knowledge in throwing, doesn't pull a muscle in his arm, and the fellow who knows how to slide and uses this knowledge doesn't sprain an ankle or strain an elbow. It is important that every player concentrate on the basic fundamentals.'

The coaches and officials who have responsibility for supervision of play must be well versed in the game. They must not only have the technical knowledge of the skills of the sport and the ability to transmit this knowledge to the players, but have an understanding of what effect the activity will have upon the players' welfare. Stafford (1942) developed a simple set of principles of supervision, which if carefully followed, offer a maximum of safety. These principles involve:

1. An understanding of the hazards involved in each activity.
2. The removal of unnecessary hazards.
3. Compensating for those hazards which cannot be removed.
4. Creating no unnecessary hazards.

The players must be furnished with proper equipment and taught how to use it properly. Regardless of budget size the key to good management is the best use of available funds. A little extra expenditure for better products will pay off over the years, for good equipment, if properly cared for, lasts longer and is more economical in the long run. Rather than outfit a team with inferior equipment, the coach should omit non-essentials and buy well-made essential items.

Health care will not be discussed specifically in this chapter. A brief statement on conditioning is given in the next section. The remaining three principles will be included in the following paragraphs which focus on positional roles.

POSITIONAL ROLES

Catcher

As stated earlier, the bare hand is most vulnerable to foul tips. Because of radical changes in the design of the catcher's mitt, catching techniques are changing. The new mitt allows one-handed catching by experienced catchers. 'The handling ease of the mitt allows the catcher to hide his arm and hand protecting them from foul tips or even wild pitches in the dirt' (Vivian, 1976).

However, young catchers must continue to use two hands, and there are many situations where experienced catchers *must* use both hands. Howard (1966) recommended that the catcher hold the rim of the glove with the bare hand or keep the bare hand folded and not clinched until the ball is in the mitt. He further recommended that the catcher place the forefinger of the gloved hand outside the mitt and use sponge rubber or a golf glove inside the mitt to ease the impact of the ball (Fig. 12/2). The catcher needs to wear a protecting mask, a chest protector, shin guards and a protective cup. There is a growing trend for the catcher to wear a hard hat under the mask. The protective equipment should fit snugly and securely (Fig. 12/3).

Because of the undue strain on the knee of the young catcher from the squatting position that is assumed on each pitch, the number of innings in which the player is used as a catcher should be limited (Fig. 12/4).

Pitcher

Pitching styles vary considerably, but the young pitcher should try to perfect a smooth delivery that will not put undue strain on his shoulder. Throwing the curve ball (spin is imparted on the ball by rotating the arm at the wrist and elbow when throwing the ball causing it to curve in flight) is a problem for pitchers and especially for the young pitcher because of the relatively late completion of bone development. Throwing curve balls by young growing players should be discouraged if not forbidden. The young pitcher should be encouraged to develop control and proper form instead.

Because of the vulnerability of the pitcher to line drives, it is important that in teaching a young person how to pitch, follow-through and balance should be emphasised. The pitcher should finish the pitching motion and immediately be in a position to receive a line drive, i.e. a solidly hit ball, most of whose flight approximately parallels the ground. Follow-through also helps to prevent sore arms.

First baseman

When the first baseman prepares to receive throws from other infielders, he should place one foot on the

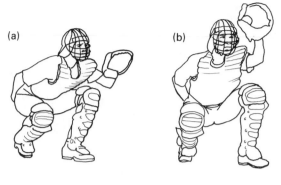

Fig. 12/2 The catcher's basic stance with no runner on base. (a) The right foot is behind the left so he can move quickly if the ball is chopped in front of the plate. The right arm is turned inward behind his back for protection and held there during a one-handed catch. (b) A protective glove with snap action helps hold the ball

Fig. 12/3 The catcher's stance with a runner on base as a pitch is received. The left arm is extended to receive the pitch with the right along the knee for protection from where it can be placed quickly into a throwing position. Alternatively the cupped right hand can be placed behind the glove and the catch performed one-handed.

Fig. 12/4 The squat position which imposes a strain on the knee joint of the catcher

inside corner of the base, giving most of the base to the runner. This will help to avoid being stepped on by the runner and keep him clear of the baseline, thereby reducing the possibility of a collision. If he is pulled off the base and has to tag the runner coming into the base, the tagging arm should be relaxed to avoid injury.

Infielders

Usually the infielder can avoid being spiked by straddling or standing directly behind the base when he is trying to tag out the runner. As the ball is caught he either sweeps (depending upon how close the runner is) or puts the glove containing the ball directly down next to the base in the line from which the runner is coming. The fielder making the tag should be sure to protect himself from getting spiked as well as run over if the runner decides not to slide. When the fielder has to tag a person running by he should tag quickly, low and then get out of the way.

In fielding ground balls the infielder should stay close to the ground and keep his eyes on the ball until he fields it. The infielder must charge towards the ball if possible. He must track the ball into the glove and remember the glove's position. If the ball is above the waist, the heel of the hand is lower than the fingers. If the ball is below the waist, the fingers are lower than the heel of the hand. When picking up the ball the glove hand should start on top of the ground and come up if necessary rather than starting above and going down. The cardinal rule in fielding a ground ball is to keep the eyes on the ball. Turning the head increases the chances of the ball hitting the fielder in the face or some other part of the head if it bounces awkwardly.

Sometimes on plays where the infielder must go from the sure footing of the infield dirt to the less secure outfield grass he may turn his ankle in his haste to get to the ball or get set for the throw. There is not much the player can do to prevent this occurrence except to check out the playing surface to know which spots are wet or slippery.

The playing surface, both dirt and grass, should be constructed and then maintained as smooth as possible for practice and games. The playing field should be inspected regularly for hazards, particularly for holes or low spots.

Outfielders

The outfield must work together as a unit. The centre fielder is the key person in the unit and should catch any ball he can unless another outfielder is in a better position. Fly balls (balls in the air) that are hit between the infielders and outfielders should be taken by the outfielder whenever possible. It is important that the fielders call out their intentions so there is no uncertainty about who is going to catch the ball.

On sunny days all fielders should wear sunglasses – infielders as well. The glove can be used also as a shield. Care must be exercised when using the glove as a shield that sight of the ball is not obstructed.

The playing field including the outfield should be enclosed with a fence. The fence should be high enough so that the players cannot fall over it. All light poles and posts should be located outside the fenced-in playing area. In many parks a warning track is installed near the fence. This allows the player to stop short of the fence or prepare to cushion the impact. Hard unyielding surfaces should be padded to protect a player when he runs into them. If at all possible when fly balls are hit over his head, the player should hurry to the fence, then turn to re-locate the fly ball and catch it.

Batters

While there is no particular batting style recommended, each batter should be in a comfortable on-balance stance and keep his eye on the ball. This should enable him to avoid being hit by a pitch thrown at him. Since helmets are required, they should be worn at all times while batting, whether in practice or in a game.

Proper batting instruction may help prevent the batter from hitting the ball against his foot or shin. Some players wear a modified shin guard for protection.

The batter should loosen up the back, shoulder, and arm muscles early in the practice or game to avoid being hampered by pulled or strained muscles. Players should swing several bats or bats with attached weights before entering the batter's box.

Base runners

In running out batted balls to first base when a turn is not going to be made, the runner should run straight ahead touching the front edge of the base with the toe. Most authorities recommend sliding into first base only when attempting to avoid a tag by the first baseman who has been pulled off the base by a wide throw.

Players should be taught the proper techniques of sliding very early. Most authorities advocate sliding feet first except under special circumstances because the risk of injury to the head, arms, or hands is great in sliding head first. The most important thing to remember is that once a player decides to slide he should complete his slide.

CONDITIONING

Baseball is unique in that only three individuals are actively involved in every pitch – the pitcher, catcher and batter. While it is true that all players should be alert on each pitch, and a few may be involved, the majority of players will not participate in most plays.

Since speed, agility, and coordination are key ingredients for success in baseball it is important that the body and particularly the arms and legs be kept in shape. During the off-season jogging and running, flexibility exercises, and sports such as handball are recommended. Before and during the season it is important that players continue running, particularly wind sprints, and stretching exercises. Each player should warm up properly for running, throwing, and batting before trying quick starts, throwing or swinging hard.

Writing in 1979, Soderholm advocated that 'The best overall conditioning programme for baseball would centre around proper strength training (and flexibility training depending on the equipment used), combined with a limited amount of sprinting, and the practice of baseball skills.'

REFERENCES

Coombs, J. (rev. Litwhiler, D.) (1967). *Baseball*, 4th edition. Prentice-Hall, Englewood Cliffs.

Hein, F. V. (1964). *Health aspects of accident prevention*. In 1963 Annual Safety Education Review. American Association for Health, Physical Education, and Recreation, Washington DC.

Howard, E. (1966). *Catching*. Viking, New York.

McConnell, M. (1960). *How to play little league baseball*. Ronald, New York.

Owen, M. (1974). Play it safe. *School Safety*, **2**, 4–6.

Polk, R. G. (1968). The frequency and causes of baseball injuries. *Athletic Journal*, **49**, 19–20, 53.

Ryan, A. J. (1962). *Medical care of the athlete*. McGraw-Hill, New York.

Soderholm, E. (1979). Striking out the myths in baseball conditioning. *Scholastic Coach*, **48**, 52–56.

Stafford, G. T. (1942). *Recreation and athletics*. In H. J. Stack and E. B. Siebrecht (eds). *Education for safe living*. Prentice-Hall, New York.

Vivian, R. W. (1976). Catching: two-handed vs. one-handed. *Athletic Journal*, **56**, 48–50.

CHAPTER 13

Dangers and demands of basketball

W. H. GEORGE WILKINSON DMS, MPhil

Basketball began in 1891 when James Naismith designed a game with minimal hazards to keep his summer athletes in good physical condition throughout the winter. The game has preserved its non-contact nature over the years while developing as a major international sport. Penalties for illegal contact, particularly violent fouls on the shooter, have become progressively severe since the first formulations of the rules of play. The result has been an effective system of control over competitive behaviour which protects participants and prevents many of the injuries associated with field games occurring. Basketball is by no means injury-free, generating its own peculiar trauma as well as injuries common to vigorous explosive effort and team games.

HOW INJURIES OCCUR

Catching the ball

As basketball demands skill in ball handling, it is inevitable that the hands and fingers are subject to trauma. Powerfully delivered passes may be imperfectly caught: this causes finger pains which may be aggravated when a player moves quickly towards the ball, thereby increasing impact speed. The phalangeal and metacarpo-phalangeal joints may be damaged in the resultant forced hyperextension. A 'stubbed finger' from a mis-catch can produce a painful joint injury, including dislocation of a finger or thumb. The cause is the compression force due to the ball striking the outstretched finger. A common practice deprecated by medical practitioners is for the coach to forcefully pull on the dislocated phalange of the finger to restore the joint.

Players closely guarded and about to receive the ball from a pass are coached to reach for it to prevent its interception. Contact on the arm by an opponent can obstruct the catch, causing a 'stubbed finger' in the process.

Catching a ball rebounding from the backboard requires a fast snatching action in which the ball is pulled from a height down into a protective position. During this action the ball may be rammed onto the fingers of an opponent contesting possession, with consequent trauma.

When finger injuries are suffered, a common practice in basketball is to tape the injured digit to the adjacent one. This acts as a splint, immobilises and protects the injured finger and allows further play.

Defensive blocking

The fingers are highly exposed to injury in any attempt to block a pass, dribble or shot. In particular, blocking an attempted outlet pass intended to travel the length of the court can lead to severe trauma through great impact speed. As a basket ball weighs 0.62kg (22oz) it constitutes a comparatively heavy missile.

Held ball situation

If a defender can legally manage to retain a grip on a ball held by an opponent a stalemate is reached. Play is resumed with a 'jump ball' which gives the two contesting players a chance to tap the ball to a team mate. Often one player is in a disadvantageous position in the 'held ball' incident. One participant may attempt to wrest possession from the other before an official intervenes. The techniques employed consist of vigorously pulling and jerking, using the arms and upper body. The player retaining a strong grip while in a mechanically poor position can injure the hands, the elbow or the shoulder joint. A natural response is to try to pull the ball horizontally around the body and away from the opponent. This occasionally leads to a characteristic Cumberland-style wrestling throw, hyperextending the elbow or shoulder joint in the process. The part the officials play in forestalling violent wrestling incidents is critical in preventing such injuries.

Falling

Falls to the floor may occur on losing balance while running or after leaping for the ball. A sudden drive towards the basket by an attacker usually calls for a countering action by the defender to stay with him or block his path. This may lead to a collision with one or both players being knocked over (Fig. 13/1). Pride suffers most in such situations, though awkwardness or lack of coordination may promote injury. Landing

Fig. 13/1 Bowled over in
contesting possession

heavily on the buttocks or the hips can cause bruising and the back of the head may hit the floor with resulting contusions or concussion; elbows, wrists and hands also may suffer painful contact with the floor. For preventive purposes gymnastic and tumbling techniques can be introduced into the training programme to teach the art of falling and rolling. If an arm is extended by a player in the attempt to break his fall, it may act as a rod which will transmit the force of the fall through the limb to the shoulder joint. Among the injuries received in this way are clavicular and scaphoid fractures and dislocations of the elbow or shoulder, particularly the acromio-clavicular or sterno-clavicular joint. A fallen player may accidentally bring down an opponent: Bachman (1970) reported incomplete tear of

a medial collateral ligament of the knee in such an incident.

Falling on the run usually means that the upper body is propelled ahead of the legs and putting an arm down to break the fall carries all of the risks already referred to. A player unable to execute a protective roll may slide along the surface of the floor incurring skin abrasions which, for obvious reasons, are called 'strawberry burns'. The practice of players is either to play on immediately or after cleansing the wounds.

Some players wear protective knee pads while others wear shorts fitted with light internal padding to protect the iliac crests. Most players prefer a feeling of lightness and mobility, and seldom wear additional items apart from hair bands, sweat bands or elasticated elbow, ankle and knee supports. Dirty floor surfaces represent a particular hazard when skin abrasions arise; open wounds incurred through contact with the floor require sterilising treatment at once.

Basketball is an extremely fast game with play often changing rapidly from end to end. Players are constantly involved in abrupt acceleration, deceleration and changes of direction. These changes put considerable stress on to the legs and their joints with the ankles and knees particularly vulnerable. Feet in poor postural positions are more susceptible to injury when subjected to abnormal stresses with unilateral weakness predisposing the weaker foot to injury (Conway, 1969).

Bachman (1970) reported that many basketball players have bony outgrowths in the lower shin, secondary to repetitive forced dorsiflexion of the ankle. The tension during violent twisting movements can result in injuries to the semilunar cartilages, the collateral or the cruciate ligaments of the knee, as well as to the ankle joint. Ankle sprain usually involves an inverted and equinous position with damage incurred to the talofibular ligament (Lunceford, 1971). The extent of the damage depends on the forces operating. This injury has been attributed to use of resin on the shoes to assist in abrupt halts and turns (Lunceford, 1964).

Another area subjected to stress is the lower back. This may be the result of repeated powerful trunk actions which combine flexion, extension and rotation from a variety of postures and occasionally landing with the body fully extended or the back arched. Excessive use of defensive techniques involving a crouched posture may place the spine at a disadvantage. For all these manoeuvres compatibility of the footwear and the type of floor is stressed. To provide constant conditions courts should be regularly cleaned of dust, sweat and grease. The practice of running the palm of the hand along the court surface or a trial sweep with a broom soon shows the state of the floor. Large halls can, during cold humid weather, experience condensation, usually in parts near to external walls and doors. Slipping and falling into a split position can lead to injuries particularly in the adductor and hamstring muscle groups, or to tendon and ligament damage in the lower limbs.

Jumping and landing

Repetitive jumping may promote patellar tendinitis or the condition known as jumper's knee. Poorly controlled landings may cause bruising of the soft tissue beneath the heel and this injury may become chronic (Blazina et al, 1973).

Jumping is performed off one foot or both feet – landing is usually executed with both feet hitting the floor simultaneously or almost together. Players are frequently trained to disregard personal safety when jumping. Taking defenders on in 'one-on-one' situations, driving into the heart of a defence and leaping upwards and in towards the basket to shoot, engaging fiercely in contesting rebound and loose-ball possession, represent areas of physical risk that players accept (Fig. 13/2, p. 108). When a player takes off on a powerful upward leap, contact by another player can cause imbalanced landing, possibly not on the feet. If in such situations his full concentration is on scoring, injury is more likely. Falling backwards with the back extended can cause considerable shock. A player may land on another's feet. It is not unknown in basketball for players to drive up and in towards the basket with a high knee lift designed to test the courage of defenders. Some coaches advocate this practice, the reasoning being that having once stood in the way of such an attacking move a player is unlikely to do so again. The knee can cause severe bruising and even fracture ribs and the defender can be knocked over backwards with injuries incurred in falling.

Play close to the basket

An attacker in attempting to score may have alternative objectives. These could be to score a basket, draw a foul or gain the rebound if the shot is unsuccessful. These objectives play a great part in the fashioning of shooting techniques. Leaping upwards and in towards the basket to shoot invariably gets the best results (Fig. 13/3, p. 109). Most profitable is the 'three point plus foul' play which occurs when a player is fouled in the act of shooting but still scores. He is awarded one free throw which if successful earns an extra point while a foul is recorded against the opponent. Some coaches encourage antagonism in defenders in practices so as to accustom and toughen attacking players to learn the art of scoring despite being fouled.

A defender may interpose himself between an opponent and the basket when a shot is made to 'screen' (or 'box') him out, while the attacker may attempt to force past. Coaches advocate a strong defensive crouch with arms held up and elbows out. After an unsuccessful shot the rebound is likely to be contested vigorously to secure possession. In such incidents the elbow represents one of the most dangerous weapons in the game. The raised elbows are usually level with the head of an opponent and therefore in forcing past or in protecting a rebound, injuries to the head can ensue. Numerous injuries attributable to accidental or intentional use of the elbows range from contusions on the skull, eye damage, fractured cheek and nasal bones to split lips and broken teeth. Cracked ribs can result from digging backwards at an opponent when being

Fig. 13/2 Demonstration of a vigorous leap upwards and inwards towards the basket before shooting

Fig. 13/3 Much of the more vigorous activity is under the basket

Fig. 13/4 'Dunking' the ball into the basket

closely guarded. A further damaging action may occur when a closely guarded attacker attempts to drive upwards and in towards the basket to score: the elbow of the shooting arm is liable in this instance to hit the defender in the face. Current tactics dictate that players attempt to release the ball as near as possible to the ring.

A player who drives hard for the basket and uses a powerful 'lay up shot' is especially exposed. On collecting the ball at the end of the dribble and taking off, the head is lifted to focus on the target. Taller players attempt on occasions to 'dunk' the ball (Fig. 13/4), or force it powerfully into the basket from above the ring. The worst foul in basketball can occur in this situation and is commonly referred to as 'tunnelling', 'bridging' or 'submarining' (Fig. 13/5). These terms describe the action of a defender who moves to assume a crouched position underneath the shooter. In this way he tunnels underneath the attacker and creates a bridge, the result being alarmingly spectacular. The defender acts as a fulcrum over which the shooter revolves forward and down. The shooter can land head first on the floor with a possibility of numerous injuries of varying severity,

Fig. 13/5 Shooter about to suffer a 'bridging' foul

the most serious being to the head and spine. Two factors contribute to the extent of the injury. A player is trained to concentrate on scoring after take off and so may be caught unprepared by the foul, while the coordination of the attacker may enable him to emerge unscathed.

ATTITUDE TO PLAY

The player

If a player competes without adequate physical preparation he is more likely to get injured. The lure of match play entices him to participate before he can safely endure the high demands of the game. Similarly, recently injured players are anxious to return to play either to maintain or regain their team position. In basketball such players often attempt to conceal the extent of their injuries. Additionally an unsympathetic attitude on the part of the coach and the non-injured players tends to discourage his complaints. Determined players attempt to participate if it is at all possible and as a result they learn to adapt their game to protect the injury. Players are sometimes known to compete through a full season with a recurring trauma, continued participation inducing the recurrence. Jammed fingers, contusions and abrasions are all considered part of the game and seldom stop the dedicated players who learn to live with them. In many cases it may be that athletes are willing to pay the price of a deteriorating condition for the current self-fulfilment that the game brings.

The coach

At a high level of competitive basketball the accent is on winning. This emphasis has repercussions in the behaviour and attitude of coaches as well as players. One of the personality types described by Ogilvie and Tutko (1971) was the 'hard-nosed coach' who attempts to produce extremely fit, highly motivated and totally controlled players. The search for success is pursued without many scruples, and training methods which attempt to develop the traits the coach desires in his team are utilised. To develop toughness and controlled aggression, practices are devised to highlight physical contact situations in which contact beyond the constraints of the rules is encouraged. The practices initially used by the Belgium national coach in 1960 provide an example of the promotion of aggression in contesting rebounds and tolerance to physical contact. The ball is tossed at the basket by the coach to initiate play, underneath which a group of players are assembled; each player attempts to gain possession of the ball and score while the others prevent his doing so; play is continuous and rules relating to travelling and drib-

bling violations are not enforced; physical contact is permissible. The practices at times become so aggressive that the coach has to part players whose tempers are high. In one-on-one practices a dribbling attacker attempts to go past a defender and score, an exceedingly common incident in competition. The coach emphasises that the attacker takes his opponent on, while the defender is allowed more than normally permissible contact and provides a strong physical challenge. Similarly, conditioned practices ensure that a team, when scrimmaging, plays the game in an extremely aggressive fashion, the coach making additional rules or conditions.

The coach may attempt to maintain motivation levels of his players by introducing punitive measures. If players or the team do not maintain certain standards they are required to do extra work or may be withdrawn from scrimmages for a period. As in all the practices designed to promote aggression the incidence of injury may be greater than in match play, since the training sessions are prolonged and there is much more contact between players.

As a rule basketball coaches are not noted for their sympathy to injured players; the tendency is to shrug off the injury as not being serious. This may be due either to lack of appreciation of and training in first aid principles or to a concern for the game in progress. The coach may well have conflict between a humane regard for his players' well-being and his desire for victory. The ignorance of coaches to the signs, symptoms and treatment of injuries may lead to either lack of immediate and appropriate action or erroneous action exacerbating the condition.

PREVENTION OF INJURIES

Techniques and tactics

Biomechanical analysis of basketball actions may reveal faulty techniques predisposing to injury. A player suffering from pain and degenerative injury can prevent further degeneration or avoid undue stress by modifying and adapting his play. A coach can protect a player by modifying his tactical role. Training schedules appropriately based can ensure gradual recovery from injury.

The control of attitudes towards fair play is largely the concern of each individual. With regard to dangerous and reckless play, the coach and the captain can exert a great deal of influence over individual players.

Players' equipment

Safety should be a major concern in the choice of playing shoes; a player should carry a variety of different designs of footwear to meet with the prevailing floor conditions. Manufacturers could market a range of footwear as a kit. Improperly fitted shoes can cause hammer toes, mallet toes and mycotic infections of the nails (Conway, 1969).

Court surface

The floor should be adequately cleaned and prepared before every training session and game. Periodic maintenance checks, particularly underneath the baskets are necessary. The floor areas near the basket endure the most wear and tear as the most vigorous activity is concentrated there. The hardwearing densely constructed gymnastic and sports hall floors are not entirely suitable for basketball play as their lack of resilience can cause sore feet and blisters, and the exacerbation and recurrence of old injuries. A standard, setting a desirable degree of friction, would represent some surety of a good grip and increase player safety.

Game control

The forming of the laws and their interpretations, officiating systems and disciplinary procedures, play a vital part in exercising control over the behaviour of players. Intentional fouls can vary in degree from merely attempting to prevent a score or by lessening his potential threat by intimidating an opponent, to seeking to seriously incapacitate him so that he is unable to take further part in the game. Basketball, with careful categorisation of fouls and deterrent penalties, and positive and precise instructions to officials, has made dangerous foul play fruitless.

Training

Training in the art of falling and rolling may prevent the occurrence of serious injuries. The training should ensure that physical conditioning for all aspects of the game is achieved.

Treatment

It is desirable that a person with adequate first aid or medical training should be in attendance at every game and training session for immediate treatment of injuries. Associations should include first aid treatment of minor injuries in the training syllabus of basketball coaches and officials. An appropriate first aid kit should be available at all times. The National Associations could arrange a section dealing with injuries at their conferences which would ensure that officials are competent to deal with contingencies. Additionally the safe return of the player to training and match play would be accelerated.

REFERENCES

Bachman, D. C. (1970). Medical aspects of professional basketball. *Illinois Medical Journal*, **137**, 149–154.

Blazina, M. E., Kerlan, R. K., Jobe, F. W., Carter, V. S. and Carlson, G. J. (1973). Jumper's knee. *Orthopaedic Clinics of North America*, **4**, 665–678.

Conway, D. H. (1969). A survey of basketball players in the Rochester area. *Journal of the American Podiatry Association*, **59**, 390–393.

Lunceford, E. M. (1964). *Basketball*. In J. R. Armstrong and W. E. Tucker (eds). *Injury in sport*. Staples, London.

Lunceford, E. M. (1971). *Acute and subacute injury*. In L. A. Larson (ed). *Encyclopedia of sports sciences and medicine*. Macmillan, New York.

Ogilvie, B. and Tutko, T. (1971). *Problem athletes and how to handle them*. Pelham, London.

CHAPTER 14

Risks in field hockey

NORMAN FOX MEd, DASE, DPE

Field hockey is a fast moving field invasive game that involves hard physical work. The heavy demands are intermittent though average energy expenditures as high as 36.5kJ/min⁻¹/65kg have been recorded (Durnin and Passmore, 1967). Good running is essential as is a readiness for explosive action and an ability to recover rapidly. Fast visual reactions while hitting, dribbling and passing the ball are desirable. There is a high requirement to handle the stick skilfully and efficiently, and the coaching and development of these attributes are important factors in injury avoidance.

Kennedy et al (1977) highlighted the incompleteness of incidence data on sporting injuries. The shortage is pronounced when the frequency, site and severity of injuries in field hockey are being considered. Authorities differ as to the degree of risk inherent in the game. At a high level of competition, Judge (1975) cited a low incidence of injury, but this level accounts for a very small proportion of the total hockey played. Blonstein (1974), listing the most dangerous sports as measured by injury rate per player, ranked field hockey fourth after rugby, soccer and gymnastics. Irrespective of the playing standard, injuries are a serious hazard in many sports particularly where the degree of competition is intense, hockey being no exception. Oliver and associates (1977), relating the experience of the Canadian medical team at the 1976 Montreal Olympic Games, claimed that competition was particularly fierce in the field hockey events at this level. They presented evidence of numerous injuries incurred to support this view.

HOCKEY RULES AND SAFETY

The skills and tactics of the game and the rules that govern play are interrelated. Rules prohibit certain manoeuvres and discipline the execution of skills. Hockey is essentially a non-contact sport yet the rule concerned with obstruction is least understood and open to various interpretations. The rule implies that a player shall not obstruct by running between an opponent and the ball, nor place himself or his stick in any way as to be an obstruction to an opponent. This therefore precludes body-charging or contact, or

shielding the ball by turning the body around it. It seems, predictably, that hockey injuries caused by body contact are relatively low, being only 3.9 per cent of total injuries in this sport (Crompton and Tubbs, 1977).

Considering that field hockey is a 'stick and ball' game, it is not surprising that 77 per cent of total injuries are implemental (Crompton and Tubbs, 1977). Players may be hit by a vigorously swung stick weighing between 0.48kg and 0.65kg (17 and 23 ounces), or struck by a hard ball travelling at high velocity. These implemental injuries occur to any part of the trunk, head, forearm, hand, leg, shin, ankle and foot and result in lacerations requiring sutures, bruising, oedema and inflammation, with accompanying pain and acute or sustained incapacity. Safety features to control the height of the ball and stick lift are incorporated into the rules of the game. These features, however, do not always inhibit the accidental or intentional breach of the rules and conventions.

To eliminate some of the risks, certain rules are applied and conventions observed to reduce dangerous play. A ball rising accidentally into the air from an imperfection of the playing area, is not governed by any rule and players are relieved when it is brought down. This does not imply that a ball in the air is illegal. The scoop, or aerial or overhead pass is frequently used. It is permissible to raise the ball in the air and over the heads of opponents, provided the pass itself is not dangerous to others, or unlikely to lead to dangerous play. Responsibility for interpreting what is dangerous is at the discretion of the umpires.

In a similar category is the act of flicking the ball so that it rises off the ground, as when a shot is taken at the goals or the ball is passed to a colleague. However, an undercutting hit, when a player has his weight on the rear foot and the head of the stick acutely angled under the ball which results in a sharply rising ball trajectory, should be immediately penalised as dangerous play. A sharply lifted ball can strike a player's face causing damage to teeth, nose or facial bones.

A rule extremely pertinent to the conduct of the game is that referring to 'sticks', which limits the fore-and-aft swing of a player's stick to shoulder height while hitting or tackling for the ball. Differences in interpretation occur due to the varying statures of players, the diverse postures adopted, and misjudgments or loss of technique under competition stress.

SITES OF INJURY

Players are exposed to various injuries during running, turning, twisting and stretching, with vulnerability at many body sites. In each injury zone the injuries can include lacerations, haematomata, dislocations, miscellaneous soft tissue injuries and fractures.

Lower limbs

Ambeganonker and Dixit (1971) claimed that the most common severe injury in hockey is dislocation of the knee caused by loss of balance when concentrating on dribbling the ball while taking evasive action from opponents. Dislocation of the ankle joint and stress fractures of the tibia and fibula associated with abrupt changes in direction and speed are also experienced. It is suggested that a principal factor in these joint dislocations and fractures is the spinal flexion demand of the game which constitutes an ergonomically unsound posture for fast controlled locomotion. This stooped position may also precipitate back complaints particularly with taller players. Minor injuries can also occur to the foot, ankle, shin, and knee by being struck with a stick or the ball.

Facial injuries

Injuries to the facial area may be caused when the ball rises abruptly in the air or a stick is swung in a high arc. Oliver and co-workers (1977) cited an example of a player at the 1976 Olympic Games who received a broken nose and facial lacerations from a stick slashed across his face. This player completed the last game of competition wearing a protective ice hockey mask and helmet. Running into the raised swing of a stick can cause furious epistaxis and fractures of the nose are commonly associated (Ambeganonker and Dixit, 1971).

GAME PHASES

Tackles

Essentially there are three types of tackles – face to face, reverse and chase. Many injuries occur when players are close together as when tackling to dispossess the player in possession. In close face to face confrontations, experienced players conventionally keep to their left to avoid a collision and the swing of the opponent's stick as the tackle to dispossess is made. The common injuries in these situations are cuts, abra-

sions and bruises to hands, forearms, knees, shins and ankles. In tackles from the reverse side it is often difficult to avoid body contact. In executing a chase tackle from the rear of a player travelling at speed who is about to strike the ball, great care is needed to avoid the backward swing of his stick. Failure to do so can result in severe stick-inflicted injuries to the nose, face and teeth.

Closed situations

Several set plays within the game heighten the injury risk. These situations include free hit, hit out and corners.

FREE HIT AND HIT OUT

The free hit and the hit out are the most frequent recurring set plays. A free hit is awarded against a player infringing certain rules. A hit out is awarded if the ball is sent out of play by the attacking team over the opponent's back line or goal line, and no goal is scored, or sent out accidentally by a defender 22.85m (25 yards) or more distant from the goal line. The hit out is taken by a defender opposite the point where it crossed the back line and usually level with the edge of the striking circle. If these hits are taken quickly, some players may be taken by surprise, not facing or watching the ball. In these circumstances there is a risk of being struck by the ball from behind. A slight delay

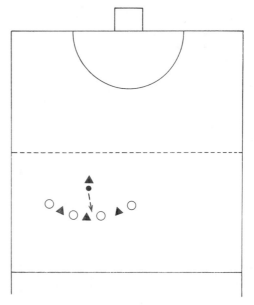

Fig. 14/1 Ringing a free hit
●=Ball ▲=Defenders ○=Attackers
→=Path of the ball

enables the opposing team to form an arc to ring the ball with three or four players, who are permitted to stand 4.57m (5 yards) from it, with defenders filling the gaps (Fig. 14/1).

The hit is usually driven hard and the intention disguised, although with an effective ring the alternatives are few. Often the only solution is to attempt to drive the ball through the ring of players. The speed of the ball, the proximity of players, combined with the frequency of this set piece, make this feature of the game one of exceptional risk.

CORNERS

The award of a corner presents the most dangerous situation in the game. A penalty or short corner is awarded for an infringement in the striking circle by a defender, or if a defender deliberately sends the ball over the back line. Goals can only be scored from within this striking circle. A long corner is given when the ball is unintentionally cleared over the back line by a defender.

The rules governing a penalty corner allow it to be taken from either side of the goal at a point on the back line 9.14m (10 yards) from goal. Six defenders are permitted to station themselves behind or just to the side of the goal, with the other five remaining beyond the half-way line. The attackers stand at the edge of the striking circle in various groups to deceive the defenders (Fig. 14/2). In the long corner, the ball is initially

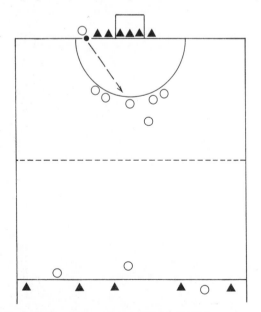

Fig. 14/2 Penalty corner taken from the left
●=Ball ▲=Defenders ○=Attackers
→=Path of the ball

hit towards the circle from near the intersection of the back and side lines.

When the ball is hit or pushed to the waiting forwards, the defenders move quickly across the circle to tackle the forward in possession before he attempts a shot. All players involved in this set piece are under great pressure. The shooter in possession has very little time to strike the ball at goal. The defenders have little time to assess the situation and take appropriate action. The ball is often struck as hard as possible towards the goal and consequently at the oncoming defenders. The velocity of a well-struck ball may be as high as $128\,\mathrm{kmh^{-1}}$ (80mph). The remaining attacking players also rush towards the goal to retrieve rebounds or deflected shots. Thus the situation demands that two opposing sets of players, perhaps totalling a dozen, run towards each other in a confined space, and a ball travelling at high velocity is hit at the goal behind them. If the shot is successfully stopped by the goalkeeper, his usual practice is to kick it clear of the circle. The ball again travels through the crowded players, this time from the opposite direction. In these circumstances, various injuries inflicted by the ball, a stick or collision with another player, particularly the goalkeeper, can occur.

INTRINSIC AND EXTRINSIC FACTORS

Apart from match-determined causes of injury, numerous other key factors can be identified. These can be broadly divided into factors intrinsic and extrinsic to the individual player.

Intrinsic factors
FITNESS
It is generally accepted that certain physiological, neuromuscular and psychomotor qualities are necessary for effective participation in sport. Neglect of these detracts from performance and predisposes the participant to injury. In contrast to some sports that have a tradition of training programmes, minimal preparation in field hockey is common even though physical fitness is perhaps the most important factor in the avoidance of exaggerated response to trauma.

POSITIONAL ROLE
Which positional role is at greatest risk is difficult to establish. However, play is most intense in and near the striking circle. The goalkeeper, although normally wearing protective equipment, is called upon to come into deliberate physical contact with the ball and must therefore play a high risk role, as do attackers who rush towards him to retrieve rebounds. Such is the nature of the game that all players are vulnerable most of the time

and are involved in most of the high risk situations that arise.

AGE AND EXPERIENCE

Field hockey can be played into middle age with the performer relying on a high level of skill and experience to avoid or minimise injury. There is an increased risk of attrition injuries particularly when running and dribbling the ball. The quality and amount of coaching, with emphasis on skilful stickwork, ball control, positional play, recognition of the spirit of the game, can all make a significant contribution to injury avoidance. Injuries due to imperfect skill development are more likely to occur with school and novice hockey players.

PSYCHOLOGICAL FACTORS

Psychological factors rendering an individual susceptible to injury are well recognised (Sanderson, 1977). Under this multifactorial influence, consideration is accorded to the interplay of personality and motivation. An important influence on the incidence of injury is an individual's commitment to competition and his willingness to take risks. The urge to win or to keep one's team place is no less in hockey than in other sports where rewards are considerable.

Extrinsic factors
CHARACTERISTICS OF OPPONENTS

Unlike combat or some contact sports, little can be done to influence or match the size, strength, speed, skill or aggressiveness of advantaged opponents. However, players should not needlessly be exposed to positional roles or levels of competition beyond their capabilities.

ENVIRONMENT

The type and condition of the playing surface can have a significant influence on injury. A player falling on some types of all-weather playing surfaces can receive severe skin abrasions. A hard surface with a worn grass cover often makes the ball ricochet and difficult to control. In heavy muddy conditions, the ball often travels short and as a result play becomes scrappy with sticks being lifted and the ball slashed as players make several attempts to move it. It is also more difficult to maintain balance on such grounds. In inclement weather, any reduction in visibility is hazardous. Rain that reduces vision also makes the ball greasy and the sticks slippery, thus hitting, stopping and stick manipulation become more difficult. Glare caused by brilliant sunshine, or failing daylight, may cause players to momentarily lose sight of the ball in critical situations.

EQUIPMENT

Reduction of risk can be achieved by the amount and quality of equipment used. With the exception of goalkeepers, hockey players are not disposed to wearing adequate protective clothing.

PROTECTIVE EQUIPMENT

Various protective items are available to reduce the incidence of injury. Observation alone confirms the need for such equipment to be more widely used in field hockey, as apart from goalkeepers few hockey players take effective protective measures. It is remarkable how little protective equipment is subject to minimum standards of safety. Field testing without controls has been the principal means of justifying the equipment for both the manufacturer and the public. It is recommended that any protective equipment purchased should be of the highest quality available.

Protective equipment for goalkeepers consists of kickers, leg guards, abdominal guard, chest guards, gloves and face mask (Fig. 14/3).

There are two types of kickers, one made of leather with half-sole and a reinforced toe cover that fits over the footwear and is secured by straps. The other is made of padded canvas that straps over the instep of the

Fig. 14/3 Goalkeeper wearing protective equipment

goalkeeper's boots. The leather type is heavier and the half-sole tends to impede the mobility and speed of the goalkeeper. The canvas instep type requires extra measures to prevent them coming loose during play but provides a satisfactory standard of protection if used with boots having reinforced toe caps.

Suitable leg guards or pads are similar to those used by wicketkeepers in cricket. Foam rubber strips worn under the pads help to prevent hard shots rebounding from them, as goalkeeping skill involves absorbing the impact and clearing the ball as it falls.

Use of abdominal and chest guards made of padded canvas and inlaid with strips of bamboo cane is advisable. These guards provide effective protection to the torso and can act as a confidence booster. Unlike lacrosse, they are not nearly as widely used by hockey goalkeepers as they should be. Although not as satisfactory, a fencing instructor's plastron affords some security to the upper torso.

There are various kinds of goalkeeping gloves available with options of padded backs and palms for left and right hands depending on stick carriage. Indoor hockey, where rapid play and artificial lighting often puts goalkeepers at exceptional risk, has promoted the use of goalkeeping face masks. Their employment has spread from the indoor to the outdoor game. Ironically the greatest disadvantage of these masks is that they reduce peripheral vision and interfere with sighting the ball.

Hockey players in outfield roles are advised to wear shin pads, similar to those worn by soccer players, which can be slipped behind stockings. Other shin

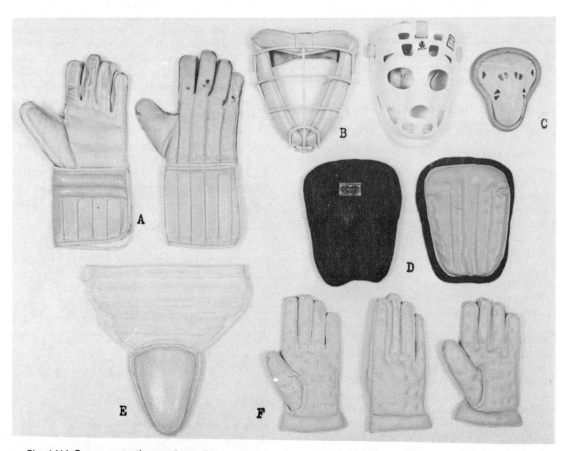

Fig. 14/4 Some protective equipment:
A. Goalkeeper's gauntlets providing wrist and forearm protection
B. Two types of goalkeeping masks
C. Male genital protector
D. Shin guards
E. Goalkeeper's abdominal guard and genital protector
F. Assorted goalkeeping gloves

pads, designed for women and affording some ankle protection, are worn outside the stockings and secured by straps. They are not popular as they interfere with running.

Male players should consider wearing a good quality genital protector or box that can be slipped into the pocket on some athletic supporters. Female players are similarly inadequately protected. Some women games players wear protective brassières and briefs with padded abdominal and hip sections. All players should consider wearing knee pads, especially on hard playing surfaces. Use of suitable mouth guards should be encouraged to prevent dental injuries. Silk and chamois leather inner gloves used by military aircrews offer some defence against minor abrasions to hands and wrists. Samples of protective equipment are shown in Figure 14/4.

The design and effects of footwear used must be of concern. High ankled canvas hockey boots providing some support are commercially available but worn by a minority. Most players wear low-cut lightweight soccer boots or training shoes, yet these designs and certain type of cleats and studs are implicated in the incidence of ankle and knee injuries. The specific footwear requirements of hockey players have, as yet, been incompletely established.

Injuries seem most pronounced at extreme levels of playing proficiency. The intensity of top competition may promote perilous play while imperfect skill development places novices periodically at risk. Common sites of severe injury are the lower limbs and face but the whole body is vulnerable. The ball and stick constitute potential causes of trauma. Besides the hazards specific to this sport, players are susceptible to many of the injuries common to field invasive games from running, turning, side-stepping, accelerating and decelerating manoeuvres.

Field hockey can be a pleasurable recreation and a challenging and demanding sport. Reduction in the incidence of injury can be achieved if the rules are adhered to, sensible precautions taken and protective equipment utilised. A commitment to personal preparation is also likely to prove fruitful in avoiding injury and enhancing enjoyment.

REFERENCES

Ambeganonker, S. D. and Dixit, N. D. (1971). *Acute and sub-acute injury: field hockey.* In L. A. Larson (ed). *Encyclopedia of sports sciences and medicine.* Macmillan, New York.

Blonstein, J. L. (1974). Injuries in sport. *Transactions of the Medical Society of London,* **90,** 20–30.

Crompton, B. and Tubbs, N. (1977). A survey of sports injuries in Birmingham. *British Journal of Sports Medicine,* **11,** 12–15.

Durnin, J. V. G. A. and Passmore, R. (1967). *Energy, work and leisure.* Heinemann, London.

Judge, H. D. (1975). *Risks in hockey.* In T. C. J. O'Connell (ed). *Injuries in rugby football and other team sports.* Irish Rugby Football Union, Dublin.

Kennedy, M. C., Vanderfield, G. K. and Kennedy, J. R. (1977). Sport: assessing the risk. *Australian Medical Journal,* **2,** 253–254.

Oliver, J. H., Mackasey, D. and Percy, E. C. (1977). Experience of the Canadian medical team at the 21st Olympiad. *Canadian Medical Association Journal,* **117,** 609–612.

Sanderson, F. H. (1977). The psychology of the injury prone athlete. *British Journal of Sports Medicine,* **11,** 56–58.

CHAPTER 15

Injuries in Rugby Union football

R. J. HARDIKER BSc; W. J. MURPHY MEd, DPE, DAE
and J. J. SHUTTLEWORTH DLC, BA, MA, PhD

THE GAME

Aggression is an essential ingredient of many sports, particularly those involving bodily contact. Aggression in man is arguably a biological necessity but it is not necessarily synonymous with violence or malice prompted by motives of revenge or hatred. In rugby football the presence of aggression and resultant violence has been the subject of an on-going debate for a considerable time. They can be manifested in most aspects of rugby including running, jumping, tackling, scrummaging, rucking and mauling. It is possible, however, to possess an aggressive attitude towards the game without the use of violence. Nevertheless injuries are an unavoidable consequence of aggression especially when it does generate violence.

It is well recognised that fitness can help to reduce the risk of injury. The fittest man on the field however, if trapped in a ruck, can be severely injured by an unscrupulous player with a disregard for the laws of the game. Invariably acts of violence come within the scope of Law 20 which relates to charging, obstruction, foul play and misconduct. Most offences against this law tend to occur in the scrum, the line-out, the ruck and the maul. These particular phases of the game constitute focal points where possession of the ball is contested, aggression is generated, violence ensues and injuries occur. These and other phases of the game require summary explanation.

Kick-offs occur at the start of each half of the game and after each score. They are taken from the centre of the field.

Drop-outs usually occur when the ball is touched down over the try line or progresses over the dead ball line to the advantage of the defending side. Drop-outs are taken from the twenty-two metre line.

In both cases the ball is usually kicked in the air towards the opposing forwards while forwards from the kicking side endeavour to reach the ball first or dispossess the catcher. Figure 15/1 illustrates a typical line-up of both teams at the kick-off.

The *scrum* is used to restart the game after certain infringements. The forwards from each side combine in the prescribed manner, and push against each other

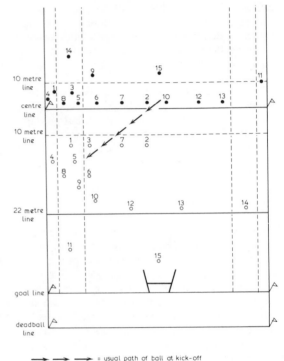

= usual path of ball at kick-off

Fig. 15/1 Diagram showing the position of players at a typical kick-off

with heads interlocked and backs arched as illustrated in Figure 15/2. The ball is thrown into the front row of the scrum where the hooker from each side attempts to scoop it back with his foot.

A *wheel* occurs when a prop forward ceases to push in a scrum and acts as a pivot around which the forward momentum revolves, turning the scrummage through an angle of 90° to the original line of direction.

The scrum is *collapsed* by a player in the front row falling to the ground, either deliberately or by accident, when both sides are exerting maximum effort. The effect is to change the direction of the force being applied by both sets of forwards. The force is redirected towards the ground instead of being maintained

Fig. 15/2 The scrummage

Fig. 15/3 The maul

Fig. 15/4 The ruck

in a horizontal plane resulting in a pile-up of bodies.

The *maul* occurs when a player from one team is stopped with the ball while still on his feet (Fig. 15/3). He then attempts to screen the ball from the opposition and release it to his own supporting players. Opposing forwards combine in an attempt to dispossess him and drive him backwards.

The *ruck* occurs when a player is grounded with the ball and individuals from both teams attempt to drive over this player and the ball so that it is made available to supporting team members (Fig. 15/4).

Risks

Few observers dispute that there are risks inherent in playing rugby. However, the element of risk can be reduced or intensified by:

1. the application of techniques, for example, collapsing the scrum, head-on tackles or 'rucking' players off the ball;
2. the manipulation of the laws, for example, Law 19 dictates that a player who is lying on the ground and
    (a) *is holding the ball*, or
    (b) *is preventing an opponent from gaining possession of it*, or
    (c) *has fallen on or over the ball emerging from a scrummage or ruck*, must immediately play the ball or get up or roll away from it. Failure to observe this law results in the award of a penalty kick at the place of the infringement.

It may be contended that if this law was applied correctly the frequent pile-ups and resultant injuries would not be seen.

3. the inculcation of attitudes in the participants, for example, a hard uncompromising attitude appears to be increasingly encouraged. Administrators are, of course, implicated: they can, after serious incidents, take positive measures by banning offenders from further participation for discretionary periods, or alternatively impose severe financial penalties.

A study of player behaviour demonstrates that more players are at risk for longer periods of time in rugby than in most field invasive games. In addition, exposure to risk is immediate due to the prescribed method of starting the game which invariably involves congregation of both sets of forwards as the ball drops from the kick-off.

Minor injuries occur regularly and neglect of these can sometimes have serious long-term repercussions. Neglect in this instance has been ascribed by Tooth (1974) to such factors as the quality of first aid available, the attitude of the coach or captain and the attitude of the player.

Serious injury has been the exception rather than the rule in rugby. Between 1968 and 1974, no cases of paralysis as a result of rugby injury in South Wales were reported. Since 1974, however, the annual average rate has been one case per season with two cases during the early part of the 1978/1979 season (Williams and McKibbin, 1978). As physical conditioning of players has become more rigorous over the years, it is probable that the increased injury incidence is due to a greater recklessness in play.

CHARACTERISTICS OF RUGBY INJURIES

There is a fair degree of discrepancy between personnel involved in playing or coaching and medical researchers as to what should validly constitute a recorded injury. It appears that the most viable operational definition incorporates the criteria of the injured player being unable to continue the game, requiring medical attention and needing a minimum recovery period of ten days (Walkden, 1975).

A systematic appraisal of the characteristics of rugby injuries requires that their type, anatomical site and relative frequency be identified prior to assessing the determinative nature of such factors as the class of rugby in which the injury was sustained, fatigue, the pitch and weather conditions, the tactics employed by the teams and the playing position. Table 1 shows the results of various studies of the site and frequency of rugby injuries.

The most frequently injured part of the body is the head and neck where lacerations and contusions tend to prevail, while the shoulder, arm, knee and ankle joints each account for approximately half that suffered by the head and neck. The trunk, which includes the back and abdomen, sustains the least number of injuries. If the body is considered in terms of larger regions a distinct pattern more clearly emerges. The lower limb, consisting of the hip, knee and ankle joints, the upper limb, consisting of the hands, arms, shoulders and collar bones, and the head and neck each account for slightly less than one-third of all injuries, the trunk being a residual region accounting for less than one-tenth and thus of relatively less significance. Injuries, therefore, are fairly evenly distributed over three main regions, although the types of injury experienced in all four regions differ appreciably.

An examination of injury types becomes more meaningful when the injured player's playing position is taken into consideration. The head and neck region experiences mainly lacerations, concussion and, to a lesser extent, haematomata and fractures. Such injury types are most frequently inflicted by means of a boot or hand. This suggests that a significant proportion are

Table 1 Review of injury frequency according to anatomical position

	O'Connell (1954) %	Micheli and Riseborough (1974) %	Roy (1974) %	Van Heerden (1976) %	Walkden (1975) %	Adams (1977) %	Davies and Gibson (1978) %
Head	21.5	} 13.0	20.5	20.9	6.5	} 16.1	19.5
Neck	2.3		–	1.5	–		5.0
Shoulder	18.3	32.0	10.0	9.2	5.25	} 32.3	13.0
Upper limb	12.8	5.0	–	12.2	–		9.0
Thorax	2.8	} 11.0	3.2	5.5	–		} 11.0
Abdomen	2.5		–	0.9	–	} 11.2	
Spine/Back	} 5.8	8.0	–	3.7	–		
Pelvis		0	–	2.5	–		
Knee	12.5	13.0	14.5	17.4	6.93	} 40.4	9.9
Ankle	11.3	8.0	13.5	10.9	5.25		} 33.1
Remainder of Lower limb	10.0	10.0	–	12.6	–		
Intermediate	–	–	38.0	2.7	76.07	–	–

Table 2 Injury frequency by position: results of three investigations

	Durkin (1977)		Van Heerden (1976)		Roy (1974)	
	Percentage	Rank order	Percentage	Rank order	Percentage	Rank order
Full-back	15.3	1	10.5	3	9.5	6
Wing three-quarter	11.9	4	12.0	2	10.5	5
Centre three-quarter	13.6	2	10.5	3	9.0	7
Outside-half	10.2	6	7.5	10	8.5	9
Scrum-half	5.1	9	14.2	1	7.0	10
Prop	9.3	7	8.4	8	9.0	7
Hooker	6.8	8	9.1	6	11.0	2
Lock forward	2.5	10	8.4	8	11.0	2
Wing forward	11.9	4	10.0	5	11.0	2
Number 8	13.6	2	8.6	7	14.0	1

deliberately inflicted; this is a widely upheld proposition which is difficult to substantiate. Nevertheless it is the forwards who receive most injuries in this region especially to the ears and face. These tend to be of a less serious nature than those suffered by the backs in the upper and lower limb regions but are far more frequent.

The game phases which predispose forwards to head and neck injuries are the binding of locks, the collapsing of scrums, the ruck and maul in pursuit of second-phase ball (a situation exacerbated by the 1977–1978 tackle law innovation permitting a player to retain possession of the ball until it touches the ground), and finally the line-out. Forwards, according to Davies and

Gibson (1978), and especially prop forwards, sustain significantly more injuries not only in the head and neck region but in all regions. There are, nevertheless, certain specific exceptions to this generalisation. Walkden (1975), for instance, ascertained that concussion predominated among the backs with the full-back alone accounting for 30 per cent of all cases. The full-back position is most at risk to injury in all regions, according to Walkden, a proposition reinforced by Durkin's (1977) investigations (Table 2). Recent kicking law innovations and tactical developments in the contemporary game can undoubtedly account for this trend with the evolution of the running, attacking, abrasive and more committed full-back as exemplified by J. P. R. Williams and Andy Irvine. The same trend would also account for the high risk factor associated with the number 8 and back row play in general identified by Roy (1974). The foraging, driving and high degree of commitment now demanded of back-row players undoubtedly explains their high rank order in injury frequency. The inter-relationship between injury site and type and forward positions is more readily identifiable in the context of first-class rugby. Durkin (1977) showed that over one-third of all injuries at this level were lacerations of which approximately two-thirds were to the scalps and faces of forwards.

Tactics employed at international and first-class competition, and which have permeated down throughout all levels of club rugby, have concentrated upon retaining possession and so called 'good ball' from first- and second-phase play. This necessitates very tight and aggressive forward play, a dearth of back play, rolling mauls, crash balls, back-row moves, and first, second and even third phase play, all of which engender situations conducive to the occurrence of head and neck injuries, especially to forwards.

In the same way that head and neck injuries are associated with forward play so also are injuries to the lower leg and shoulder girdle shown to be related to playing positions in the back division. Backs on the whole, including the scrum-half and full-back, experience less frequent but more serious injuries located mainly in the shoulder, knee and ankle joints. Injuries of a less severe but still incapacitating nature, such as muscle tears, seem also to be the prerogative of backs.

By far the most prevalent types of injury in the upper and lower limb regions are ligamentous and cartilaginous; they account for nearly one-third of the injuries in these regions and double that of fractures, sprains, tears and strains. Damaged ligaments are the most common soft tissue injury and they are experienced mainly in the knee and ankle and, to a lesser extent, the shoulder joints. Torn cartilages, on the other hand,

occur half as frequently and tend to be located almost exclusively in the knee joint, with the exception of rib cartilages which are damaged relatively infrequently. The leg is also the main location of such less severe injuries as tears, haematomata, sprains and strains which occur with such frequency that precise diagnostic information is lacking. Nevertheless, they cause considerable disruption to the continuity of players' performances.

Backs are the major recipients of soft tissue injuries sited in the leg. This can undoubtedly be accounted for by the velocity at which the player is running when tackled, the sudden changes in direction executed in swerving and side-stepping and recent innovations in boot and stud design. The crash tackle has also largely replaced the more traditional techniques, particularly in the centres. The impact force absorbed by the lower leg is considerable and contributes to the incidence of ligamentous and cartilaginous injuries to the knee and ankle. This situation has been compounded by the popularity of both low cut boots, which afford little stability to the ankle joint, and more effective traction-inducing studs. Modern studs effectively anchor the knee and ankle joints while permitting the upper leg to rotate either in a tackle or during sudden changes in direction, thereby inducing cartilaginous and ligamentous damage. Centres are especially susceptible to these circumstances as they are the recipient of lateral tackles from the opposition back-row, head-on crash tackles from opposing centres, sudden forceful changes of direction executed in making a break, and violent twisting at the base of mauls in which they have been caught.

Fractures and dislocations dominate the types of injuries found in the upper limb. Fractures of the hand, arm and clavicle and dislocations of the fingers and shoulder, especially acromio-clavicular separation, are commonly experienced by backs. The scrum-half is particularly vulnerable to fractures and dislocations of the metacarpals, phalanges, radius and ulna, a result of harassment by the boots of opposing forwards around the scrum and line-out. It is the shoulder joint, however, which experiences most damage in this region. It accounts for one-quarter of all joint injuries, similar to that of the ankle and second only to the knee in which one-third of joint injuries are sited. Dislocation, particularly acromio-clavicular and, to a lesser extent, sterno-clavicular separation and fracture of the clavicle each account for nearly 40 per cent of shoulder injuries, the backs being again the main recipients.

The crash tackle contributes significantly to the high incidence of shoulder injuries among backs. Both the execution of the tackle, where a direct blow is imparted by the shoulder, and the aftermath, where the tackled player is liable to fall heavily on the point of the shoulder joint, are circumstances where either fracture or dislocation occur. The centres and full-back are most at risk followed by the wings and fly-half. The latter under contemporary strategy is rarely called upon to tackle, relying upon his back-row to execute this task while lying deep in order to effect tactical kicks. Nor is he liable to be subject to incessant crash tackles as the off-side law constrains his opposing back-row. The techniques involved in executing and receiving a tackle are thus instrumental in determining the prevalence of shoulder joint injuries. When tactics place emphasis on retaining possession, backs tend to lie up flat and hit their opposite numbers hard and high in an attempt at dislodging the ball, thereby making it available for their own back row to initiate counter-attacks or second-phase. These tactics unquestionably enhance the likelihood of shoulder injuries and it is the backs who are in the forefront of the aggressive high velocity crash tackling in the modern game.

Another relevant factor, in addition to tactics, is the playing surface. Hard surfaces heighten the number of shoulder injuries as the unyielding surface affords little protection at the point of impact. Conversely, a wet and muddy ground inhibits the likelihood of ankle and knee joint injuries as it provides little purchase for studs, thereby allowing the lower leg to rotate freely. Upper limb region fractures and dislocations are similarly reduced on yielding surfaces. Van Heerden (1976) found that over 70 per cent of injuries occurred on dry surfaces while Roy (1974) reported over 80 per cent of knee injuries occurred on dry, firm pitches.

The fast, hard and competitive nature of the modern game together with bigger and fitter players has resulted in a constantly increasing number of injuries. It has been suggested in the context of soccer that the more committed a player is to tackling the less likely he is to sustain injury (Thomas and Reilly, 1975). Experience in rugby is that increased competitiveness and its attendant commitment appears to have led to increased aggression, a win-at-all-costs attitude and dirty play. Training is more frequent and intense, and injuries occurring during practice sessions now account for one-third of the total. Fatigue is a factor in this context, and as it increases during a game, concentration, technique and physical resilience decline. The last quarter has consequently been found by Davies and Gibson (1978) to attract nearly half of the injuries sustained during first-class games.

The constantly evolving laws of rugby will in future determine to a significant extent the site, frequency and type of injuries experienced. Attempts at keeping the game open by restricting kicking outside the 22 metre line have resulted in the full-back being brought into play more often and thus receiving more injuries. The tackle law has diminished the importance of the ruck, enhanced that of the maul and created the collapsed maul, thereby increasing the likelihood of hand, face and head injuries arising from trampling and scraping. The gradual retreat of the mark and its eventual possible disappearance could conceivably encourage the increase in high tactical kicks, thereby endangering the full-back even more. Rugby appears to be in a perpetual state of flux in terms of its tactics, laws and code of ethics. These factors in turn regulate the characteristics, site, frequency and type of rugby injury.

INJURIES IN SELECTED GAME PHASES

It should already be apparent that certain features of play precipitate injury. Some examples of game phases likely to produce trauma include the kick-off, line-out, scrummage, ruck and maul.

Kick-off

The side receiving the kick-off is exposed to a full frontal charge by opponents. Back injury is quite common when the player fielding the ball is isolated and turns his back to the advancing forwards in an attempt to shield the ball.

Line-out

In the line-out the contestants for the ball engage in elbowing their opponents resulting in facial and upper-torso injuries (Fig. 15/5, p. 124). In addition, dumping or up-ending of a player who is airborne results in shoulder damage when making contact with the ground. Scrum-halves can be rendered particularly vulnerable in this phase when presented with a badly delivered ball and exposed to forwards advancing through the line.

Scrummage

Injuries in the scrummage result from various causes:

1. The scrum may collapse. The front rows are then particularly exposed to serious neck and spinal damage. Although illegal, this has developed into an effective strategy to counter the wheel and the eight man drive.

2. The opposing front rows charge into one another at the commencement of a scrum; head and facial damage often ensues.

3. Wheeling of the scrum can produce tension of the neck and trunk. Here, injuries associated with the collapsed scrummage may also be experienced.

Due to the necessity of binding, the ears of the back five players often develop haematomata or 'cauliflower

Fig. 15/5 The line-out with possession being contested

ear'. In addition the aggression associated with front row play often prompts exchanges of punches. Hookers who are pillared between their props sometimes fall the victims of punches, kicks, and even eye gouging from unscrupulous opposing second row forwards.

Ruck and maul
Second-phase play as constituted by the ruck and maul is a component of the game in which the incidence of maliciously induced injuries is high.

In an endeavour to get possession of the ball in the ruck, players on the ground are walked on. In addition, if they interfere with efficient retrieval of the ball they are often scraped or raked out of the ruck away from the ball as well as being stamped upon.

In the process of wresting the ball from opposing players, fingers may be damaged in the maul. Sometimes eyes are gouged and mouths maliciously ripped. The equally illegal practices of charging into mauls and pulling opponents from them also occurs.

Tackling
Injuries are sustained by both the tackler, due to incorrect techniques, and the tackled person, due to severity of the tackle or subsequent landing. Tackling from the front, side and rear can produce facial injuries if the tackler's head is incorrectly positioned. The tackled player often suffers injuries to the menisci of the knee and the ligaments of the ankle and knee. Osteoarthrosis may be a long-term effect. In addition, incorrect landing techniques frequently produce fractures and dislocations in the acromio-clavicular and sterno-clavicular articulations.

Crash tackles in which two opponents meet head-on can result in a multiplicity of facial and upper torso injuries. The dangerous and illegal stiff-arm tackle produces similar results although confined to neck and facial areas.

Running, side-stepping and swerving
Although no inter-personal contact is involved, these skills, practised mainly by backs, can damage the knee and ankle joint. The likelihood of injury is increased by the traction afforded by a firm pitch and by the length (and thus traction) of studs and the low (and thus supportive) sides of boots. Such injuries which result from rapid tension, flexion and extension of the hip, knee and ankle joints may be obviated by modifications to equipment and the playing surface.

Fielding the high-ball
The full-back is exposed more than any other position in catching a high kick from the opposition in the face of advancing opponents. This partially explains the high risk nature of the position. Upon being hit by several of his opponents while attempting to simultaneously watch the opposition and catch the ball, the full-back is liable to suffer any one of numerous injuries.

PROTECTIVE CLOTHING

Traditionally, the use of protective clothing to prevent injury in rugby has not been widely accepted. The use of shoulder pads is illegal except in special circumstances at the discretion of the referee. Shin pads are

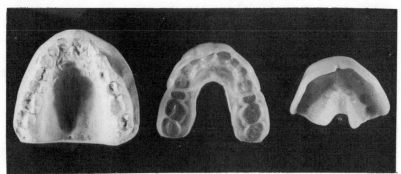

Fig. 15/6 Examples of mouth protectors showing individually moulded types

used by hookers and prop forwards while bandages and strapping are used liberally to fortify joints, particularly those of the hand and ankle. Injuries to the ankle are further intensified by the universal adoption of the lightweight, low cut boot.

The piece of preventive equipment which has made the biggest impact in recent years is the gum shield. Individually moulded types are preferable (Fig. 15/6). Mouth protectors can reduce the incidence and severity of facial fracture and protect teeth. It is also claimed that they reduce the incidence of concussion because they modify the transmission of the blow through the temporo-mandibular joints (Williams, 1975).

In certain areas, mini-rugby participants are forced to wear mouthguards, while in some countries insurance coverage requires that these protectors must be worn.

Only a selection of situations which can generate risk within the game of rugby union has been covered. No attempt has been made to describe the numerous situations which may arise outside of these set game phases and which may intensify risk. To some extent these are common to other field invasive games and contact sports.

The total milieu of the game decrees that all players are vulnerable. The qualities required in a rugby player were perhaps best summed up by Craven, the South African coach (Crawford, 1978):

'A player must be hard because he is expected to play against hard men and he must make contact with hardness. A player will experience bumps and jolts and he will fall or be flung to the ground like a rag. Players will fall on him and even tread on him. Elbows, knees or even hard heads will strike him without pity, and if the player has a faint heart these things will hurt him and even frighten him.'

One crucial problem which faces the administrators of rugby football is how to stop or even reverse the trend towards violent play. If a suitable answer is found to that problem then, hopefully, injuries within the game will be reduced both in numbers and severity.

REFERENCES

Adams, I. D. (1977). Rugby football injuries. *British Journal of Sports Medicine*, 11, 4–6.

Archibald, R. M. (1962). An analysis of rugby football injuries in the 1961/1962 season. *Practitioner*, 189, 333–334.

Crawford, S. A. G. M. (1978). New Zealand rugby: vigorous, violent and vicious. *Review of Sport and Leisure*, 1, 64–84.

Davies, J. E. and Gibson, T. (1978). Injuries in Rugby Union football. *British Medical Journal*, 2, 1759–1761.

Davies, R. M., Bradley, D., Hale, R. W., Laird, W. R. E. and Thomas, P. D. (1977). The prevalence of dental injuries in rugby players and their attitude to mouthguards. *British Journal of Sports Medicine*, 11, 72–74.

Durkin, T. E. (1977). A survey of injuries in a first-class Rugby Union football club from 1972–1976. *British Journal of Sports Medicine*, 11, 7–11.

Hawke, J. E. and Nicholas, N. K. (1969). Dental injuries in rugby football. *New Zealand Dental Journal*, 65, 173–175.

Micheli, L. J. and Riseborough, E. M. (1974). The incidence of injuries in rugby football. *Journal of Sports Medicine*, 2, 93–98.

O'Connell, T. C. (1954). Rugby football injuries and their prevention: a review of 600 cases. *Journal of the Irish Medical Association*, 34, 20–26.

Roy, S. P. (1974). The nature and frequency of rugby injuries: a pilot study of 300 injuries at Stellenbosch. *South African Medical Journal*, 48, 2321–2327.

Thomas, V. and Reilly, T. (1975). *The relationship between anxiety variables and injuries in top-class soccer.* Proceedings European Sports Psychology Congress (Edinburgh).

Tooth, R. M. (1974). Prevention of injury in rugby. *Australian Journal of Sports Medicine*, 5, 29–32.

Van Heerden, J. J. (1976). An analysis of rugby injuries. *South African Medical Journal*, **50**, 1374–1379.

Walkden, L. (1975). The medical hazards of rugby football. *Practitioner*, **215**, 201–207.

Williams, J. P. R. (1975). *Prevention of rugby injuries.*

In T. C. J. O'Connell (ed). *Injuries in rugby football and other team sports.* Irish Rugby Football Union, Dublin.

Williams, J. P. R. and McKibbin, B. (1978). Cervical spine injuries in Rugby Union football. *British Medical Journal*, **2**, 1749.

CHAPTER 16

Soccer injuries

TONY O'NEILL BSc, MB, BCh, BAO

The basic elements of soccer involve running, turning, jumping, tackling, kicking and heading the ball. The injuries which occur in this sport, as in any other body-contact game, result from direct blows or from indirect mechanisms. The rules of soccer do not permit outfield players to touch or control the ball with their arms or hands and so much of the trauma seen occurs to the lower limbs. The goalkeeper is in a separate category and his injuries tend to be more general, as he is allowed to use his hands and, in addition, his role often calls for him to dive at the feet of players thereby exposing more of his body to potential injury. Because of the international character of soccer, matches are played on widely varying surfaces and in all kinds of climatic conditions.

HEAD AND FACIAL INJURIES

The soccer player is susceptible to direct blows to the head and face from another player or from the ball. Although the regulation football weighs only 15oz (430g) it can travel at high velocity and if it strikes the face or head at close range, injury may result. A player standing 10 yards (9.1m) from the ball facing a free kick is liable to be hit on the face or head by the ball, and some players, if they choose to turn their backs on a free kick, may be struck on the back of the head by the ball. Apart from a direct blow from the ball, poor heading technique may also produce minor injury at the point of contact.

Accidental clashes of heads while jumping to head

Fig. 16/1 The goalkeeper in attempting to punch the ball clear may cause injury to the head or face of opposing forwards (photographs by courtesy of the Liverpool Echo)

the ball are common and are particularly likely to occur where players are in close contact with each other, for example, in the penalty area for corner kicks or facing goal kicks, throw-ins or free kicks. During the course of play, a player may be kicked on the head by an opponent if he puts his head down too low to head a ball which he should really have kicked. A goalkeeper attempting to punch the ball clear may miss his target and instead strike another player on the head or in the face (Fig. 16/1). The goalkeeper himself can sustain a head injury diving at the feet of an incoming player or going down to collect a low ball. He also may be knocked off-balance near an upright and is therefore liable to strike his head off the post.

The scalp, eyebrows and lips are common sites of head and facial lacerations in soccer. Nosebleeds, nasal fractures, fractured cheekbones and damage to teeth are also seen and are usually due to direct blows from the ball or from another player. Serious injuries of the eye are rare.

In all cases of head injury, concussion is a possibility and every head injury must be regarded as being potentially serious.

SPINAL AND BACK INJURIES

Neck injuries

Fortunately, injuries to the cervical spine are not often seen in soccer. However, a player who falls awkwardly on his head and who injures his neck may sustain a possible serious lesion, and should be managed accordingly. There are recorded cases of goalkeepers who suffered fractured cervical vertebrae as a result of diving at players' feet.

Other spinal injuries

Injuries to the thoracic and lumbar spine are very rare but must be suspected in the case of severe trauma to the back. These usually result from severe kicks.

Soft tissue injuries

Soft tissue injuries of the back occur quite commonly in soccer due to indirect mechanisms such as jumping or twisting, which cause muscular or ligamentous strains, or due to direct trauma such as a blow from another player. The sacro-iliac joint which connects the pelvis with the spinal column may be the site of chronic injury in soccer players due to strain of the ligaments in the region or in association with osteitis pubis, a condition of the pubic bones in the front of the pelvis. Sacro-iliac strain normally presents as low back pain localised to one or other side which has been troubling the player for a time.

CHEST INJURIES

Chest injuries in soccer generally involve the ribs, rib cartilages or muscles of the rib-cage. Direct trauma is the most common cause and the goalkeeper is more susceptible than the outfield players. Injuries to the lower ribs may sometimes damage the underlying kidneys. Bruising of the ribs results from a contusion and an x-ray is required to differentiate this from a fracture.

ABDOMEN

Probably the most common and least serious abdominal injury seen in soccer is when a player is 'winded' following a blow to the lower abdomen from the ball or from another player's boot. The player usually recovers within a few minutes. Rarely, the abdominal organs may be injured. The liver and spleen in the upper abdomen are protected by the lower ribs and muscle, and the kidneys which are situated on the back wall of the abdomen lie beneath the lower posterior ribs. Severe trauma, such as a knee in the back at the angle under the ribs, can cause damage to the kidney. A goalkeeper may be particularly susceptible to this situation in a crowded goalmouth when stretching for a ball, as this part of his body is left relatively unprotected. It is sometimes difficult to distinguish between a severe muscle injury and possible kidney damage, but the presence of blood in the urine indicates that kidney damage has occurred. The muscles of the abdominal wall can be strained when a player tackles an opponent or when he jumps or twists awkwardly. Rarely a footballer may develop a hernia subsequent to stress injury of the lower abdominal muscles.

PELVIS

'Groin strains' are a common finding in soccer players but the term may be applied by footballers to a number of different conditions. Strains of the upper attachments of the muscles of the lower limb may be the reason but another condition which can be responsible is osteitis pubis which occurs particularly after football games, or similar exercise involving a lot of hip rotation (Williams, 1978). Tenderness is found over the symphysis pubis.

The male genitalia, near the pelvis, are vulnerable to direct blows and while most injuries resolve without complication, occasionally a haematocoele may develop; this is characterised by increasing pain, swelling and tenderness of the scrotum, due to the internal bleeding. In soccer a player may sustain this injury if, during a tackle, legs get tangled and an opponent's leg damages the 'fixed' scrotum. It may also occur from a direct blow. Players protect their genital regions with the hands when setting a defensive wall against a free kick close to goal.

UPPER LIMB

Injuries to the upper limb account for a small percentage of soccer injuries in general but the goalkeeper is particularly susceptible. Fractures, dislocations and subluxations are usually caused by falling on the outstretched hand, the point of the shoulder or wrist, or from direct trauma. The collar bone (clavicle) may be fractured by a direct kick or by falling on the outstretched hand. Partial dislocation (subluxation) of the acromio-clavicular joint (between the acromion process of the scapula and the collar bone) can result from a fall on the point of the shoulder. Goalkeepers are likely to sustain fractures of the hand and fingers. Dislocations of the shoulder and elbow joint are uncommon but dislocation of the finger joints is often seen and is usually caused by a player falling awkwardly on his fingers, or by the ball striking the hand.

LOWER LIMB

Most of the injuries occurring in soccer involve the lower limb.

Fractures

The commonest fracture seen is probably due to a direct blow to the lower part of the tibia and fibula. In soccer, the practice of 'going over the ball' whereby an opponent strikes a player on the shin with his boot rather than playing the ball is an illegal act. However, it does occur and may result in a fracture. A goalkeeper diving at the feet of an inrushing forward may fall across the player's legs in such a way as to cause a fracture (Fig. 16/2). Fractures due to indirect mechanisms are also seen. A full-back who turns acutely can catch his foot in the ground and cause damage to his ankle which may involve fracture of the lower end of the fibula. A soccer injury which frequently occurs is that of a sprained ankle in association with a fracture further up the fibula, often due to a foul tackle. Fractures of bones in the feet and of the toes are usually due to direct blows such as another player striking the foot or occasionally from striking a ball which is blocked by an opponent's foot. Young players are susceptible to fractures of the epiphyses or growing points of the bone.

Thigh injuries

Superficial injuries to the skin occur frequently in soccer players when the pitch is hard with little grass on it or when the game is played on synthetic grass like Astro-turf. The sliding tackle in soccer in these conditions can result in quite severe 'grass burns' or 'Astro-burns'.

Muscle injuries of the thigh involve the quadriceps group (on the front of the thigh), the hamstring group (on the back of the thigh) and the adductor group (on the inside of the thigh). Muscle strains of the quadriceps group occur most commonly during the kicking movement but also in sprinting and in overstretching for the ball. This type of injury is often seen in the early part of the season where too much kicking is done with poorly conditioned muscles. More severe types of muscle strain in this region are rupture of muscle or herniation of muscle, usually due to excessive strain.

Muscles of the 'hamstring' group tend to be damaged during sprinting and overstretching, and also in kicking. Hamstring strains are encountered throughout the year but appear to be particularly common when conditions underfoot are soft. Injuries to the long

Fig. 16/2 In diving across the feet of an inrushing forward, the goalkeeper may cause injury to himself or his opponent (photographs by courtesy of the Liverpool Echo)

muscles of the adductor group are less common but usually are caused by a player overstretching for the ball. It should be emphasised that many of these muscle injuries can occur just as frequently in training as in match situations. While most muscle strains are limited to tears of the fibres, in some cases the origin or insertion of a muscle may be detached and a fragment of bone avulsed at the site of the attachment. In children these injuries may be severe.

Direct blows to the thigh, particularly from the foot or knee of another player are another prevalent injury. Painful bleeding in the tissues can result in haematoma formation and the condition known as 'charley-horse' or 'dead leg' may be sufficiently uncomfortable as to prevent a player from taking further part in a match.

A complication of a thigh muscle injury, particularly after a direct blow, is myositis ossificans in which part of the muscle tissue becomes ossified.

Knee injuries

The knee joint is susceptible in soccer not only to direct trauma but also because stresses and strains of the knee joint mechanisms occur during the game. The main bone of the lower leg, the tibia, is fixed on the ground by the studs of the football boot. It is unable, therefore, to rotate outwards on forced extension or to rotate inwards on forced flexion with the bodyweight in motion. It is consequently vulnerable when subjected to sudden external violence.

Injuries to the cartilages of the knee are usually caused by a combination of rotatory movement and compression (Smillie, 1970). If, for example, the foot is fixed to the ground, and an adduction strain is superimposed, the cartilage may tear because of pressure from the lower part of the thigh bone, i.e. from the medial femoral condyle. Rotation strains on the knee, seen when a player turns quickly, may be of such severity that the cartilage is unable to absorb the stress and it tears. The player therefore who turns sharply on the fixed foot while weight-bearing and who subsequently complains of pain in his knee may have damaged a cartilage. Symptoms such as collapse and locking of the joint may be further evidence of a cartilage injury.

The collateral ligaments on each side of the knee give stability to the joint. When the leg is stretched, e.g. in tackling, the joint is extended and these ligaments are more vulnerable to injury. An opponent striking or falling against the outstretched leg of a player can cause such severe strain to the joint that the ligament on the opposite side of the same knee may be torn. If a player's foot is 'fixed' in a tangle of legs he may fall to one side producing a similar mechanism which can damage the ligament. When a player goes with another for a '50/50'

ball and the stresses transmitted up the leg on contact are of sufficient intensity, the knee ligaments may be damaged.

Less serious injuries occur when a rotatory strain affects the knee when it is slightly flexed. The twisting injury can happen, of course, when the player is not weight-bearing. The lateral ligament on the outside of the knee is relaxed when the knee is flexed and is therefore not subject to rotation strains. It is likely to tear when the knee is exposed to sudden and powerful inward movement of the lower leg relative to the thigh.

Within the knee joint are two small ligaments, the cruciate ligaments. The anterior cruciate ligament can be torn when a player who, in the process of heading the ball, is knocked off balance while jumping in the air and falls to the ground with his leg twisted under him. This ligament is often damaged when the medial cartilage is torn. The posterior cruciate ligament may tear when a force of sufficient magnitude is directed against the flexed knee striking the upper front part of the tibia and driving it backwards. If a goalkeeper's body strikes the lower leg of an inrushing player in such a way as to produce the necessary force, this injury can result.

The patella or knee cap is seldom fractured in soccer but it may be dislocated if a player receives a kick to the inside border of the patella.

Calf muscle injuries

Direct blows from a player's boot are common but the muscle can be strained when, for example, a player is jumping. Unfit players appear to be more prone to this type of injury. Cramp is a condition where the calf muscles go into spasm and it is seen usually towards the end of games and in unfit players.

Achilles tendon injuries

A kick to the tendon can produce painful tenderness and swelling. Indirect injuries range from partial or complete rupture (usually due to an explosive movement) to inflammation of either the tendon or the surrounding tissues which may become chronic.

Ankle injuries

Direct trauma to the ankle joint is common largely because of the nature of the game. Inversion injuries of the ankle joint, however, are also common and result in damage to the ligaments on the outside of the ankle. Classically a player who lands awkwardly on his ankle or who, while running, 'goes over on his ankle' develops an ankle sprain which may be of such severity as to avulse part of the bony attachment of the ligaments. 'Footballer's ankle' is a condition where exostoses (bony growths) are found in the joint, and these can be dislodged into the joint causing a persistent painful ankle. Repeated trauma to the ankle joint is believed to be responsible for this condition.

Foot injuries

Fractures of the foot may result from violence or from stress. A direct blow is not necessary to produce the fracture which can occur secondary to running continuously on hard surfaces. These stress fractures occur particularly in the metatarsal bones and are sometimes referred to as 'march fractures'. The toes are also likely to be fractured by direct blows.

The toenail may be damaged and a sub-ungual haematoma may result producing acute pain.

The tendons of the foot bruise if subjected to a blow and this injury may simulate a fracture. The ligaments in the foot are also subject to strains. These injuries can result when two players attempt to kick a ball at the same time or from a player striking an opponent's foot.

Blisters on the toes and soles of the feet are seen especially at the beginning of the season and in conditions where the grounds are hard. Friction between the boot and the skin causing pressure on the skin is responsible.

THE ENVIRONMENT AND SOCCER INJURIES

As in most other field games, the environment and prevailing climatic conditions may play a role in the mechanism of soccer injuries. Muscles are believed to be more likely to suffer strain in conditions of extreme heat or cold. Tendon injuries and inflammatory-type injuries of the muscles of the lower leg show an increased incidence on hard grounds. Wet weather, producing muddy conditions underfoot may predispose to muscle strains. Pools of water on the pitch can be a hazard if the ball suddenly stops dead in the water; two players going for the ball, unable to correct their timing, can clash and a fractured leg or ankle results. Frost-affected grounds or excessively dry grounds, which are not rolled, can cause inversion type injuries of the ankle joint or more serious injury due to the ball running awkwardly, as the bumpy playing surface may be full of ruts and hard uneven ridges. Blisters on the toes and the soles of the feet are more liable to develop in these types of conditions. Severe grass burns or Astro-burns are inevitable consequences of soccer being played on hard or synthetic surfaces. Injuries resulting from players clashing with each other due to poor visibility are likely to occur where soccer is played under inadequate floodlights. In hot climates, insufficient protection of players with prophylactic electrolytes and water renders them liable to heat stroke or heat cramps. Because muscles and joints are often stiff after a night's rest, there may be a greater likelihood of injury in the morning.

PREVENTION OF SOCCER INJURIES

Soccer players who are not physically fit are more likely to suffer from indirect muscle injuries. A flexibility routine to stretch muscle is essential in training, and strengthening of muscle is necessary to protect it when certain movements are being carried out in the game. For example, the neck muscles should be conditioned for heading the ball and the abdominal muscles for tackling. Weight training should be carefully supervised.

Many soccer players have 'tight' hamstring muscles and are predisposed to strains of these muscles as a result. Most clubs insist that warm-up exercises are done prior to training and matches, and provide special facilities for this purpose.

Correct technique is necessary not only to play the game well but also to cut down the incidence of injury. A player who does not tackle properly may injure either himself or his opponent. Basic tactical knowledge is also necessary. A player who passes a ball to another who at that point has no chance of avoiding an opponent's tackle, may cause his team mate to be injured. Players who fail to communicate verbally with each other may collide when going for the same ball.

Equipment

Equipment is another factor in the prevention of injury. The soccer boot with its low cut heel means that the soccer player is susceptible to ankle injuries. Nowadays the studs of the boot are checked by the referee prior to a game to ensure that sharp points do not act as a potential source of injury to another player. Shin guards should always be worn to protect the tibia and fibula from direct injury. The genitalia can be protected to some extent by the wearing of swimming trunks or jock-straps. Rings, chains or medals should not be worn while playing soccer as they may injure the wearer himself or another player. Tie-ups should not be too tight or they may bring on cramp. Boots should be correctly fitting, or painful blisters may result. The modern soccer ball is lightweight and without laces, and so the problems caused by the old leather ball which became unduly heavy in wet weather are no longer with us – nor are the problems caused by the lace of the old-style ball and the metal 'eyes'.

The pitch should be in good condition and there should be no debris lying on it which could cause lacerations or abrasions.

A modification of the rules of the games and the dimensions of the pitch together with the use of a lighter ball is necessary where children are involved. Players in this category should be evenly matched as regards age, size and physique.

Good refereeing and intelligent interpretation of the Laws of the Game will reduce injury to a minimum and will eliminate dangerous play. All players should be in good health and should have received inoculation against tetanus.

The training programme should be carefully planned to provide a balance between all the components necessary for fitness. A footballer, when he is injured, should be handled by qualified personnel so as to prevent complications. Initial measures such as the application of ice to the injury, proper cleaning of wounds should be carried out to improve the player's recovery prospects. A player returning from injury should be completely rehabilitated to prevent recurrence of the injury. He should not be asked to play before he has made a full recovery.

REFERENCES

Smillie, I. S. (1970). *Injuries of the knee joint*. Churchill Livingstone, Edinburgh.
Williams, J. (1978). *Injury in sport*. Bayer, Haywards Heath.

SECTION 4

Injuries in selected individual sports

CHAPTER 17

Common injuries in track and field athletics – 1. Racing and jumping

M. McDERMOTT MB, BCh, BAO and T. REILLY BA, DPE, MSc, PhD, MIBiol

Track and field embraces a wide range of activities and has close relatives in cross-country and road racing. Apart from race-walking (20km and 50km) and marathon running, all events are held within the confines of athletic stadia, a fact that itself brings attendant problems. The constantly improving performances in javelin, hammer and discus events may endanger adjacent competitors and spectators unless the programme is carefully planned and recommended safety procedures abided by. This chapter concentrates on running, hurdling and jumping events while the throws are considered in Chapter 18.

The abilities fundamental to track and field participation discussed here are running and jumping. These impose requirements of repetitive locomotion, powerful explosive action and efficient execution of technique to varying degrees. These basic abilities may be performed with appreciable modification as, for example, in the hurdler's economical and rapid clearance of the barrier. Alternatively they are called upon serially in other events – the long jumper reaches high speeds in the run-up, coordinates powerful muscle action in the take-off and demonstrates skill in aerial movements and landing, all performed to optimal biomechanical specification.

The nature of track and field competition ordains that the trauma associated with physical contact is rarely found among participants. However, preparation for the sport has, over the last two decades, become progressively more rigorous while competition itself has increased in intensity. The season is prolonged providing better opportunities to achieve personal best performances which in turn accentuate individual strain. The majority of injuries occur in training, 60 per cent of the problems of runners being associated with training error (James et al, 1978). The proportion of jumpers' complaints originating in training and practices is probably greater still. Causal factors and injuries common to running and jumping are considered before those related to specific athletic events.

COMMON CAUSAL FACTORS

The increasingly acknowledged injuries throughout track and field events may be attributed to four major causes apart from fitness – quality of surfaces, excessive training loads, innate musculo-skeletal deformities and inadequate footwear.

Surface quality

Unfortunately the majority of long distance racing and training is now performed on hard often uneven roads. These provide inadequate compliance for the athlete's legs. Continuous running on severely cambered road will cause excessive forces to be exerted on the inside leg resulting in Achilles tendon and possibly ankle and knee joint problems.

Track racing is gradually becoming almost exclusively confined to synthetic surfaces. Although conducive to faster times and better wear the stiffness in these materials has been implicated in joint and tendon injuries (Haberl and Prokop, 1974). Grass provides an altogether gentler surface on which the distance runner especially should frequently train.

Hill training is a basic part of most athlete's programmes. This again imposes musculo-tendonous strains, particularly on the Achilles tendon in climbing and on thigh muscles in descending.

Jumpers are likewise prone to surface-induced injury. The high jumper must be especially careful to avoid losing balance when forced to take off on a wet synthetic surface. Similarly the broad jumper must be wary when confronted with adverse climatic conditions or uneven approach runs.

Excessive training loads

The heavy training currently indulged in brings various overuse injuries. Stress fractures, shin splints and Achilles bursitis all arise from accumulated impact loading. Jumpers are not excused vulnerability, encountering their own specific exertion injuries such as proximal tibial stress fractures.

Musculo-skeletal deformities

Minor deformities which normally go unnoticed often come to light as a result of participation in athletics. Examination of patients with recurrent knee pain may, for example, reveal genu varum or patellar instability. These otherwise occult defects are spotlighted when a strenuous training programme is undertaken.

Footwear

A proportion of injuries are caused by inadequate footwear. Blisters occur when the feet overheat in ill-fitting shoes. Thin soled flat road racing shoes place unnatural strains on the foot in general and the athlete who sacrifices safety for speed often regrets it later. Conversely, thick soled shoes with broad flared heels or a heel roll and wedged mid-sole are found to protect the Achilles tendon in many victims. As first contact is mostly on the outside border of the shoe, for some leg geometries wide shoes may cause unwanted moments about the leg and ankle.

Most present-day track shoes afford little heel protection and have considerable room for design improvements. The sole should be flexible, tough but soft enough to provide cushioning. Excessive training in spikes can cause plantar fasciitis and precipitates recurrent foot strains.

INJURIES COMMON TO THE RUNNING EVENTS

Achilles tendon

From the preceding section it is clear that the Achilles tendon with its surrounding tissues is damaged with depressing frequency by competitive athletes. This tendon connects the powerful plantar flexors in the calf to the calcaneus. It is surrounded by a delicate membrane, the paratenon. Deep to its bony insertion is a bursa which can become infected or inflamed.

Five basic categories of injury are described:

COMPLETE RUPTURE

This fortunately is a rare occurrence in healthy athletes but causes extreme pain and disability when it happens. Typically, the rupture is of sudden onset during violent contraction of the plantar flexors as in steep uphill running, during the acceleration phase in a sprint start or driving off the long jump board. The patient is unable to walk on tip toe and there is a characteristic 'step' in normal heel outline.

Surgical repair is recommended in an active athlete.

PARTIAL RUPTURE

Partial rupture is a recognised clinical entity and is perhaps present in athletes who never seek medical aid.

The rupture at time of occurrence may cause acute pain, otherwise it tends to cause a lack of thrust in running or jumping. Examination may reveal a small lump on the tendon and some wasting of the attached muscles.

ACHILLES TENDINITIS

Here there is an inflammatory reaction deep in the tendon fibres and the athlete experiences discomfort on jogging. X-ray is normal and the only physical sign is tenderness on pinching the affected tendon. The athlete is advised to ease down in training at the first sign of tendon pain. Fortunately most cases resolve with rest and adequate heel protection. Injection of the tendon with steroids is potentially dangerous and may cause complete rupture.

ACHILLES PERITENDINITIS

In this condition there is inflammation in the paratenon and tissues surrounding the tendon. There is pain and swelling in this area. Most cases settle with rest and steroid infiltration around the tendon.

With recurrence of attacks, fibrosis develops between paratenon and tendon proper. Characteristically, there is soft tissue swelling and the athlete complains of morning stiffness. Surgical clearance is then indicated.

BURSITIS

Less commonly, painful bursitis may develop at the Achilles tendon insertion. Steroid and hyaluronidase injections usually clear up this condition successfully.

Chondromalacia patellae

This is a very common condition among sportsmen and adolescent females. The undersurface of the patella degenerates as a consequence of friction between it and the femoral condyle (usually the lateral). The condition causes gradually increasing pain on knee flexion with particular difficulty descending stairs and running.

The underlying cause is attributed to a mechanical defect in the functioning of the extensor muscle group and minor local bony deformities. In the advanced case there is wasting of the vastus medialis with marked crepitus on flexing the knee.

As in virtually all knee conditions quadriceps strengthening exercises are helpful. The natural history of the disease is variable. The adolescent variety tends to resolve with time: the unfortunate athlete may go through a gamut of enforced rest, local steroid injections and an assortment of foot supports in an attempt to find a cure. If symptoms persist and the disease progresses, operative intervention is usually necessary if the athlete is to remain in his sport (Sim and Detenbeck, 1972). Fortunately, only relatively few who fail to respond to an adequate trial of conservative treatment are found to need surgery (Dehaven et al, 1979).

Shin splints

This is a blanket term used to cover a variety of conditions causing pain and disability. These include stress fractures of the tibia and fibula and also musculo-tendonous problems. Shin splints are caused by poor conditioning, unaccustomed over-exertion and training on hard surfaces. Persistent bend running with marked lean, as in indoor racing, is another recognised cause (Rasmussen, 1974).

THE ANTERIOR TIBIAL SYNDROME

The tibialis anterior is entirely clothed in a sheath which does not allow this muscle to hypertrophy normally with training. There is impairment of blood supply on exercise producing shin pain. The condition responds well to surgical treatment.

ANTERIOR TIBIAL TENOSYNOVITIS

Here there is a thickening of the sheath surrounding the tendon of tibialis anterior with consequent pain and stiffness. Again, surgical decompression proves rewarding.

MEDIAL TIBIAL SYNDROME

The medial tibial syndrome describes a common cause of athletes' leg pains. Pain is located at the inner border of the tibia. X-ray and isotope scanning are needed to differentiate this injury from tibial stress fracture as the site and symptoms are similar. The injury occurs almost exclusively in runners on elevating training mileage and arises from increased pressure in the deep flexor muscles due to prolonged exercise. The pathogenesis has been attributed to chronic ischaemia inside the medial fascial compartment (Orava and Puranen, 1979). Most cases heal without any specific treatment with rest and adaptation to training. Fasciotomy may be necessary in athletes with chronic exertional ischaemia in the medial fascial compartment failing to respond to conservative treatment.

STRESS FRACTURES OF TIBIA AND FIBULA

In this condition a transverse or longitudinal fracture of the cortex of the tibia or fibula occurs. Middle-distance runners moving on to high mileage regimes are especially vulnerable. Fatigue fracture of the fibula shaft arises from excessive repetitive pounding from running on hard surfaces. X-rays are often negative due to the lack of displacement but there is marked bony tenderness on examination. Due to increased local metabolism, the uptake of particular isotopes at the fracture site increases before the radiological signs of the fracture can be seen. Hence isotope scanning can be used for diagnosis.

Rest offers a complete cure. A training pause of four to six weeks is usually sufficient for treatment of leg stress fractures.

Foot pain

There are numerous conditions causing foot pain in runners. Considerable variation exists in foot structure between athletes. Podiatrists believe that a majority of lower limb, and indeed back injuries are due to inherent foot defects. The somewhat enigmatic condition known as Morton's foot has also been held responsible for many foot problems. Here, there is either a short first or long second metatarsal bone with excessive tendency to pronate the foot. Orthotic appliances are often successful in relieving the symptoms.

Other conditions associated with foot pain include bone spurs, tenosynovitis of the various foot tendons, plantar fasciitis and foot strain with chronic synovitis of the small foot joints. All of these conditions may be traceable to footwear which is either too tight or provides inadequate support. Treatment is directed to developing foot mobility and strength along with adopting appropriate footwear. Bone spurs may require surgical removal if especially troublesome.

Verrucae (warts on the soles of the feet) and tinea pedis (athlete's foot) can both plague athletes using communal washing facilities. Verrucae respond to liquid nitrogen application and surgical removal under local anaesthetic. Tinea pedes, causing maceration of the skin between the toes, responds to antifungal applications. This condition recurs if treated inadequately.

INJURIES IN SPECIFIC RUNNING AND JUMPING EVENTS

Sprinting

MUSCLE INJURIES

Muscle tears are particularly common among sprinters. Localised tears or strains occur where a muscle exerts quick, powerful and often poorly coordinated contraction. Hamstring, thigh adductor and quadriceps muscle tears are precipitated by violent exertion mostly at the start and towards the finish of the sprints. At the start, the runner may be generating up to 6hp in his desperation to accelerate (Wilkie, 1960). Impaired coordination near the finish produces agonist/antagonist mismatch and consequent soft tissue injury. Suspect hamstrings may give way in mid-race due to overstretching in attempting to retain a fluent style at full speed.

Muscles acting on two joints are especially at risk, for example rectus femoris and the hamstrings. Tearing may occur in the belly of these muscles or in the musculo-tendonous junctions. Intramuscular tears promote rapid accumulation of blood within the muscle with consequent severe pain and spasm. Treatment is directed at reduction of this haematoma and its rapid absorption. Several specialised techniques are involved but there is a consensus of opinion that cold and pressure are of most benefit.

Gentle exercise is undertaken as soon as possible with careful graduation to a full course of joint movement. Stretching is crucial to preventing scar tissue formation and development of adhesions. There are adjuvant therapies to this basic routine – massage, ultrasound, short wave diathermy and cryotherapy – all having their proponents either singly or in combination.

Adequate time must be allowed for healing – pain is a warning signal which is perilous to ignore. The athlete should undertake a fitness test prior to resuming full training. Unfortunately, hamstring injuries have a tendency to recur in sprinters and become chronic. Hence attention to stretching exercises before and after activity is advocated in the athlete who has suffered a pulled muscle.

JOINT INJURIES

Sprinting imposes great strain on individual leg joints particularly where the stride is imperfectly balanced and where repetitive bend running is practised. The joint most frequently strained is the knee. Tearing of the medial and lateral collateral ligaments and the cruciate ligaments may occur, albeit uncommonly. Rotational strain arising from poor surfaces or inadequate footwear may cause tearing or rippling of the menisci. Early attention by a specialist in sports medicine is desirable, rather than 'running through' the pain with the support of bandaging.

The ankle joint together with the shin bones bear the brunt of excessive bend running as in prolonged 200m and relay practices. Over-use of cinder tracks particularly in spiked shoes can lead to synovitis of the small joints of the foot. Foot hygiene with particular attention to toenails is again important.

Distance running
MARCH FRACTURE

The condition owes its name to its initial observation in military recruits. It refers to the development of a stress fracture in the second or third metatarsal bone as a result of prolonged walking or running. Rest is indicated to relieve pain and allow the fracture to heal.

KNEE INJURIES

Injuries specific to the knee in distance runners are diverse. The number of acknowledged conditions is constantly increasing and ranges from simple sprain to rarer entities like tendoperiostitis in the lateral femoral condyle and the iliotibial tract friction syndrome (Orava, 1978).

Patients occasionally complain of knee pain without any localising signs. This may in fact be a secondary injury which occurs as a result of injury elsewhere, for example Achilles tendinitis in the other leg. Knee problems in females may be related to the more acute articulation of the femur because of the broader pelvis. This induces a more lateral sway of the body when running (Klafs and Lyon, 1978). A tendency in young female runners to take the lower leg and foot over to the side when swinging through should be corrected since it results in additional stresses on the medial aspect of the knee joint on ground contact.

SCIATICA

This condition appears to occur with increased frequency in distance runners, possibly as a result of uneven running gait, jumping off kerbs, running downhill or generally transmitting shock through the vertebral column. The symptoms are pain and weakness of the leg, particularly in the hamstrings, which develop on exercise. The pain or numbness in the hamstrings may shift position over time. Some afflicted athletes mistake the condition for a pull in this muscle group. The usual cause of this form of sciatica is intervertebral joint irritation. It generally responds to rest for a few days and anti-inflammatory agents.

Prolapse of the intervertebral disc is a more serious cause of sciatica. It may require operative intervention if it fails to respond to conservative treatment.

HEAT INJURY

Heat stress is an almost constant accompaniment to marathon running and race-walking in hot humid conditions. Body temperature rises and a proportion of cardiac output, subserving the body's thermoregulatory needs, is shunted to the skin to be cooled making less blood available to the working muscles. Sweating is the primary mechanism for loss of body heat in these conditions, heat being lost when the sweat is evaporated on the skin surface. Marathon runners may lose four to five litres of fluid during a race, amounting to six to ten per cent of bodyweight. Endurance capacity is further adversely affected in that plasma is also lost with reduction in total blood volume, which in turn promotes further temperature increments. The work rate must be retarded to avoid overheating.

Heat distress can be of varying severity. Heat cramps are the result of dehydration with loss of fluid, electrolytes and salt, the muscles employed in the exercise being primarily affected. Heat exhaustion is characterised by body temperature of about 40 °C (104 °F), extreme tiredness, breathlessness, dizziness and tachycardia. These symptoms result from a reduced sweat production. Heat stroke is more serious, characterised by body temperatures of 41 °C (105.8 °F) or higher, cessation of sweating and total confusion or loss of consciousness. As thermo-regulation has priority over control of body water (Åstrand and Rodahl, 1977) hypohydration can be driven so far as to threaten life in hot conditions if water is not available. Eventually coma and death ensue if the victim is left untreated. Immediate replacement of body fluid is required and cooling by ice cube application.

Attention is directed towards adequate race and pre-race nutrition and fluid intake. Clothing should be brief, light in colour and loose woven. Early warning symptoms preceding heat injury should be heeded including pilo-erection on chest and upper arms, chilling, throbbing head, unsteadiness, nausea and dry skin. Since the body adapts to heat, acclimatisation should be explored where possible. If exposure to heat lasts for several weeks ingestion of salt tablets is advised; 5 to 15g of salt per day depending on diet, climate and degree of exercise is sufficient (Åstrand and Rodahl, 1977). Race organisers should pre-arrange with medical personnel for the care of possible cases of heat injury.

FOOT CONTUSIONS

These arise from direct trauma to the heel and forefoot with bruising of the tissues between the bones and skin. Again, inadequate footwear and hard surfaces are implicated. Cross-country runners encountering sections of road in mid-race are liable to bruising of the plantar aspect of the foot if spikes are worn. Use of rippled soles or waffle-sole designs for these road and country courses is advisable.

SPIKING WOUNDS

These predominate in the bustle of middle distance track races and crowded cross-country starts. The areas commonly involved are the heels, instep and the front of the shins. Immediate cleansing and dressing is usually required. The victim would be wise to have an anti-tetanus injection if not previously innoculated.

Hurdling

Hurdling may be described as sprinting with a modified stride for clearing the barrier. Apart from great speed, the high hurdler needs a long stride to permit a three-stride rhythm between clearances. Besides, the taller individual with a high leg length/trunk length ratio has an advantage in that the centre of gravity is raised less to effect hurdle clearance. Females are not handicapped to the same extent in that the effort in clearance is relatively easier because of the lowered hurdle heights. Efficient clearance involves keeping the centre of gravity as low as possible, spending minimal time in the air and landing so as to quickly initiate the running rhythm for further clearances. For this, great flexibility particularly in the hip, groin and back is called for.

The hurdler suffers many of the injuries incurred by the sprinter. Hamstrings are liable to injury if the athlete has to overstretch between barriers to retain the correct stride pattern. This may arise from one poor clearance where momentum is lost or in racing against the wind. Flexibility in the hamstrings is desirable because they are stretched in the lead leg in clearance. Groin strain may occur in the trailing leg action and flexibility here is also essential. A sample of exercises for the lead and trail leg is shown in Figure 17/1. A further precaution is for the hurdler to clear a series of phantom barriers during warm-up, emphasising lead and trailing leg motion alternately.

The shin of the leading leg may be bruised in clearance if take-off is too near the barrier. The medial aspect of the knee or the medial malleolus of the trailing leg may be grazed in clearance. Some coaches employ protective pads on the hurdler's knee and ankle, though this may encourage imperfect technique (Reilly, 1977). If the trailing leg hits the hurdle, the leading leg may land short with the foot abruptly jammed into dorsiflexion. Tearing of the medial belly of the gastrocnemius may result from this sudden dorsiflexion with the knee extended.

Tear of the adductor magnus or gracilis may be caused by imbalanced clearance and overstretching, resulting in landing on the leg with the thigh in forced abduction. Ankle sprain can result from imbalanced landing with the foot in an inverted and inwardly rotated position. Damage is usually to the lateral collateral ligament (O'Donoghue, 1970), though less frequently avulsion of the tip of the lateral malleolus is found (Miller, 1971).

Spiking wounds are mostly self-inflicted in adjusting to errors in stride pattern. Abrasions associated with falling heavily on cinder or tartan are found when the required rhythm and balance are lost. The fatigue of anaerobiosis may be a causal factor, particularly in the low hurdles race, contributing to a variety of injuries associated with errors of coordination. Repetitive bend running in training for the 400m hurdles may lead to

Fig. 17/1 A selection of flexibility exercises for the hurdler

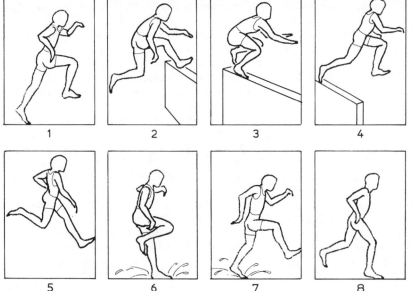

1   2   3   4

5   6   7   8

Fig. 17/2 Illustration of the technique used by a steeplechaser taking the water jump

strain of the collateral ligaments of the knee.

Good technique is also required of the steeplechaser who, unlike the hurdler, cannot afford to hit the stouter barriers he must cross. Finger and wrist injuries as well as limb abrasions are found in falls after physical contact during clearance. It is sensible to step on the barrier top if the approach run is hampered by other runners as can happen in the early laps. Falls in the water jump can be physically costly, often causing damaged ankles or metatarsal fractures. It is important

to accelerate in approaching the jump so as to step easily onto and drive off the barrier top. Good technique involves landing in the water with the lead leg and stepping out of it in the first running stride so that only one foot gets wet (Fig. 17/2). It is wise to practise water-jumping under conditions of fatigue so errors in technique do not creep in over the final laps of competition. Chronic foot injuries may result from repetitive poor landings if training shoes offer insufficient support.

JUMPING

The broad jumps

In the long jump and triple jump the athlete exploits the kinetic energy developed in a fast run-up to achieve some vertical lift in a jump or hop, step and jump for horizontal distance. Since performance is measured from the end of a fixed take-off board, take-off should be as near this point as possible. Efficient aerial technique is important to secure effective landing and avoid falling backwards on contacting the ground. Speed, muscular strength and power are pre-requisites for these events and must be painstakingly developed during the off-season.

Hitting the take-off board consistently requires many hours of repetitive practice. Since stride length can vary with wind conditions and track surface an absolute distance of approach will not work for all conditions. Jumpers generally use check-marks at the beginning and early on in the approach since marks near the board only serve to slow the approach and distract the performer from the explosive effort needed there. Attempts to correct missed strides during the run-up can lead to hamstring tears or injury from later faulty take-off or landing. Problems associated with uneven run-ups are ameliorated with the use of all-weather surfaces.

Contusions involving the soft tissue between the calcaneus and the shin may result from repetitive jumping since the take-off leg is planted heel first in long jumping. The triple jump initial thrust involves a more flat-footed plant. Practitioners in both events may use shortened approach runs in training to avoid the fatigue of repeated full-scale run-ups. Some indoor facilities for top jumpers incorporate declining approaches so speed is gained more quickly. Aerial technique is facilitated with take-off from a springboard which allows more time in the air for skill acquisition.

Groin and lower back injuries may result from imperfect landings in the sandpit. Lower back injuries are especially common in triple jumpers from inefficient absorption of the shock of the landing at each phase (Reilly, 1977). Landing efficiently from the hop must simultaneously incorporate an optimal drive into the step with the same proviso obtaining on landing from the step and thrusting for the jump.

Ankle and knee sprains are possible on uncontrolled landing in the long jump or at any phase of the triple. Meniscus damage in the final triple phase may result from landing heavily if the affected leg undergoes rotational torsion with the knee flexed. Injury can occur to the lower limbs in this phase at club level if the competitor fails to reach the pit. Poor landing facilities can account for severe and unnecessary lower limb injuries. A deep and even pit of fine grain sand is an effective shock absorber and must be well maintained.

Female long jumpers tend to incur a greater proportion of overstrain injuries than their male counterparts. It is likely that the male musculo-skeletal system is better suited to the explosive effort required. Emphasis should be placed on off-season strength training regimes to improve the quality of the female athlete's muscle, tendon and bone so that she is better prepared to withstand the stress of the competitive season.

High jump

The high jumper needs great explosive leg strength for vertical propulsion after a controlled run-up. The ability to spring is demanded irrespective of the style employed and typically accounts for about 90 per cent of the height attained. The remainder is due to efficient lay-out crossing the bar, top jumpers using either the straddle or the flop method. In the straddle, approach is at an angle of about 35° and take-off is almost opposite the near upright. The final stride is long with a pronounced heel plant to increase thrust. Take-off demands vigorous ilio-femoral and knee extension, powerful plantar flexion, great hip flexibility to allow a high swing of the lead leg before losing ground contact, and coordinated use of the arms. Clearance is effected by straddling the bar face down and rolling over to land on the side. Wrist and acromio-clavicular sprains have been eliminated with the use of foam landing mats.

The flop gets its name from the ungainly landing on the back or back of the neck after clearing the bar draped crossways and face upwards. The approach is much longer and faster than in the straddle, is curved in its final part and take-off is from the outside rather than the inside leg. Safe landing beds are imperative for floppers. These must be positioned correctly by officials to ensure that the jumper does not slide over the sides or between beds where separate modules are used.

The take-off leg is more vulnerable as it provides the leverage in the jump. Stress from the muscular contractions can lead to muscle or joint injuries. 'Jumper's knee' describes tendinitis of the patellar or quadriceps tendon at the inferior or superior poles of the patella respectively (Roels et al, 1978). The condition occurs also in broad jumpers. An aching type of pain appears insidiously after practice and subsequently at the beginning and termination of a work out. If allowed to go on with intense activity over a prolonged period the jumper may eventually incur a disastrous complete rupture of the tendonous attachment (Blazina et al, 1973). Knee damage is promoted in the flop with forced outward rotation from having to simultaneously twist the take-off leg and rotate the lower body. Lower back pain may also result from poor alignment at take-off.

The deltoid ligament on the medial aspect of the ankle can be damaged in inexperienced jumpers concentrating on aerial technique too early and planting the take-off foot abnormally abducted and everted. Moulded fibre heel pads have minimised complaints of calcaneal periostitis and contusions of soft tissue in the take-off foot. With insufficient heel support irritation of calcaneal plantar bursa, calcaneal periostitis and bony spurring on the heel present chronically.

Strain of the connective tissue of the iliopsoas muscle is common. Chronic muscle injuries have been reported in this hip flexor, the adductor magnus and longus and biceps femoris (Dickinson, 1971).

Bone injuries include avulsion fracture of the ischial tuberosity in straddlers because of the forceful upward swing of the lead leg. Another complaint is periostitis or epiphysitis at the distal attachment of the iliopsoas on the femur and at the ischial attachment of biceps femoris. Osgood Schlatters disease or epiphysitis of the tibial tubercle is sometimes found related to jumping in youngsters.

Stress fractures of the navicular bone of the foot may occur if the take-off foot is persistently planted parallel to the bar in using the flop technique. This bone forms the final block of the longitudinal foot arch and bears the brunt of the compression and shear forces produced. Strengthening the intrinsic foot muscles, planting the foot tangentially to the run-up and use of an extended heel cap in the take-off shoe have been advocated to avoid this injury (Krahl and Knebel, 1979).

Pole vault

Pole vaulting requires great all-round strength, flexibility, speed, coordination, agility and no small amount of fortitude. The athlete develops great speed in the run-up while carrying the pole pointed ahead, which he plants firmly in the metal or wooden box and drives off the ground in a forward and upward action onto the pole (Fig. 17/3). During flight he rides the pole to which he has imparted kinetic energy, the degree of bend in a flexible pole depending principally on take-off velocity. After a hanging phase behind the arch of the pole, the vaulter rocks back by whipping his feet upwards with bent knees and dropping his shoulders backwards before turning and pushing off at the top of the vault to a flyaway or piked crossing. The release of the pole must be exquisitely timed so that the maximum energy has been taken back from it. Best performances have been found to be characterised by a pronounced bending of the pole, similar rates of pole

bending and pole straightening and marked changes in the athlete's potential energy and kinetic energy of translation as the pole straightens (Hay, 1971).

All top vaulters use fibre glass poles selected to fit their weight, and employ hand holds and hand spreads to suit individual physiques. Metal poles are still used by novices since flexible poles are of little advantage below 3m or so. Technique varies with these different types but the fundamental swinging action can be learnt using a metal pole. Performances at major meetings well exceed the height of a double-decker bus, so that, mindful of the speed and precise timing required, it is easy to appreciate the risk involved in this event.

The approach run may induce muscle pulls if warm-up has been inadequate. Top vaulters tend to use an extensive routine of stretching exercises for muscles involved at the run-up, take-off, ascent and push off the pole. Keeping warm and supple at championships presents a unique problem in that competition may be drawn out for three, four or five hours or more. The muscles pulled in the build-up run tend to be hamstrings, adductors and, less frequently, the soleus and gastrocnemius. Bruising on the side of the leg can occur in inexperienced vaulters if the pole is persistently carried against it.

Breaking a pole during flight from the spectacular bend it gets is a nightmare of all vaulters. When this happens the athlete is usually fired out of control towards the landing beds. One of the dangers is of being impaled on the broken end. In the majority of cases he emerges physically unscathed after his nerve shattering experience.

If the drive at take-off is poor, momentum may be insufficient to carry the vaulter over the landing beds, in which case swinging back on the pole allows him to come down unharmed in a controlled fashion. A poor plant, badly coordinated take-off or a cross-wind may propel him against the uprights with resultant damage on contact. Severe injury can occur when the athlete pulls out without crossing the bar and just fails to contact the landing module on descent.

The back muscles contribute at take-off and need systematic development. In flight, abdominal muscles may be injured from the forceful contraction needed to reach the hanging position. Injury to the shoulder muscles can also occur from their involvement in the ascent. Chronic tendinitis of the rotator cuff muscles is sometimes found.

One of the obvious dangers on landing is of being hit by a dislodged crossbar. Minor or moderately severe sprains of the ankle or the extremities of the spine can occur if the landing is not flat, despite provision of energy absorbing materials. Bruises to the heel on landing may result in chronic soreness in schoolboys using

Fig. 17/3 Vaulting with a flexible fibre-glass pole

poor landing beds even at moderate heights. Attention at all levels should be given to the security of uprights, the provision of landing mats conforming to competition requirements and the prevailing weather conditions. Storage and proper maintenance of poles will help ensure their integrity and grip for effective and safe performance.

The running and jumping events arguably provide the most glamorous competitions in the world of sport. The urge to emulate their athletic hero often urges ambitious runners and jumpers to step up dramatically their volume of training in the mistaken belief of a linear relationship between quantity of training load and quality of ensuing performance. In effect they pass the thin line separating training from straining and pay a severe penalty in incurring injury. A more cautious approach to increasing training load is advocated as well as the adoption of preventive measures in the conditioning regime. A conservative attitude is supported also when the danger signals of injury are first displayed. A reduction in training load and symptomatic control at this phase proves highly beneficial in the long term.

REFERENCES

Åstrand, P. O. and Rodahl, K. (1977). *Textbook of work physiology*. McGraw-Hill, New York.

Blazina, M. E., Kerlin, R. K., Jobe, F. W., Carter, V. S. and Carlson, G. J. (1973). Jumpers knee. *Orthopaedic Clinics of North America*, **4**, 665–678.

Dehaven, K. E., Dolan,W. and Mayer, P. J. (1979). Chondromalacia patellae in athletes: clinical presentation and conservative management. *American Journal of Sports Medicine*, **7**, 5–11.

Dickinson, A. L. (1971). *Chronic injury: track-high jump*. In L. A. Larson (ed). *Encyclopedia of sports sciences and medicine*. Macmillan, New York.

Haberl, R. and Prokop, L. (1974). Aspects of synthetic tracks. *Biotelemetry*, **1**, 171–178.

Hay, J. G. (1971). Mechanical energy relationships in vaulting with a fibre glass pole. *Ergonomics*, **14**, 437–448.

James, S. L., Bates, B. T. and Osternig, L. R. (1978). Injuries to runners. *American Journal of Sports Medicine*, **6**, 40–50.

Klafs, C. E. and Lyon, M. J. (1978). *The female athlete*. C. V. Mosby, St Louis.

Krahl, H. and Knebel, K. P. (1979). Foot stress during the flop takeoff. *Track Technique*, **75**, 2384–2386.

Miller, S. J. (1971). *Acute and subacute injury: hurdles*. In L. A. Larson (ed). *Encyclopedia of sports sciences and medicine*. Macmillan, New York.

O'Donoghue, D. H. (1970). *Treatment of injuries to athletes*. W. B. Saunders, Philadelphia.

Orave, S. (1978). Iliotibial tract friction syndrome in athletes – an uncommon exertion syndrome on the lateral side of the knee. *British Journal of Sports Medicine*, **12**, 69–73.

Orave, S. and Puranen, J. (1979). Athletes' leg pains. *British Journal of Sports Medicine*, **13**, 92–97.

Rasmussen, W. (1974). Shin splints: definition and treatment. *Journal of Sports Medicine*, **2**, 111–117.

Reilly, T. (1977). Some risk factors in selected track and field events. *British Journal of Sports Medicine*, **11**, 53–56.

Roels, J., Martens, M., Mulier, J. C. and Burssens, A. (1978). Patellar tendinitis (jumpers knee). *American Journal of Sports Medicine*, **6**, 362–368.

Sim, F. H. and Detenbeck, L. C. (1972). Injuries of knee in athletes. *Minnesota Medicine*, **55**, 881–885.

Wilkie, D. H. (1960). Man as a source of mechanical power. *Ergonomics*, **3**, 1–8.

CHAPTER 18

Track and field – 2. The throws

T. REILLY BA, DPE, MSc, PhD, MIBiol

The throws provide contrasting spectacles in the respective events of shot, javelin, discus and hammer. In common, they demand finely tuned skills and great explosive power in execution. Throwers tend to be muscular and large, except in the javelin where body size is sacrificed for speed. The attempts to prohibit acquisition of mass by ingestion of anabolic steroids have gained universal support so that individuals can compete on fairer terms. The application of sensitive measures of drug detection (Beckett and Cowan, 1979) has, hopefully, begun to eliminate illegal steroid use. Strength and body size can also be increased by weight training which is an essential part of most throwers' preparation and the occasion of many injuries. Safety procedures in handling and lifting weights should be rigidly adhered to and athletes should never work alone in the weight training room.

The throws are unique in the track and field calendar of events in that bystanders and spectators as well as competitors are exposed to risk. This applies especially to the discus, hammer and javelin where distances in the region of 70, 80 and 90m are reached respectively. Rules for competition dictate that practices are limited in location and that implements are carried and not thrown back in retrieval. All implements must fall within a restricted sector for a throw to be valid. This sector is roped off to avoid accidents in the shot and javelin. In the case of the discus and hammer, both of which involve turning before release, a cage or enclosure prevents the implement from flying off in the unwanted directions. The rules for competition strongly recommend the use of a cage of specified dimensions to promote spectator safety. Needless to say it must be well maintained by ground staff. Dissatisfaction is sometimes expressed with the C-shape of the hammer cage since it does not effectively account for different handed throwers or the turning of the hammer wire outside the head on release. A U-shaped cage increasing in height towards its front has been suggested (Johnson, 1979). A dramatic illustration of the inadequacy of the current cage was provided by a Russian competitor at the Montreal Olympic Games whose throw bounced off the track immediately in front of the assembled 5 000m runners.

Group practices also constitute a source of danger where safety considerations should be paramount. Youngsters can, for example, be taught javelin throwing in a cohort and must retrieve the implements as a group once the last individual has thrown. The teacher/coach must insist that the javelin is carried so that its metal head is not liable to cause injury. All bystanders should be aware of impending throws and keep clear of the landing areas. In discus throwing groups, left-handed individuals should be placed together at the left end of the line. If safety procedures are ingrained in the early years they will have become second nature by the time the athlete reaches senior competitive level.

A recurrent aetiological feature in throwing injuries is incorrect technique. For this reason the important performance principles will be covered for each of the throws. Additional detail is provided to present a flavour of the events.

SHOT PUTT

The shot putt is close to a pure power event and attracts individuals of great size and muscularity. A sphere 16lb (7.25 kg) weight (4 kg for women) is impelled from a circle 7ft (2.13m) in diameter. A lighter shot is used in junior competition: at senior level no allowance is made for differences in bodyweight. Other things being equal, the greater the body size the greater the advantage in putting so that until weight categories are introduced for this event an element of unfairness will exist. A progressive increase in the size of putters in the major Games over the last two decades or so underlines this. An increase in weight via the muscular mass rather than body fat is preferred for greater power production.

Recognition of the importance of lean body mass has encouraged illegal ingestion of anabolic steroids to increase muscle size. The extent to which steroids have been used by putters of international standard must remain speculative. However, credence must be given to the admissions after retirement by numerous élite performers of extensive use of these drugs and acknowledgment of their adverse side-effects. Alternatively, body size may be legally increased by adoption of weight training regimes to boost muscle hypertrophy or by exorbitant energy intake levels. The high protein diets of many top throwers may have deleterious long-term effects as a result of the large cholesterol contents.

The rules for the event dictate that the putt is made from the shoulder close to the chin and that the arm shall not be dropped below this position or be brought behind the line of the shoulder. Besides body size, the major determinants of performance are the acceleration of the shot before release and the angle of release, which optimally is about 40°. Acceleration of the shot is enhanced by moving it as far as possible across the circle. Consequently three main techniques have developed from the basic side-on stance of Fonville and Fuchs in the 1940s. Firstly, the step-back involves a quick glide across the circle with the legs crossing scissor-like while in the air. The O'Brien method, named after the Olympic champion of 1956 and 1960, is favoured by most top throwers and coaches (Fig. 18/1). Finally, the Baryshnikov spiral involves turning as in a discus throw and requires even more adroit balance as control of the body after release of the shot tends to be difficult. All methods ultimately arrive at a fundamental throwing posture with the chin, knee and supporting big toe in virtual vertical alignment prior to

further rapid and upward acceleration of the shot. Putting correctly from this basic position from a standing throw is essential before the refinements of the glide can be coached or if later injuries from poor technique are to be avoided.

The power for putting is generated by forced extension of the knee and hip, augmented by back extension and supplemented by successive shoulder, arm, wrist and finger involvement in the final pushing action. Coordination of muscle action in these segments must be finely timed for efficient performance and so each is liable to injury.

Lower limbs

Muscle tears in the lower limbs are rare but may occur from loss of balance in the glide or attempts to avoid fouling the stopboard after release. Wet concrete circles and poorly gripping footwear are often implicated. In cold conditions competitors may retain track-suit bottoms during putts and keep warm in the intervals between to avoid muscle pulls. The rotational movement in the glide across the circle may endanger the meniscus of the knee.

Back injuries

Back injuries may originate from using heavy loads in weight training and are aggravated in throwing prac-

Fig. 18/1 The sequence of actions in shot putting. The elbow must be taken through high and behind the shot for efficient and safe performance

tices. Improper timing of the sudden violent contraction of the back muscles can lead to tears from their attachment or through the muscle belly. Reflex spasms of uninjured muscles provide some protection. Sprains of the ligaments may occur with the more serious back muscle injuries (Littin, 1971). Rupture of the back extensors and avulsion fractures of the cervical and thoracic spines have also been reported (Groh, 1972).

Shoulder and upper arm

The shoulder is a common site of injury, probably as a result of its intrinsic instability. Development of the muscles around the joint provide a measure of security. Injury, due to imperfect timing, can occur in any of the rotator cuff muscles which fasten the humeral head in the glenoid cavity. These may be damaged at their origin, mid-portion or attachment at the greater tuberosity of the humerus with possible avulsion fracture here. The most common tendon injury is that of the long head of the biceps.

Muscle tears at the elbow include those from origins at the humeral epicondyles. Immediate pain is felt at the side of the joint. Avulsion fracture of the olecranon has also been found (Groh, 1972). The predisposing technique faults may be poor synchronisation of the arm and trunk muscles, taking the throwing elbow through too low or ahead of the shot, or overcompensation from dropping the shoulder on the non-throwing side.

Lower arm

Sprains of the ligaments of the wrist are almost widespread in shot putters which is evident in the frequent use of supports for this joint in practices. The wrist bears the weight of the shot and, additionally, is put through an extreme degree of forcible flexion. Pain is immediate and usually accompanied by mild swelling; the injury is therefore easily recognisable. Tenderness may be located either at the distal end of the radius or at the ligamentous insertion in the metacarpals.

The fingers contribute in gripping the shot throughout and in the final propulsive effort. The extensor tendons of the terminal phalanges are especially liable to damage. Injury to the tendon of the long extensor of the thumb is also possible if the thumb is not correctly positioned on the side of the shot.

JAVELIN

The javelin is thrown from behind a scratch line after utilising an approach run to gain momentum. This linear acceleration in the run-up is supplemented by transitional steps and arm movement, all in the line of intended throw. The complex interplay of segmental action is founded on a basic throwing posture with the body forming a bow-like shape. This is attained by withdrawing the spear over two strides behind the body in transition from the run-up, coming down heel first after a high knee-lift two strides later ahead of

Fig. 18/2 The throwing base in the javelin event. Any tendency to throw round-arm must be avoided

bodyweight. A wide throwing base is achieved in reaching out with the lead leg for the other to drive the hip forward on the throwing side. The throwing action is completed by taking the shoulder through quickly, the elbow high and over the shoulder and the lower arm through late in a flail-like action, the spear being released over or in front of the non-throwing foot (Fig. 18/2). The optimum angle of release varies with the type of implement used.

According to Hay (1973) the speed of release is by far the most important single factor in determining the distance thrown. Since acceleration of the implement is enhanced with increasing range of movement during the throw, mobility at the shoulder, back and hip is all important. Specific exercises to increase the extent of movement are desirable. A solid support in the heel plant during the penultimate foot placement helps set up a stable throwing base. The heel spikes in the javelin boot assist this purpose though repetitive practising of the final strides on hard surfaces can cause contusions in the soft tissue of the heel.

Coaching the correct throwing technique at an early stage is essential if injuries in the propulsive arm are to be avoided. This starts with the proper grip on the missile binding and the provision of a good launching platform from an elevated palm. The throw itself is grossly similar to baseball pitching or bowling in cricket and the correct motor pattern can be introduced by throwing a cricket ball. Other useful drills might include throwing for accuracy at 15 to 20m against an incline or throwing from a kneeling position. Greater strength is promoted if the coach provides some resistance on the tail of the missile in a standing throw preventing its release or by strategic use of medicine ball throws. Strength, power and speed of limb movement are more important than body size in this event, as many top throwers are only moderate in build.

Probably the most frequent fault in novices is the tendency to throw round arm rather than with a high lead of the elbow over the shoulder. As a result the medial collateral ligament of the elbow joint can be strained. A side arm throw with the arm abducted parallel to the ground and the elbow in 90° flexion swinging through at the level of the shoulder similarly exposes the medial ligament to considerable strain. Damage appears to be cumulative rather than from a single incident. Recurrent minor strains of the ligament are characterised by pain on the medial aspect of the joint before extension of the elbow begins when the medial ligament is transmitting most force. The pain interferes with performance to varying degrees, rapidly resolves with rest but returns on further practices. The intensity of training must be reduced and the underlying fault corrected.

Another fault of novice throwers is a tendency to let the wrist only get out to the side beyond the line of the elbow joint when throwing. At the end of the throwing action the forearm is pronated sharply to prevent the whip of the javelin. According to Littin (1971) this aggravates the strain on the medial collateral ligament of the elbow. The combination of forceful elbow extension with forearm pronation may cause a pivoting of the ulna in the trochlea, forcing the olecranon medially with increased pressure on the medial side because of the long arm of the ulnar shaft. Littin referred to reports of transient paralysis of the ulnar nerve in some javelin throwers and fractures of the olecranon. Repeated stress of this type can lead to the formation of bony spurs on the medial side of the elbow. Careful attention to the positioning of the wrist under the cord grip once the javelin is withdrawn, and a correct pull through the long axis of the missile is essential for prevention.

Elbow pain is experienced by almost every competitor at some time varying from slight discomfort to symptoms severe enough to stop participation. Even accomplished javelin throwers may hyperextend the elbow at the end of the throw, impinging and injuring the tip of the olecranon process against the floor of the olecranon fossa. The symptoms result from a single errant throw and are completely disabling (Miller, 1960).

Groh (1972) reported that rupture of the pronator teres is often found in specialists in this event. This injury is probably a result of imperfect alignment of the javelin before the throw commences. In the final phase of elbow extension and pronation the flexor muscles and pronator teres act as a brake to achieve a trip-up effect (Waris, 1946). Other common findings include rupture of the tendon of the long head of the biceps and of the tendon of the long extensor of the thumb (Groh, 1972). This last injury probably results from a faulty grip on the binding.

DISCUS

Discus throwing originated in the Greek Games thirty centuries or so ago and was included in the first of the ancient Olympic Games. It was among the events in the programme of the first revised Olympic Games in Athens in 1896 and is today moderately well supported by both sexes at all competitive levels. The discus is platter-shaped, weight 2kg for senior men's and 1kg for senior women's competitions with lower weights for juniors and youths. It is thrown from a circle 98.5 inches (2.5m) in diameter normally of concrete whose final surface is lightly stippled to give a firm footing without retarding the thrower's movements.

In modern discus throwing the athlete starts at the rear of the circle facing opposite to the eventual direction of throw. The discus is held against the palm and wrist with the fingers evenly spaced, the pads of their ends curled over the lip of the discus. The grip should be relatively relaxed so that the implement is not tightly held or the wrist cocked to avoid chronic tendinitis: supination is not required to prevent the discus from falling once it is kept in motion. This applies while preliminary relaxed swings are taken with the discus at arm's length before it is finally withdrawn as far as possible with the trunk twisted to the side. In the last preliminary swing the throwing shoulder is twisted right back while the arm is also extended behind the line of the shoulder as far as possible with the discus held at shoulder height. Flexibility in the trunk and shoulder is necessary to allow this. Bodyweight in this coiled position is supported on an extended right leg. An orthodox thrower then flexes the supporting knee, shifts bodyweight onto a flexed left leg and begins to move to the left across the circle in a semi-running stride. As the thrower spins in rotation in getting across the circle, the discus is held back in the outstretched arm so its angular velocity can be maximised. Proportionally long arms provide the athlete with a mechanical advantage which is apparent in the builds of top throwers (Tanner, 1964). The rotation culminates in a strong throwing position from which the discus is slung. This running rotation technique is illustrated in Figure 18/3.

Fig. 18/3 The early part of the running rotation across the circle. A firm foothold is essential at this stage, while the knee of the supporting leg is under strain

The run across the circle combines a thrust from the left leg with a lift from the right thigh, the thrower arriving at about the centre of the circle. By the time the right foot lands, the hips lead the shoulders which the discus in turn trails. The left leg scissors rapidly past the right landing heel first at the front of the circle. This allows the thrower to drive the right side of the body powerfully against a left side in a long throwing action with the chest at right angles to the direction of the throw. The thrower reaches out in delivering the missile opposite the right shoulder in a final squeezing action of wrist and fingers assisted by the lift from vigorous extension of the legs. The discus parts off the index finger which spins it clockwise, this gyroscopic effect increasing the distance of the throw by keeping the missile flat in flight. The throw is best if delivered into the prevailing wind while optimal angle of release varies with wind conditions between 30 to 40°. On release the feet normally reverse to retain balance within the circle.

To avoid injuries arising from poor technique it is important that the correct actions be coached from the beginning. Repetitive practices of winding up for a standing throw are usually effective in establishing the basic action. In the standing throw the athlete faces the direction of flight with the feet balanced slightly wider than hip width apart. Bowling the discus helps novices get the correct release off the index finger. They may also learn by tossing it vertically in an underarm action, catching it and repeating. Use of a rubber discus can help keep strain from repetitive spinning off the fingers. Rupture of the extensor tendons of terminal phalanges is common in this event (Groh, 1972). A discus strapped onto the hand can help in learning to execute the turn. The strap prevents release and allows concentration on balance and footwork without the need for retrieval. Efficient rotation is important so that the torque on the menisci of the knee is minimised.

Holding the discus correctly in an extended arm serves to avoid the wrist injuries associated with putting and those associated with elbow hyperextension in javelin throwers. Conditioning exercises for the major muscle groups of the body are recommended for this event. Strength and power of the thigh, back and shoulder musculature should be developed, since these groups are integrally involved in the coordination of a good throw. As with the shot putt, the rotator cuff muscles are liable to injury in sudden forceful contractions. Since top throwers rely heavily on weight training for strength development, it is again emphasised that such regimes should be conducted with care to avoid injury.

HAMMER

The hammer is technically the most complex of the throws and is the only one restricted to male competitors. The basic skills take years to perfect so that top hammer throwers tend to be older than their counterparts in other throwing events. In general they are also stockier in build than discus or shot putt specialists, a feature that facilitates balance in turning prior to release.

The hammer is thrown from a circle 7ft (2.13m) in diameter. The implement consists of a 16lb (7.25kg) ball at the end of a 4ft (1.22m) spring steel wire. The handle is connected to the head by a swivel and to the grip by means of a loop. The orthodox thrower holds the hammer by placing the left hand inside the right with the handle resting on the middle joint of the fingers. When high release speeds are reached blisters and skin abrasions result unless a glove is worn on the inside hand. A leather glove on this hand is permitted while most throwers additionally bind the middle portions of the fingers with adhesive tape.

The throw starts with the athlete at the rear of the circle, his back towards the direction of release with the hammer resting on the ground behind his right foot. A series of preliminary swings are taken before the thrower enters his first turn. At least three turns are taken by seasoned throwers to maximise the acceleration of the hammer head before it is released into a 45° sector (reduced to 40° by recommendation of the IAAF Technical Sub-committee, 1979). The athlete, in turning quickly, is forced to sit back against the hammer as the centrifugal forces exerted on him increase with successive turns. The speed of turning increases progressively while the counter-balancing movements of the body become more pronounced. The athlete is coached to keep the arms fully extended, sit back and keep the weight over the left foot to retain balance and continuous acceleration. In the turns the athlete spins around the left foot while each time the right comes down in a pawing-like action. Good footwear is needed for protecting the soles of the feet as the spin is made on the left heel with the turn taken up in rolling fashion at the small toe: the right foot turns on the ball of the foot. The right foot retains contact with the ground for as long as possible allowing the shoulders to lead the hips and causing a transverse abdominal stretch which can then be exploited. Errors in timing at this phase may injure the transverse abdominal muscle. The hammer is delivered at the high point of the final turn at about shoulder level. The usual angle of release is about 40 to 45° to the horizontal. Figure 18/4 illustrates the turning action in a good throw.

The novice progresses from simple swings to learn-

Fig. 18/4 Turning in the hammer throw. The athlete must exert great force to counteract the outward pull of the hammer as it rotates, and retain balance. The left foot may fold underneath on delivery and is vulnerable at that point

ing to turn. Giddiness is overcome by focusing on one point during each rotation. A shortened wire is often used in the early stages to facilitate learning. The delicate interplay of footwork must be coordinated with the powerful leg, back and shoulder muscle action to perfect the turn. The rotational and linear forces must be integrated in explosively executing the throw. If release is marginally retarded the shoulder joint is particularly vulnerable as the hammer attempts to rip away from its tether. According to Groh (1972) pectoralis major, trapezius and the rhomboids are common locations of injury. Back extensor muscles, cervical and thoracic vertebral spines are also susceptible.

Many hammer throwers' injuries originate in the strenuous strength training programmes these specialists employ. As weight training is usually conducted close to maximal efforts, special attention to safety is needed. Practice sessions tend to be lengthy during which errors in technique creep in from fatigue especially underturning or overturning. To pre-empt any accident arising from such episodes training should be conducted according to the safety recommendations of the rules book.

All throwing events demand highly specialised techniques as well as fast explosive actions. The most effective injury-preventive mechanism is correct skill acquisition achievable over painstaking practices. Use of portable video-tape machinery in training sessions for immediate feedback of performance is a valuable coaching aid to eliminating faults. Timing and coordination of the various body segments are essential if each is to make maximal contribution towards the total effort. Strength training of involved muscle groups is recommended in conjunction with establishment of the correct motor patterns. Specific flexibility and balance are other requisites for effective injury prevention.

A thorough warm-up prior to competition is advised. This need not include all-out throws since experience suggests that maximal efforts are best left until the competition. As this may be prolonged it is important to keep warm and supple in the intermissions between trials. In all the events a good grip on the implement should be secured, especially in wet conditions. Use of resin on the hands is permitted to effect this while a towel for drying the implement is an important item to complete the athlete's kit.

REFERENCES

Beckett, A. H. and Cowan, D. A. (1979). Misuse of drugs in sport. *British Journal of Sports Medicine*, **12**, 185–194.

Groh, H. (1972). *Sport injuries and damage to the locomotor system.* In O. Grupe, D. Kurz and J. M. Teipel (eds). *The scientific way of sport.* Springer Verlag, New York.

Hay, J. G. (1973). *The biomechanics of sports techniques.* Prentice-Hall, Englewood Cliffs.

Johnson, C. T. (1979). Hammer safety. *Athletics Coach*, **13**, 18–25.

Littin, L. O. (1971). *Acute and subacute injury: weights.* In L. A. Larson (ed). *Encyclopedia of sports sciences and medicine.* Macmillan, New York.

Miller, J. E. (1960). Javelin thrower's elbow. *Journal of Bone and Joint Surgery*, **42**, 788–792.

Miller, S. J. (1971). *Acute and subacute injury.* In L. A. Larson (ed). *Encyclopedia of sports sciences and medicine.* Macmillan, New York.

Tanner, J. M. (1964). *The physique of the Olympic athlete.* George Allen and Unwin, London.

Waris, W. (1946). Elbow injuries of javelin throwers. *Acta Chirurgica Scandinavica*, **93**, 563–575.

CHAPTER 19

Risks in selected outdoor water based activities

T. REILLY BA, DPE, MSc, PhD, MIBiol and F. H. SANDERSON DCC, BEd, MA, PhD

Water based activities constitute a source of popular recreation as well as skilled sport, and embrace an assortment of indoor and outdoor events. Locations include swimming and diving pools, rivers, marina, watersport centres, lakes, off-shore resorts and open seas. Of current indoor sports, swimming has a long tradition founded on military preparation; diving and water-polo are well established Olympic sports; while octopush – a form of hockey played underwater – is a comparatively recent innovation. Rowing and canoeing are both strenuous river sports, wild-water canoeing being the most robust form. Various surfing and skiing competitions have evolved from leisure pursuits, the inaugural water ski championships taking place in France in 1949 after the formation earlier that year of the International Water Ski Union. Wind surfing employs a sail on a surf-board, its proponents suffering frequent immersion. Sailing and yachting races have been expanded well beyond the traditional shorter distances, presenting novel hazards as well as challenges to participants.

In many of the newer water sports regular recreational participation requires expertise in craft handling as well as swimming proficiency, though particular activities may safely be enjoyed by non-swimmers if sensible precautions are taken. Surfers and water skiers, for example, can wear a secure life-belt but are still strongly advised to learn to swim. Hire facilities at most resorts make the water sports open to practically all-comers who seek the experience without necessarily any prior conditioning. Development of inland water facilities has meant that enthusiasm has progressed beyond the sporadic recreational participation on the coastline. Proliferation of motor boats on the waters has brought attendant risks of collision and increasing concern for traffic control. The British Water Ski Federation, for example, lays down procedures when more than one boat is on the same stretch of water.

Risk of death by drowning is omnipresent. Watersport fatalities were found to account for 43 per cent of total accidental recreational deaths in Scotland in one year (Moncur, 1973) and for 21 per cent in Japanese high school students, over an eight year period (Izeki, 1973). In most cases, these are avoidable

through insistence on standard and sensible safety precautions and eschewing unfamiliar and dangerous waters. These rates are still relatively low when the vast numbers of recreational participants are considered, while fatality is rare in watersport competitions. Strains and sprains associated with the muscular effort of heavy repetitive anti-gravity work are not found since the body mass is buoyed up in the water. For this reason exercise in water is often recommended in rehabilitation for land sports. Competitive watersports produce low injury rates, the incidence being less than two per cent of all sports injuries in the study of Crampton and Tubbs (1977). The injuries characteristic of a selection of outdoor watersports are now presented. The risks and injuries in diving and competitive swimming are covered in Chapter 20.

WATER SKIING

Proficiency in water skiing ranges from the baseline of the beginner to the tricks and stunts of the professional. Beginners commence with two skis, the standard size being 165cm long and 16.5cm wide with fins 20cm long by 7.5cm deep. Wider skis are needed for larger body builds and ideally their size is also adjusted for age and sex. Adjustable footpieces of moulded rubber retain the feet firmly in place during take-off and skiing but dislodge easily in emergencies. A waveborne errant ski can however cause concussion if hitting the head of an individual who has fallen.

Initial skill acquisition can be enhanced by land drills prior to entering the water. These might include sitting in a squat position on skis, holding on to a rope and slowly standing erect while resisting the pull of the instructor at the other end. With suitable land drills and instruction most learners can ski for a distance on their first day without the frustrations and discomfort of frequent failures. In the start position great leg strength is required to hold the skis in position in front of the body with knees flexed. The quadriceps contract forcefully as the body rises, the adductors help keep skis parallel as the boat accelerates abruptly and the hamstrings prevent excessive forward pull. In consequence, novices are often stiff on the day following their early practices. Learners should be coached to immediately release the tow rope once balance is irretrievably lost to avoid being dragged along the water. Mild injuries mostly occur with beginners, so consideration and care on the driver's part can help prevention.

Proficiency develops relatively quickly as the skier masters criss-crossing the wake. This allows greater velocities than the usual 40kmh^{-1} of the boat to be achieved. At this stage sharp turns of the boat should be avoided by the driver, especially while the skier is outside the wake. For providing the necessary abrupt acceleration at take-off and for towing adults an outboard motor of 50 to 75hp is best. The skier may then graduate to mono-ski by discarding the unwanted one in the water. A safer but more skilful manoeuvre is to start with one ski from standing in shallow water, so avoiding the danger of leaving floating skis unattended. The skier then progresses to using shoe skis or riding on discs and later to barefoot skiing where speeds of 130kmh^{-1} are reached by experts. The greater the speed the greater is the hazard, and the harder is the impact with the water on falling. Because of the greater speeds they employ, barefoot skiers need padded wet-suits, usually made to measure, for protection in falls on smooth waters.

Competitive water skiing may require contestants to ski between six buoys in a mono-ski slalom run, the speedboat entering and leaving through the gate buoys. Special muscular effort is demanded in rounding the buoys. This is achieved by combining the actions of arms, shoulder and back in drawing the rope handle towards the trunk and braking the ski with thigh and leg muscles by pushing its rear end outwards and leaning in to turn. Hitting the buoy at this point can result in abrasions, lacerations and rib fractures (Bass, 1971). On rounding the buoy, torsion injuries to the ankle may occur if the bindings slip or elbow and shoulder strains from longitudinal forces applied to the limbs if the rope slackens.

Alternatively, long distance competitions involve skiing out to sea and turning at a gate to return towards shore. Appreciable isometric strength and endurance in the arms, shoulders and legs is needed as well as balance. Speeds approaching 100kmh^{-1} are common in internationals where the minimum race distance is 50 nautical miles (90km). The first buoy must be at least 2.4km (1.5 miles) from the start to allow the field to spread out while competitors must at all times ski within the wake of their own boat. Each boat is required to carry a variety of safety equipment; this includes a suitable anchor and line, fire extinguishers, compass, flares, paddles, ignition cut-out fastened to the driver, and buoyancy aids. Two crew members are

required; both must wear a life-jacket with inherent buoyancy and a fluorescent orange crash-helmet. The skier wears a lightweight plastic helmet which must cover the ears for protection in the event of a fall sideways. The slits in the helmet must be large enough to allow good hearing, but not so large that water rushes in with such force that the ear drum is perforated. The average rope length is about 45m though longer ropes are used in Australia and USA in races in calm lakes and rivers.

The tactic used by Italian skiers of wrapping the rope handles round the body to take the strain off the upper limbs has been banned from international use on safety grounds. A technique introduced by Australian competitors to allow greater endurance gained international acceptance in 1979: both handles are placed behind the lower back at about hip height and held by one hand while the other holds an additional forward handle (Fig. 19/1).

Fig. 19/1 Special towing line handles for long distance water skiing

In water ski jumping, competitors take off from a ramp 150cm high for boys and females and 180cm for men. Pre-ramp velocities approach 100kmh^{-1} which may increase further with reduced friction between skis and wood or plastic ramps while distances exceeding 40m are jumped in major events. Extensive abrasions are likely if the skier misses the end of the ramp but hits the side, or prematurely falls and is carried up the ramp by the momentum developed. The sides of ramps should be covered with protective shields which deflect bodies on impact courses. As he rises up the ramp he must counteract a downward force estimated at three times his body weight to prevent bunching at the hips and knees and develop thrust for the jump

(Bass, 1971). If balance is lost in the air the greatest dangers are in being hit by a flying ski and in landing awkwardly.

Greater impact forces on landing (6.5G for 95 milliseconds(ms)) than at take-off (5.0G for 95ms) were reported by Reid and colleagues (1978) for men at the Canadian championships. They concluded these forces were insufficient to result in direct injury to healthy athletes but that frequent exposure to these impacts could prove hazardous to the water ski jumper. They cited findings of considerably higher incidences of flexion/compression injury to the lumbar dorsal spine, including anterior wedging of the vertebral bodies, narrow disc spaces and osteochondroses of the vertebrae than in the general population.

After landing from a bad jump the skis may begin to sink at the rear as the rope slackens. When it becomes taut the skier may suddenly be pulled violently forward off his bindings on to his own skis and suffer head or facial lacerations (Bass, 1971). Protective helmets would prevent such injuries. Another cause of injury could be skis crossing on landing after balance is lost in mid-air.

Overall championships incorporate slalom, jumping and trick-skiing into a combined event. Tricks may involve turning 180° or 360° at a time, turning while crossing the wake or with the tow rope hooked around the foot. Competition involves two 20 second(s) runs before a panel of five judges. Champion amateurs may eventually become professionals and display other tricks working with a partner or in echelon and coordinating manoeuvres. Injuries may be caused by the ski, the rope or from loss of balance. Skis used are 1m long, 15cm wide with rounded ends slightly turned up and no fins. Since trick-skiing requires difficult operations and exceptionally high skill, it is imperative that routines should only be attempted after considerable instruction. Adverse sequelae are mostly brought about from taking undue risks. Though severe injuries do occur in water skiing their incidence is low when the large numbers participating are considered.

Falling awkwardly is an obvious cause of sprains, joint dislocations and ligament tears in all forms of water skiing. Falling forward in a spreadeagled posture with arms outstretched leaves the shoulder joint especially vulnerable. The best procedure for the beginner to adopt is either to attempt to sit or roll over. In learners, the skis begin to part sideways before loss of control and the abduction force applied may damage medial knee ligaments or medial and lateral ligaments of the ankle. Landing in a splits position may produce ruptures in abductor muscles and capsular sprains of the hip and is common to jumping, slalom and recreational skiing.

The nylon tow rope, usually about 23m long, may cause lacerations or friction burns at take-off or in falling by pulling across exposed skin at any body part. For safety, the slack is taken up at the start of a run prior to rapid acceleration and care taken that the rope is unwound and floating freely in front of the skier. The whiplash effect of a broken rope may cause similar effects and possibly sever a finger tip (Bass, 1971). Tendon injuries to fingers may also occur if caught in the tow ropes or handles.

The driver should be skilled and accompanied so that both the path ahead and the skier behind can be under surveillance. A wide rear view mirror can assist as does a communication code between skier and boat operators using recommended hand signals. O'Brien et al (1978) reported paralysis in the deltoid and extensor muscles of right arm and wrist after their patient was thrown in the air with the arm forced backwards when another boat cut across his tow rope. Collisions between boats are less frequent than accidents from hitting fallen skiers or swimmers. Collisions with solid objects such as floating debris, submerged rocks, or hitting a dock or pylon of a jetty due to misjudgment of distance may produce a variety of injuries.

Boat propellers can be lethal, causing amputations or fractures of extremities. This could happen if both driver and accompanying observer are looking behind and is completely avoidable. Sleight (1974) reported severe multiple injuries in a skier run over by the driver dazzled by the sun's reflection as he returned to pick him up after a fall. Skiers are more conspicuous in the water if they hold up a ski while drivers should steer away from areas occupied by casual surfers and swimmers. Water skiers are separated from other water users in controlled club practices. Most countries legislate to prohibit skiing in a channel close to shore and watersport centres have recognised capacities.

Falling may induce forceful entry of water into body cavities. Sinusitis and otitis media can arise from water entering the nose or ears. A perforated ear drum can present complications as the tympanic membrane may not completely repair. Bathing caps afford ear protection while ear plugs may only be forced deeper into the aural canal. The rectum may suffer if the individual falls in a sitting position and rectal douches occur if rising from a crouched starting posture is delayed. Ramey (1974) reported intra-rectal tears in a female skier after falling and dislodging her bikini to one side. Vaginal douches can produce salpingitis with risks of later sterility. Neoprene rubber pants provide adequate protection for experienced and novice skiers and may be lined with reinforced nylon.

Moore (1964) reported two fatalities from fracture-dislocation of the cervical spine on falling when coming into land at high speed. Paterson (1971) found dislocations of the fifth and sixth cervical vertebrae with locked facets and temporary quadriplegia when a skier hit a submerged sandbank and a crush fracture of the body of the fifth cervical vertebra in another individual falling on coming in to land and hitting his head on a bank concealed below the water's edge. Soft internal organs can be damaged from the quick deceleration in crashing on to the shore or jetty. These accidents can be prevented by approaching gently and parallel to the beach until running out of speed.

ROWING AND CANOEING

Rowing

Rowing constitutes strenuous physical exertion placing high demands on aerobic and anaerobic mechanisms (Di Prampero et al, 1971; Hagerman et al, 1975). The total energy requirement for rowing an international 2 000m course has been estimated to be approximately 250kcal or 1 046kJ with an 18 per cent contribution from anaerobic processes at top speeds (Jackson and Secher, 1976). These authors found single sculls to be more costly in energy production than doubles or coxless pairs at a similar velocity. Performance is faster in doubles where each partner uses two sculls than in coxless pairs where each individual uses one oar. Olympic oarsmen tend generally to have high absolute maximal oxygen uptake values (Nowacki et al, 1969; Di Prampero et al, 1970). Great force is also required (Secher, 1975), the strain on the oar reaching 80 to 100kg in the study of Tokyo Olympic rowers (Ishiko, 1971). The primary source of power is the thrust of the legs supplemented by the vigorous action of the back and transmitted through the shoulders and arms to the oar. Rowing skill is demonstrated in economy of effort and in coordinated team-work. The sport provokes relatively few serious injuries and these are mainly due to faulty technique. Muscle tears and back injuries to ligaments or muscles may occur in land training or in lifting the shell from the water. The characteristic injuries associated with water work are back injuries, tenosynovitis and blisters.

Both the legs and the back are used vigorously with each stroke (Fig. 19/2). Muscle injury particularly in the lower back can be due to repetitive training, since fatigue can only be alleviated by introducing breaks and hence disrupting the rhythmic movement. Too much forward swing can lead to strain in the back or shoulder muscles before the powerful leg action commences the sequence. Abdominal muscles may be injured when underdeveloped in the early stages of training or if the rower lies too far back at the finish of the stroke. Besides transmitting the force developed to

Fig. 19/2 The rowing action demands vigorous muscle action from the legs and back

the oars the arm muscles place and retrieve the oars in the water. All rowing techniques require good coordination of the muscles involved with the blade taking firm hold of the water and releasing cleanly. Movement of the oars of a crew above the water is found to be nearly uniform in top rowers but this does not ensure uniformity of movement of oars in the water which is more difficult to perfect (Ishiko, 1971).

Tenosynovitis or tendinitis in the sculler or oarsman usually involves inflammation of the extensor tendons of the forearm. Pain is felt while the hand is dorsiflexed during feathering the oar as the blade is taken parallel to the water surface to reduce air resistance (Schwartz, 1971). The hand farthest up the oar achieves this by rotating the oar handle. A practical measure to avoid aggravating the inflammation is for the oarsman to change sides, a solution not applicable to scullers. Tenosynovitis may also be attributable to gripping the oar too tightly on the inside hand. In this case a more relaxed hold is advised. Treatment of the condition on recurrence is far less straightforward and specialist sports medical attention should be sought.

A pervasive affliction of rowers is blisters, particularly of the hands and buttocks. Novices, especially females, are susceptible. Vulnerability is greatest at the beginning of a period of training before the hands harden. A simple bandage may be adequate in treating finger blisters while a tight-fitting leather glove can be worn for protection while the palms heal. If blisters continually recur on the palms the technique is probably faulty. Blistered buttocks can be afforded some protection by wearing tight-fitting underpants which help to reduce friction on the skin. This area may also be blistered if training is prolonged in wet conditions while heels may suffer from contact with wet socks. Blisters should always be carefully treated, especially if the skin is broken. Sound hygiene, and daily laundering of kit is recommended in order to avoid infection. A less frequent complaint is abrasions on the back of the calf. These may be prevented by adjusting the seat height.

Canoeing

Canoeing and kayak paddling involve various forms of speed and wild-water events in specially designed crafts. The kayak has a pointed bow and stern, and low sides and is covered except for the cockpit. In sprint competitions the paddle has double blades for alternate use on each side of the kayak while the operator adopts a long-seated position. Flat water competitions range from 500 to 10 000m for men and 500m is the standard international distance for females. In wild-water disciplines slalom competitions are held on rapid rivers over a course designated by a number of gates each consisting of two poles suspended vertically between 1.3 and 3m apart. Competition, normally lasting 3.5 to 4.5 minutes, involves the negotiation of gates in a pre-determined order, and forward and reverse paddling in upstream and downstream manoeuvres. In wild-water down-river racing the competitor encounters a succession of rapids through which he chooses his own route while competition duration may vary between 13 to 35 minutes. The Canadian (C1) canoe is paddled on one side from a kneeling position. The wild-water events emphasise muscular endurance as well as strength in the trunk, shoulders and arms and skill in handling the craft.

The greatest hazards in canoeing and kayak paddling are drowning and exposure to cold. A life-jacket made of closed-cell vinyl or unicellular plastic foam is an important item of equipment for the canoeist. The ability to aright a capsized craft quickly is important and is usually developed in the early stages of learning. Even top canoeists capable of efficient first time canoe rolls, view immersion in hazardous winter spate with concern. Attendant symptoms can include severe fore-head pain, breathing and speaking difficulties as well as visual disturbance, dizziness and disorientation (Baker and Atha, 1977). Clothing with appreciable insulation is recommended when training in cold conditions. Close-fitting wet suits of foam neoprene, vinyl thermal socks, cotton sweat pants and fish-net underwear afford protection against exposure. A wet suit also helps to prevent the lacerations which are possible when capsizing in rapids. In these circumstances, protective headgear is essential. Skill in esquimautage is especially important to allow recovery in traversing in rocky rapids.

The functional curvature of the spine in the direction opposite the paddling side is likely to become permanent where paddling is exclusively on one side of the craft (Fig. 19/3). The dorsal musculature develops asymmetrically as it hypertrophies and shortens on the paddling side while becoming lax and more spare on the opposite side. The spinal column may become slightly scoliotic as a result but corrective exercises can facilitate even bilateral development.

The immediate interface between the individual and equipment used accounts for many of the ailments suffered. Gripping the paddle too tightly can cause blisters on the hand. An incorrect grip may eventually provoke tendovaginitis in the forearm. Boils on the buttocks may follow abrasions and infection after lengthy periods using a wet seat or poorly fitting pants. Lesions and abrasions can also occur on the outside of the legs from contact with the inner side of the craft. Bursitis of the knee may afflict individuals operating from a kneeling position as in C1 rowing.

Pelle (1971) listed myalgia in the forearm muscles and acute or chronic pains in the shoulder joint as typical aggravations. The joint is likely to be unduly strained on the paddling side if improper technique is used. Extended practice of eskimo rolls is a possible cause of sinus infection (Brown, 1971).

SURFING

Risk of injury in surfboarding has been estimated at 1 per 17 500 surfing days – an incidence well below most sports (Allen et al, 1977). The most frequent cause of injury is being hit by a loose board. Injury from one's own board characteristically occurs when surfacing after being thrown into the water. Trauma can include a maxillo-facial fracture, abdominal and eye injuries and varying degrees of renal contusion if struck in the flank. Allen and associates reported a fatality due to severing of the carotid artery by a skeg from a loose board.

Surfboard leashes or 'ding-strings' minimise the chances of injuring others but increase the likelihood of

Fig. 19/3 Asymmetrical muscular development may occur in the power canoeist from repetitively paddling on one side

self-injury. Serious injuries including toe amputation, lacerations and blunt trauma have been reported (McDanal et al, 1976). Near-drowning is another potential hazard (McDanal et al, 1977).

The original Malibu boards, about 3m long and 14 to 16kg weight, were paddled out from a kneeling posture. After one season surfing nodules have been found in the pressure points on the tibial tuberosity. These lesions are generally bilateral and appear to be a bursal cyst of the subcutaneous infrapatellar bursa (Cragg, 1973). A rubber suit extending over the knee prevents trauma. The shorter fibre-glass boards (2m long or less and weighing between 9kg and 5kg) can be paddled prone and avoid this injury. The standard 23cm keel or skeg on most current boards gives better stability but make a loose board more dangerous. The smaller boards produce more stress on the elbow, being more difficult to paddle. Epicondylitis can result and can also occur due to frequent mounting of the board or holding on to it as waves break (McDanal and Anderson, 1977).

The turbulence of large ocean waves forces water into the ear canals of the surfer. Exposure to cold ocean water for many years can be an important aetiological factor in hyperostosis. This usually manifests with a diffuse rounded bony protuberance of the anterior and posterior osseous canal wall (Seftal, 1977). The stimulation of new bony growth is usually bilateral in surfers. Septal estimated that surfing for two hours each day for four to five days a week in water between 10 to 15.5 °C

would take 7 to 10 years to develop moderately severe ear canal hyperostosis.

It is easy to appreciate the attraction of outdoor water based activities especially to urbanised communities and during sun-drenched summers. The seas, lakes and rivers have a characteristic lure that may obscure the dangers inherent in engagement in aquatic recreations. In general, risk factors may be associated with the individual, the craft used, the weather and water conditions or with the particular activity. Responsibility is placed on the shoulders of the participant for thorough prior organisation and sensible judgement.

It is important that the safety procedures outlined by the relevant sports association be carefully adhered to. Life-belts and fail-safe systems should be used where advised as well as appropriate protective clothing. Proficiency in swimming should be developed and at least an elementary knowledge of life-saving is important. Attention is also directed to craft maintenance and courtesy to other water users. Correct technique in the specific skills of the sport should be acquired in the early stages of participation. In the more rigorous water sports, land drills should be executed efficiently to avoid injury promotion and the need for physical conditioning appreciated. With a sound preparation for outdoor water sports, confidence and enjoyment can only be enhanced by a safety conscious approach to participation.

REFERENCES

Allen, R. H., Eiseman, B., Strachley, C. J. and Orloff, B. G. (1977). Surfing injuries at Waikiki. *Journal of the American Medical Association*, **237**, 668–670.

Baker, S. and Atha, J. (1977). A survey of disorientation and other problems among canoeists following immersion in cold water. *British Journal of Sports Medicine*, **11**, 179.

Bass, A. L. (1971). *Acute and subacute injury: water skiing*. In L. A. Larson (ed). *Encyclopedia of sports sciences and medicine*. Macmillan, New York.

Brown, J. M. (1971). *Acute and subacute injury: kayak*. In L. A. Larson (ed). *Encyclopedia of sports sciences and medicine*. Macmillan, New York.

Cragg, J. (1973). Surfers' nodules. *British Journal of Clinical Practice*, **27**, 418–419.

Crampton, B. A. and Tubbs, N. (1977). A survey of sports injuries in Birmingham. *British Journal of Sports Medicine*, **11**, 12–15.

Di Prampero, P. E., Pinera Limas, F. and Sassi, G. (1970). Maximal muscular power, aerobic and anaerobic, in 116 athletes performing in the XIXth Olympic Games in Mexico. *Ergonomics*, **13**, 665–674.

Di Prampero, P. E., Cortili, G., Celentano, F. and Ceretelli, P. (1971). Physiological aspects of rowing. *Journal of Applied Physiology*, **31**, 853–857.

Hagerman, F. C., McKirnon, M. D. and Pompei, J. A. (1975). Maximal oxygen consumption of conditioned and unconditioned oarsmen. *Journal of Sports Medicine and Physical Fitness*, **15**, 43–48.

Ishiko, T. (1971). *Biomechanics of sport*. In *Medicine and sport*, Vol. 6: Biomechanics 11. Karger, Basel.

Izeki, J. (1973). Statistical observation on sudden deaths in sport. *British Journal of Sports Medicine*, **7**, 172–176.

Jackson, R. C. and Secher, N. H. (1976). The aerobic demands of rowing in two Olympic rowers. *Medicine and Science in Sports*, **8**, 168–170.

McDanal, C. E., Anderson, B. S. and Sims, J. K. (1976). Ding-string injuries. *New England Journal of Medicine*, **295**, 287.

McDanal, C. E. and Anderson, B. (1977). Surfer's elbow. *Hawaii Medical Journal*, **36**, 108–109.

McDanal, C. E., Rosario, M. D., McDanal, J. O., McNamara, J. J., Anderson, B. S., Springer, W. N. and Sims, J. K. (1977). Near drowning from ding-string surfboarding; a case report. *Journal of the American Medical Association*, **238**, 398.

Moncur, J. (1973). A study of fatalities during sport in Scotland (1969). *British Journal of Sports Medicine*, **7**, 162–163.

Moore, A. T. (1964). *Water skiing*. In J. R. Armstrong and W. E. Tucker (eds). *Injury in sport*. Staples Press, London.

Nowacki, P., Krause, R. and Adam, K. (1969). Maximal oxygen uptake by the rowing crew winning the Olympic Gold Medal 1968. *Pflugers Archiv*, **312**, 66–67.

O'Brien, M., Bonner, F. J. and Bonner, J. F. (1978). Electromyographic evaluation of a water skiing injury. *British Journal of Sports Medicine*, **12**, 142–144.

Paterson, D. P. (1971). Water skiing injuries. *Practitioner*, **206**, 655–661.

Pelle, L. (1971). *Acute and subacute injury: canoeing*. In L. A. Larson (ed). *Encyclopedia of sports sciences and medicine*. Macmillan, New York.

Ramey, J. R. (1974). Intrarectal tear with bleeding from water skiing accident. *Journal of Florida Medical Association*, **61**, 162.

Reid, J. G., Kopp, P. M. and Verhoeven, A. P. (1978). *Impact forces on water ski jumpers*. In E. Asmussen and K. Jørgensen (eds). *Biomechanics* V1-B. University Park Press, Baltimore.

Schwartz, R. A. (1971). *Acute and subacute injury: rowing*. In L. A. Larson (ed). *Encyclopedia of sports sciences and medicine*. Macmillan, New York.

Secher, N. H. (1975). Isometric rowing strength of experienced and inexperienced oarsmen. *Medicine and Science in Sports*, **7**, 280–283.

Seftal, D. M. (1977). Ear canal hyperostosis – surfer's ear. *Archives of Otolaryngology*, **103**, 58–61.

Sleight, M. W. (1974). Speedboat propeller injuries. *British Medical Journal*, **2**, 427–429.

CHAPTER 20

Background to injuries in swimming and diving

T. REILLY BA, DPE, MSc, PhD, MIBiol and STANLEY MILES CB, MSc, MD, FRCP, FRCS

Water constitutes an alien environment for man whether his sport or recreation is on the surface or underneath it. Reports testify to the inherent hazards in underwater endurance records due to anoxia (Craig, 1962; Dumitriou and Hamilton, 1964), while drowning can occur in shallow water and lung rupture is possible at 2m depth.

Bradycardia is demonstrated on immersion in water; Irving (1963) reporting a decrease from 110 beats min^{-1} to 36 beats min^{-1} in humans. It is reflexly initiated and represents an important adaptation to diving mediated by cardiovascular control centres in the brain.

Apart from drowning there are three major determinants of injury in the water. The first is associated with the physical laws of pressure, the second is occasioned by the barrier presented by the water surface on impact while the third is thermo-regulatory needs of the organism. These factors, along with those specific to the activity are now considered in swimming and diving.

SWIMMING

Swimming is a relatively injury-free sport and was found to be the safest of 11 surveyed in four northern England counties (Weightman and Browne, 1975). Over one year, 64 per cent of the clubs reported no injured members. As it does not involve the vigorous anti-gravity work of locomotor sports, swimming tends to escape the musculo-tendonous injuries of repetitively elevating and lowering body mass. For this reason it serves usefully in the rehabilitation of other athletes. Since bodyweight in water is reduced to only a few kilograms, swimming is also a common exercise for the physically handicapped.

Injuries associated with contact sports are found in the swimming pool sports of water polo and octopush. The former is often played by competitive swimmers. It occasions nasal and facial injuries from being hit by the ball and elbow injuries associated with poor throwing action.

Top swimmers tend to be younger than élite participants in other sports. Training demands are great, distances of 15 to 20km per day being covered by international competitors. These are characterised by high aerobic capacities especially when measured in a swimming flume (Holmer, 1978) as the activity engages practically all major muscle groups of the body. With the strenuous regimes undertaken particularly by young females the conclusion of the detailed Swedish study of Åstrand and associates (1963) that intensive swimming has no gynaecological ill-effects must be reassuring to parents.

Since many injuries are common to the various swimming strokes, the trauma to different anatomical locations are considered in sequence.

Head injuries

Common head injuries include bruises and cuts (Weightman and Browne, 1975). Conjunctivitis was found common after swimming in chlorinated water in girls aged 12 to 16 (Åstrand et al, 1963). This can be avoided by using suitably designed goggles or less chlorination. Water purified by ozone rather than chlorine is increasingly accepted by swimmers.

A frequent complaint is otitis externa, an inflammatory disease of the auricle and external auditory canal. Essentially, it is a skin condition attributable to dermatitis or psoriasis. Skin scales and other debris from dermatitis accumulate in the ear, tending to absorb water and affect the integrity of the lining. Similarly wax may partially block the auditory canal and prevent drainage. Infection may be primarily bacterial, fungal or both. The most important aetiological factor is prolonged exposure of the canal to water. Water temperatures higher than 20°C (68°F) increase the incidence of otitis externa in children swimming regularly especially in high humidity (Munro, 1978). Drying the ears with cotton swabs after training provides protection. Jones (1971) outlined a series of alcohol dilutions for preventing the condition.

Shoulder

The main power in swimming comes from the shoulder girdle except in the breast stroke where the leg kicks are at least as important as the arm strokes. It is not surprising to find the most frequent site of musculo-tendonous injury is the shoulder. Tendinitis of this joint is most common on free style and backstroke (Merino and Llobet, 1978). The complete rotation of the arm in these strokes makes the supraspinatus muscle most vulnerable. Injury to the trapezius alone is found in breaststrokers who do not suffer from the tendinitis associated with 'swimmer's shoulder' (Kendall, 1964).

Kennedy et al (1978) reported impingement injuries involving both supraspinatus and biceps tendons in free style and butterfly swimmers leading to degenerative changes in those tendons. They are reflected in symptoms of pressure impingement on the rotator cuff as the swimmer approaches the phase of maximal abduction in each style. Discomfort is first noticed after swimming; it may progress to pain during and after training and finally to pain which is severe enough to affect stroke performance. The swimmer could still train using the style that does not cause pain. Alternatively, temporary minor alterations in hand entry angle, height of recovery or training mileage may work. Kennedy (1978) reported that in swimmers resistant to conservative therapy, transcutaneous nerve stimulation can be successful. Dominguez (1978) reported relief of chronic disabling symptoms that failed to respond to prolonged conservative remedies by resection of the coracoacromial ligament.

Prevention may lie in a good set of stretching exercises for the shoulder girdle prior to training and a long warm-up of easy distance swimming before any sprinting. Strengthening of the shoulder muscles would also seem to be important.

'Apprehension' shoulder is found frequently in back-strokers (Kennedy et al, 1978). The patient has immediate misgivings, anxiety and pain in the acute phase of the backstroke turn. This is due to dislocating the humeral head onto the rim of the glenoid cavity with the shoulder in full abduction and external rotation as the hand is used to push off the wall. The format of the turn can be modified if the apprehension becomes unbearable.

Back

Butterfly swimmers appear to be the most affected by low back pain because of the mechanical stress on the lumbar spine. This is due to the vigorous extension of the back and the strong dolphin kick. This stroke incidentally is most costly from the standpoint of mechanical efficiency (Holmer, 1974). Well-trained butterfly specialists seem to have stronger spinal extensors than spine flexors, attributable to the special breathing action and the dolphin kick (Mutoh, 1978). It is assumed that the butterfly stroke requires vigorous spine extensors which would cause increased lumbar

lordosis, this in turn giving rise to low back pain. Mutoh considered that since specific training may start at an early age before muscular development is complete, repeated trauma to the lumbar spine may cause spondylolysis or intervertebral disc degeneration.

Strengthening the muscles of the lower back is recommended in butterfliers. This can be achieved by appropriate weight training. Good spinal flexibility should also be developed. It is further advised that other swimming styles should be included in the workouts of specialists in butterfly.

Lower limb

Knee complaints are typically related to the breast stroke. There is a constant build up in tension in the tibial collateral ligament as the forces in knee extension, valgus stress and terminal external rotatory stress are applied in sequence in the whip-kick of the stroke (Kennedy, 1978). The result is a chronic ligamentous irritation and the kick may need to be modified so there is less external rotation of the tibia. Alternatively the breaststroker may introduce other styles into the training programme.

Another injury associated with breast stroke, especially in unfit individuals, is straining of the coronary ligaments of the medial meniscus. This results from the forced separation of the medial articular surface of the tibia from the medial femoral condyle (Kendall, 1964). Strain of the adductor longus is also a feature of this stroke because of the powerful adduction of both legs from a position of wide abduction, concomitant with full extension of hips, knees and ankles. This injury is usually unilateral.

Particularly with the backstroke and flutter kick, inflammation of the extensor tendons along the dorsum of the feet occasionally occurs. The cause is chronic overuse in the extreme plantar flexed position. It is relieved by local measures and modification of the kick.

Hand

Turning may produce traumatic synovitis of the interphalangeal joints following contact with the wall with the fingers extended. Sprains of the wrist and flexors of this joint occur more commonly, particularly in breaststrokers (Kendall, 1964). Attention is directed towards skills' practice in executing the turn. Backstrokers are more likely to misjudge the finish and collide with the end of the pool than other stroke specialists.

MARATHON SWIMMING

Long distance swimmers present different anthropometric features from their Olympic counterparts. The typical male channel swimmer has about 22 per cent bodyweight as fat compared with 10 per cent in top swimming pool competitors (Pugh et al, 1960). Normally large depots of body fat are not conducive to high performance achievement in sport but the long distance swimmer provides an exception. Firstly, since bodyweight is buoyed up in water the excess mass as fat does not impair performance. Secondly, as almost half the body's fat is laid down subcutaneously this layer provides useful insulation in immersion. Because females contain on average more body fat than men it is hardly surprising that many of the outstanding marathon swimmers are women. Marathon swimmers tend also to be muscular, as muscles provide the strength needed for great endurance and insulation additional to fat.

The average human is not equipped for spending lengthy periods in water so that hypothermia is the main danger in marathon swims. These may be swimming pool endurance attempts, where cold stress is minimised, or cross-channel, cross-lake and ocean swims. To supplement the insulation properties of their body fat, channel swimmers often coat their skin with grease or lanolin for further protection. The swimmer also takes the rigours of weather into consideration in timing attempts. The higher the water temperature the better, since heat is lost by conduction and convection much more rapidly in water than in air. Where record attempts must be abandoned because of cold exposure, further heat loss must be prevented while warm drinks and glucose assist heat production. In all circumstances alcohol must be avoided as it promotes vasodilation of the skin blood vessels with further loss of heat.

The Catalina Channel, between Catalina Island and southern California, and the English Channel are two of the more famous routes. These crossings require a coordinated team approach. A support boat accompanying the swimmer takes responsibility for navigation in ocean or channel swims. A captain familiar with local waters is needed – coach and swimmer depending on his advice before setting the time of the attempt. American swimmers are usually accompanied by two expert paddlers to help guide the swimmer in following the boat.

Preparation for professional marathon swims involves year round training. In the off-season six hours may be spent daily in the water six days a week, later increased to nine to ten hours per day. This can be split between two work-outs as well as between pool and ocean training. As the major events approach ocean swims up to 45km may be covered.

Though in ultra-long duration exercise fat is the preferred source of fuel, ocean swimmers currently use the carbohydrate loading regime employed by marathon runners the week before competition. Apart from its benefits in boosting energy stores it may also help in retaining thermo-equilibrium. Fluid intake is important: Klafs and Lyon (1978) reported that a fluid-electrolyte drink works well with American swimmers. Though these do not feel like eating much during activity, biscuits help to overcome the salty sea-water taste.

HIGH DIVING

Albrand and Corkill (1976) described what they called a 'summer epidemic in young men' of broken necks from diving accidents. Typically the victims dived headlong into shallow water, the depth of which they had not checked. In some cases damage was caused by rocks hidden in shadows below the surface. The carelessness of victims is well exemplified by Burke's (1972) case of a youth who dived off a notice board warning swimmers not to dive because of the water's shallowness. Accident locations include rivers and garden pools as well as resorts. Indoor swimming pool supervisors are well aware of the hazard if boisterous youngsters attempt to dive without suitable tuition. The inexperienced tend not to lock the thumbs so that the arms part on entry with the head unprotected against the force of the water.

Competitive diving is a short duration sport, the entire performance from commencement of the diver's approach to surfacing after entry occupying less than 10 seconds whether from a 3m springboard or 10m platform. For this reason Olympic divers tend to have much lower aerobic power values than their swimming colleagues and are substantially lighter (Shephard, 1978). The highboard event demands jumping power, agility and gymnastic ability in contrast to the intense cyclical actions of the swimmer. The more compact frame allows the diver to rotate more quickly in spinning aerial movements. Since style is an integral component of performance which is rated by a panel of judges on a 21 point scale, the execution of the dive must be graceful as well as technically meritorious. Evaluation is on the basis of the approach, the take-off, technique and grace in the air, and entry into the water.

At take-off the diver must achieve height off the board. In the air, turning decreases the body's moment of inertia and increases its angular velocity: this enables the diver to somersault, possibly with a complete or partial twist, before preparation for a controlled entry. In emerging from a tucked position to enter the water at about $50 kmh^{-1}$ fully extended, the angular velocity is reduced as the extension of the body increases its moment of inertia. In a backward dive the performer swings the arms upward and backward prior to leaving the board while a piked aerial position involves shoulder and hip flexion with the knees straight and toes pointed.

Good technique is paramount to successful and safe performance. Many of the aerial acrobatic movements can be practised on a trampoline where a safety harness can be employed. This avoids the hazards associated with repeated impact on water and permits greater devotion to particular manoeuvres than in a similar period over water. A critical safety aspect is to ensure that alignment prior to entry into the water is correct. For this the diver needs good shoulder flexibility as well as flexibility in back and hip extension and plantar flexion. Flexibility in trunk flexion should be developed to facilitate the piked and tucked positions in the air.

Other protective measures include strengthening the muscles that open and close the piked and tucked positions: these muscle groups are also used to maintain body alignment and avoid inadequate or too much rotation before the rigid body enters the water. Isometric exercises are recommended for all muscle groups which keep the body straight on entry and include arm, shoulder, legs and trunk muscles. These contractions can be practised while hanging from a horizontal bar. Lee (1971) proposed that youngsters should not do any high diving until they could hold a handstand and were strong enough to clasp the hands so firmly overhead that the coach is unable to forcefully and suddenly separate the hands externally. The clasped hands and extended arms serve to protect the diver by separating the water and allowing the head and remainder of the body to follow their path. The stomach muscles must be developed sufficiently to keep the back straight on striking the water, so preventing hyperextension of the back.

A disc injury may result if a sway back occurs prior to entry. Groher (1973) reported degenerative changes of the small spinal joints in divers resulting from the strain on the lumbar spine after imperfectly executed dives with hyperflexion or hyperextension on entry. The incidence of dorsal pain was less in the younger divers suggesting fatigue fractures in persistent microtrauma to be responsible. Violent movement of the body into the piked or tucked position while in the air may also cause lower back pain. Blast injuries to the chest wall and lungs may follow hitting the water absolutely flat from the high board. This typically happens with the inexperienced who may land either on the stomach or back. The abrupt pressure changes may produce severe shock, bruising of the chest wall and bleeding from the nose. Broken pulmonary blood vessels are usually reflected in the diver's spitting blood. Darda (1971) included sprained shoulders and

hands, and black eyes among injuries on landing from failure to lock the upper limb joints correctly. Foot first entries from the 10m platform may cause sprained ankles.

The most serious injuries quite plainly occur on entry into the water. Faults earlier in the dive may be to blame while various injuries can occur earlier on also. Wrist fractures may result from hitting the board with the hands, and sprained ankles are experienced from loss of balance on either forward or backward take-off from the springboard (Darda, 1971). Head injuries may also occur from hitting the board or platform if descent is too near the apparatus.

The diver is by no means immune to soft tissue injuries. Shoulder injuries can accompany lower back strain from the jarring of repeated forward take-offs in platform diving. Shin splints may be caused by constant use of poorly mounted non-flexible springboards or excessive bouncing on flexible springboards (Darda, 1971). The flexors of the forearm, triceps and the trapezius are particularly prone to hyperextension injuries from failure to adopt the correct entry posture (Kendall, 1964). According to Darda pulled deltoids are common in beginners while triceps injuries are typically found in the more mature competitors. Quadriceps tendon strains and quadriceps strains periodically occur so that this functional unit should be developed by appropriate strength training.

Probably the most publicised diving trauma on impact is ear drum rupture. This can occur in progressing to an advanced aerial twist or in a timing error. In major competitions gently bubbling water around the point of entry provides a visual reference to help the timing. Shephard (1972) reported a ruptured ear drum in a Canadian highboard diver, believing the initial collapse of the Eustachian tube to have developed during aircraft flight to the competition. Ear irritations and infections as found in swimmers also prevail. Special attention is directed to the care of ear conditions and sinusitis.

SKIN DIVING

Man cannot breathe underwater and any unaided excursions beneath the surface are limited in time by the need to hold the breath. Normally this is for two or three minutes only. Experienced professional oriental pearl divers may perform as many as 30 dives an hour to 20m, even in temperatures as cold as 10°C (50°F) (Rahn, 1965).

A further limitation is pressure. Though human tissues like those of a fish are incompressible and unaffected by depth, the human body contains air filled spaces – the respiratory system, the middle ear and the sinuses. When man descends under water, the air must reduce in volume according to Boyle's Law if it is to remain in pressure equilibrium with surrounding tissues, which it must to avoid damage. The sinuses and middle ear connect with the respiratory system whose response is the key factor in diving.

The normal atmospheric pressure at the ocean surface is 760mmHg or 1atm. The same pressure is exerted by a column of sea water of 10.07m (or 10.33m fresh water). Thus a man under 10 metres of water will be subject to a pressure of 2atm, for practical purposes, and for every further 10 metres he descends a further atmosphere of pressure will be added.

This fact puts a further limit on the potential of the skin diver who goes under water without any artificial aid. An average man entering the water would take a maximum inspiration of say 4.5 litres. This together with the residual lung volume of 1.5 litres would give him a total lung volume of 6 litres at the surface. If he descended to 30m he would be subjected to a pressure of 4atm, a fourfold increase. If the air is to remain at the same pressure as the surrounding water its volume must be reduced to 1.5 litres, i.e. to the residual volume by contraction of the chest wall. This is a change from full inspiration to full expiration while breath holding. On return to the surface the chest re-expands.

Any attempt to go deeper than this is dangerous. If the chest volume cannot further decrease, air in the lungs will remain at the same pressure while that of surrounding tissues and blood will increase with that of the surrounding water. This 'thoracic squeeze' is accompanied by pulmonary oedema, congestion and haemorrhage.

Similarly, if the links between the sinuses and the respiratory system, or the Eustachian tubes are blocked, equalisation of pressure during the dive is impossible and excessive pain and physical damage, e.g. a ruptured ear drum, may occur.

For the skin diver, breath holding ability and pressure changes put a time limit of two to three minutes and a depth limit of 30 metres on each dive. Furthermore, and this is true for all forms of diving, an ability to clear the ears to equalise pressure in the middle ear with that of the external ear is essential and easily achieved with practice. Freedom from chronic or acute infections of the upper respiratory tract is mandatory. Ear plugs should not be used as these may be forced into the aural canals. If goggles or helmets are used these must have facilities for equalising the pressure within to that of the surrounding water.

Breath holding is limited in man by a rise in the partial pressure of CO_2 (PCO_2) in the alveolar gas and arterial blood and a fall in O_2 partial pressure (PO_2). Of these two the former is more important. Without it a fall in PO_2 may depress the respiratory centre before it responds to the peripheral low PO_2 stimulus and allow anoxic unconsciousness to prevail. Because of this it is possible to prolong breath holding time by vigorous hyperventilation which washes out the CO_2 then in the alveoli and delays the ultimate stimulation of its re-accumulation. Under water there is an increase in PO_2 due to the depth increase in respiratory gases so that more is available to maintain consciousness during the prolonged breath holding period. Unfortunately, when the increasing PCO_2 does promote the demand to re-breathe and the diver turns to the surface, the ascent reduces the pressure of the respiratory gases and in consequence the PO_2 on which consciousness depends. If this is lost, the diver drowns. Many lives have been lost among enthusiastic spear fishermen following hyperventilation prior to the underwater dive. This practice must be understood and condemned.

Skin diving equipment is usually confined to simple masks and fins. Additionally, a snorkel tube may be used for breathing near the surface. Masks incorporating safety glass are recommended to avoid breaking glass on hard underwater objects. Forceful clenching of the teeth on the mouth of the snorkel may result in tempero-mandibular joint disorder causing earache as referred pain (Williams and Sperryn, 1976). Coral cuts and abrasions on sharp coral edges are common. A spear gun or hand spear must be used with care as these can easily penetrate arms, legs and abdomen. Injuries from marine life can vary from jelly-fish stings to mutilation from predatory fish depending on the locality.

SCUBA DIVING

To overcome the restrictions of breath holding and increasing pressure with depth, apparatus must be provided to ensure a continuous supply of air, or other breathing mixture, at a pressure equal to that of the water in which the diver is operating. Air is a mixture of 21% oxygen and 79% nitrogen. Both these gases are soluble in the blood and diffuse throughout the tissues. When air is breathed at atmospheric pressure as on land the oxygen and nitrogen dissolved in the tissues are in equilibrium with the partial pressures of those gases in the lungs. At depths where the air must be supplied at increased pressure the increased partial pressures of the two gases in the lungs drive more of each into the blood and tissues. For safe diving therefore any adverse effects of these two gases must be considered as must also the effects of changes in pressure and volume. These changes and possible countermeasures have been described in detail by Miles and Mackay (1976) and are listed as follows:

Pressure and volume changes (Boyle's Law)

The limiting effects of these changes on the skin diver have already been described. To overcome them for other divers, air must either be pumped down from the surface to reach him at his working pressure or be carried by him in cylinders from which demand values controlled by the pressure of the surrounding water will deliver air at the correct pressure. The compression of air needed means that at depth the volume of gas delivered is less than it would be if released at the surface, i.e. the greater the depth the diver is working the shorter will be the life of the supply cylinder. Careful monitoring of available supply and its rate of use is therefore important.

Density

Increasing the pressure of a gas increases proportionally its density. Air breathed at a depth of 30m will, for example, be four times as dense as that breathed at the surface. This means a great increase in effort by the respiratory muscles to move this air in and out of the lungs due to the resultant increase in resistance of denser air in the respiratory tract. To overcome this may need a conscious effort if CO_2 retention is to be avoided. The experienced diver will control his breathing pattern and ensure that his work load is regulated to avoid short bursts of extreme activity. Competitive sports involving time, speed and supreme effort underwater are physiologically unacceptable. The game of 'octopush' is carried out in the relatively shallow water of the swimming pool.

The professional diver who must work at deep depths overcomes the density problem by replacing the nitrogen in the air he breathes with helium, a much lighter gas.

Nitrogen narcosis

As with increasing depth, nitrogen is breathed at a greater partial pressure so more of this gas dissolves in the blood and diffuses into the tissues. Here it has a marked narcotic effect on the central nervous system producing a deterioration of function with slowing of mental processes and intellectual function (Bennett, 1972).

The first mild sensation of euphoria (raptures of the deep) is felt at about 30m but there are considerable individual variations. The scuba diver who is largely responsible for his own safety should limit his depth to 50m for this reason. The commercial 'Standard Diver' with his helmet and heavy boots may go much deeper because his safety is wholly dependent upon the surface attendants who pump air down to him and are able to pull him up if things go wrong. His skills however do diminish with increasing depth.

The deep diving professional can avoid the hazards of nitrogen narcosis, as he does of density, by replacing the nitrogen in his air with the less narcotic helium.

Oxygen toxicity

To breathe pure oxygen on the surface will in several hours produce chronic pulmonary irritation but at a depth of 10m, where twice as much would dissolve in blood and tissues, the threshold of oxygen poisoning is reached earlier. As little as 20 minutes' exposure would produce lip twitching and epileptiform convulsions. This fact very much limits the use of pure oxygen to relatively shallow depths and, in general, it is not acceptable for sports diving though it may be used by cave explorers to pass through flooded links between compartments. 'Assault' swimmers may use it in wartime for planting mines on enemy ships because it can be used as a fully closed circuit with canisters of soda lime absorbing the CO_2. As such, there is no give away stream of escaping bubbles.

Since the effect is due to increased oxygen partial pressure it follows that if air is breathed at increasing depth a time will come when the PO_2 therein will reach the danger limit. This in fact occurs at about 100m when oxygen poisoning could become a hazard.

The problem is overcome in deep diving by reducing the proportion of oxygen in the mixture breathed to ensure an acceptable PO_2. For example, at a depth of 200m a mixture of 4% oxygen in helium would be acceptable.

Decompression

The problems of descent described above can be controlled without difficulty. The greatest problem is that of returning safely to the surface.

During the descent the gases breathed, oxygen, nitrogen and by the deep divers, helium, because of increased pressures pass through the lungs to the blood and tissues until ultimately – and this may take many hours – a new equilibrium is established and no further transfer takes place. During this period, however, the absorbing gases can *only* enter the body through the lungs but when the pressure is released during the final ascent the resulting pressure reduction is felt throughout the body. When this occurs the dissolved gases must come out of solution. Although much of this can take place by release from the blood as it passes through the lungs this may not be sufficient to prevent the excess gas coming out of solution in various parts of the body with actual bubble formation. This may have disastrous results. It is essential therefore to ensure that return to the surface is sufficiently controlled to avoid this happening and that the excess gases can leave via the lungs. In practice, oxygen, because it is used up in

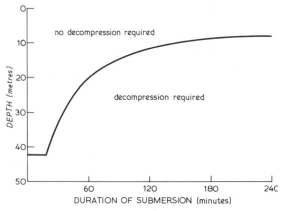

Fig. 20/1 Time limits for decompression at various depths

the body's metabolic activity, is not a problem. Nitrogen and helium however are, the former only being of concern to the sports diver.

In practice it is found that for the depths within the normal range of the sports diver it is possible to surface directly and safely from depth provided that the time at depth is limited according to the curve in Figure 20/1. Thus it is possible to remain at 50m for seven minutes or 20m for 45 minutes and so on. If these times are exceeded the ascent must be interrupted by a series of pauses (or stops) according to a calculated schedule. Generally speaking it is possible to ascend two-thirds of the way to the surface before the first stop is necessary and thereafter the stops may increase in length at 3m intervals as the surface is approached. Diving manuals contain tables which give divers a profile for a safe ascent according to depth of dive and time on the bottom. Where repeated dives are made the deepest depth is used in calculation and bottom times added together, though if the interval exceeds two hours modifications are allowed, these too being found in the manuals.

It is obvious that for deep and lengthy dives a great deal of time must be spent in decompression. In commercial practice advantage is taken of the fact that a new equilibrium of saturation with gas under pressure is achieved in time and divers may then remain at this level almost indefinitely. By living for many weeks in pressurised cabins they are able to carry out repeated diving sorties for one single, though prolonged, decompression routine at the end of the period of saturation. The only application this technique of saturation diving may have to sport is in the provision of some form of pressurised underwater holiday camp in attractive under sea areas such as the Australian Barrier Reef.

This is still a dream of the future but not without possibilities.

It is, however, during periods of ascent and decompression that most of the diving problems occur. These can vary from the acute effects of burst lung to a wide range of decompression sickness.

DECOMPRESSION SICKNESS

Ever since diving became a practical proposition decompression sickness has been an unwelcome complication. Pains following the dive, usually in joints or limbs and often crippling, were known as 'the bends', and were an accepted hazard. Since the introduction of decompression tables, following the work of Haldane (1922), the problem has been largely brought under control and today, provided the diver sticks to established codes of practice, there is little to fear.

In order of severity and danger the following problems may present according to the extent and distribution of bubble formation.

'*Niggles*' are minor pains or discomfort in and around joints often with fleeting mottley rashes. These are neither severe nor significant and respond to palliative treatment without re-compression.

'*Bends*' are the more severe joint pains and the commonest form of decompression sickness. They usually occur quite soon after leaving the water but may be delayed for several hours. For treatment they need a planned programme of re-compression in a suitable chamber, the object being to decrease the size of bubble by pressurisation and facilitate dispersal by a prolonged period of decompression.

'*Staggers*' is the name used when there is involvement of the spinal cord or brain with varying degrees of muscular or sensory paralysis. A paraplegia is not uncommon. These spinal or cerebral 'bends' are the serious results of bubbles released within the brain or cord. If not treated early permanent disabilities may result. More intensive therapeutic schedules are needed and in the final stages of decompression oxygen may be used.

'*Chokes*' describe the irritating cough and respiratory distress which may result from bubble formation within the pulmonary alveolar circulation. This is usually temporary and needs little treatment other than rest.

Bone necrosis may occur at the ends of long bones and occasionally produce a severe arthritis. It is unknown in the sports diver but common in the caisson worker or deep diver who is careless in the application of diving schedules. It is a delayed condition presenting even years after exposure.

Finally there is the dangerous condition of '*burst lung*' or *pulmonary barotrauma*, first described as a hazard for crew men escaping from a sunken submarine. It is a real problem for the diver who must discard a faulty breathing apparatus and surface unaided. In so doing the natural reaction is to hold the breath until the surface is reached. Air confined in the chest during ascent cannot expand freely as surrounding pressure is reduced so that as the surface is reached there is an excessive intrapulmonary pressure. When the diver relaxes his chest muscles there is sudden chest expansion and release of air. Lung tissue may be torn and some air pass into surrounding tissue producing emphysema or, more significantly, enter the pulmonary circulation through torn blood vessels. Such bubbles will pass directly to the left side of the heart and from there enter the arterial circulation. Such air emboli may reach and obstruct the vessels of the coronary or cerebral circulation almost immediately causing unconsciousness or even death. Treatment is instant re-pressurisation. To avoid the risk of burst lung the diver (or submariner) should relax during ascent. The expanding air can then escape as a prolonged and comfortable expiration.

Diving manuals include therapeutic recompression tables to meet all these emergencies but expert medical supervision is also needed. This can usually be obtained from Naval Diving Schools or established commercial diving centres. Many sports diving clubs have experienced doctors available. In emergencies where a pressure chamber cannot be reached an unhappy and unsatisfactory compromise is to return the diver to the water to a depth as near as possible to what would produce the needed therapeutic pressure. If a burst lung victim cannot be immediately recompressed he should be placed in a head down position on his left side to encourage air bubbles to gravitate away from the coronary and cerebral circulations.

SAFETY

From the above it will be realised that certain guidelines are needed for the safety of the sports diver:

1. He should be a good swimmer.
2. He should never dive alone.
3. His diving apparatus should be maintained with great care. Its efficient working is essential to survival.
4. He should follow closely the instructions and schedules appropriate to the dive.
5. When a dive is planned the availability of the nearest pressure chamber and a source of expert advice should be known.
6. 'Free ascent' should not be practised unless

facilities for immediate recompression of casualties are available.

In well planned recreational diving today decompression sickness is a rare event. It must be kept that way by training and safe practice.

DROWNING

The end result of any mishap in water is frequently drowning. On land, when consciousness is lost by accident, death is rare and perhaps only 1 in 100 will die. In water, loss of consciousness has a death rate of 1 in 3.

The physiology and treatment of drowning is well documented (Practitioner, 1979). All divers should become experts in rescue and resuscitation both respiratory and cardiac.

In addition to the mishaps peculiar to diving already described, other contingencies may occur. Drowning may follow attacks in the water of acute respiratory illness, epilepsy, heart attack and physical injury, e.g. shark attack, cuts from motor boat propellers or spear guns. It thus follows that the diver must at all times be in perfect health. Periodic medical examination with chest x-ray is part of the diver's way of life and freedom from temporary illness at the time of the dive is essential, particularly respiratory illness. Even a common cold is unacceptable.

THE 'SPORTS DIVER'

Though often regarded as a sport, diving does not really offer competition. It is a satisfying and health giving recreation but most of all it gives access to a completely new environment opening up wide opportunities of cultural interest. These include underwater photography, marine biology, fishing, archeology and treasure hunting in old wrecks. Above all because of the absolute dependency of the diver on his attendants and team mates it fosters a rewarding spirit of understanding comradeship.

It is obvious that swimming and diving present grave dangers if indulged in recklessly. Each of the activities covered has its own preventive protocol and safety check-list which should be followed. Emergencies are always possible so to have club members skilled in life-saving and first aid is essential.

Injury considerations are embracing ranging from fatality on the one hand to fungus infection on the other. Infections such as athlete's foot are water borne and thrive in damp areas such as exist around swimming pool edges. These can be extremely irritating whether as acute inflammation or a chronic condition with reddening and scaling of skin. Plantar warts or verrucae may be picked up easily in similar conditions. Feet should always be dried carefully while an antifungoid powder aids prevention. As with the whole range of water sports, attention to personal hygiene and a safety consciousness are rewarded by uninterrupted enjoyment of one of nature's abundant assets.

REFERENCES

Albrand, O. W. and Corkill, G. (1976). Broken necks from diving accidents: a summer epidemic in young men. *American Journal of Sports Medicine*, **4**, 107–110.

Åstrand, P. O., Engstrom, L., Eriksson, B. O., Karlberg, P., Nylander, I., Saltin, B. and Thoren, C. (1963). Girl swimmers. *Acta Paediatrica*, Supplementum, **147**, 1–75.

Bennett, P. B. (1972). *Nitrogen narcosis*. In L. Zanelli (ed). *British Sub-Aqua Club diving manual*. Riverside Press, London.

Burke, D. C. (1972). Spinal cord injuries from water sports. *Medical Journal of Australia*, **2**, 1190–1194.

Craig, A. B. (1962). Underwater swimming and drowning. *Journal of Sports Medicine and Physical Fitness*, **2**, 23–26.

Darda, G. E. (1971). *Physical activity: sports, games and exercises: diving*. In L. A. Larson (ed). *Encyclopedia of sports sciences and medicine*. Macmillan, New York.

Dominguez, R. H. (1978). *Coracoacromial ligament resection for swimmer's shoulder*. In B. Eriksson and B. Furberg (eds). *Swimming medicine* IV. University Park Press, Baltimore.

Dumitriou, A. P. and Hamilton, F. G. (1964). Underwater blackout – a mechanism of drowning. *American Academy of General Practice*, **29**, 123–125.

Groher, W. (1973). Low back pain in divers. *British Journal of Sports Medicine*, **7**, 100–102.

Haldane, J. S. (1922). *Respiration*. Clarendon Press, Oxford.

Holmer, I. (1974). Physiology of swimming man. *Acta Physiologica Scandinavica*, Supplementum **407**.

Holmer, I. (1978). Physiological adjustments to swimming. *Geneeskunde en Sport*, **11**, 22–26.

Irving, L. (1963). Bradycardia in human divers. *Journal of Applied Physiology*, **18**, 489–491.

Jones, E. H. (1971). Prevention of 'swimming pool ear'. *Laryngoscope*, **81**, 731–733.

Kendall, P. H. (1964). *Swimming*. In J. R. Armstrong and W. E. Tucker (eds). *Injuries in sport*. Staples, London.

Kennedy, J. C. (1978). *Orthopaedic manifestations*. In B. Eriksson and B. Furberg (eds). *Swimming medicine* IV. University Park Press, Baltimore.

Kennedy, J. C., Hawkins, R. and Krissof, W. B. (1978). Orthopaedic manifestations of swimming. *American Journal of Sports Medicine*, **6**, 309–322.

Klafs, C. E. and Lyon, M. J. (1978). *The female athlete*. C. V. Mosby, St Louis.

Lee, S. (1971). *Clinical examination: diving*. In L. A. Larson (ed). *Encyclopedia of sports sciences and medicine*. Macmillan, New York.

Merino, J. P. and Llobet, M. (1978). *Insertion tendonitis among swimmers*. In B. Eriksson and B. Furberg (eds). *Swimming medicine* IV. University Park Press, Baltimore.

Miles, S. and Mackay, D. E. (1976). *Underwater medicine*. Adlard Coles, London.

Munro, J. G. C. (1978). Otitis externa in swimmers. *Australian Journal of Sports Medicine*, **10**, 26–29.

Mutoh, Y. (1978). *Low back pain in butterfliers*. In B. Eriksson and B. Furberg (eds). *Swimming medicine* IV. University Park Press, Baltimore.

Pugh, L. G. C. E., Edholm, O. G., Fox, R. H., Wolff, H. S., Harvey, G. R., Hammond, W. H., Tanner, J. M. and Whitehouse, R. H. (1960). A physiological study of channel swimming. *Clinical Science and Molecular Medicine*, **19**, 257–273.

Rahn, H. (1965). *Physiology of breath hold diving and the Ama of Japan*. Publication 1341, National Academy of Sciences, Washington, DC.

Shephard, R. J. (1972). *Alive man: the physiology of physical activity*. C. C. Thomas, Springfield, Illinois.

Shephard, R. J. (1978). *Human physical working capacity*. Cambridge University Press, London.

Symposium on drowning (1979). *The Practitioner*, April and May issues.

Weightman, D. and Browne, R. C. (1975). Injuries in eleven selected sports. *British Journal of Sports Medicine*, **9**, 136–141.

Williams, J. G. P. and Sperryn, P. N. (1976). *Sports medicine*. Edward Arnold, London.

CHAPTER 21

Injuries in combat sports

G. R. McLATCHIE MB, ChB, FRCS, CPSG

The popular combat sports considered in this chapter are boxing, karate, wrestling and judo. Although these sports produce relatively few injuries compared to others, until recently karate has had a high incidence of disabling injury (Weightman and Browne, 1975; McLatchie, 1976; McLatchie and Fitzgerald, 1979). The injuries can be serious often necessitating a long period off sport or work before recovery is complete.

The range of injury produced by these sports is wide – from a bruise to a brain injury – but certain of them carry particular risks. These sports and their resultant injuries are now considered in detail and the mechanism, emergency treatment, and possible methods of prevention discussed.

BOXING

The 'noble art' has been an attraction since Greek and Roman times. Boxing mania was so intense at the end of the eighteenth century that even the storming of the Bastille was relegated to the back pages of the London papers because it clashed with a popular heavyweight contest! Although extremely popular until the Second World War the sport lost prestige and now only about 7 000 bouts are staged in the United Kingdom per year.

It has always been a target for criticism by both the lay public and, in particular, by the medical profession because of the injuries which can occur in the course of a bout or as a result of continued participation in the sport. The very nature of boxing in which two contestants confront each other and attempt to land blows on a particular target must of necessity cause injury. Such injuries can be reduced to a minimum by improvement in equipment and technique but there will always remain a number of injuries which will require prompt and adequate medical attention.

The instruments of attack, the hands, and the target of attack, the head, are the most common sites of injury; indeed injury to other areas or organs is rare. The mechanism of injury is illustrated in Figure 21/1.

Head injury

Head injury is the most important boxing injury. The 'punch drunk' syndrome was first described by Martland in 1928, since when medical supervision has been mandatory. The efficacy of this is such that boxing now

Fig. 21/1 The mechanism of boxing injury. The hands and the head are the most common sites

ranks eleventh as a cause of serious injury in sport (Weightman and Browne, 1975). Regular medical examinations of professional boxers, including electroencephalography, are now carried out. If a boxer is 'knocked out', a minimum period of four weeks must elapse before he can take part in further bouts.

When death occurs following head injury it is nearly always due to intracranial bleeding and, according to Green (1978), subdural haemorrhage into one of the middle cranial fossa is the most common finding. These bleeds are thought to be due to prolonged battering and for this reason most amateur bouts last only three rounds whereas professional bouts still last ten to fifteen rounds.

Previously traumatic encephalopathy or 'punch drunkenness' was commonly seen in the slugging boxer or sparring partners (Williams and Sperryn, 1976). Its onset is insidious and clinical signs are difficult to detect. The deterioration in the boxer can best be observed in the ring. His movements are slowed, he stands on a broad base and with impaired reflexes he is less able to avoid a blow. At a later stage he seems drunk. He is fatuous, emotionally labile and has slurred speech. Memory and intellect become impaired and eventually even moral sense is lost. Pathologically there is progressive ventricular dilatation with diffuse cerebellar and cerebral neuronal degeneration. The neurological features have been ascribed to petechial haemorrhages in or near the brainstem and to the diffuse cerebral changes already described. Repeated minor trauma is thought to be the cause (Roberts, 1969).

Orbital and eye injuries

Serious eye injury is rare but cases of retinal detachment, paralytic diplopia (double vision) and optic atrophy have all been reported (Doggart, 1965; Rugg-Gunn, 1965). Following such injuries retirement is mandatory. The eye injury most commonly encountered is due to head butting or from the boxing gloves; this results in either abrasion or laceration of the cornea or peri-orbital cuts, i.e. cuts around the region of the eye. The diagnosis of corneal abrasion can be made by instilling into the eye, a drop of fluorescein which stains the abrasion. Most small abrasions heal in two to three days and a pad may be worn for that period. Peri-orbital cuts may require suture thus forcing withdrawal from the bout.

Nose bleeds and nasal fractures with dislocations of the nasal septum are fairly common. These produce the typical boxer's nose (Fig. 21/2) with considerable cosmetic deformity. Fractures of the mandible and facial bones do occur but are also unusual. Haematoma of the pinna, i.e. the broad upper part of the external ear, producing 'cauliflower ear' is also unusual because early aspiration and the injection of proteolytic enzymes allows early resolution.

Hand injuries

Fracture or fracture-dislocation of the base of the first metacarpal is a common injury. The reasons for this are the position of the thumb in a separate compartment of the glove coupled with poor technique in delivering a blow; it may also occur through heavy contact with the

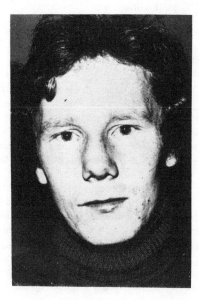

Fig. 21/2 Boxer's nose (lateral and anterior views). There is flattening of the nasal bones from previous fractures with dislocation of the nasal septum

ring floor. These injuries require manipulative reduction and occasionally surgical treatment because they are unstable injuries. The necks of the second and fifth metacarpal bones are the next most commonly sustained fractures. After reduction three to four weeks' immobilisation in a dorsal slab is all that is required.

Prompt medical attention and better informed refereeing has contributed much to the reduction in the incidence of boxing injuries. This must be maintained and improved to defend the sport against adverse criticism.

KARATE

Karate is one of the oriental martial arts and has become very popular as a sport in recent years mainly through the film industry and television. It is estimated that there are 28 000 people who practise the various styles of karate in Great Britain today. Until 1977 the British team held the world title.

Contests are of two types: controlled and full contact. In the controlled or traditional sport a competition lasts only two or three minutes. Points are scored when a blow – either a punch or a kick – breaks through an opponent's defence to reach his head, face or trunk. A half-point or a whole point is scored, depending on the power of the blow and the part of the target to which it is delivered. Punches and kicks are 'pulled' before contact is made so, theoretically, injury should be rare. The full contact sport is self-explanatory with rounds of three minutes duration like boxing.

Injuries do occur but especially in the controlled sport. Many are accidental due to poor control or judgement; some are intentional. They fall into three main groups:

1. Cranio-facial and cervical injuries
2. Visceral injuries
3. Limb injuries.

Cranio-facial and cervical injuries

Lacerations, abrasions, nose bleeds and black eyes are common and only cause withdrawal from the contest when bleeding is persistent or the eye is closed due to peri-orbital swelling. Steristrip or sutures to lacerations and adrenalin packs for serious nose bleeds are effective methods of treatment. Nasal fracture can occur and present with the features of 'boxer's nose'. Fracture of the malar bone has been reported by Serres et al (1973) – the affected man presented with a palpable depression on the right side of his face and suffered from double vision. He also had paraesthesia (tingling) due to nerve entrapment over the affected side of his

face. After the cheek bone was elevated the symptoms settled.

Concussion and skull fracture are the most worrying head injuries. Both can be caused by uncontrolled blows but also by the occiput striking a hard floor after a fall. Therefore, padded flooring is essential at all competitions. Cervical injury, in the form of dislocation, has occurred when spinning kicks have been used. Many associations have now outlawed such manoeuvres and their use in competition is actively discouraged (Fig. 21/3).

Fig. 21/3 Cervical injury can result from a variety of illegal back kicks. The attacker has rotated through 360° to gain momentum

Visceral injuries

The thoracic viscera can be damaged from direct blows producing a pneumothorax (lung collapse). The abdominal viscera are also vulnerable. Cantwell and King (1973) reported a single case of subcapsular haematoma of the liver in a woman who had received a combination of blows to the right subcostal region during her second karate lesson. She became ill six weeks later and a laparotomy (exploration of the abdomen) was performed. This revealed a large stellate laceration of the capsule on the dome of the right lobe of the liver. An organising haematoma with 1 500ml of altered blood was aspirated.

Splenic rupture has been observed following heavy round house kicks to the left posterior and lower thoracic region. The patients so affected became profoundly shocked. Splenectomy was indicated in both cases (McLatchie, 1979). Renal trauma from the same technique also occurs but to date only haematuria has been observed with no renal damage evident on intravenous urography.

Blows to the solar plexus are common but recovery is rapid in almost every case (30 to 90 seconds). However, one case of acute traumatic pancreatitis with a serum amylase of greater than 12 000 International Units has occurred. The patient recovered with conservative treatment (McLatchie, 1979a).

Testicular injury, due to uncontrolled kicks, is acutely painful and forces retirement from competition. The use of proper groin guards diminishes this risk. Those injured have the consolation that their opponent is disqualified for using an illegal technique. Spontaneous recovery is the rule.

Injuries to the limbs

Peripheral nerve injuries are occasionally seen (McLatchie, 1977); the nerve affected is the ulnar nerve at the elbow and its deep branch in the hand. The lesion results from attempts to block kicks or from hardening the hands on firm objects (Nieman and Swan, 1971). The radial nerve is also injured by high kicks to the middle third of the upper arm. Footsweeps occasionally produce superficial peroneal nerve palsy, the foot striking the leg in the region of the fibular neck. Paraesthesia over the distribution of the nerve results, but weakness and wasting of muscle groups have also been reported. Recovery time varies from hours to weeks but is complete.

Digital dislocations and sprains occur during attempts to parry blows when the affected digit is hyperextended. If no fracture is suspected reduction should be carried out and immobilisation in a boxing glove bandage allows the participant to continue fighting.

Thumb injuries are also common. 'Gamekeeper's thumb' and 'karate thumb' (McLatchie, 1977) both occur as well as the previously mentioned Bennett's fracture dislocation. In 'gamekeeper's thumb' the ulnar collateral ligament is avulsed from the base of the proximal phalanx with the wedge of bone. In 'karate thumb' it is the radial collateral ligament which is affected. The former requires surgical fixation since it is potentially unstable, the latter requires conservative treatment. Puncher's knuckle (Sperryn, 1973) is seen in many karatekae who toughen their fists on firm pads.

Fascial compartment compression of the leg and quadriceps haematoma are a serious group of injuries noted especially in the Kyokushinkai knock-down style. (This is one of the five original Japanese karate styles in which a score is recorded if one knocks down his opponent. Therefore, low hard kicks to the shins and thighs of the opponent are practised in order to weaken him.) Severe bruising of the large muscles of the thighs can be a chronic source of pain if subsequent calcification, myositis ossificans, occurs. Traumatic anterior tibial compartment syndrome (fascial compartment compression) may require surgical treatment since the viability of the limb is threatened. Ice packs, elevation and bandaging the limb considerably relieves pain and reduces swelling. Withdrawal from the competition is mandatory.

Knee injuries are also quite common in karatekae. In performing a technique such as the roundhouse kick there is a degree of rotation on a fixed tibia which produces tears of the menisci. This mechanism is similar to that of football knee injuries. The patient usually presents with a history of pain, usually in the medial joint compartment and occasionally jamming of the knee. On examination a small effusion is often found. If the symptoms become chronic, meniscectomy is sometimes necessary.

Through the Martial Arts Commission, medical cover is now available at karate competitions. Rules regarding fitness to compete are laid down with the result that the incidence of injury has been considerably reduced (McLatchie and Morris, 1977). Recommendations for medical officers attending karate contests are described in detail elsewhere (McLatchie, 1979b).

JUDO

Judo, the way of gentleness, has been popular in Great Britain for more than thirty years. It is an Olympic sport and an effective method of self-defence. Serious injury is indeed rare and results most often from the floor techniques in which the opponent can be strangled unconscious if he does not submit.

It is popular among children, in whom a special type of sprain which is known as 'pulled elbow' may be found. In this condition the radial head is pulled out of its annular ligament. The symptoms are pain and tenderness over the radial head associated with limitation of pronation and supination. Treatment is simple: firm alternate pronation and supination with the elbow held at a right-angle allows the radial head to 'click' back into position. Post-traumatic sequelae do not occur.

A much more serious but very rare elbow injury can occur, the mechanism of which is a fall with the elbow hyperextended and the forearm pronated. It is a serious fracture-dislocation often confused with the more common Monteggia fracture. The lesion consists of a fracture of the radial head or neck with associated olecranon fracture and/or dislocation of the elbow joint. The treatment is surgical and prognosis unfortunately poor, osteoarthrosis being a late sequel (Fig. 21/4). Figure 21/5 shows the mechanisms of injury.

Other minor injuries which occur include scratches, mat burns and minor soft tissue sprains. It is not usual for these to prevent further participation. If breakfalls are inadequately performed there is the possibility of cervical injury (Fig. 21/6). The judoka must therefore learn how to breakfall efficiently before taking part in randori (free fighting) in which dislocations of both minor and major joints such as the shoulder and the elbow have been witnessed (Williams and Sperryn, 1976).

WRESTLING

Wrestling is one of the oldest known sports. At amateur level two styles, Graeco-Roman and freestyle, are practised. In the Graeco-Roman style the use of the legs is forbidden and only holds above the waist allowed. Freestyle permits the use of any fair hold and has a code of rules which describes such holds. Current medical control is efficient. The contestants have to

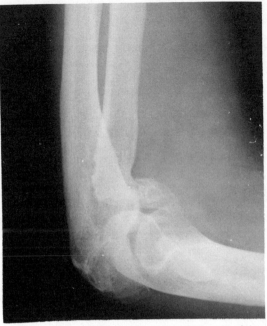

Fig. 21/4 Radiograph showing osteoarthrosis of the elbow joint

Fig. 21/5 A breakfall performed badly in judo leads to fractures of the radial head due to the force of a fall being directed along the radius. Flexion of the elbow then follows and the olecranon process impacts upon the ground producing a fracture. This is a combined lesion

Fig. 21/6 The mechanism of a skull fracture. In combat sports following a knock-out blow from a sweep, the opponent falls backwards striking his head on a hard floor

undergo pre-match medical examination and to maintain adequate hygiene, namely, be clean shaven with short hair and short nails. Serious injury is rare and even in the professional sport, with no holds barred, there have only been two deaths in Great Britain during the last 40 years (Green, 1978). One of these was due to myocardial infarction and the other to a serious head injury.

A well-known hazard in this sport is cervical injury. This can occur if one contestant falls heavily on his opponent when he is 'bridging' (Fig. 21/7). Gabashvili (1971) reported four deaths from cervical injury but none have been reported in Great Britain. Strict adherence to the rules is vital if such injuries are to be avoided. As in boxing and karate, fractures and fracture dislocations of the metacarpo-phalangeal joints of the thumb are common, requiring surgical intervention to produce a stable joint.

Chronic injuries are also seen and these usually affect the shoulders with innumerable minor muscle sprains, and the knees where meniscus and ligamentous injuries occur and are a source of persistent trouble. They often present with effusion, laxity and pain.

The Sumo wrestlers of Japan present an interesting

Fig. 21/7 The risk of cervical injury is obvious if the wrestler's opponent falls on him when he is bridging

range of injuries. In this professional sport the participants are 'reared' from a young age in establishments known as 'stables' to prepare them for their sport. They eat a special high fat diet and, unlike other Japanese, grow very tall and become enormously obese. Their training is intensive. Their hands are subjected to repeated trauma against padded posts as they practise their training techniques. As a result of this, stiffness of the metacarpo-phalangeal and proximal phalangeal joints of the fingers and thumbs occurs. They are also said to present with a 'punch drunk' like syndrome in later life due to repeated concussions from butting each other in competition. Some are also reported to be partially sighted as a result of this. They have short lives, usually to the mid-forties, with a higher incidence of pancreatitis and myocardial infarction than the general population.

PREVENTION OF INJURY

In the combat sports many injuries result when a competitor is tiring; therefore, cardiovascular fitness is especially important. The acquisition of skill through persistent practice decreases the risk of injury. It allows the individual to read the situation and realise the risk involved. It also allows the development of efficient movement patterns to the level of conditioned reflexes. Efficient warm-up is probably another factor which reduces the possibility of injury. The exact mechanism of this is not known but it may help to 'settle the nerves' and to prime muscle groups for action.

Protective clothing is advised in the martial arts, especially in karate. The use of gumshields, groin guards and pads for the fists, shins and feet has markedly reduced the incidence of injury in this sport (McLatchie, 1977). In boxing too, facial injury is lessened by wearing a proper fitting gumshield. The use of headgear in sparring and a padded or sprung flooring contributes much to the prevention of serious head injury (Schmid et al, 1968). For wrestling and judo, padded flooring is also in use.

Control of the competition by a strict referee is vital. The competitors should be aware of the rules and the referee's judgement should be upheld by the governing body of the sport. The combat area is not an excuse for assault. Illegal moves should be penalised by disqualification; in no sport is injury more likely to result than in the combat sports if illegal techniques are resorted to.

In summary a participant should be fit, skilful, informed of the rules of his sport, controlled and he should wear recommended protective clothing.

REFERENCES

Cantwell, J. D. and King, J. T. (1973). Karate chops and liver lacerations. *Journal of the American Medical Association*, **224**, 1424.

Doggart, J. H. (1965). *Eye injuries.* In A. L. Bass, J. L. Blonstein, R. D. James and J. G. P. Williams (eds). *Medical aspects of boxing.* Pergamon Press, Oxford.

Gabashvili, I. (1971). *Death of sportsmen in the Georgian S.S.R., 1955-70.* In Abstracts of XVIIIth World Congress of Sports Medicine (Oxford).

Green, M. A. (1978). *Injury and sudden death in sport.* In J. K. Mason (ed) *The pathology of violent injury.* Edward Arnold (Publisher) Ltd., London.

Martland, H. S. (1928). Punch drunk. *Journal of The American Medical Association*, **91**, 1103-1107.

McLatchie, G. R. (1976). Analysis of karate injuries in 295 contests. *British Journal of Accident Surgery*, **8**, 132, 134.

McLatchie, G. R. (1977). How to treat karate injuries. *Medical News*, **9**, 12.

McLatchie, G. R. (1979). *Serious injuries at karate contests.* (Unpublished observations, Glasgow Royal Infirmary.)

McLatchie, G. R. (1979a). Surgical and orthopaedic problems in sport karate. *Medisport*, **1**, 40-44.

McLatchie, G. R. (1979b). Recommendations for Medical Officers attending karate competitions. *British Journal of Sports Medicine*, **13**, 36-37.

McLatchie, G. R. and Fitzgerald, B. (1979). *A survey of sports related injuries attending Glasgow Royal Infimary.* (Unpublished observations, Glasgow Royal Infirmary.)

McLatchie, G. R. and Morris, E. W. (1977). Prevention of karate injuries – a progress report. *British Journal of Sports Medicine*, **2**, 78-82.

Nieman, E. A. and Swan, P. G. (1971). Karate injuries. *British Medical Journal*, **1**, 233.

Roberts, A. H. (1969). *Brain damage in boxers.* Pitman Medical Publishing Co. Ltd., Tunbridge Wells.

Rugg-Gunn, A. (1965). *Eye Injuries.* In A. L. Bass, J. L. Blonstein, R. D. James and J. G. P. Williams (eds). *Medical aspects of boxing.* Pergamon Press, Oxford.

Schmid, L., Hajek, E., Votipka, F., Teprik, O. and Blonstein, J. L. (1968). Experience with head-gear in boxing. *Journal of Sports Medicine and Physical Fitness*, **8**, 171-173.

Serres, P., Calas, J. and Guilbert, F. (1973). Karate and fracture of the malar. *Review of Oral and Maxillo-facial Surgery*, **74**, 177-178.

Sperryn, P. N. (1973). Traumatic bursitis in a boxer's hand. *British Journal of Sports Medicine*, **7**, 103.

Weightman, D. and Browne, R. C. (1975). Injuries in eleven selected sports. *British Journal of Sports Medicine*, **9**, 136-141.

Williams, J. G. P. and Sperryn, P. N. (1976). *Sports medicine.* Edward Arnold (Publishers) Ltd., London.

CHAPTER 22

Injuries in racket sports

F. H. SANDERSON DCC, BEd, MA, PhD

The sports which will be particularly considered are tennis, badminton and squash although the information will be of relevance to other less popular racket sports. Generally, these sports would be described as 'minimum hazard' in terms of injury rate (Eastwood, 1964) in comparison with, for instance, American football, soccer, or even basketball. However, there are a range of injuries which do tend to be associated with particular demands of racket sports. Tennis, badminton, and squash all require frequent changes of direction in a confined space which involve abrupt deceleration and fast acceleration. Consequently, the ankle, knee and thigh are the sites of most lower extremity injuries among racket players. Other injuries arise from the fact that the upper extremity is used unilaterally, the shoulder and elbow being particularly vulnerable. The racket itself can be a lethal weapon, and the ball or shuttle is a particularly dangerous missile. Hence, head and eye injuries are not uncommon.

Because of this similarity of injuries across racket sports, the chapter is sectioned in terms of specific injuries rather than in terms of specific sports. The relative incidence of injuries within racket sports will be apparent from the particular emphases within sections. The practical causes of injuries are discussed, together with suggestions as to how their occurrence may be avoided or reduced.

HEAD AND EYE INJURIES

The most common head injury is facial laceration, usually caused by a widely swinging racket and, although it does occur in tennis and badminton doubles play, is, for obvious reasons, most prominent in squash. Jonah Barrington suffered cuts around the left eye on 17 occasions in eight years play, with his opponent's follow-through causing most of the problems (Barrington, 1973).

Although facial lacerations can be traumatic, a more serious problem can arise from ocular injuries sustained in play. The partner's racket in doubles play or the opponent's racket in squash account for some eye injuries but the majority are attributable to the ball or the shuttle. In squash, North (1973) and Cobb (1977)

found that approximately 30 per cent of eye injuries were caused by the racket and 70 per cent by the ball. In badminton, Chandran (1974) reported a ball-racket ratio of 6:1 in a total of 63 cases examined. Eye injuries in tennis are less frequently sustained with the overwhelming majority caused by the tennis ball in the doubles game (Burstein, 1963; Seelenfreund and Freilich, 1976).

Generally, spectacle wearers appear to be more at risk of serious injury. Ingram and Lewkonia (1973) examined squash players and found that 70 per cent of the most seriously injured were spectacle wearers. Seventeen per cent of North's (1973) sample of squash players with ocular injuries had broken spectacles. Not wearing the corrective lenses during play is not the answer as near-sighted individuals are most at risk (Chandran, 1974). Those who need ocular correction should wear plastic or toughened glass safety lenses with a sturdy frame (Ingram and Lewkonia, 1973; Vinger and Tolpin, 1978); Ingram and Lewkonia (1973) and Koetting (1971) further suggested that contact lenses may reduce injury risk although Vinger and Tolpin (1978) took a contrary view. Blonstein (1975) was concerned enough about the injury risks that he tentatively suggested the use of protective headgear incorporating a visor in squash. Additional sound but ominous advice offered by North (1973) was that one-eyed individuals should be warned of the risks. Burstein (1963) argued that such individuals should be *prevented* from playing potentially hazardous sports. A similarly heavy handed approach has been adopted by at least one American university where athletes are required to wear safety lenses for high-risk sports (Rachun, 1969).

Examining the factors which are contributory to ocular injury in racket sports, it appears that inexperience is of major importance. In badminton, eye injuries usually result from the shuttle hitting a player following a smash hit, and Chandran (1972) noted that the most vulnerable players in this situation were between 11 and 20 years old. In tennis, the doubles player at the net is particularly vulnerable when inadequately instructed in the techniques of protecting himself from the rapidly played ball. In squash, it is likely that most of the eye injuries could be prevented by improved technique and a more rigorous enforcement of the rules.

Squash players are particularly exposed to head and ocular injuries because two players are hitting the ball hard within a confined area and without a net to separate them. Hence, high degrees of skill, cooperation and sportsmanship are necessary in order to minimise injuries. Problems arise with the inexperienced or unwary player who takes his eye off the ball during rallies. Particularly when the ball is in the rear of the court and his opponent is behind him, this player is vulnerable when he finally does turn to see where the ball is. Inexperience is likely to be a factor in several

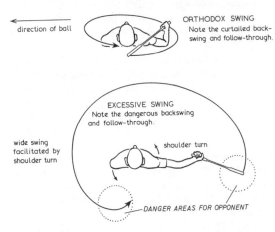

Fig. 22/1 Views of orthodox swing and excessive swing in forehand drive in squash

Fig. 22/2 The striker whose swing is somewhat excessive, has nevertheless been crowded by his opponent. This situation is common where a left-handed player is involved

other dangerous situations; when a player attempts a vicious reverse angle volley off the serve of an opponent who is already moving to the centre of the court; when a player has an excessive follow-through of the racket after the shot (Fig. 22/1); when a player is 'crowded' by his opponent (Fig. 22/2); when a player 'turns' in the back corner and plays the ball; when a player obeys the natural tendency to play the ball at all times. Sound coaching can reduce these problems. A player should be encouraged to watch the ball until the opponent is playing the shot and he should be instructed in good stroke technique which will help prevent excessive racket swing and dangerous mis-hits. Additionally, he should learn to be cooperative on court, allowing his opponent 'fair view and freedom of stroke' and always refraining from playing a ball which might be considered dangerous to his opponent. In view of the safety problems created by left-handed players, coaches should advise players on the ways in which tactics must be adapted for the left-handed opponent. Officials should warn players about dangerous play and should not hesitate to employ the ultimate sanction of disqualification against the minority who create danger as an intimidatory tactic.

These suggestions can help reduce injury risk but a protective device for the eyes could provide complete safety. Difficulties may arise in persuading players to wear them.

SHOULDER AND BACK INJURIES

Shoulder injuries

Injuries to the shoulder are fairly common in racket sports (Williams, 1978) because of the regular and excessive leverage forces to which the region is subjected. Players are prone to clinical conditions experienced by baseball players, only to a less extreme degree. In particular, the action of the tennis serve and the overhead smash in all racket sports can broadly be likened to the throwing action of the pitcher. Hence, during the backswing phase in the racket sports, the insertions of the anterior deltoid and pectoralis major muscles may be injured by severe tension (Novich and Taylor, 1972). In the impact and follow-through phases, the fully stretched scapular insertions of the posterior deltoid, rhomboid major and long head of the triceps may suffer trauma because of the overload. Anterior dislocations of the gleno-humeral joint as a result of the tennis serve have been documented (Novich and Taylor, 1972). An injury associated with constant motion of the shoulder as occurs in racket sports, is bicipital tenosynovitis (O'Donoghue, 1970).

Priest and Nagel (1976) examined 84 world-class players and found that more than 50 per cent had had shoulder symptoms at some stage. Anterior rotator cuff symptoms were most common, particularly among the males. The serve was associated most often with anterior cuff discomfort followed by the overhead smash and the backhand. They maintained that symptoms resulted from impingement of the cuff caused by abduction of the arm, but Bernhang (1976) felt that rotation of the shoulder, through approximately 200° in the case of the serve, coupled with maximal abduction, caused the symptoms. He further suggested that the reduced incidence of the injury among females is attributable to greater joint flexibility, allowing easier external and internal rotation.

It appears that the main cause of injury in this region is a faulty technique deriving from over-vigorous stroke playing. As in most sports skills, there exists a speed/accuracy trade-off and too much emphasis on speed, particularly when there is inadequate supporting musculature and flexibility, leaves the player vulnerable to injury. Preventive measures entail placing emphasis on accuracy of serving and stroke-making, initially at the expense of speed. The latter can be increased as a function of increased strength and flexibility.

Back injuries

Any sudden and severe change from spinal extension to flexion or vice versa can lead to back strain. The problem is exacerbated by simultaneous torsional movements of the upper body. For example, acute strain can be caused by an abrupt change of movement to make a recovery shot with consequent high torque overloading the attachments of the dorsal spinal ligaments (Sicular, 1971). Supple (1971) observed lumbar strain resulting from use of the complex American twist service in tennis. Back injuries are as likely to be linked with inadequate warm-up, lack of fitness, fatigue and climatic conditions as poor technique.

ELBOW AND WRIST INJURIES

The elbow is a frequent site of complaint in racket players. Priest et al (1977) found three main regions around the elbow at which symptoms occur in tennis players – the lateral epicondyle, the medial epicondyle, and the groove of the ulnar nerve. They found that medial symptoms were more common than lateral symptoms in top tennis players. The main cause of medial problems was the serve, with cubital tunnel pain being associated with the spin serve. Other than avoiding excessively strenuous serves and reducing the spin, it appears that there is little that the good tennis player can do to prevent medial symptoms. The problem is much less severe among club players.

In squash, medial symptoms are relatively infrequent but would be associated with 'wristy' forehand shots played from postures of marked anatomical weakness. As well as problems with the medial epicondyle, this kind of action may lead to strains of the forearm flexors and sprain of the wrist in extreme cases. In squash, the remedy lies in playing with a cocked wrist for the whole of the stroke. Similarly, if this technical principle is not observed on the backhand stroke, acute strain and tenosynovitis of the forearm extensors may result.

Lateral epicondylitis, or classic 'tennis elbow' is by far the best documented injury. The syndrome was first described in the 1870s, and since then many explanations have been offered for its occurrence. Nirschl (1974a) commented that 'the concepts of massive overload, multiple repetition, quality of tissue, age, potential hormonal imbalance (in women) and available strength, endurance, flexibility, as well as mechanical joint design, all play their respective roles'. Interacting with these factors are the equipment used and the skill level of the player.

Equipment related factors have often been associated with the occurrence of elbow injuries. Plagenhoef (1970) implicated head-heavy rackets whereas others stress the damaging effects of an abrupt change of racket type, especially from light to heavy (e.g. Slapak, 1964). Williams and Sperryn (1976) suggested that a change from wood to steel without an accompanying change in technique is causative. Clearly, this factor needs further investigation in the light of Priest's (1976) finding with a large sample of tennis players that the occurrence of symptoms was highest in those using wood rather than steel or aluminium rackets. To add to the aetiological confusion, Steiner (1976) argued that the type of racket is not a significant factor in elbow injuries. He also suggested that the size of the racket handle is of minor importance. However, several experts hold a contrary opinion. Williams and Sperryn (1976) suggested that whereas the tennis grip size is near-optimal the badminton grip size may be incorrect. Nirschl's (1977) investigations have led him to suggest a reliable method of determining the correct racket handle size of the tennis racket – the circumference equalling the distance from the proximal palmar crease along the radial border of the ring finger to the tip of the ring finger. The same formula cannot be applied to badminton and squash because of the important differential influence of impact forces, forearm strength, racket weight, and so on, across the three games. Research is needed to identify optimal grip sizes in badminton and squash. In the absence of specific information, it is best to adopt as large a grip as is comfortable.

Excessive string tension has also been mentioned as a causative factor in elbow injury in that the ball impact vibrations transferred to the arm are increased (e.g. Nirschl, 1977). Generally, relatively light and non-rigid rackets with moderate string tension should be preferred. Gut is preferable to synthetic stringing (Novich and Taylor, 1972). Plagenhoef (1970) recommended a gut tension in the tennis racket of approximately 56lb (25.4kg), whereas Nirschl (1974b) advised conventional stringing with sixteen gauge gut at 52lb (23.6kg). This discrepancy can be explained in terms of the greater gut tension requirement of the advanced player.

Most information on causative factors in elbow injury relates to inadequate techniques and the specific physical demands of racket games. During games, extensor overload is caused by the powerful repetitive hyperextension movements of the arm linked with vigorous rotary movements of the forearm. Although tennis elbow can be caused by pronation or supination of the forearm in racket games, it tends to be associated with pronation. More specifically, Nirschl (1975) maintained that extensor overload can occur in all positions from full pronation of the forearm to neutral. The reason presented was that tennis professionals are less prone to tennis elbow than amateurs in that they tend to avoid pronation strokes and use the extremity less for power and range of motion.

Somewhat surprisingly, Priest et al (1977) found that among amateurs, tennis elbow was more common in higher ranking players. However, epicondylitis can be caused by both poor technique, more common among low-ranked amateurs, and by cumulative effects of powerful hitting associated with the higher ranking amateurs and the professionals. Slapak (1964) argued that the club player's elbow symptoms are linked with mishitting, whereas the good player may succumb to the combined effects of fatigue and overuse.

The technical problems particularly associated with the backhand stroke are exacerbated by the common strategy of playing the ball or shuttle early. This demands precise timing but without the advantage of time for elaborate preparation of the stroke. Mistiming may well involve extensor overload, particularly if the missile is hit off-centre and the torque is increased beyond a manageable level. A tighter grip would be needed to counteract the inability to find the sweet spot and the resultant increased vibrational shocks transmitted to the arm may be a cause of tennis elbow (Hatze, 1976). There is also indirect evidence that moderate players are likely to suffer local fatigue because of unnecessarily sustained grip pressure, a situation which would leave them more vulnerable to the development of elbow symptoms. Bernhang et al

(1974) found that better tennis players have a short-duration maximum grip pressure which is also coordinated more closely with ball impact. It seems that tennis and squash players particularly should be more discriminating in the application of maximum grip pressure, and that learners should use only moderate grip tightness to diminish the effects of torque recoil forces being transmitted to the elbow.

Poor backhand stroke production in tennis and squash is characterised by the predominant use of the forearm extensors as the power source for the stroke rather than correct weight transference and shoulder muscle power. Nirschl (1975) noted that the faulty backhand in tennis is often accompanied by an exaggerated backhand grip with the thumb placed behind the handle for additional power. Such a combination of factors means that the player tends to pronate the forearm and punch at the ball with the extending elbow and wrist. Bernhang et al (1974) referred to this as the 'leading-elbow' stroke (Fig. 22/3) which they noticed in players afflicted with tennis elbow.

An additional outcome in squash is for the players to employ a very wristy backhand to achieve the necessary power. If the ball is missed, or even mistimed, the extensor overload resulting from a wristy stroke will be high. Similarly, high overload exists where a backswing is negligible or absent as a means of disguising a stroke, as for example when a squash player at the front

Fig. 22/3 The 'leading elbow' stroke is common among tennis players afflicted with lateral epicondylitis. A similar kind of stroke occurs in squash when a player hits a backhand volley close to his chest, either because his footwork is faulty or because he has insufficient time to make adjustments

of the court whose arm is fully extended and pronated to play a short shot, suddenly plays a lob to the back with a flick of the wrist (Fig. 22/4a). The wrist is necessarily used in badminton but the consequences are less severe because of the relatively light racket and missile.

Preventive measures must come through sound coaching; specifically they will involve learning to extend the power source to the shoulders and incorporating transference of weight to the leading foot on impact. Moreover, the swing should begin early so that these aims can be accomplished more easily. It is clear that the forces acting on the extensors can be greatly reduced with the two-handed tennis backhand, and the fact that this stroke is employed successfully by world class players suggests that its widespread introduction should be encouraged.

THIGH, KNEE AND LOWER LEG INJURIES

Thigh injuries

Strains of the adductor group of muscles on the inner side of the thighs and the iliopsoas muscles are frequent in racket sports. Particularly in badminton and squash, deep lunging movements are required which involve severe eccentric contraction of adductors and maybe over-active contraction of the iliopsoas. For right-handed squash players, the adductors of the right leg are affected as it is this leg which tends to lead in the deep lunges to the front of the court (Fig. 22/4b). The deep lunge is a valuable aspect of play in that it can often save time in reaching the ball and recovering to the middle of the court. As it must remain part of the racket player's repertoire, systematic flexibility exercises and a thorough pre-match warm-up are recommended as a means of reducing the risk of adductor strain.

Knee and lower leg injuries

As in other sports which demand twisting, turning and sudden changes of speed and direction, knee injuries are quite common in racket sports. Sprains of the medial or lateral menisci and ruptures of the cruciate ligaments have been observed in tennis players (Supple, 1971). Williams (1978) noted 15 cases of racket players with chondromalacia of the patella among a sample of 100 sportsmen with this injury. It can be caused by repeated abrupt checking of the extended knee and reversal of direction or as a consequence of synovitis of the joint (O'Donoghue, 1970). An awareness of optimum footwear traction, together with relevant strength and flexibility training will help minimise the occurrence of trauma associated with the inherent stresses of racket games. Some authorities recommend knee strapping where strain is a possibility (e.g. Reahl, 1967).

One of the most common lower leg injuries among racket games players is calf muscle strain. Sometimes referred to as 'tennis leg', it usually involves a rupture of the medial gastrocnemius belly (Arner and Lindholm, 1958). It occurs when the foot is in maximal plantar flexion and is exposed to violent dorsiflexion while the knee joint is extended. The fact that the injury commonly occurs in middle-aged sportsmen suggests that diminishing strength and flexibility are contributory factors. Froimson (1969) faulted the flat-heeled tennis shoes which allow exaggerated dorsiflexion, thereby tightening the heelcord and encouraging gastrocnemius rupture.

(a)

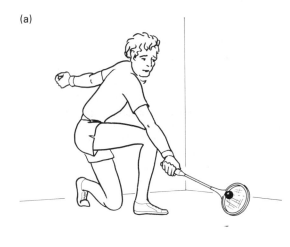

(b)

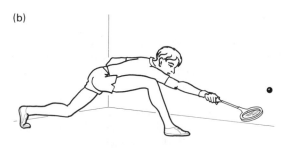

Fig. 22/4 Squash player in the act of lobbing the ball to the back of the court with a flick of the wrist. With the forearm pronated, this stroke places great strain on the forearm extensors (a). The player is also demonstrating the most common forward lunging movement – right leg leading – which is responsible for the majority of adductor strains (b)

FOOT AND ANKLE INJURIES

Foot injuries can be minimised by a reliance upon durable and well-fitting footwear. Too often, especially with new or ill-fitting footwear, players develop calluses and friction blisters on the tops of the toes or the balls of the feet. Bruising of the heel or 'black-heel' (Benjamin, 1973) can result from a combination of poor footwear and hard playing surfaces. Cushion-soled socks or more than one pair of socks is recommended and special care should be taken in the selection of footwear. There should be a fixed cushioned sole with arch support and there should be room for only minimal lateral and horizontal movement of the foot. If too much movement is possible, then the usually excellent traction of modern footwear can cause the foot to be forced into the front of the shoes when the player suddenly stops. This condition, sometimes described as 'tennis toe' involves haemorrhage beneath the toenails (Gibbs, 1973). The fact that ingrown toenails can also occur in such circumstances suggests that proper care of the feet is also essential.

Ankle injuries, mainly strains and sprains, are fairly common in racket sports and this too may be in some measure due to the design of modern footwear, e.g. too much traction, too low cut. The player is often required to change direction laterally which can place overload on the lateral ligaments of the ankle. Some sports shoes, either through wear or design fault, exhibit a rounded continuity between the sole and the upper at the lateral aspect which increases the likelihood of lateral rotation of the foot (Fig. 22/5). Vulnerability would be present, for instance, when a player moving to the right suddenly uses his right foot to check his stride and moves to the left. The foot is forcibly inverted and the momentum of the weight passes over the outside of the joint. The ankle is at its most vulnerable when the foot is simultaneously plantar flexed.

McCluskey et al (1976) described how lateral ligament sprains can result from a bowstringing of the tight Achilles tendon when the foot is in extreme dorsiflexion. They recommended heelcord stretching exercises as a preventive measure. Heelcord tightening accompanied by a violent movement of the toes causes rupture of the Achilles tendon. Berson et al (1978) found that this injury constituted approximately 18 per cent of lower extremity injuries in squash players, whose average age was 39.5 years. In view of the fact that exaggerated dorsiflexion is implicated in ankle sprains, and ruptures of the Achilles tendon and gastrocnemius, it seems that there is a need for a specially designed shoe with an elevated heel, which would be particularly desirable for middle-aged racket players.

In cases where there is a known weakness of the ankle, strapping is sometimes recommended. However, controversy exists as to the ultimate benefits of strapping. Reahl (1967) suggested that in sports where the ankle is vulnerable, strapping should be mandatory. Wiecher (1967) and Williams and Sperryn (1976) were less convinced, arguing that there will be an increasing dependence effect with relevant muscles tending to atrophy. Wiecher further stated that strain may be transferred to the knee because of the constraining effects of the strapping. However, Garrick and Requa (1973) found a decreased frequency of ankle sprains over two seasons in basketballers using ankle strapping and no consequent increase in knee strains.

Only those injuries which are most commonly associated with racket sports have been dealt with. Of course, racket players occasionally sustain contusions, dislocations, fractures, and so on, but the incidence of such injuries does not warrant their inclusion here.

The risk of incurring many of the injuries described can be reduced or eliminated by a sensible appreciation of safety on court. In tennis, badminton, and particularly squash, there must be an awareness of the need for cooperation between players in a competitive environment. Equipment must be well-maintained and appropriate for the particular conditions, e.g. shoes with soles suited to the playing surface, a racket grip with a non-slip quality, and so on. A strict enforcement of the rules should complement these measures.

Other injuries are caused by technical deficiencies, inadequate flexibility and muscular development, fatigue, and extreme overuse. The remedies are self-

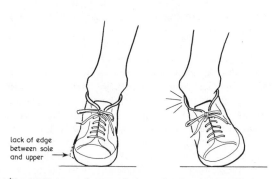

lack of edge between sole and upper →

Fig. 22/5 Inversion sprain in racket sports. In this case, the player is using the plantar flexed right foot to check movement right and initiate movement to the left. The foot is forcibly inverted with weight passing over the outside of the joint. Lack of an edge on the lateral aspect of the sole will enhance the likelihood of injury

explanatory, but usually difficult to initiate systematically. Expert advice is necessary for the avoidance or removal of technical faults and for the planning of relevant strength and flexibility training programmes. Players should resist the temptation to continue playing when extremely fatigued, as the muscles are more vulnerable to overload stresses per se and the player is more likely to error and technical deficiency.

Overuse injuries usually involve a progressive deterioration and players should seek medical advice, or at the least, restrict activity, at the first signs of discomfort.

It is likely that the incidence of many common racket sport injuries will be reduced in the future as a function of improved facilities, equipment, coaching, off-court training, player awareness, and, not least, by the increased sophistication and availability of sports medicine facilities.

REFERENCES

Arner, O. D. and Lindholm, A. (1958). What is tennis leg? *Acta Chiropida Scandinavica*, **116**, 73–75.

Barrington, J. (1973). *Barrington on squash*. Stanley Paul, London.

Benjamin, E. S. (1973). Black heel. *South African Medical Journal*, **47**, 919.

Bernhang, A. M. (1976). Editorial Comment on Priest & Nagel's paper on 'Tennis shoulder'. *American Journal of Sports Medicine*, **4**, 40–42.

Bernhang, A. M., Dehner, W. and Fogarty, C. (1974). Tennis elbow: a biomechanical approach. *Journal of Sports Medicine*, **2**, 235–260.

Berson, B. L., Passoff, T. L., Nagelberg, S. and Thornton, J. (1978). Injury patterns in squash players. *American Journal of Sports Medicine*, **6**, 323–325.

Blonstein, J. L. (1975). Eye injuries in sports. *Practitioner*, **215**, 208–209.

Burstein, F. (1963). Ocular injuries in sports. *Journal of Sports Medicine and Physical Fitness*, **3**, 25–30.

Chandran, S. (1972). Haphaema and badminton eye injuries. *Medical Journal of Malaya*, **26**, 207–210.

Chandran, S. (1974). Ocular hazards of playing badminton. *British Journal of Ophthalmology*, **58**, 757–760.

Cobb, A. (1977). Eye injuries in squash rackets. *Squash Player International*, **6**, 11.

Eastwood, F. R. (1964). Hazards to health: athletic injuries. *New England Medical Journal*, **271**, 411–413.

Froimson, A. I. (1969). Tennis leg. *Journal of the American Medical Association*, **209**, 415–416.

Garrick, J. G. and Requa, D. K. (1973). Role of external support in the prevention of ankle sprains. *Medicine and Science in Sports*, **3**, 200–203.

Gibbs, R. C. (1973). 'Tennis toe.' *Archives of Dermatology*, **107**, 1114.

Hatze, H. (1976). Forces and duration of impact and grip tightness during the tennis stroke. *Medicine and Science in Sports*, **8**, 88–95.

Ingram, D. V. and Lewkonia, I. (1973). Ocular hazards of playing squash rackets. *British Journal of Ophthalmology*, **57**, 434–438.

Koetting, R. A. (1971). Contact lenses and the athlete. *Journal of School Health*, **41**, 75–77.

McCluskey, G. M., Blackburn, T. A. and Lewis, T. (1976). Prevention of ankle sprains. *American Journal of Sports Medicine*, **4**, 151–157.

Nirschl, R. P. (1974a). Discussion of Bernhang et al's paper on 'tennis elbow: a biomechanical approach'. *Journal of Sports Medicine*, **2**, 258–59.

Nirschl, R. P. (1974b). The etiology and treatment of tennis elbow. *Journal of Sports Medicine*, **2**, 308–323.

Nirschl, R. P. (1975). Etiology of tennis elbow. *Journal of Sports Medicine*, **3**, 261–263.

Nirschl, R. P. (1977). Tennis elbow. *Primary Care*, **4**, 367–382.

North, I. M. (1973). Ocular hazards of squash. *Medical Journal of Australia*, **1**, 165–166.

Novich, M. M. and Taylor, B. (1972). *Training and conditioning of athletes*. Lea and Febiger, Philadelphia.

O'Donoghue, D. H. (1970). *Treatment of injuries in athletes*. Saunders, London.

Plagenhoef, S. (1970). *Fundamentals of tennis*. Prentice-Hall, New Jersey.

Priest, J. D. (1976). Tennis elbow: the syndrome and a study of average players. *Minnesota Medicine*, **59**, 367–371.

Priest, J. D. and Nagel, D. A. (1976). Tennis shoulder. *American Journal of Sports Medicine*, **4**, 28–40.

Priest, J. D., Jones, H. H., Tichenor, C. J. C. and Nagel, D. A. (1977). Arm and elbow changes in expert tennis players. *Minnesota Medicine*, **60**, 399–404.

Rachun, A. (1969). Vision and sports. *Sight-Saving Review*, **38**, 224–226.

Reahl, G. E. (1967). Soft tissue injuries of the knee and ankle. *Maryland State Medical Journal*, **16**, 66–71.

Seelenfreund, M. H. and Freilich, D. B. (1976). Rushing the net and retinal detachment. *Journal of the American Medical Association*, **235**, 2723–2726.

Sicular, A. (1971). *Acute and subacute injury in squash tennis*. In L. A. Larson (ed). *Encyclopedia of sports sciences and medicine*. Macmillan, New York.

Slapak, J. (1964). *Tennis elbow*. In J. R. Armstrong and W. E. Tucker (eds). *Injury in sport*. Staples Press, London.

Steiner, C. (1976). Tennis elbow. *Journal of the American Osteopathy Association*, **75**, 6, 575–581.

Supple, C. J. (1971). *Acute and subacute injury in tennis*. In L. A. Larson (ed). *Encyclopedia of sports sciences and medicine*. Macmillan, New York.

Vinger, P. F. and Tolpin, D. W. (1978). Racket sports: an ocular hazard. *Journal of the American Medical Association*, **239**, 2575–2577.

Wiecher, F. J. (1967). Examination treatment and conditioning of athletic injuries of the lower extremities. *Journal of the American Podiatry Association*, **57**, 509–514.

Williams, J. (1978). *Injury in sport*. Bayer, Haywards Heath.

Williams, J. P. G. and Sperryn, P. N. (1976). *Sports medicine*. Edward Arnold, London.

CHAPTER 23

Cycling injuries

W. MOORE BSc, and J. A. FOWLER BA, MCSP, DipTP, SRP, MBIM

The notion that prevention is better than cure applies equally to cycling as to any other sport. In cycling, injuries can be avoided not only by anticipation and skilful riding but also by attainment of the correct position on the bicycle and by ensuring that the bicycle is in first class working order. Fitness also plays a part since some injuries result from congenital abnormality, weakness or lack of the specific physiological requirements for the event undertaken.

There are however two main causes of cycling injuries – the position on the bicycle and crashes. Before these can be considered in any detail the cycling action must first be outlined.

THE CYCLING ACTION

Cycling is a balancing activity with a large amount of effort being spent keeping the machine upright, the rider representing a top-heavy unit. The base is some 1.2m long, 2.5cm wide and rounded and moveable; it defies all requisites of stability in a stationary position. Only when forward momentum is secured, is balance possible. The able track performer who balances in one place is not completely stationary as there is an interplay between right and left pedals, and the position of the front wheel.

The rider cannot depend entirely on the forward momentum but must keep the gravitational line close to the wheel line. The faster the speed, the easier it is to make adjustments when lateral deviations of the gravitational line from the wheel line occur; however, the faster one goes the harder one falls when these lateral adjustments are not made and crashing results. A very large number of the body's muscles are involved in maintaining balance.

The racing cyclist may be likened to a runner who is only partially weight-bearing, encumbered by a crouched restricted position anchored by the hands and feet. Less fixation is given by the perineum and ischial tuberosities which frequently come off the saddle. Forward movement is begun by lower limb extension, the foot in contact with and fixed to the pedal by toeclip and strap. The extension is started in the quadriceps muscle followed by extension of the hip by the gluteal muscles. Plantar flexion of the ankle by the gastrocnemius and soleus muscles is made more effective by the ball of the foot being over the pedal spindle. A combination of clawing, using the anterior tibial muscles as the pedal comes up, and pushing by the bodyweight as the pedal descends, increases effectiveness but aggravates the problem of balance.

In utility cycling, or when using a fixed wheel, recovery of the leg is achieved by allowing relaxation of the extensor muscles; the foot then rides up passively and the leg is flexed. To reduce inefficiency it is necessary to pull the foot upwards with the tibialis anterior; then the gastrocnemius helps flex the knees. At the same time there is strong flexion at the hip using the psoas and iliacus muscles. The trunk is bent forward by gravity and controlled by the back extensors, thus reducing wind resistance; when moving fast the abdominal muscles are working strongly to stabilise the pelvis thereby allowing more efficient use of the legs in pedalling.

Figure 23/1 (p. 184) shows the activity of six muscle groups during one revolution of the pedals and reinforces the biomechanical analysis with those from EMG profiles (Faria and Cavanagh, 1978).

Turning is fairly simple but requires complex muscle action and weight shifting. If the turn is too sharp, forward momentum causes the front wheels to skid and the rider falls. When turning, the cyclist leans to the inside of the curve to counteract centrifugal forces. The greater the speed the greater the curve and the greater is the lean required.

The arms are very important even though they have been neglected in the past in terms of strength training. The arms provide the force through the hands and handlebars which prevent the front wheel wobbling. They also play a crucial role in the power drive of the legs; even by just gripping the bars the trunk is made more stable and so the leg muscles act more ably. By pulling on the handlebars this stabilising of the trunk is enhanced.

The legs are thus the driving force assisted by the arms but unlike the runner no dynamic arm action is possible except in controlling the machine. The trunk is relatively stable and the muscle work of the arms and

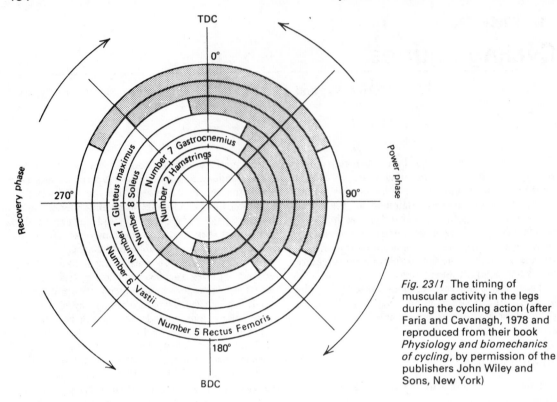

TDC

0°

Recovery phase

270°   90°   power phase

Number 7 Gastrocnemius
Number 2 Hamstrings
Number 1 Gluteus maximus
Number 8 Soleus
Number 6 Vastii
Number 5 Rectus Femoris

180°

BDC

Fig. 23/1 The timing of muscular activity in the legs during the cycling action (after Faria and Cavanagh, 1978 and reproduced from their book *Physiology and biomechanics of cycling*, by permission of the publishers John Wiley and Sons, New York)

trunk is mainly isometric or dynamic within a small part of the inner range of movement.

The position of the bicycle will differ slightly with the branch of the sport followed. There is an optimum, which when adopted will be less likely to produce injury from propelling the machine. These positions are well detailed in the handbooks of the British and Italian Cycling Federations. They cover variations for time trialling, track and road racing and cyclo-cross.

It must be borne in mind that cycling is an endurance sport, the shortest distance being 1km lasting just over one minute and the longest up to 800km (500 miles) in a 24-hour period. In addition there are multi-stage races, single stage and multi-heat events. A single stage event can involve covering distances up to 580km (362 miles) with 100 to 240km (62 to 150 miles) per day in a multi-stage event lasting for three weeks. A cyclo-cross rider will cover 24km (15 miles) or so and will have some injuries in common with the cross-country runner. Each specialty has its own specific fitness requirements and training schedules should be designed accordingly.

TRAUMA DUE TO POSITION

Broadly speaking, trauma affects the fixed parts of the body due to the cyclist's position but some moving parts can be affected because of poor alignment or faulty equipment. The more fixed parts are the feet, buttocks, back, chest and the upper limbs. The moving joints are the ankle, knee and hip, and there is some associated movement of the head and the elbow. The handlebars are so designed as to give four or five alternative positions so that the fixed postures of the upper limbs and trunk can be altered.

Fixed body parts
FEET

The feet should be enclosed in good quality leather shoes with a thick sole. These should fit closely and even be a little on the tight side when new, as the leather tends to stretch with use. If the sole is too thin there is an insufficient base for attaching shoe plates and the pressure of the pedal is carried through the sole of the foot and makes it sore. Insufficient anchorage

Fig. 23/2 The feet are fixed to the pedals by the shoe plates and toe straps; the toe strap buckle positioned on the top. The ball of the foot is placed over the pedal spindle

can cause the plates to move, altering the position of the foot on the pedals. When this happens it will lead to mal-alignment and to problems at the ankle, knee and hip. Shoes that are excessively tight can rub causing blisters and corns which will require an Elastoplast dressing or the services of a chiropodist.

The feet are held fixed to the pedals by the shoe plates and toe straps (Fig. 23/2). The toe straps are usually in a line drawn from the head of the fifth metatarsal to just behind the head of the first metatarsal. If the toe strap buckle is not placed on top of the foot, pressure may be exerted at the little toe. Soreness, pain, corns or an exostosis (bony outgrowth) can occur as a consequence; the problem can be avoided by having thicker leather at this part of the shoe.

BUTTOCKS AND CROTCH

The greatest problem in this area is associated with poor hygiene. This part gets very hot and sweaty during a long ride and if not properly washed may lead to infection and so to saddle boils. To this can be added the danger of grit and dirt being thrown up from the road especially when wet and this can lead to increased friction and perineal soreness. Soreness may also be caused if the saddle is too high or too far back so that the rider sits on the point and the narrow section. It is essential to have a good position and it is advisable to wear good quality shorts with a chamois seat insert next to the skin. It may also be appropriate to layer lanolin on the chamois to reduce friction.

Saddle soreness is an acute panniculitis, i.e. inflammation of the superficial fascial tissue, progressing to a localised area of fat necrosis. The immediate treatment

is to puncture the lesion with a sterile needle to relieve oedema. If allowed to become chronic it produces ulceration and chronic infection (Williams and Sperryn, 1976). Surgical spirit will keep the perineum clean and harden off the skin.

Occasionally the urethra is damaged from a direct astride blow to the perineum. This may be a partial or complete rupture presenting as a painful swelling. These injuries are serious and need immediate investigation and the rider advised not to pass urine (Williams and Sperryn, 1976).

Priapism, a persistent painful erection, can occur due to pressure on the pudendal nerve from a badly fitting saddle pushing into the perineum. Treatment is sedation and replacement of the saddle (Williams and Sperryn, 1976).

Soreness of the ischial tuberosity can be due to inflammation of the bursa which separates the tuberosity from the gluteus maximus (Stahl, 1978). It is fairly rare as the bursa is often not present, but the soreness seems to be caused by a combination of continuous minor trauma from bouncing on the saddle and repetitive use of the gluteus maximus. Often, after a prolonged period of riding, pain is experienced in the region of the ilium, above and posterior to the head of the femur; palpation over the buttock reveals spasm in the gluteus medius and minimus. One explanation is an ischaemia of the hip abductors due to their use while pedalling and to compression from the gluteus maximus.

TRUNK

All cyclists at some time or another experience backache which is usually in the lumbar region, the sacro-iliac or thoracic area. There appears to be four main causes:

1. Spasm of the extensors of the spine arises as a result of prolonged periods in an unnatural position leading to a relative ischaemia. It can be relieved while on the bicycle by moving more, and the onset can be delayed by a progressive resistance exercise regime. Deep massage or ultrasound to the affected area is successful.

2. Tension on the posterior longitudinal and interspinous ligaments can occur after muscles weaken through fatigue or where there is mis-alignment; later pain can occur or aching will follow. Massage will relieve the ache but stronger muscles are needed. As with the extensor spasms, pain diminishes when activity is terminated.

3. A more serious but rarer problem is that of protrusion and prolapse of the intervertebral disc. The prolapse or protrusion presses posteriorly or posterolaterally and impinges on the dura of the emerging

Fig. 23/3 The racing posture of the cyclist

spinal nerve or the spinal cord (Cyriax, 1978). At best, there is a mild ache and at worst paraesthesiae or anaesthesia. Specialist treatment is required from a doctor and a physiotherapist. It will help to learn to use the legs in lifting; to keep the back straight when off the bicycle and to have strong muscles. A good saddle position (Fig. 23/3), correct sized frame and the avoidance of sudden twists or jerks are essential.

4. Spondylolisthesis is the displacement of one vertebra on the one below, and may not be the cause of any symptoms during a lifetime. However, the condition may lead to a secondary disc lesion or may itself cause symptoms usually of central backache. It is due in part to stretching of the posterior ligaments of the lumbar intervertebral joints, and some days the back may ache, sometimes it may not (Cyriax, 1978).

UPPER LIMB

The gleno-humeral and acromio-clavicular joints are subjected to minor trauma which later leads to arthrotic changes. There is perhaps an ache when riding which may continue for sometime afterwards. The condition is aggravated by subluxation of the acromio-clavicular joint which can occur in a crash.

Subluxation with associated osteoarthrosis is treated by infiltration with hydrocortisone and procaine and this can afford some relief even after long-standing problems. Short wave diathermy or ultrasound may often relieve the symptoms for long periods; they will also relieve associated muscle spasm.

Occasionally, because the arm is held in abduction at the shoulder an associated tenosynovitis develops at the long head of the biceps. It can be relieved by deep transverse massage to the tendon as it lies in the bicipital groove or, if particularly severe, it may be infiltrated with hydrocortisone and procaine.

Three associated muscles at the elbow joint, extensors carpi radialis longus and brevis, and brachialis, may show spasm and a continual ache when riding may be experienced. These muscles are under tension during pushing and pulling on the handlebars and are subject to minor trauma which is transmitted through uneven road surfaces. Deep massage and ultrasound provide relief but it is imperative to have strong flexible muscles.

The wrist is a source of minor aches and pains which again are associated with continual minor trauma. Short wave diathermy or ultrasound to the wrist and passive movements for the accessory range of movement of the joint, are helpful. Sometimes tenosynovitis of abductor pollicis longus and extensor pollicis longus develops; this appears to be due to holding the handlebars for long periods with the thumb abducted and flexed around the bars, and again there is associated minor trauma. The flexors and extensors of the wrist can also be affected. If rest does not achieve relief then deep massage and ultrasound will.

The ulnar nerve is vulnerable at the point at which it enters the palm. Pressure occurs between the handlebars and the hypothenar eminence; this pressure is sometimes increased by riding over uneven terrain or going over pot-holes. Symptoms produced range from anaesthesia and paraesthesiae in the ring and little fingers to weakness of the grip. Prevention is by frequently altering the position of the hands on the handlebars (Faria and Cavanagh, 1978). Permanent changes will need specialist attention from a doctor and a physiotherapist.

The fingers are often affected by the cold and then they become very stiff; occasionally they suffer traumatic osteoarthrosis. Massage and short wave diathermy will help but more easily, frequent active movements while riding can be beneficial. The hands should be protected when training or racing in cold conditions by suitable mitts.

Associated with fixture

THE ANKLE

Cyclists seldom suffer ligamentous injuries at the ankle joint through riding; but there are three tendons associated with the ankle joint which can cause sufficient nuisance as to preclude training and racing.

Peritendinitis of the Achilles tendon occurs with intermittent attacks of acute pain which may in some cases gradually become continuous. It is usually an early season problem especially if insufficient attention has been paid to off-season training. The causes are numerous but they all imply overuse. This injury is seen in the single stage rider who changes to multi-stage events; time trialists who move to the longer competitive distances or the rider who changes from one type of terrain to another. The cyclist who trains on the flat and only occasionally rises from the saddle enters a multi-stage event which involves increased distances and climbing mountains; this means that the rider becomes like a runner for long periods, dancing up and down on the pedals for several days. Specialist physiotherapy is required for the early tendinitis (Cyriax, 1977); if, later, a paratenon develops surgery will be required (Williams, 1967; Williams, 1976). The problem may be eased by wearing a raised heel on the shoe to relax the calf muscles when off the bicycle. Training on the bicycle should be progressive at 50 per cent to 75 per cent of racing pace increasing the distance by 3 to 5km (2 to 3 miles) each day from 9km (5 miles) upwards. Climbing hills and getting out of the saddle must be avoided. The prevention of this peritendinitis is to give thought to training over all kinds of terrain. Cyclo-cross should not be attempted without some running training.

Tenosynovitis of the tibialis anterior and extensor hallucis longus may also be seen in the cyclist. These tendons are affected as they cross the ankle joint. They are treated by transverse frictions or by infiltration of hydrocortisone, and rest.

THE KNEE

The menisci are not normally affected in bicycle riding but damage occurs in training off the bicycle or while playing other sports. The coronary ligaments can suffer strain as a result of the femur pushing forward steadily on the tibial plateau. It is usually associated with the use of high gears especially in long distance events. Transverse frictions produce quick and effective results. The pain or ache that occurs behind the patella can be that of chondromalacia patellae (Fulford, 1969) or a weak vastus medialis muscle, allowing alteration of the line of pull of the patella on the femoral condyles. In chondromalacia, the central medial articular facet on the posterior surface of the patella is eroded, while in a weak vastus medialis the upper medial facet is similarly affected (Williams, 1971). A bent pedal spindle or loose cotter pin can cause the same problem by allowing mal-alignment at the knee. Very often the pain can be cured by strengthening the quadriceps group, first by straight leg raising and then by progressive resistance exercises. Mechanical faults in the bicycle should be corrected: the cranks must be straight and at right angles to the bottom bracket, the pedal spindles must be at right angles to the cranks, and the shoe plates must be aligned so that the foot rests squarely on the pedal and not at an angle.

It is common for cyclists to develop very painful knees due to the cold weather as a result of wearing shorts too early in the year. It is an easy condition to avoid but difficult to overcome. The answer is to cut down the mileage and to keep the knees covered for as long as possible. Racing in wet weather especially around country lanes causes grit and mud to be thrown up at the rider. This gets lodged in the shorts and works its way into the material. Eventually there is increased friction at the perineal and the adductor regions with ensuing soreness. It is advisable to buy good quality racing shorts with fairly long legs so that there is minimum chafing between thighs and the saddle.

TRAUMA DUE TO CRASHES

Causes of crashes

On the whole, cyclists are skilful at maintaining balance and many crashes are avoided: however, there are some situations in which they become unavoidable and these occur in all branches of the sport. There are two main factors – firstly, loss of adhesion between the road surface and the tyres leading to loss of balance and, second, loss of balance through any other cause including professional fouls.

LOSS OF ADHESION

On a steep descent speeds of 80 to 96kmh^{-1} (50 to 60mph^{-1}) are reached allowing little time for contact between road surface and tyres. A gust of wind can cause a wobble and then loss of adhesion. Wintry conditions, loose gravel or strong winds, either alone or in combination, can also lead to loss of adhesion. On very steeply banked tracks this loss of contact has spectacular results and may be caused by just a few spots of rain. Equipment is often implicated in loss of adhesion. Tyre tread may be poor, worn out and not replaced for reasons of finances, carelessness or laziness. Tyres can also roll off. Neglect amounts to almost a criminal offence and so all tyres are inspected before track and road meetings to see that they are firm. Occasionally accidents will happen – taking a corner too fast or at too great an angle may cause the tyre to be forced off the rim and cause a crash.

LOSS OF BALANCE

The deliberate fouls which cause crashes are, fortunately, very rare and remediable on a 'tit for tat' basis. The very nature of the sport tends to militate against fouling as the culprit may be worse off by being involved in the resultant crash. The main cause of loss of balance is lack of skill which applies more to schoolboy and junior events than to senior level. Switching, i.e. the swinging aside of a cyclist to adjust to the sudden change of position of the rider in front, is the biggest single factor; at fast speeds there is insufficient time to move out of the way. The fact that the rider behind may not be able to avoid the switch may also be due to lack of skill, poor judgement in travelling too close to his opponent, or being not good enough to avoid the move. There is also the domino effect, i.e. one rider knocks another who knocks another until it becomes impossible to avoid a crash no matter how skilful the riders are. The more skilful riders will be able to exercise sufficient control on poor surfaces even when they are exhausted. It is during the period of exhaustion that some crashes occur due to lack of control or loss of concentration. A pedal may accidentally be put into the wheel of an adjacent rider; lines may be changed so that adhesion is lost on corners; another rider is interfered with; or the rider runs off the road. Occasionally, pressure may be such that a rider has to concentrate so hard in single-mindedly pursuing a good time or chasing the escaping group, or trying to catch the bunch after a puncture, that he fails to see a parked vehicle and collides head-on with it. A tight echelon in a cross-wind constitutes a potentially dangerous situation where a lapse of attention can be physically costly.

Many mechanical factors can contribute to crashes by causing imbalance. The most common is snapping cranks or pedal spindles with a resulting lurch to one side. Going over pot-holes can cause wheels to collapse, while breaking seat pillars also causes serious problems.

Trauma associated with crashes

The incidence of crashes is highly unpredictable in any one event. A crop of injuries, because of a multiple pile up rather than a solitary severe case, is usual (Black, 1970). The injuries run the whole gamut of the orthopaedic spectrum. The common fractures are those of the clavicle, scaphoid and the lower end of the radius and ulna. One or two cases of a fractured neck of femur in young cyclists have been recorded (Stahl, 1978). The skull is sometimes fractured with fatal results. The shoulder joint is most frequently dislocated with subluxations of the acromio-clavicular and sterno-clavicular joints being recorded (Stahl, 1978). A likely cause is a direct blow on the shoulder after being thrown from the machine.

Grazes, abrasions, gravel rashes, friction burns are common cycling injuries and always occur as a result of contact with the road surface after crashing. Most, if not all of the riders involved in a crash will have one or more of them, depending on their speed and position when it happens. Although the wound (especially a friction burn) remains clean for up to four hours, it is most important that it is kept clean afterwards. A friction burn is more likely to occur on the track where

there is a greater chance of more sophisticated treatment being available. On the other hand a graze with gravel rash can occur on the open road when the rider is competing in a long distance or stage of a multi-stage event. In this case it has been found useful to spray the affected area – mostly the greater trochanter, thigh, knees and shins – with an anaesthetic spray, usually incorporating iodine powder. The wound can then be covered with Netelast while the rider is still moving on tow. There is thus little loss of continuity and the psychological 'pack barrier' (i.e. the tendency to give up) is avoided. If it has not already been done on the move, it is essential, later, to scrub the area of the rash so that all debris and grit is removed. It is *not* advisable to use cotton wool as the small strands may be left behind and become foci for infection. The ability of the rider to continue may be paramount and infiltration with local anaesthetic is advisable to ensure a restful night. It is not usual to apply more than a spray while the rider is on the move. The wound must be well covered to prevent secondary infection and further friction from clothing.

If there is bruising and contusion without an open wound, the area is covered with a hyaluronidase and heparinoid ointment (Lasonil); (Movelat gel or cream).

MISCELLANEOUS INJURIES

There is a risk of conjunctivitis from spray dust and grit thrown up from the racing surface. The problem is not helped, especially on hot dry days, by sweat dripping into the eyes. Regular bathing with Optrex Eye Lotion is soothing and preventive. To avoid aggravating the condition, it is advisable to hand up grit-free wet sponges while the rider is on the move to maintain body fluids so that reduction of eye lubrication does not occur.

In common with chondromalacia patellae, sinusitis seems to be an occupational hazard to cyclists. The major cause is continual irritation of the nasal mucosa from grit and dust; it may also be due to an increase in mucous secretions as effort increases circulation. It is essential to prevent retention and infection of these secretions by blowing the nose properly so that the nares are not held together when blowing: if they are held together pressure forces material into the sinuses and even into the bronchi.

Extreme effort, especially in hill climbing on cold winter days, can produce the phenomenon known as 'effort bronchitis'; breathing becomes harsh with audible bronchial sounds. There is an increase in pulmonary secretions and much frothy white sputum is produced. The result can resemble an asthmatic attack;

indeed, Dekker and Groe (1957) suggested that the secretions of asthma are produced in this way by compression of the trachea and major bronchi when muscular effort increases intrathoracic pressure. The problems soon settle after exertion; if abnormal secretions are not cleared there may be danger of chronic bronchitis.

Corns are due to ill-fitting shoes and wrongly aligned shoe plates so that the foot is not snugly fitted into the toeclips. The strap of the toeclip is a causal factor if pulled too tightly. Corns are best avoided by having well-fitted shoes which do not cause pressure and which allow the feet to spread.

During cold wet weather poor circulation exacerbates chilblains. The condition is not helped by inappropriate shoes and socks which do not afford protection against the weather. Vitamin K taken in accordance with instructions is helpful as is the wearing of socks and shoes without holes but with a fleecy lining in the winter.

Because the need to keep a sharp lookout and to watch opponents involves constant backward glances, minor injuries can occur in the cervical spine. In the United Kingdom, where driving is on the left-hand-side, spasm of the left sternocleidomastoid muscle may develop causing torticollis (wry neck); for those who ride on the right-hand-side of the road, this will develop on the right side. After a hard day's ride there may be a general neck ache which can be relieved by traction and massage. Occasionally, torticollis may result from a sudden displacement of the disc or appear gradually overnight (Cyriax, 1977). Both Cyriax (1977) and Maitland (1977) have described treatments for this condition.

SAFETY

The racing cyclist is a skilful handler of the bicycle at speed and must have a sound body to propel the machine. The nature of the sport demands a mechanically sound bicycle; gears should be well-adjusted, the chain correctly aligned, the wheels should be true, the tyres secure and the brake blocks should be changed frequently. Adjustments to suit the individual should be made to saddle height, handlebar width and the length of extension.

A lot of problems in cycle racing are caused through crashes so a few brief do's and don'ts will be useful.

Do's

DO brake before a corner and never on it, especially in wet conditions.

DO take a smooth line using as much road as is safe to do.

DO look over the shoulder of the man in front.

DO look for changes in formation when changing direction.

DO look ahead for oncoming traffic when in an echelon, or when spread from gutter to gutter.

DO move to the correct side when working in a small group.

Don'ts

DON'T ride too close to the wheel in front.

DON'T look behind while in a bunch or group.

DON'T ride into a non-existent or rapidly closing gap, especially during a sprint.

DON'T change your line in a corner unless absolutely necessary.

DON'T look down at the wheel in front.

Attaining cycling fitness is time-consuming because of the long training and racing distances involved. It is important that as much consideration is given to the care of the machine as to the body, otherwise fitness may be wasted because of mechanical defects.

REFERENCES

Black, W. A. (1970). Cycling injuries. *British Journal of Sports Medicine*, **3**, 105–107.

Cyriax, J. (1978). Textbook of orthopaedic medicine. Volume 1, *Diagnosis of soft tissue injuries*. 7th edition. Baillière Tindall, London.

Cyriax, J. and Russell, G. (1977). *Textbook of orthopaedic medicine*. Volume 2, *Treatment of soft tissue injuries*. 9th edition. Baillière Tindall, London.

Dekker, E. and Groe, J. J. (1957). Asthmatic wheezing, compression of the trachea and major bronchi. *Lancet*, **1**, 1064.

Faria, I. E. and Cavanagh, P. R. (1978). *Physiology and biomechanics of cycling*. John Wiley and Sons, New York.

Fulford, P. (1969). Chondromalacia of the patella. *British Journal of Sports Medicine*. **3**, 198–202.

Maitland, G. D. (1977). *Vertebral manipulation*, 4th edition. Butterworths, London.

Stahl, T. (1978). Personal communications.

Williams, J. G. P. (1967). Causes and prevention of Achilles peritendonitis in middle and long distance runners. *British Journal of Sports Medicine*, **1**, 16–17.

Williams, J. G. P. (1971). Diagnostic pitfalls in the sportsman's knee. *Proceedings of the Royal Society of Medicine*, **64**, 640–641.

Williams, J. G. P. and Sperryn, P. N. (1976). *Sports Medicine*. Edward Arnold, (Publishers) Ltd., London.

Williams, J. G. P., Sperryn, P. N., Boardman, S., Street, M., Mellett, S. and Parsons, C. (1976). Post-operative management of chronic Achilles tendon pain in sportsmen. *Physiotherapy*, **62**, 256–259.

SECTION 5

Orthopaedic aspects of sports injuries

CHAPTER 24

The physiology of injured skeletal muscle

R. J. MAUGHAN BSc, PhD

The functional unit responsible for bodily movement or the generation of static force is composed of a skeletal muscle, its tendonous attachments and the bones onto which these tendons are inserted. In this chapter, attention will be focused on the response of muscle tissue to injury, to the exclusion of a coverage of injuries to tendon and bone.

Skeletal muscle accounts for about 40 per cent of the total bodyweight of the average adult male, and a slightly lower proportion in the adult female. Most of this muscle tissue is located close to the body surface, usually overlying the rigid components of the skeletal system. Because of this, it is likely that the application of external violence to the body will result in muscular damage. Newman et al (1969) found that in a population of 1 847 patients suffering from sports injuries, 14 per cent of the cases involved injury to skeletal muscle. The implications of this for the athlete are obvious, since all sporting activity requires involvement of at least part of the muscle mass. The competitive athlete is also particularly susceptible to muscular injury as a result of acute or chronic overuse. Inability to train or compete due to injury is a personal catastrophe for the serious athlete, and the aim of treatment must be to minimise the initial damage and to maximise recovery. An understanding of the physiological effects of trauma on skeletal muscle must form the basis of successful treatment.

STRUCTURE AND FUNCTION OF MUSCLE

In cross-section, the light microscope reveals the muscle as consisting of bundles of individual fibres enclosed within the fascia, a tough collagenous sheet which forms an outer connective tissue sheath. Within this outer sheath, the epimysium, the fibres are grouped in bundles, each normally containing 20 to 40 fibres and each being surrounded by a less substantial envelope of connective tissue, the perimysium. Each fibre is enclosed within a fine collagen network, the endomysium. Large muscles may contain many thousands of fibres, although the very smallest muscles consist of only a few fibres grouped together. Irrespective of the size of the muscle, each fibre is between 20

and 80μ in diameter (Bendall, 1969). Figure 24/1 illustrates the different levels of organisation within the muscle.

In longitudinal sections of skeletal muscle, the light microscope reveals the characteristic cross-striations of the fibres: further detail can be resolved by use of the electron microscope (Fig. 24/2). Each fibre is composed of a large number of myofibrils, each 1 to 1.5μ in diameter. The myofibril can be considered as the basic contractile unit of the muscle cell. The myofibril itself is composed of bundles of microfilaments. The striated appearance of the muscle is due to the composition of the microfilaments, the light region is due to the presence of the protein actin, the dark region being composed of another protein, myosin. It is the physical and chemical properties of these proteins which enable the muscle to shorten or to generate tension. These phenomena occur not as a result of contraction of any of the physical structures of the muscle but because of a relative sliding motion of the microfilaments.

Also present within the fibre are other structures essential for the normal functioning of the cell. All striated muscle cells contain nuclei located along the length of the cell immediately under the cell membrane. Mitochondria within the cell are responsible for the maintenance of the oxidative energy supply. Also present is a delicate internal membrane system, the sarcotubular system, which is involved in the control of the initiation of contraction in response to a nervous impulse. Substrate depots are present in the form of glycogen granules and lipid droplets. The blood supply to the muscle consists of an extensive network of capillaries which surrounds the fibre, the capillary density being higher in trained than in untrained muscle (Andersen, 1975).

The mechanical properties of the muscle depend upon the existence of the contractile apparatus, but the activity of the contractile components is modified by the presence of elastic components in the muscle. The series elastic component lies not within the muscle itself but within the tendons into which the muscle fibres are inserted and which attach the muscle to the bone. The parallel elastic component is due to the presence of the non-contractile structures of the

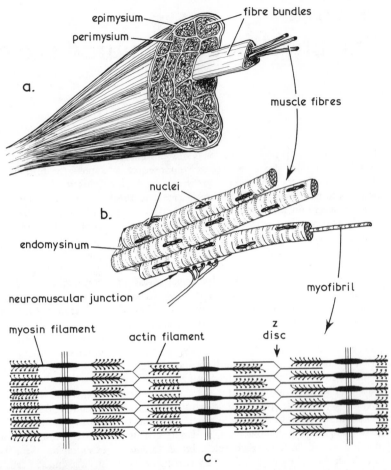

epimysium

perimysium

fibre bundles

muscle fibres

a.

nuclei

b.

endomysinum

neuromuscular junction

myofibril

myosin filament

actin filament

z disc

c.

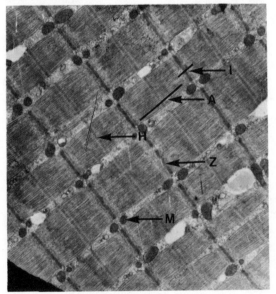

I

A

H

Z

M

Fig. 24/1 The structure of skeletal muscle as revealed by the light microscope.
(a) Whole muscle in transverse section showing organisation of connective tissue and muscle fibres
(b) Individual muscle fibres revealing characteristic cross-striations and nuclei
(c) Ultra structure of muscle fibril showing individual protein filaments

Fig. 24/2 Electron micrograph showing part of a muscle fibre taken from human vastus lateralis (magnification 29,250 times). The regular array of the myofibrils can be clearly seen. Each fibril consists of alternating light I bands consisting of actin filaments and dark A bands consisting of myosin filaments overlapping with actin filaments. In the light H zone in the middle of each A band only myosin filaments are present. In the middle of each band is a Z disc, which serves to maintain the regular spacing of the filaments. Abundant mitochondria (M) are present in this muscle section. The small dark granules in the inter-filament spaces consist of glycogen (Photograph by courtesy of H. H. Eichelberger, University of Aberdeen)

muscle, including the cell membranes, sarcotubular system and connective tissue. These elastic elements have the effect of damping the contractions produced by the contractile apparatus which must first stretch the elastic tissue before shortening or load bearing can occur.

EFFECTS OF TRAUMA ON SKELETAL MUSCLE

Muscle injuries can occur as a result of intrinsic factors generated from within the muscle, or from extrinsic factors which originate outside the tissue. Both of these types of factors can result in damage to the muscle fibres, to the associated connective tissue or to the vascular system. Tearing or rupture of the muscle as a result of excessive stretch or of a direct blow on the surface of the muscle may be complete, in which case loss of function is also complete due to loss of structural continuity. Such cases are, however, relatively rare. Rupture of the muscle appears to be most common in the region of the muscle-tendon junction (Burry, 1973) and will be visible as a bunching of the muscle due to retraction from the severed region. It is not clear why the muscle-tendon junction should be weaker than the belly of the muscle itself. Tears, strains and pulls of the muscle describe cases of partial rupture in which the damage is restricted to a limited number of fibres.

Associated with the damage to the contractile components of the muscle, rupture of connective tissue and blood vessels normally occurs at the site of the injury, leading to the formation of a haematoma. If the epimysium remains intact, blood escaping from damaged capillaries is retained within the muscle, leading to a rise in intramuscular pressure and associated pain and loss of function. Because the blood remains within the muscle such an outcome is termed an intramuscular haematoma. If the injury has resulted in splitting of the fascia, an interstitial haematoma is formed, in which the increase in pressure is avoided due to the escape of blood into the interstitial spaces. As a result, the effects of an interstitial haematoma in terms of pain and disability are generally less severe than those produced by an intramuscular haematoma, although it may produce rather spectacular discolouration of the skin either in the region of the wound or further down the limb.

RECOVERY AND REPAIR OF DAMAGED TISSUE

The repair of damage to skeletal muscle involves two separate processes which shall be dealt with separately; the first of these involves the formation of non-contractile collagenous fibres, the second depends on the capacity of the muscle tissue for regeneration.

Following injury, the tissue is infiltrated by macrophages. These cells are converted to fibroblasts which proliferate rapidly in the damaged area. Existing fibroblasts also rapidly divide. This proliferation appears to result from the inactivation of inhibitory substances which are normally present in healthy tissues. An increase in the number of fibroblasts in the region of a wound has been observed to occur within 24 hours of wound infliction (Dunphy and Udupa, 1955). These fibroblasts secrete a soluble protein precursor of collagen and, in their mature form, these cells remain in the tissue as fibrocytes. The process of maturation is accompanied by an irreversible shortening of the fibrocytes, leading to the tendency of muscle wounds to heal short. The strength of this scar tissue progressively increases, reaching a maximum some months after its initial formation (Douglas, 1966). Because it is non-contractile, this fibrous tissue cannot contribute to the generation of tension by the muscle, but it allows the undamaged muscle to fulfil its normal function.

It was established by Gay and Hunt (1954) that skeletal muscle possesses the capacity of regeneration to the extent that complete reunion of transected fibres is possible if the cut ends of the fibres are closely opposed following sectioning. They suggested that the majority of the cut fibres in the muscles which they studied had successfully reunited. It should, of course, be realised that surgical sectioning of muscle produces a clean cut through the fibres, whereas muscle lacerations sustained in the sporting situation seldom involve simple transection of the fibres, but are usually associated with considerable damage, which makes it impossible to oppose accurately the damaged ends of fibres.

There is a widespread misconception that muscle is incapable of regenerative repair. Experimental work on animals has, however, demonstrated that skeletal muscle possesses a high capacity for regeneration (Carlson, 1968; Carlson and Gutman, 1972). Carlson performed a series of experiments in which complete animal muscles were removed, minced into small (1mm^3) pieces and re-implanted in their original sites. He showed recovery of the muscle begins almost immediately and follows a sequence of events similar to those undergone by normal muscle in the post-natal period. Morphological changes can be observed within two to three days, with the appearance of myoblasts around the edges of the minced tissue. Progressive regeneration takes place during the succeeding weeks, spreading through the muscle mass, and re-attachment to the existing tendon stumps takes place. The original fibres degenerate and disappear, and cross-striations begin to appear in the new developing fibres. The contractile properties of the muscle also gradually return, the first responses being observed about seven to eight days after the operative procedure; it is at about this time that the presence of cross-striations in the immature fibres is first noted. Although functional re-innervation of the regenerating muscle occurs, complete recovery in terms of strength is not achieved. Each of the new fibres possesses almost normal functional characteristics, but the new muscle contains relatively few fibres and large amounts of connective tissue. The total tension which the muscle is capable of producing is therefore less than that of normal muscles. These experiments do, however, demonstrate that mature muscle is capable of recovery by regeneration. The experiments quoted here were done, for obvious reasons, on animals rather than on human subjects, but there seems to be little doubt that the results are generally applicable to mammalian skeletal muscle.

Occasionally, the process of recovery and repair is complicated by bacterial infection of the wound or by the formation of serum filled cysts resulting from incomplete re-absorption of the haematoma. In such cases, surgical drainage may be required. A more serious complication is the development of myositis ossificans. This ossification process is due to the invasion of the haematoma formed at the time of injury by osteoblasts which are probably derived from the damaged periosteum. Maturation of these cells leads to the formation in the muscle of an open network of bone. The patient will experience symptoms of pain, swelling and disability. If this condition is present, exercise of the affected limb should be strictly avoided, as this may result in further damage and increased ossification (Ellis and Franck, 1966). It is quite probable that the associated pain will result in disinclination on the part of the subject, but it should be realised that vigorous massage may be equally dangerous.

PHYSIOLOGICAL EFFECTS OF TREATMENT

The object of any treatment given to the injured athlete must be to minimise damage in the short term and to maximise recovery in the long term. In the immediate post-injury phase, this should be accomplished by attempting to eliminate bleeding at the site of injury and by preventing movement which might aggravate muscular damage. The first of these objectives is normally achieved by the application of cold or pressure, or both. By increasing the local tissue pressure as a result of bandaging to the point at which it exceeds the systolic pressure, occlusion of the blood vessels in the area below the bandage will occur. Application of cold in the form of proprietary cold packs, sprays or ice has a two-fold effect. Firstly, blood flow is

decreased as a result of a decrease in local metabolic rate due to the decreased temperature of the tissues. This mechanism, however, is of little importance compared with the reflex inhibition of blood flow which occurs. In response to stimulation of cold receptors, probably in the form of free nerve endings in the skin, a reflex mechanism exists whereby local vasoconstriction takes place as a result of contraction of the smooth muscle lining the arterioles. If the application of cold is too severe and prolonged, accumulation of vasoactive metabolities will occur as a result of anaerobic metabolism. This will normally overcome the cold-induced reflex vasoconstriction, and a period of high local blood flow ensues. This in turn gives way to vasoconstriction and a cyclical pattern of alternate high and low blood flow is observed. However, the net effect is an overall decrease in local blood flow, and a combination of cold and pressure is strongly recommended if intramuscular bleeding is suspected. The American Medical Association Committee on the Medical Aspects of Sports recommended application of cold during the first 24 to 48 hours after injury (Hein, 1969). Williams and Sperryn (1976) advised that pressure be applied and maintained for 48 to 72 hours.

Most injuries are presented for treatment only after some time has elapsed, and are consequently too late for first aid treatment. The aim in these cases, as indeed in all cases, must be to obtain maximum restoration of function, normally in the shortest time possible, as the sportsman is invariably anxious to return to training and competition. A wide choice of treatments is available, and each case must be considered on an individual basis. The aim of these treatments is generally to stimulate local blood flow, and in this respect, local heating, massage and exercise are all effective.

Application of heat from infra-red sources is widely used, but for heating of deep tissue structures, this method is rather ineffective. Ultrasound treatment is effective in producing localised heating in deep structures, but tends to produce its effects most markedly in underlying bone rather than in muscle (Bass, 1969). Dyson et al (1970), however, showed that ultrasound therapy was effective in promoting healing of experimental lesions.

Massage with ice (cryokinetics) has been suggested as a treatment for chronic injuries in addition to its use in the immediate post-injury phase (Grant, 1964; Laing et al, 1973). There is no satisfactory explanation for the beneficial effects which this treatment has been reported to produce.

Surface massage has a two-fold effect, by promoting re-absorption of any haematoma which may be present and by stimulating blood flow in the affected area. In conjunction with massage, a gradual return to exercise should be undertaken. This can take the form initially of stretching exercises against gentle resistance and may take the form of active stretching of the muscle by the patient or of externally applied manipulation to the joints. Rylander (1969) has proposed that a more vigorous exercise programme than that normally recommended is effective in promoting recovery. Except in cases of myositis ossificans, rest will normally delay recovery, and is not to be recommended.

It has been suggested that administration of anti-inflammatory drugs, such as oxyphenbutazone (Blazina, 1969), indomethacin, phenylbutazone, meferamic acid and flufenamic acid (Bass, 1969) are effective in aiding rehabilitation. In contrast to these reports, a double-blind study by Huskisson et al (1973) showed that indomethacin treatment was not superior to a placebo administered to injured football players.

EFFECTS OF TRAINING AND DISUSE ON SKELETAL MUSCLE

Sports injuries, by definition, occur to sportsmen and sportswomen, and it should be recognised that the muscle of the trained athlete is different in some respects from that of the normal non-athletic individual. The aim of a training regime is to produce an adaptive response which will facilitate the performance of exercise. If the athlete is prevented from training by injury, these processes are reversed, and a de-training effect is observed. Training and fitness are obviously specific to individual sports, and the characteristics of the endurance athlete are quite different from those of the heavyweight weightlifter. The endurance athlete has a highly developed cardiovascular system: the increased dimensions of this system facilitate an increased oxygen delivery to the working muscles. In addition, the oxidative capacity of the muscle is enhanced by an increased concentration of the enzymes and co-factors involved in oxidative energy supply. These adaptations result in an improved ability to maintain a high level of energy production without the onset of fatigue. The training programme of the athlete whose event is based on strength rather than endurance is designed to increase both muscle mass and the strength of the muscle per unit cross-sectional area. These aims can be achieved independently by a careful choice of the training stimulus.

The full effects of a training programme become apparent over a period of months or years rather than weeks. It is of interest, therefore, to note that Saltin et al (1968) found that the maximum oxygen uptake, a measure of endurance capacity, was decreased by approximately 26 per cent in response to 21 days bed rest. In the rat, immobilisation of a limb resulted in a rapid decrease in the concentration of enzymes involved in oxidative energy production; these responses to disuse occurred in an exponential fashion, one half of the total decrease being complete in four to six days (Booth, 1977). Similar changes in the weights of individual muscles in the immobilised limb were also recorded. Thus the decrease in both endurance and strength is extremely rapid when compared with the time necessary to produce the training effect. It is for these reasons that absence from training due to injury should be minimised.

Skeletal muscle is a highly specialised tissue, adapted for the performance of physical work in the form of movement or tension generation. Injury to muscle may result from acute or chronic overuse, or from the application of external violence. Injury may take the form of damage to the contractile apparatus, but often also involves rupture of the vascular system, and consequent extravasation of blood leading to an increase in intramuscular pressure and associated pain. The repair and recovery processes involve a degree of regeneration of muscular tissue and the formation of fibrous scar tissue.

Treatment should aim to eliminate further damage by restricting movement in the immediate post-injury phase and limit bleeding by application of cold and pressure. During the recovery phase, massage and heat application should be used in conjunction with a gradual return to normal activity. The return to full training should be accomplished as rapidly as is possible in order to minimise the de-training effect which accompanies muscular disuse.

REFERENCES

Andersen, P. (1975). Capillary density in skeletal muscle of man. *Acta Physiologia Scandinavica*, **95**, 203–205.

Bass, A. L. (1969). Treatment of muscle, tendon and minor joint injuries in sport. *Proceedings of the Royal Society of Medicine*, **62**, 925–928.

Bendall, J. R. (1969). *Muscles, molecules and movement*. Heinemann, London.

Blazina, M. E. (1969). Oxyphenbutazone as an adjunct to the conventional treatment of athletic injuries. *Clinical Medicine*, **161**, 19–22.

Booth, F. W. (1977). Time course of muscular atrophy during immobilisation of hind limbs in rats. *Journal of Applied Physiology*, **43**, 656–661.

Burry, H. C. (1973). *Soft tissue injury in sport*. In J. H. Wilmore (ed). *Exercise and sports sciences reviews*. Academic Press, New York.

Carlson, B. M. (1968). Regeneration of the completely excised gastrocnemius muscle in the frog and rat from minced muscle fragments. *Journal of Morphology*, **125**, 447–471.

Carlson, B. M. and Gutmann, E. (1972). Development of contractile properties of minced muscle regenerates in the rat. *Experimental Neurology*, **36**, 239–249.

Douglas, D. M. (1966). *Wound healing*. Churchill, London.

Dunphy, J. E. and Udupa, K. N. (1955). Chemical and histochemical sequences in the normal healing of wounds. *New England Journal of Medicine*, **253**, 847–851.

Dyson, M. Ford, J. B., Joseph J. and Warwick, R. (1970). Stimulation of tissue regeneration by pulsed planewave ultrasound. *Institute of Electrical and Electronic Engineers Transactions of Sonics and Ultrasound*, **17**, 133–140.

Ellis, M. and Frank, H. G. (1966). Myositis ossificans traumatica: with special reference to the quadriceps femoris muscle. *The Journal of Trauma*, **6**, 724–738.

Gay, A. J. and Hunt, T. E. (1954). Reuniting of skeletal muscle fibres after transection. *Anatomical Record*, **120**, 853–871.

Grant, A. E. (1964). Massage with ice (cryokinetics) in the treatment of painful conditions of the musculoskeletal system. *Archives of Physical Medicine and Rehabilitation*, **45**, 233–238.

Hein, F. V. (1969). Continuous cold application for athletic injuries. *Journal of the American Medical Association*, **207**, 962.

Huskisson, E. K., Berry, H., Street, F. G. and Medhurst, H. E. (1973). Indomethacin for soft tissue injuries. *Rheumatology and Rehabilitation*, **12**, 159–160.

Laing, D. R., Dalley, D. R. and Kirk, J. A. (1973). Ice therapy in soft tissue injuries. *New Zealand Medical Journal*, **78**, 155–158.

Newman, P. H., Thompson, J. P. S., Barnes, J. M. and Moore T. M. C. (1969). A clinic for athletic injuries. *Proceedings of the Royal Society of Medicine*, **62**, 939–941.

Rylander, C. R. (1969). Rehabilitation of the injured athlete. *Delaware Medical Journal*, **41**, 271–273.

Saltin, B., Blomqvist, C., Mitchell, J. H., Johnson, R. L., Wildenthal, K. and Chapman, C. B. (1968). Response to exercise after bedrest and after training. *Circulation*, Supplementum, **7**.

Williams, J. G. P. and Sperryn, P. N. (1976). *Sports medicine*. Edward Arnold, London.

CHAPTER 25

Back and neck injuries

J.D.G. TROUP PhD, MRCS, LRCP

Spinal injuries may be considered under three headings:

1. Injuries, mainly to non-bony tissues, in which the spine remains stable.

2. Injuries which make the spine sufficiently unstable to put the spinal cord or nerve roots at risk.

3. Injuries of the vertebral column with gross neurological damage and imminent deformity.

Minor injuries in the first category far outnumber the others. This is not to imply that there is a direct relationship between the severity of musculo-skeletal trauma and the amount of neurological damage. The cord can be transected without fracture or dislocation and a severely fractured spine may leave the cord

unharmed, though clearly at risk (Holdsworth 1963, 1970; Roaf, 1976; Bodnar, 1977; Vigouroux et al 1978).

Fractures vary greatly in severity, some occurring without symptoms at the time of injury or later. Similarly with non-bony injuries: often the onset of pain is delayed for a day or so after injury. There are two reasons for this. First, there is an inhibitory mechanism available on the field of battle which prevents the painful stimuli from being transmitted to the cortex for recognition; and secondly, the intervertebral disc and the facets of the apophyseal joints are not supplied with nerves and can thus be injured without pain. There is another category of back or neck injury altogether in

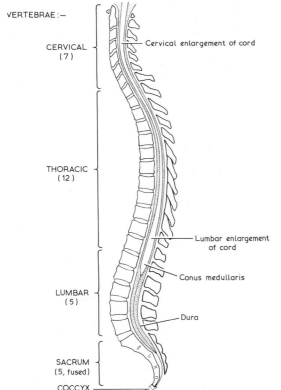

VERTEBRAE :—

CERVICAL (7)

Cervical enlargement of cord

THORACIC (12)

Lumbar enlargement of cord

Conus medullaris

LUMBAR (5)

Dura

SACRUM (5, fused)

COCCYX

Fig. 25/1 (left) The vertebral column showing the spinal cord and dura within the spinal canal

Fig. 25/2 Anatomical features of the sacrum and lower three lumbar vertebrae

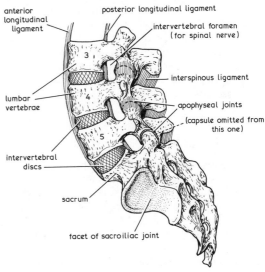

anterior longitudinal ligament

posterior longitudinal ligament

intervertebral foramen (for spinal nerve)

interspinous ligament

lumbar vertebrae

apophyseal joints

(capsule omitted from this one)

intervertebral discs

sacrum

facet of sacroiliac joint

which there is an unexpected onset of the symptoms of an injury in the absence of a truly accidental occurrence, often when bent down. In these cases part of the vertebral column or its connective tissue support have become unduly susceptible to injury. This can arise because of degenerative change. It can also occur after exposure to 'conditioning' factors: for example, loading prolonged enough to produce 'creep-effects' – stiffening the spine and making it less capable of absorbing energy.

Non-bony injuries can also be severe. If the ligaments of the neural arch of the vertebra are ruptured the column is unstable even in the absence of fracture or dislocation. Moreover, one of the most common reasons for disability after a non-bony injury is the consequent mechanical irritation of the nerve roots. The reason for this wide spectrum is the proximity of nervous, bony and connective tissue in a relatively confined space (Figs. 25/1 and 25/2). This is why it may be vital to be able to distinguish between the injury which is stable and the one which is not. Any suspicion of local pain and weakness or numbness in the limbs following injury must be treated with respect. Because of the risk of converting a serious injury into a disaster, the patient must be handled with the greatest care. This caveat applies with equal force to patients who are unconscious or those with head injury because the force required to injure the head is in many cases more than enough to damage the neck at the same time.

Prevention of spinal injuries depends on an understanding of the biomechanics of the spine and of the causative mechanism; and on supervision wherever obvious dangers abound, for example at swimming baths or in contact-sports. Recovery after injury (especially where nervous tissue has been at risk) depends on the speed with which possibility of injury is appreciated, on the skill with which first aid is applied and the patient then transported, as well as on the efficiency of management of the diagnostic and therapeutic services.

FUNCTIONAL ANATOMY

The strength of the vertebral column

Stripped of its muscles and ligaments the spine is an unstable structure but the vertebral column together with its supporting tissues serve a number of mechanical functions. First of all they form a highly mobile structure. They protect the spinal cord and nerve roots from direct injury. Moreover they are able to withstand considerable compressive, tensile, shearing and torsional forces. All the tissues of the spine are plastic; that is to say they deform when stress is applied. When, therefore, the spine is subjected to impact on falling or being struck some of the energy can be dissipated safely into plastic deformation and some into intervertebral motion – provided that the spine has not been unduly stiffened by age, disease or any other cause.

The spine is relatively resistant to injury when exposed to single modes of force such as purely flexor, extensor or compressive force, but more susceptible if the modes are combined or if there is a torsional component (Roaf, 1960; Holdsworth, 1970). In addition, the strength of the spine depends very much on the time factor, being inversely proportional to the duration of the applied load (Perey, 1957).

When the compressive force exceeds the osmotic pressure of the intervertebral disc, 'creep-effects' take place. Tissue fluid is expelled, the disc narrows and stiffens; and the dynamic characteristics of the intervertebral joint-complex are modified accordingly (Kazarian, 1975). Creep-effects are not produced only by 'excessive' loading: loss of vertebral height has been recorded in healthy young male adults after loading the shoulders for 20 minutes with 9kg (Fitzgerald, 1972). Creep-effects are accelerated if the loaded spine is then exposed to vibration (Kazarian, 1972) – the phenomenon of 'vibro-creep'.

When the applied force is of brief duration, the probability of injury is related to the magnitude of peak acceleration and to the jerk or rate of increase of acceleration (Hodgson et al, 1963). The risk of injury after a single, rapid axial loading depends on where the force is applied, on the constraints on the body after application as well as the characteristics of the individual spine. The probability of fracture after ejection from a fighter aircraft at, say, $200\,\mathrm{ms^{-2}}$ may be as much as 1 in 5. The risks are less, though still far from negligible in parachuting where the deceleration on landing is of the order of 50 to $60\,\mathrm{ms^{-2}}$ (Murray-Leslie et al, 1977). In parachuting such loadings are isolated. In sports such as cross-country motor-cycling or power-boat racing the frequency of impact can be expected to cause vibro-creep, susceptibility to injury increasing throughout the duration of exposure (Allen 1976).

The 'conditioning' factors which make back injury more likely are therefore prolonged static loading, vibratory stress and repetitive impacts and shocks. Unhappily there are too few valid data to indicate safe limits for any of these hazards, and none for the periods of recovery which should be allowed. Individual capacity for spinal stress varies greatly, depending on the size and physical characteristics of the vertebral column, on muscular strength, experience and skill and on the presence or absence of degenerative changes and other abnormalities.

The biomechanics of the spinal canal

Understanding spinal mobility entails more than a knowledge of the kinematics. In the context of spinal injuries it is important to note the effects of motion on the tissues within the spinal canal: on the spinal meninges, cord and nerve roots. The normal range of movement imposes linear and volumetric changes on the canal and the tissues within it must adapt accordingly.

On fully flexing the spine the cervical spinal canal is increased in length by 20 to 30 per cent compared with full extension, the increase being greater on the posterior than the anterior wall of the canal (Fig. 25/3).

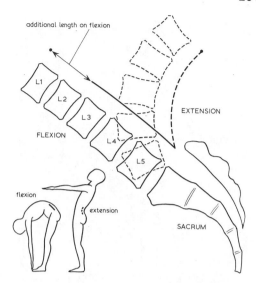

Fig. 25/4 Diagram from radiographs of the lumbar spine taken in flexion and extension with the images of the sacrum superimposed: showing lengthening of the lumbar canal on flexion

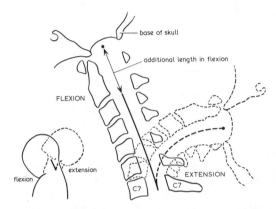

Fig. 25/3 Diagram based on lateral radiographs of the cervical spine taken in flexion and extension showing the increase in the length of the spinal canal on flexion

Likewise on lateral flexion, the convex side of the canal becomes longer than the concave. The spinal meninges are thereby stretched on flexion, further stretched on the convex side on lateral flexion and pulled tight by added rotation. The spinal dura mater (the outer meningeal layer forming the tube enclosing the subarachnoid space, cord and nerve roots) is relatively inextensible; on extension it is lax and when stretched by flexion tends to follow the shortest route within the canal. The cord and nerve roots are semi-fluid and readily deformable. Thus the cord becomes longer and narrower in cross-section when stretched. Similar mechanical changes in the lumbar region impose comparable changes on the lumbar spinal dura and nerve roots (Fig. 25/4) likewise on cord and dura in the thoracic spine though mobility there is less. The effects are not locally restricted: the increased tension in cord and dura on flexing the neck is transmitted caudally and are detectable in the lumbar region (Breig, 1978) (Fig. 25/5, p. 202).

Changes in the length of the canal are accompanied by changes in its lumen. The posterior part of the disc and the ligamenta flava are stretched on flexion but in extension are lax and tend to bulge into the canal, so making it narrower.

The significance of these changes is twofold. First, an injured spinal cord or nerve root may be further damaged by flexion of the neck. At the site of a fracture or dislocation there may be oedema of soft tissues, bleeding and the formation of blood clots or fragments of bone encroaching on the canal. This may be enough to restrict the blood supply to the cord. If the cord is then stretched across the site of injury by flexion and lateral flexion or rotation, additional and permanent damage can be caused. If the cord has been severed, the cut surfaces are drawn apart by flexion (Breig, 1978) allowing a blood clot to form between them (Fig. 25/5). Secondly, the narrowing of the canal on extension accounts for the compressive injuries to the cord from hyperextension injuries. Full extension after injury causes further compression while added lateral flexion and rotation is likely to compress the nerve roots in the intervertebral foramina, particularly at the site of injury.

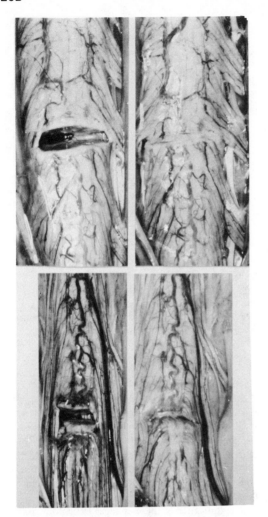

Fig. 25/5 Experimental transection of the cord in a fresh cadaveric specimen in the cervical region (upper right and left) and at lumbar level (lower right and left): on the right (upper and lower) the cervical spine is extended and the cut surfaces of the cord are apposed; on the left the neck is flexed, separating the cut surfaces at both cervical and lumbar levels. (Fig. 67A from Breig (1978, op. cit.))

SPINAL CORD AND NERVE ROOT INJURIES

Spinal cord injuries

The cord lies in the spinal canal of the cervical and thoracic regions ending at the level of the first, or second, lumbar vertebra (see Fig. 25/1). The commonest sites for injury are at the fifth/sixth cervical and twelfth thoracic/first lumbar levels. In both sites the cord is relatively larger because of the origins of the great nerves of the upper and lower limbs respectively;

and at both sites fractures and fracture-dislocations are common. If the spine is forcibly extended and compressed, the cord may be injured by a pincer action; while a flexion-distraction injury could lead to overstretching and rupture. Alternatively, the cord can be damaged without evidence of either fracture or dislocation.

If the patient is conscious the symptoms of injury to the cord are weakness and numbness in the limbs. In an unconscious person, bruising and laceration about the head, face or trunk are indications that the spine – and therefore the cord – may have been injured. In most cases, signs of damage to the nervous system are maximal immediately after injury, though not invariably. Later development of signs of cord damage may be due to post-traumatic oedema, to want of skill during first aid handling and transport or to haemorrhage.

First aid for spinal cord injuries (Guttmann, 1976)

Whenever a spinal cord injury is suspected, warn the patient not to move. Unless there is some overwhelming danger to compel it, the patient should *never* be moved without adequate help. Any handling must be slow, gentle and skilled. At least three, preferably four or five, people are needed. The danger is very great when rescuing an injured person from water after bathing and diving accidents (Kewalramani and Taylor, 1975) which are a common cause of paraplegia in sport (Steinbruck and Paeslack, 1978). Any supervisors and attendants who may find themselves responsible for first aid must be trained to prevent rough handling of the neck.

If the patient is conscious, pain at the site of injury may help to locate it. If arms and fingers can be moved but not legs, the injury could be thoracic or thoracolumbar. If there is no finger movement but the wrist can be extended and the elbow flexed but not extended, the lesion is likely to be lower or mid-cervical. Absence of all upper limb movement points to an upper cervical injury.

The patient should be moved in one piece, taking care to avoid any flexion, extension and rotation. If the breathing is satisfactory, he can be moved to a supine position, keeping the head in a straight line with the body and maintaining normal spinal curves with pads or rolled-up clothing which can be gently introduced to support the neck and lower back; with further padding each side of the head to prevent rolling. The stretcher must be rigid. Hard objects should be removed from pockets to prevent the development of pressure sores, and soft padding applied to stop rubbing of knees, ankles, elbows and hands. The patient must then be transferred to a spinal injuries unit.

In cases where there is any difficulty with breathing it may be life-saving to have the patient not supine but lying on the side, though this makes support of the spine more difficult. The whole length of the spine must be kept horizontal with padding below the neck and lower back, but maintaining the normal curvature. The main problem is to keep the limbs, pelvis and shoulders stable. They will have to be strapped to prevent rotation. It is vital in such cases to keep a clear airway but when aspirating or intubating the patient the head and neck must be kept straight and not bent back.

Nerve root injuries

Fractures of the vertebral neural arch or fractures and fracture-dislocations caused by lateral flexor, rotatory or shearing forces may be accompanied by injury to the nerve roots; either within the canal or typically, in the intervertebral foramen. In a neck injury associated with traction on the shoulder the spinal dura mater may be ruptured and the nerve root torn from the cord, though it is possible for cervical roots to be torn without injury to the dura when violence is done to the neck alone (Sunderland, 1974). In the lumbar region traction injuries to the roots are uncommon though they occur in some cases of pelvic fracture (Barnett and Connolly, 1975).

UNSTABLE INJURIES

Instability of the spine may be defined as the loss of its ability to move without damage or irritation of the spinal cord or nerve roots and without the development of deformity (White et al, 1976).

After injury, stability depends mainly on the integrity of the ligaments of the neural arch and on the function of the muscles which support the spine. But it is not possible to judge from the external appearance of laceration or bruising whether a given injury is stable or not: in many disastrous injuries the skin remains unmarked and there is no visible deformity. Stability can only be established by meticulous clinical and radiological examination. In the field, the danger is that an unstable injury without initial neurological damage could be allowed to become displaced and so damage the spinal cord or nerve roots. For anyone who has fallen from a height, been thrown or violently struck and who is unconscious, the first aid care must be as for a spinal cord injury: likewise for a conscious person with a severely injured back, head or neck even in the absence of numbness and weakness of the limbs.

The actual mechanism of injury (Roaf, 1976) may prove to be valuable evidence for the surgeons and radiographers at the accident and emergency department. In many cases, for example, thoraco-lumbar fracture-dislocation caused by flexion-rotation of the trunk, there is a typical mechanism of injury. The evidence of reliable witnesses may help to speed the diagnosis.

Fractures

About 1 in 10 fractures are unstable, instability occurring because of concomitant injury of the supporting ligaments and, on a longer term basis, in those cases in which the existence of a fracture makes the slow development of deformity possible because of gradual strain of the supporting ligaments.

The most unstable of all is the fracture-dislocation caused by flexion-rotation injury or by rotational shear to the trunk (Fig. 25/6a) with accompanying rupture of the posterior ligaments and sometimes further fracture in the neural arch. The typical site for this is the

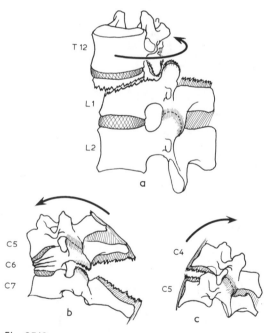

Fig. 25/6
(a) Rotational fracture-dislocation at T12/L1 with shearing fracture across the body of L1, and rupture of capsular and interspinous ligaments: it is wholly unstable
(b) Flexion injury at C6 causing wedge fracture of body and rupture of posterior ligaments: unstable in flexion and rotation and liable to anterior slip
(c) Extension injury at C4/5 with rupture of the disc and anterior longitudinal ligament: unstable in extension

thoraco-lumbar region. It is wholly unstable, deformation is imminent if not present and this type of fracture accounts for 95 per cent of the paraplegics at this spinal level (Holdsworth, 1963).

A purely flexor injury which causes a wedge fracture of the body and rupture of the posterior ligaments becomes unstable in flexion (Fig. 25/6b) and the extensor injury with fracture of the arch and rupture of the anterior longitudinal ligament is unstable in extension (Fig. 25/6c).

Children are more supple than adults and their heads are proportionately larger. For these reasons, among others, they are less liable to spinal fracture in sport than young adults. However, the incidence of fractures in children differs in that they are relatively commoner in the atlas and axis – notably the odontoid process (Fig. 25/7b) and the neural arch (Fig. 25/7c) of the axis – and in the mid-thoracic region (Sherk et al, 1976; Hegenbarth and Ebel, 1976). A danger with children is

that they may be able to get up with full use of their limbs and yet have an unstable fracture. Neck pain after a fall cannot be ignored and the problem in children is that it is often difficult to elicit a clear account of the injury.

Dislocations

The force on the spine which dislocates it is necessarily enough to rupture some or all of the ligaments of the neural arch, to an extent depending on the direction of dislocation and on whether it affects one or both apophyseal joints. They are commonest in the cervical region, lumbar dislocation being relatively rare, the direction of instability depending on the dislocating force. Though in some cases of unilateral dislocation, there is locking of the affected facet, it remains potentially unstable.

Dislocations also occur in combination with fractures, the most unstable being the type caused by flexion-rotation. Some fracture-dislocations remain stable in one direction depending on the ligaments left intact: for example, the extension fracture-dislocation of the neck in which it remains stable in flexion (Holdsworth 1963, 1970).

Ligamentous ruptures

A number of spinal injuries consist in ligamentous rupture either without dislocation or with a reducible dislocation in which the vertebrae separated under strain. The latter type may be seen in some patients with lateral flexion injury of the neck (Roaf, 1963), flexion injury of cervical and lumbar vertebrae with posterior ligament rupture or extension injury with rupture of the anterior longitudinal ligament: in such cases there may be a compression fracture contralaterally or on the opposite side to the rupture in flexion or extension injuries or the 'tear-drop' fracture of the vertebral body in cervical extension injuries (Holdsworth, 1963).

Rupture of the transverse ligament of the atlas allows anterior atlanto-axial subluxation which jeopardises the cord and it is almost always caused by head injury (Fielding et al, 1974) (Fig. 25/7d).

STABLE INJURIES

Stable fractures

The majority of spinal fractures, and this includes compressive or wedge fracture of the vertebral body, are stable. It even includes the 'burst' fracture in which a mainly compressive force disrupts the vertebra but leaves the ligaments intact (Holdsworth 1963, 1970). Healing is seldom a problem in wedge fractures and in the young, subsequent growth may eliminate the wedg-

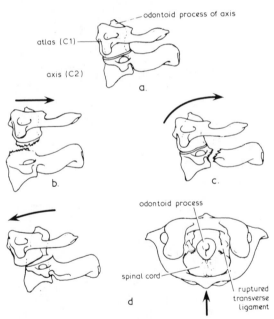

Fig. 25/7
(a) Normal anatomy of C1 and C2
(b) Fracture of the odontoid process of the axis with posterior displacement
(c) Fracture of the neural arch of the axis 'the hangman's fracture'
(d) (left) Rupture of the transverse ligament of the atlas with anterior atlanto-axial subluxation;
(right) Superior view of the atlas with the spinal cord, showing the ruptured ligaments and the odontoid process

ing. This is not to say they should be ignored because they affect the future capacity of the spine to withstand injury (Kazarian, 1978). Experimentally it is possible to crush a vertebra to 50 per cent of its normal height and yet to see it recover (Kazarian and Graves, 1977). Not surprisingly, it is possible to miss such fractures when first x-rayed: they only become evident at a later stage when bony callus becomes visible (Crooks, 1970).

The other common type of stable fracture is that of the bony processes of the vertebra. Spinous and transverse processes can be fractured by violent muscular effort in accidental events, and this may also be true of fracture of an inferior articular process. They heal most often by fibrous union and seldom create problems: if indeed they are ever diagnosed. A comparable fracture is of the part of the neural arch between the articular processes, a defect known as spondylolysis (see below). If it is bilateral there is a tendency for the body of the affected vertebra and the column above it to slip forward a little in relation to the one below. In some cases they heal by bony union but mostly by fibrous tissue. As the interspinous ligament and the intervertebral disc remain undamaged, the defect leaves the spine basically stable (Troup, 1977).

Fatigue failure

Like metal, bone may fracture after exposure to repeated heavy loading because of fatigue failure. In athletes it is not uncommon for it to occur in the tibia and metatarsals, and it is one of the causes of lumbar spondylolysis (Hutton et al, 1977). It is present in three to four per cent of the adult population and appears to be commoner in gymnasts, parachutists, wrestlers, divers, weightlifters, professional dancers and other athletes (Krenz and Troup, 1973; Wiltse et al, 1975). The commonest site is at the fifth lumbar (Fig. 25/8). The defect is usually trouble free, being a frequent chance finding in symptomless people; although there is a greater likelihood of irritation of a nerve root when spondylolysis is at the fourth lumbar (Jackson et al, 1978). The amount of anterior slip (spondylolisthesis) from this cause is unlikely to merit attention. Only if the defect is unstable in the sense that there appears to be neither bony nor fibrous union, or if there is nerve root irritation, is treatment likely to be needed in a patient with chronic pain.

NON-BONY INJURIES

Injuries to the muscles and ligaments of the back and neck, sprains of the synovial apophyseal joint or to the intervertebral disc in the early stages of degeneration are common.

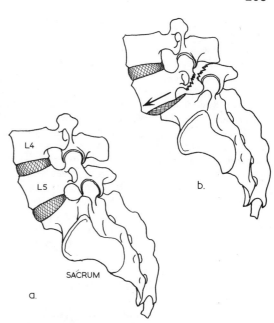

Fig. 25/8 Lumbar spondylolysis
(a) Normal appearance
(b) Defect in the interarticular or isthmic part of the neural arch of L5 with resulting spondylolisthesis of L5 on the sacrum

In the healthy spine the disc itself – the nucleus pulposus and the annulus fibrosus – are relatively strong: initial damage is to the epiphyseal plates and the underlying trabecular bone of the vertebral body (Roaf 1960, 1976). In the apophyseal joints most injuries consist of sprains of the capsular ligament but the trauma may extend to the cartilaginous facets of the articular processes. It is believed that if these microtraumata to disc and facets are repeated there will be an early onset of degenerative changes (Farfan, 1977; Hansson, 1977). Degeneration normally occurs without causing symptoms, the reason being that these same weight-bearing tissues of the spine have no nerve supply and can be injured without pain. Once the disc has begun to degenerate its dynamic behaviour changes: it responds more quickly to compressive loading and its susceptibility to injury is increased (Kazarian, 1975). The nucleus of the disc may then prolapse through the epiphyseal plate into the body, so creating a Schmorl's node, or through the annulus postero-laterally: again, probably without immediate pain. If and when the neighbouring tissues are adversely affected by the injury, pain and muscle spasm may begin to develop.

The majority of people with non-bony injuries of the spine recover whether they are treated or not. Of the others, some fail to lose their pain, or they become liable to repeated attacks. In the latter case it may be because the spine, like some would-be-footballers' knees, is constitutionally just not fit for the rapid motions and heavy loadings which some sports demand. In cases of persistent pain, there may be a mechanical irritation secondary to the injured apophyseal joint or disc which affects the nerve root either within the spinal canal or as it emerges through the intervertebral foramen: an occurrence which is more likely in those with small spinal canals (Porter et al, 1978). In this way symptoms of pain (though pain is not invariable), weakness or numbness may develop in those parts of the back or limb supplied by the affected nerve root. In many young people with lumbar disc prolapse irritating a nerve root, the symptoms may only be a little backache and stiffness in the leg. In the lower back the fourth and fifth lumbar and first sacral roots are commonly affected, causing symptoms referable to the sciatic nerve. Similar lesions occur in the neck, though less commonly, the lower cervical roots being liable to irritation with consequent pain, weakness or numbness in the arm.

The management of back and neck injuries

Because of the closeness of the joints of the spine and of their distance below the skin, normal clinical examination alone seldom leads to a very precise diagnosis – and spinal radiography is mainly of value in excluding serious disease or fracture. Further investigations are elaborate and costly, some entail a risk of minor complications and the full diagnostic approach is usually reserved for those who have not responded to conservative therapy.

The treatment for an acute back or neck injury is rest; most people being more comfortable on a firm bed. When moving about, a cervical collar or an 'instant' lumbar corset is helpful and not difficult to improvise. Food and drink should be cut down to limit the number of visits to the lavatory. If the pain spreads to the limbs, if there are urinary problems or if the pain is crippling, patients should be advised to call the doctor. Anti-inflammatory drugs are usefully prescribed at this stage, with analgesics, relaxants or sleeping pills as the situation demands.

Most acute attacks begin to abate within three or four days but symptoms are likely to persist in minor form and it is prudent to avoid any activity which exacerbates them. A truly accidental injury such as a fall may leave the back sensitive for two or three months, so it is as well to beware of any handling or postural stresses or exercises which are painful until the lesion has settled down. Mobility in the pain free ranges should, however, be maintained particularly in the lower limb after lumbo-sacral injuries for there is a risk that immobility too rigidly enforced will lead to the formation of adhesions around the nerve roots because of the locally painful irritative state. This is one of the causes of sciatic pain following a lumbar injury.

After the pain has subsided it is important to regain normal mechanical function and to retrain the supporting musculature, including all the muscles of the abdominal wall and of the hips, which may have become weak after back pain inhibited their normal usage. A satisfactory exercise programme following back injury is included in a book published by the Consumers' Association (1978).

PREVENTION OF SPINAL INJURIES

Prevention of spinal injuries in sport is first a matter of skilled supervision and training. It can also be tackled ergonomically by improving the design of sports equipment. Finally, it may be approached by the adoption of medical screening to identify those who are susceptible to spinal injury.

Broken necks and tetraplegia due to diving into overcrowded or shallow water are avoidable if attendants know the rules and can apply them. Falls from horses, motor-cycles or the ring are difficult to prevent because the various interacting factors are less controllable – as in many competitive games. Nevertheless, the skill to adapt to the unexpected situation is partly a matter of training. This may be difficult at the beginning of the season, as in rugby (Williams and McKibbin, 1978). Training is most likely to be fruitful in preventing non-bony injuries in situations in which the individuals at risk are in full control, as in weightlifting or for manual work in general (Charlesworth et al, 1978).

The application of ergonomics to the design of sporting equipment should be a reliable preventive method provided other dangers are not created. Head injuries, for example, can be reduced in number and severity by wearing a helmet but only provided that the physical risks remain the same. If its use leads to the development of new tactical and training methods – if the helmet is used for butting or is aggressively handled – the increased leverage may cause neck injuries which might not otherwise have happened, as in American football (Okihiro et al, 1975; Albright et al, 1976; Torg et al, 1977). Protecting the spine with special equipment is impossible without producing other effects, for example, hampering mobility, some of which may interfere with performance. Apart from the belt worn by weightlifters which conceivably augments the effects of increased intra-abdominal pressure in relieving back-stress, or the brace worn by motocross-riders to make the vibratory effects on the spine more tolerable, protective equipment for the spine in sport is of limited value.

Medical and radiological screening is considered essential in work entailing a high risk of spinal injury (Kazarian, 1978). There are those who prove to be more susceptible to injury than others and if they could be identified reliably, the incidence of spinal injuries would fall. However, this implies that certain individuals shall be deprived of their chosen sport. There is, moreover, no justification for exposing healthy, symptom free young people to the radiation needed for lumbar spinal radiography. The risks for cervical radiography are probably acceptable. For the lumbar spine, therefore, routine radiography cannot be accepted. There might be exceptions for sports such as parachuting, but only where there is a high injury rate. Medical screening which includes radiography applies mainly to those who have had a spinal injury and who need advice about the future.

PROGNOSIS AFTER SPINAL INJURY

Once an episode of back or sciatic pain has been reported in the general population, a further attack becomes three or four times more likely. And so, probably, for the neck. The reasons are not clear. The problem has a neurophysiological component arising from memory storage; there may be a psychogenic factor serving to reinforce the pain; or it may be that the first attack was inadequately treated in that spinal functions may not have been fully restored though the pain itself had been satisfactorily relieved. People who have had previous back or sciatic pain are likely to have stiffer spines and to have dynamically weaker muscles (Troup et al, 1974; Nummi et al, 1978), but these are generalisations which may not apply to an individual. There are undoubtedly many who hurt themselves at sport and simply retire from it. Those who present problems are the ones who are loath to give up their sport but are bedevilled by either successive injuries or pain which is enough to spoil their performance. Regrettably there is no body of scientific evidence on which to base advice to these people: only the rather subjective qualities of medical experience and acumen together with a biomechanical understanding of the sport.

The first thing is to be able to reassure the individual that there is no serious disease in the spine: this may mean investigations including radiography. The diagnostic problem concerns the nature of the mechanical derangement in the spine and its possible neuro-physiological effects. The prognosis depends on experience of the natural history of the condition. Pain after an old injury may require that the spine be x-rayed in extreme positions as a test of normal stability. Symptoms in the limbs can be tested electrophysiologically to record the conductivity of nerve roots if they have been damaged or irritated. The response to anti-inflammatory drugs and to the various physical therapeutic methods should be assessed. Then, taking into account the personality of the patient, it is usually possible to make a prognosis, give advice and perhaps suggest further treatment. Where there is a reasonable hope of returning to training, full athletic rehabilitation should be a matter of collaboration between trainer, physical therapist and physician.

REFERENCES

Albright, J. P., Moses, J. M., Feldick, H. G., Dolan, K. D. and Burmeister, L. F. (1974). Non fatal cervical spine injuries in interscholastic football. *Journal of the American Medical Association*, **236**, 1243–1245.

Allen, G. R. (1976). *Progress on a specification for human tolerance of repeated shocks*. Royal Aircraft Establishment: Working Paper for International Standards Organisation, ISO/TC 108/SC 4/WG 2 (UK/Allen-6) August 1976.

Barnett, H. G. and Connolly, E. S. (1975). Lumbosacral nerve root avulsion: report of a case and review of the literature. *Journal of Trauma*, **15**, 532–535.

Bodnar, L. M. (1977). Sports medicine with reference to back and neck injuries. *Current Practice in Orthopaedic Surgery*, **7**, 116–153.

Breig, A. (1978). *Adverse mechanical tension in the central nervous system. An analysis of cause and effect. Relief by functional neurosurgery*. Almqvist and Wiksell International, Stockholm.

Charlesworth, D., Hayne, C. R. and Troup, J. D. G. (1978). *Lifting instructors' manual*. The Back Pain Association, Teddington, Middlesex.

Consumers' Association (1978). *Avoiding back trouble*. Consumers' Association, London.

Crooks, L. M. (1970). Long term effects of ejecting from aircraft. *Aerospace Medicine*, **41**, 803–804.

Farfan, H. F. (1977). A reorientation in the surgical approach to degenerative lumbar intervertebral joint disease. *Orthopaedic Clinics of North America*, **8**, 9–21.

Fielding, J. W., Cochran, G. van B., Lawsing, J. F. and Hohl, M. (1974). Tears of the transverse ligament of the atlas: a clinical and biomechanical study. *Journal of Bone and Joint Surgery*, **56-A**, 1683–1691.

Fitzgerald, J. G. (1972). *Changes in spinal stature following brief periods of shoulder loading. IAM Report No: 514*, Royal Air Force Institute of Aviation Medicine.

Guttmann, L. (1976). *Spinal cord injuries: comprehensive management and research*, 2nd edition. Blackwell Scientific Publications, Oxford.

Hansson, T. (1977). The bone mineral content and biomechanical properties of lumbar vertebrae: an *in vitro* study based on dual photon absorptiometry. Doctoral thesis, University of Göteborg, Sweden.

Hegenbarth, R. and Ebel, K-D. (1976). Roentgen findings in fractures of the vertebral column in childhood: examination of 35 patients and its results. *Paediatric Radiology*, 5, 34–39.

Hodgson, V. R., Lissner, H. R. and Patrick, L. M. (1963). Response of the seated human cadaver to acceleration and jerk with and without seat cushions. *Human Factors*, 5, 505–523.

Holdsworth, F. (1963). Fractures, dislocations and fracture-dislocations of the spine. *Journal of Bone and Joint Surgery*, 45-B, 6–20.

Holdsworth, F. (1970). Fractures, dislocations, and fracture-dislocations of the spine. *Journal of Bone and Joint Surgery*, 52-A, 1534–1551.

Hutton, W. C., Stott, J. R. R. and Cyron, B. M. (1977). Is spondylolysis a fatigue fracture? *Spine*, 2, 202–209.

Jackson, A. M., Kirwan, E.O'G. and Sullivan, M. F. (1978). Lytic spondylolisthesis above the lumbosacral level. *Spine*, 3, 260–266.

Kazarian, L. E. (1972). Dynamic response characteristics of the human vertebral column. *Acta Orthopaedica Scandinavica*, Supplementum 146.

Kazarian, L. E. (1975). Creep characteristics of the human spinal column, *Orthopaedic Clinics of North America*, 6, 3–18.

Kazarian, L. E. (1978). *Standardization and interpretation of spinal injury criteria*. AMRL-TR-75-85, Wright-Patterson Air Force Base, Ohio.

Kazarian, L. E. and Graves, G. A. (1977). Compressive strength characteristics of the human vertebral centrum. *Spine*, 2, 1–14.

Kewalramani, L. S. and Taylor, R. G. (1975). Injuries to the cervical spine from diving accidents. *Journal of Trauma*, 15, 130–142.

Krenz, J. and Troup, J. D. G. (1973). The structure of the *pars interarticularis* of the lower lumbar vertebrae and its relation to the etiology of spondylolysis: with a report of a healing fracture in the neural arch of a fourth lumbar vertebrae. *Journal of Bone and Joint Surgery*, 55-B, 735–741.

Murray-Leslie, C. F., Lintott, D. J. and Wright, V. (1977). The spine in sport and veteran military parachutists. *Annals of the Rheumatic Diseases*, 36, 332–342.

Nummi, J., Järvinen, T., Stambej, U. and Wickström, G. (1978). Diminished dynamic performance capacity of back and abdominal muscles in concrete reinforcement workers. *Scandinavian Journal of Work, Environment and Health*, 4, Supplement 1, 39–46.

Okihiro, M. M., Taniguchi, R. and Goebert, H. W. (1975). Football injuries of the cervical spine and cord. *Hawaii Medical Journal*, 34, 171–174.

Perey, O. (1957). Fracture of the vertebral end-plate in the lumbar spine: an experimental biomechanical investigation. *Acta Orthopaedica Scandinavica*, Supplementum 25.

Porter, R. W., Hibbert, C. S. and Wicks, M. (1978). The spinal canal in symptomatic lumbar disc lesions. *Journal of Bone and Joint Surgery*, 60-B, 485–487.

Roaf, R. (1960). A study of the mechanics of spinal injuries. *Journal of Bone and Joint Surgery*, 42-B, 810–823.

Roaf, R. (1963). Lateral flexion injuries of the cervical spine. *Journal of Bone and Joint Surgery*, 45-B, 36–38.

Roaf, R. (1976). *Biomechanics of injuries of the spinal column*. In P. J. Vinken and G. W. Bruyn (eds) *Handbook of Clinical Neurology*, Volume 25: *Injuries of the spine and spinal cord*, Part I pp. 123–40. North-Holland Publishing Company, Amsterdam.

Sherk, H. H., Schut, L. and Lane, J. M. (1976). Fractures and dislocations of the cervical spine in children. *Orthopaedic Clinics of North America*, 7, 593–604.

Steinbruck, K. and Paeslack, V. (1978). Paraplegie durch sport – und badeunfalle. *Zeitschrift fur Orthopädie und ihre Grenzgebiete*, 116, 697–709.

Sunderland, S. (1974). Meningeal-neural relations in the intervertebral foramen. *Journal of Neurosurgery*, 40, 756–763.

Torg, J. S., Truex, R. C., Marshall, J., Hodgson, V. R., Quedenfeld, T. C., Spealman, A. D. and Nichols, C. E. (1977). Spinal injury at the level of the third and fourth cervical vertebrae from football. *Journal of Bone and Joint Surgery*, 59-A, 1015–1019.

Troup, J. D. G. (1977). The etiology of spondylolysis. *Orthopaedic Clinics of North America*, 8, 57–63.

Troup, J. D. G., Hodgson, S. and Shannon, H. S. (1974). *The prevention of spinal disorders in dockworkers*. Unpublished report from the TUC Centenary Institute of Occupational Health and the Institute of Orthopaedics, University of London to the National Dock Labour Board.

Vigouroux, R. P., Guillermain, P. and Verrando, R. (1978). Neurotraumatologie d'origine sportive.

Neurochirurgie, **24,** 347–350.

White, A. A., Southwick, W. O. and Panjabi, M. H. (1976). Clinical instability in the lower cervical spine: a review of past and current concepts. *Spine*, **1,** 15–27.

Williams, J. P. R. and McKibbin, B. (1978). Cervical spine injuries in Rugby Union football. *British Medical Journal*, **2,** 1747.

Wiltse, L. L., Widell, E. H. and Jackson, D. W. (1975). Fatigue fracture: the basic lesion in isthmic spondylolisthesis. *Journal of Bone and Joint Surgery*, **57-A,** 17–22.

ACKNOWLEDGEMENTS

My thanks to Professor Robert Roaf for his guidance with this chapter and to Mrs Dorothy Paul for its presentation.

Figure 27/5 is reproduced from *Adverse mechanical tension in the central nervous system. An analysis of cause and effect. Relief by functional neurosurgery*, by kind permission of the author, Professor Alf Breig and the publishers, Almquist and Wiksell International, Stockholm.

CHAPTER 26

Injuries to the shoulder region

LISLE THOMPSON TD, MchOrth, FRCS

ANATOMY

The shoulder joint (gleno-humeral joint)
MOVEMENTS

The articulation of the head of the humerus with the glenoid cavity of the scapula forms the shoulder joint. This is a ball and socket joint and movements in any direction are easily obtained. Attached to the edge of the glenoid cavity and serving to deepen it is a rim of fibrocartilage known as the glenoid labrum. Stability of the joint depends on the muscles which surround it; the ligaments contribute little to the joint's stability (Fig. 26/1).

MUSCLES AROUND THE SHOULDER JOINT

(a) The subscapularis muscle covers the front of the shoulder joint and is attached to the lesser tuberosity of the humerus and to the bone about half an inch below it. It is a medial rotator of the shoulder.

(b) The supraspinatus tendon lies above the shoulder, and the muscle initiates the action of abduction.

(c) The infraspinatus muscle lies above and behind the shoulder joint. It is a lateral rotator of the shoulder.

(d) The teres minor lies behind the shoulder joint. It is a lateral rotator of the shoulder.

The tendons of the supraspinatus, infraspinatus and teres minor muscles are inserted into the greater tuberosity of the humerus from above downwards. The four muscles (a, b, c, d) give stability to movements of the shoulder by synergistically steadying the head of the humerus in the glenoid cavity thus preventing it from slipping and skidding. These muscles are frequently referred to as the 'rotator cuff'. There is no support by muscle below the joint and the capsule is lax to allow abduction of the arm. It is through this weak part that the head of the humerus escapes when a dislocation occurs.

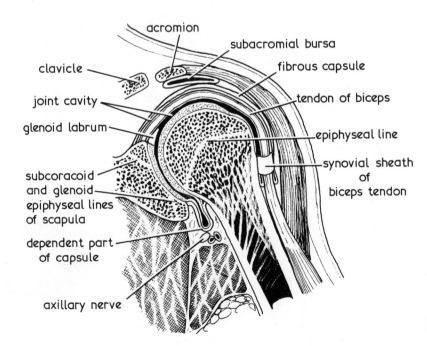

Fig. 26/1 Coronal section of the left gleno-humeral joint

The latissimus dorsi, teres major and pectoralis major give some support to the front and inferior part of the shoulder joint as they converge on the bicipital groove and its ridges. If there is a fracture in the upper humeral shaft, the tendency, therefore, will be to pull the humerus towards the trunk with displacements of the lower fragments inwards at right angles to the axis of the humerus. These muscles are powerful adductors of the shoulder.

The deltoid muscle, as it runs from the clavicle and acromion to the deltoid tuberosity of the humerus, surrounds the lateral aspect of the joint, and contributes to the natural shape of the shoulder. It is a powerful abductor of the shoulder.

LIGAMENTS (FIG. 26/2)

(a) Capsule ligament: this is thickened anteriorly to form the gleno-humeral ligaments. These consist of three bands of longitudinal fibres on the internal surface of the front of the capsule.

(b) Glenoid ligament: this deepens the glenoid cavity.

(c) Coraco-humeral ligament: this lies anteriorly, and on the upper aspect of the joint. It fuses with the supraspinatus tendon as it blends with the capsule.

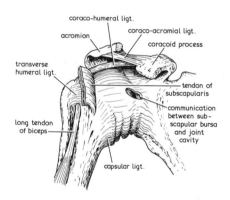

Fig. 26/2 The ligaments of the gleno-humeral joint

BURSA

There is a large bursa beneath the acromion process and deltoid, the floor being formed by the supra- and infraspinatus tendons.

The sterno-clavicular joint

This is a synovial joint of the plane type with the medial end of the clavicle articulating with the manubrium of the sternum and the first rib.

MOVEMENTS

Movements occur only in association with movements of the shoulder and the arm; the sternal end of the clavicle always moving in the opposite direction to the acromial end. The stability of the joint depends almost entirely on the ligaments which surround it; the shape of the joint contributing little in the way of stability.

LIGAMENTS

(a) The superior ligament or the inter-clavicular ligament, runs from one clavicle to the other and is attached to the top of the sternum between the two joints.

(b) The posterior ligament is only a weak ligament running from the clavicle to the sternum.

(c) The anterior ligament is a comparatively weak ligament running between the sternum and the clavicle.

(d) The inferior ligament or the strong rhomboid or costoclavicular ligament attaches the clavicle to the sternal end of the first rib.

There is a complete meniscus dividing the joint into two cavities.

The acromio-clavicular joint

This is a small synovial joint between the lateral end of the clavicle and the acromion. The plane lies antero-posteriorly, but the joint slopes downwards and medially so that the clavicle tends to override the acromion laterally. The front and back of the joint are covered by the attachments of the deltoid and trapezius muscles respectively. Together with the sterno-clavicular joint these two joints form the shoulder girdle.

MOVEMENTS

Movement of this joint only occurs with movement of the arm or shoulder. Stability depends on the ligaments which support this joint, the articular surface providing no stability.

LIGAMENTS

(a) The superior ligament is fairly strong and lies superiorly.

(b) The inferior ligament is a strong ligament lying inferiorly.

(c) The coraco-clavicular ligaments, i.e. the trapezoid and conoid ligaments, bind the lateral end of the clavicle to the coracoid process. Through this ligament the weight of the arm is transmitted to the clavicle, and thence to the axial skeleton. The tone of the trapezius, levator scapulae and the rhomboids support the weight of the upper limb.

INJURIES OF THE SHOULDER JOINT

Supraspinatus injuries

SUPRASPINATUS TENDINITIS

The patient may or may not have a history of injury to the shoulder for the mechanism is an abduction strain. The patient complains of pain near the insertion of the deltoid muscle in to the humerus when abducting the arm between 70° and 120°. Above and below that arc the movements are pain free.

On examination a painful arc of movement is found. There is no pain on movement in other directions as would occur in an arthritis of the joint. There is no loss of movement as would occur following a periarthritis, when adhesions had formed in the joint and capsule. There is no loss of power such as would follow a rupture of the supraspinatus tendon. X-rays of the shoulder show no abnormality.

In the immediate painful phase the shoulder should be rested in a collar and cuff sling. Physiotherapy with short wave diathermy or ultrasound may help relieve the pain; movements are encouraged as the pain becomes less. An injection of 2% Xylocaine and Depo-Medrone (60mg) and analgesics plus anti-rheumatic drugs such as phenylbutazone (Butazolidin) and indomethacin (Indocid) are helpful.

SUPRASPINATUS CALCIFICATION

The patient presents with a painful shoulder. The pain is referred to the deltoid insertion and often beyond that point. The pain can be very severe and limit all movements of the shoulder joint.

On examination the shoulder is stiff and painful; abduction is to about 60° only. X-rays show deposits of calcium salts of carbonate and phosphate in the supraspinatus tendon.

Treatment is as for tendinitis. An injection of Xylocaine and Depo-Medrone will help to relieve the pain. Physiotherapy in the form of short wave diathermy or ice packs is helpful. Sometimes operative treatment to remove the calcium, either by needling the mass or opening the mass with a scalpel, may be required to relieve the pain.

RUPTURE OF THE SUPRASPINATUS TENDON

This often occurs in the older patient and can follow an abduction strain which is often trivial.

On examination the patient *cannot* abduct the shoulder – all he can do is to raise it. If he lies on his back he can lift the arm forwards because the biceps tendon is still intact. X-rays usually show degenerative changes in the joint.

In mild cases which are seen early, the arm is immobilised in an abduction frame for 8 to 12 weeks. In the more severe cases which are seen early, repair of the ruptured tendon and capsule, perhaps with excision of the acromion, is required. In the later cases operative treatment is of little value and conservative management is all that can be offered.

The biceps tendon

BICEPS TENDINITIS

The patient presents with painful stiffness of the shoulder. The pain is felt more to the front of this joint, and the tendon of the biceps muscle is painful.

On examination there is tenderness over the biceps tendon in its groove and pain when the muscle is stressed. The pain is felt at the front of the joint and into the biceps muscle.

Short wave diathermy and ultrasound help the painful tendon and an injection of Xylocaine and Depo-Medrone into the bicipital groove near the biceps tendon relieves the pain. Graduated exercises are begun as the pain becomes easier.

RUPTURE OF THE BICEPS TENDON

The tendon of the long head of the biceps muscle may rupture suddenly on lifting a weight or it may occur spontaneously. The patient often has had pain at the site of rupture for some time before the actual rupture occurs. The rupture occurs either in the bicipital groove (extracapsular) or at the upper margin of the glenoid (intracapsular). At the time of the rupture the patient feels a sharp pain at the top of the shoulder spreading down to the upper arm. The arm feels weak and the biceps muscle will bulge in the lower half of the upper arm. Rarely, the rupture occurs spontaneously and unknown to the patient.

Treatment is usually by conservative measures. If there is marked weakness of the arm, an operation to suture the stump of the distal end of the tendon to the periosteum of the humerus will help to give the biceps muscle some stability.

Periarthritis of the shoulder

The symptoms of pain and stiffness may occur after a trivial injury or strain. At other times they may arise spontaneously. The condition tends to affect the older person. The pain is diffuse and not localised to the deltoid insertion.

On examination, shoulder movements are limited by muscle spasm unlike the stiffness of a true arthritis. Abduction and external rotation are affected principally; tenderness is not confined to the tuberosity of the humerus. In the later development of the condition, movements are limited by the formation of adhesions between the gliding surfaces of the ligaments and muscles of the joint finally producing a frozen shoulder.

In the early stages, physiotherapy in the form of heat and short wave diathermy is helpful. *Active* movements are encouraged but not *passive* movements which will only irritate the joint. Anti-rheumatic and pain relieving tablets will help the pain and a hydrocortisone injection will also be of value. When the pain has gone, a manipulation of the shoulder under a general anaesthetic will relieve the stiffness due to adhesions, but this would only be carried out when the pain has gone and the adhesions are avascular.

Dislocation of the shoulder

ANTERIOR DISLOCATION

This type of dislocation is caused by a fall which forces the arm into abduction leaving the head of the humerus out of the glenoid cavity anteriorly through the inferior part of the capsule. In this way the head of the humerus lies anteriorly below the coracoid process of the scapula. It is the most common form of dislocation and can occur in a wide variety of sports.

On examination the normal rounded contour of the shoulder is absent and the head of the humerus can be felt just below the coracoid process. An x-ray examination confirms the position and excludes a fracture. Physical examination must exclude any danger to the brachial plexus or to the circumflex nerve.

The Hippocratic method of reduction is the safest way to reduce the dislocation under a general anaesthetic. Kocher's method can be used but great care is needed to avoid stretching the nerves around the shoulder joint. The arm is held by the side with a collar and cuff sling for three weeks.

The Hippocratic method of dislocation reduction was first described in about 600 BC. The technique consists of putting a pad in the axilla and pushing on this pad with the unbooted foot, at the same time pulling in a longitudinal direction the arm of the affected side. The final stage of reduction is obtained by lifting the humeral head into the glenoid by pressure from the foot. This manipulation is carried out under a general anaesthetic. This method is probably the safest way to reduce a dislocated shoulder and is less likely to damage any nerves or blood vessels surrounding the shoulder joint.

Kocher's method was first described over a century ago and was designed for reduction without a general anaesthetic. It requires great care as stretching the nerves around the shoulder joint, especially when reduction is carried out under a general anaesthetic, is a real hazard. The method consists of first externally rotating the humerus using the flexed elbow as a lever; this brings the head of the humerus under the glenoid and near the tear in the capsule and rotator cuff. The elbow is now adducted towards the mid-line, further lifting the head of the humerus nearer the glenoid. The final stage of reduction is obtained by internally rotating the humerus using the flexed elbow as a lever.

POSTERIOR DISLOCATION

This dislocation is caused by a fall or blow over the front of the shoulder as might occur in a heavy frontal shoulder charge in field games or a fall in motorcycling. It may be caused by a fall causing internal rotation of the humerus as well as forcing the head of the humerus backwards. It is rarer than the anterior dislocation.

Examination can be difficult, as the shape of the shoulder may appear normal, but if examined carefully the head of the humerus can be seen and felt more posteriorly than the normal, with the coracoid process being more prominent. X-rays in two planes will give confirmation. It is important to note that the x-ray may appear to be normal on first inspection.

Reduction is obtained by traction with external rotation of the arm. To avoid re-dislocation the shoulder is *not* fixed in internal rotation but in a light plaster spica with the shoulder in some 40° of abduction and external rotation. The elbow is placed at a right angle. The plaster is removed after about three weeks and gentle exercises begun.

FRACTURE DISLOCATION OF THE SHOULDER

Dislocation with fracture of the greater tuberosity of the humerus is treated as for an anterior dislocation of the shoulder joint. The fracture of the greater tuberosity usually reduces itself at will at the time of reduction of the shoulder by the Hippocratic method. The treatment is the same as for an anterior dislocation with immobilisation in a collar and cuff sling under the clothes for three weeks.

Dislocation with a displaced fracture of the humeral neck is more difficult to treat. Traction of the limb in the Hippocratic manner with the arm in 50° of abduction is carried out using an image-intensifying screen. The head of the humerus is palpated in the axilla and reduced into the glenoid cavity if possible. Care must be taken of the axillary vessels and nerves. Failure may need an open operation, but this is difficult and may be dangerous in the hands of the inexperienced surgeon.

RECURRENT DISLOCATION OF THE SHOULDER

This may occur after a severe type of anterior dislocation with a lot of soft tissue damage. The anterior part of the capsule is torn from the glenoid cavity and the labrum is detached anteriorly.

The condition can be limited by adequate immobilisation for three weeks in the early stages with the arm in full internal rotation. There may also be a small crush fracture in the posterior lateral aspect of the humeral head which can be seen in special x-rays. This condition allows the shoulder to dislocate easily in abduction with external rotation.

Treatment is by surgical repair either by the Putti-Platt type which tightens the anterior capsule and muscles of the shoulder, or Bankart's operation which attaches the capsule to the bare anterior wall of the glenoid (Bankart, 1938).

INJURIES OF THE SHOULDER GIRDLE

The acromio-clavicular joint

This joint is injured by a fall on the point of the shoulder, a common occurrence in rugby football.

On examination there may be a mild sprain of the joint with tenderness over the joint line. If the coracoid ligaments have been torn then the lateral end of the clavicle will be elevated. This is more marked if the patient stands up and the joint is palpated while the patient holds a weight in the hand. X-ray examination confirms the displacement, the films being taken in the erect position and the joint stressed by holding a weight in the hand on the injured side.

The easiest way to manage the injury is to hold the joint in the reduced position using a pad over the lateral end of the clavicle and under the point of the elbow with strapping to compress the two points. The arm is put in a full sling with a pad in the axilla. Pain may later be treated with ultrasound and hydrocortisone injections if it persists. Rarely operative treatment with fixation of the joint with Kirschner wires is required. (Kirschner or 'K' wires are used in orthopaedic surgery to apply skeletal traction to a fractured bone or to hold fragments together.) The mild cases with only a strain of the joint require a sling for a week or so when the joint has not been subluxated.

Most injuries of this joint settle with no pain. There may be some displacement but this does not seem to matter with regard to function. Persistent pain may require an excision of the outer end of the clavicle.

Fracture of the clavicle

This injury is caused by a fall on the point of the shoulder as might occur in rugby football or a horse-riding accident. It may also result from falling on the outstretched hand.

On examination the fracture site can be felt easily under the skin. The inner fragment is pulled up by the sternocleidomastoid muscle and the outer fragment is depressed by the weight of the arm. There is overlap of the fragments. The fracture occurs usually in the middle third of the bone. X-rays confirm the fracture.

The injury is best treated by a figure-of-eight bandage re-applied every second day. The arm is supported in a full arm sling and the fracture is united in three to four weeks.

In rare cases involving the outer third of the clavicle, the coraco-clavicular ligaments are torn. This allows the medial end of the fractured clavicle to be elevated and a pad and strapping over the medial end of the fracture and under the elbow is required to correct the displacement.

The sterno-clavicular joint

This joint may also be injured in falling on the point of the shoulder and the inner end of the clavicle is usually displaced anteriorly. In the few cases when the displacement is posterior, the clavicle may press under the trachea. This requires urgent reduction because of respiratory embarrassment.

On examination this dislocation is easily seen and palpated. The dislocation is confirmed by x-rays.

The dislocation is easily reduced but it is difficult to maintain the reduction. It is best treated with a figure-of-eight bandage and a collar and cuff sling for about three to four weeks. In the anterior type injury operative repair is not indicated. The rare form of posterior dislocation with pressure on the trachea or the great vessels calls for urgent reduction, and in this type of case a repair of the anterior capsule is required.

Fractures of the scapula

This type of injury usually occurs after a direct injury to the scapula. The displacement is slight due to the muscles which surround the bone, but fractures of the underlying ribs may occur. An avulsion fracture of the coracoid process may occur in throwing injuries; a fall on the point of the shoulder may fracture the acromion or glenoid neck.

On examinaed there is pain and tenderness at the site of the fracture and this is confirmed by x-rays. If the neck of the scapula is fractured, pain, but no tenderness, may be found due to the overlying thick band of muscle.

Muscles prevent much displacement of the fracture and treatment is to immobilise the shoulder in a full arm sling for a few days after which exercises should be begun as soon as possible to prevent stiffening of the shoulder joint.

In sport, injuries to the shoulder are common. They may be major with a dislocation or a fracture of the bones about the joint or they may be minor when only soft tissue is damaged. The minor injuries often produce persistent pain and stiffness due to damage to the rotator cuff, or a painful arc syndrome. These are the muscles which produce the stability of the shoulder joint which, without their help, is unstable. External rotation is an essential component of abduction and this movement of external rotation must be encouraged by active movement and *not* by passive movement. As the pain in the shoulder decreases, so the amount of active movements can be increased. If the shoulder is persistently stiff and painful, exercise has probably been too vigorous and should be decreased. The shoulder should never be manipulated to relieve stiffness of the joint in the presence of pain.

REFERENCE

Bankart, A. S. B. (1938). The pathology and treatment of recurrent dislocation of the shoulder joint. *British Journal of Surgery*, **26,** 23–29.

CHAPTER 27

Injuries to the elbow

LISLE THOMPSON TD, MchOrth, FRCS

ANATOMY OF THE ELBOW JOINT

The bones of the forearm, the radius and ulna, articulate with the lower end of the humerus at the elbow. This is a hinged synovial joint which has a natural stability. Only flexion and extension of the elbow joint are possible, movement occurring about a transverse axis. Supination and pronation of the forearm are obtained through the superior radio-ulnar joint which is a type of ball and socket joint acting with the inferior radio-ulnar joint. The shafts of the forearm bones are connected by fibrous interosseous bands, the radius moving on the ulna around a vertical axis (Fig. 27/1).

Ligaments

1. The lateral ligament is attached, above, to the lower part of the lateral epicondyle of the humerus and below, to the annular ligament.

2. The medial ligament is due to thickening of the capsule that completely invests the joint. It passes from the front of the medial epicondyle of the humerus to the medial edge of the coronoid process of the ulna.

3. The posterior ligament is due to capsular thickening.

4. The annular ligament of the superior radio-ulnar joint receives strong bands from both the lateral ligament and the anterior ligament. It encircles the head of the radius and retains it in contact with the radial notch on the ulna. In this way movement between these two bones is permitted at the joint.

Muscles

Posteriorly are the triceps tendon and the anconeus tendon which lie to the outer side of the olecranon. They are extensors of the joint. The superficial flexor group of muscles and the pronator radii teres lie to the medial side. To the lateral side lie the superficial

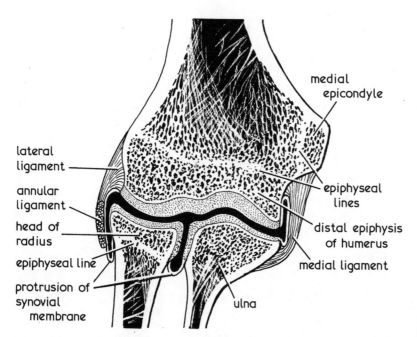

Fig. 27/1 Coronal section of the elbow joint

lateral ligament

annular ligament

head of radius

epiphyseal line

protrusion of synovial membrane

medial epicondyle

epiphyseal lines

distal epiphysis of humerus

medial ligament

ulna

extensor group of muscles. They are weak supinators of the forearm but strong extensors of the wrist and fingers. Anteriorly are the brachialis muscle, which is attached to the coronoid process of the ulna, and the biceps tendon which is attached to the bicipital tuberosity of the radius where there is a bursa. These muscles are strong flexors of the joint.

SPECIFIC SPORTS INJURIES TO THE ELBOW

Tennis elbow

This injury can occur in golf and fishing as well as in racket sports. The condition affects the extensor muscle origin from the lateral side of the elbow joint. It follows a minor strain in energetic use of the forearm from pronation to supination. The patient complains of pain which spreads from the lateral epicondyle of the humerus often to the forearm muscle. It is brought on by overuse of the extensor and supinator muscles of the forearm and is relieved by rest.

On examination there is tenderness over the lateral epicondyle of the humerus at the site of the extensor muscle origin of the forearm muscles or along the lateral ligament. The pain is brought on by supinating the forearm against resistance. X-rays are usually normal but in long standing cases there may be some calcification in the tissues around the extensor origin.

TREATMENT

1. Rest in the early stage and a short cock-up splint will help.

2. An injection of hydrocortisone and local anaesthetic into the painful area is given. The injection may have to be repeated.

3. Physiotherapy with ultrasound may help.

4. Resting of the arm in a plaster of Paris cast.

5. Manipulation of the elbow under a general anaesthetic, forcing the elbow into full extension with the forearm pronated and the wrist fully flexed.

6. Operative treatment:

(a) Lengthening of the extensor carpi radialis brevis.

(b) Freeing the extensor origin from the lateral epicondyle of the humerus may be required in stubborn cases.

(c) Excision of the thickening discoid fibro-cartilage from the joint and the synovial membrane may be required.

Golfer's elbow

This condition affects the flexor tendon origin from the medial epicondyle of the humerus and becomes chronic with scar tissue formation. Signs and symp-toms are the reverse of a tennis elbow with pain on extending the wrist with the arm in full supination. The left arm is the one usually affected in right-handed golfers, but the injury can occur in other sports.

TREATMENT

This is as for a tennis elbow, by rest and physiotherapy. An injection of hydrocortisone and local anaesthetic is helpful. Manipulation in a reverse manner to that of a tennis elbow may be required under a general anaesthetic.

Thrower's elbow

In this condition there is a whiplash injury of the elbow when hyperextension causes the olecranon to come in contact with the olecranon process in the lower humerus. This may cause a fracture or an epiphysitis. This injury is seen in baseball, cricket, as well as field events.

TREATMENT

In the early stage, treatment is rest from throwing. It may need a plaster of Paris cast for three to four weeks. Occasionally excision of bony fragments may be required.

Javelin thrower's elbow

This is a strain of the medial ligament of the elbow caused by a round arm type of throw. Treatment is to rest the arm and correct the throwing fault by coaching the athlete to lead with the elbow. Physiotherapy and a hydrocortisone injection may be required.

Dislocation of the elbow

This results from a fall on the outstretched hand caus-ing the lower end of the humerus to pass forwards over the coronoid process of the ulna and the head of the radius. This tears the brachialis muscle and joint cap-sule producing a *posterior* dislocation. An *anterior* dislo-cation occurs in a similar fashion. X-rays are used to confirm the dislocation.

Under a general anaesthetic the dislocation is reduced and the position checked by x-ray. The arm is immobilised in a collar and cuff sling for three to four weeks.

COMPLICATIONS

These include:

1. Calcification in the brachialis muscle. This is sus-pected when the range of movements stop increasing.

2. The medial epicondyle may be trapped in the joint after reduction and must be looked for on an x-ray check.

3. There may be damage to the median and ulnar nerves.

'Pulled elbow'

In this condition the head of the radius is pulled out of the annular ligament and is likely to occur in sports such as judo.

On examination there is pain and tenderness over the head of the radius. Movements of supination and pronation of the forearm are limited.

TREATMENT

The elbow is flexed to a right angle and the extended wrist is grasped. Then, pushing in the long axis of the forearm, the forearm is alternately supinated and pronated until the head of the radius clicks back.

FRACTURES OF THE ELBOW

Fractures of the olecranon

These are of two types:

1. Direct injury which results from a fall on the point of the elbow especially on a hard playing surface. The olecranon may be comminuted by the force of the fall or the fracture may be a transverse type with subluxation due to the pull of the triceps.

2. Indirect injury which may occur in throwing events due to the vigorous action of the triceps tendon on its insertion. This leads to pain on extending the elbow and is felt over the olecranon. This pain may have a sudden onset or may increase gradually over a week or so. On examination there is pain and tenderness over the olecranon. X-rays confirm the fracture.

TREATMENT

If there is displacement, the fracture must be reduced and fixed internally using a screw or tension wire banding. The arm is immobilised in a sling until the wound is healed; then gentle exercises are commenced. Full activity can be resumed when the fracture is radiologically united.

Fracture of the lateral epicondyle of the humerus

This occurs from a sudden contracture of the extensor muscles of the forearm and is an avulsion fracture. There is pain and tenderness over the lateral epicondyle of the humerus with swelling later. There is pain on extension of the wrist against resistance. X-rays show the fracture which may be displaced.

TREATMENT

If the fracture is undisplaced, immobilisation in a collar and cuff sling for three to four weeks until the pain has subsided is all that is required. If the fragment is displaced it must be reduced and is then sutured with strong catgut or fixed with small 'K' wires. Activities are resumed when the fracture has united and the wires are removed.

Fracture of the medial epicondyle of the humerus

This is caused by a valgus strain of the elbow with the contraction of the flexor muscles of the forearm. It may also occur as a complication of a dislocation of the elbow. The fragment may remain in the joint after the elbow has been reduced.

There is pain and tenderness over the medial epicondyle of the humerus and pain when the wrist is flexed against resistance. The fracture and the position of the fragment is confirmed by x-rays.

TREATMENT

If there is medial displacement, immobilisation in a collar and cuff sling for three weeks is required followed by a gradual increase in exercises. Full activity may be resumed when there is no longer any pain or tenderness.

Fracture of the capitulum of the humerus

This is caused by a fall on the outstretched hand. The head of the radius (which may also be damaged) causes the capitulum to fracture.

There is pain and swelling about the elbow with tenderness over the head of the radius. X-rays confirm the fracture.

TREATMENT

If there is no displacement the arm is immobilised in a collar and cuff sling for three or four weeks. If there is displacement of the capitulum, it should be replaced. The head of the radius will help to keep the capitulum in position but if unstable the fragment may be sutured into place with catgut or held in position with 'K' wires. Sometimes reduction is not possible because of comminution and then the fragment must be excised.

Fracture of the coronoid process of the olecranon

This may occur after falling on the outstretched arm and is probably associated with a transient dislocation of the elbow.

There is pain, swelling and stiffness in the elbow. The fracture which is rarely displaced is confirmed by x-rays.

TREATMENT
Immobilisation in a collar and cuff sling for three to four weeks followed by gradual increase in exercises is required.

Fracture of the head of the radius
This fracture is caused by falling on the outstretched hand, the head of the radius being driven against the capitulum.

There is pain and tenderness over the head of the radius with loss of supination and pronation of the forearm as well as loss of some flexion and extension. Diagnosis is confirmed by x-rays.

TREATMENT
If there is a crack fracture with minimal displacement of the fragment, a collar and cuff sling is applied for three weeks followed by exercises to encourage supination and pronation as soon as pain permits. When there is displacement of the fracture with comminution the head of the radius must be excised. Care is taken to ensure that all the fragments are removed. Failure to remove the head of the radius in these fractures will limit supination and pronation of the forearm. The patient can return to full activities in about six to eight weeks after the operation which should be carried out as soon as convenient after the injury.

Supracondylar fractures of the humerus
There are two types of supracondylar fracture of the humerus.

1. The most common is an extension type of injury when the elbow with the lower fragment of the humerus is driven backwards on the humerus.

2. The less common type is a flexion injury with the proximal end of the lower humerus being driven below and behind the lower humeral fragment and elbow joint.

The elbow swells quickly on injury, but immediately after the injury the bony parts can be palpated in the fractured area. It is noted that the triangle formed by the medial and lateral epicondyle of the humerus and the point of the olecranon remains an equilateral triangle. This equilateral triangle is disrupted in a dislocation of the elbow joint. There is pressure upon (or a rupture in some rare cases) the brachial artery which leads to loss of blood supply to the forearm, especially to the flexor muscles. This may lead to Volkmann's ischaemia if the fracture is not reduced quickly.

Volkmann's ischaemia occurs when the blood supply to the flexor muscles of the forearm is diminished by spasm of the brachial artery due to irritation of this blood vessel by the fractured humerus. It is recognised by flexion of the fingers with pain in the forearm and pain when the flexed fingers are passively extended. The radial pulse at the wrist is weak and the hand and fingers are swollen and discoloured. There may also be damage to the medial or ulnar nerves at the time of the fracture due to their close approximation to the elbow joint.

Myositis ossificans affecting the brachialis muscle may occur causing stiffness of the elbow. This stiffness may be severe and persist, causing contracture of the fingers and wrist.

TREATMENT
Urgent reduction of the fracture to avoid a vascular catastrophe is required. It is usually carried out under general anaesthetic. Following reduction the arm is immobilised in a collar and cuff sling for about four to six weeks, when exercises are begun. Open reduction may be required if there is any difficulty in obtaining reduction of the fracture or if there is impairment of the circulation after closed manipulation of the fracture.

The muscles surrounding the elbow joint are strong when acting together and with the natural stability of the hinged joint make an extremely stable articulation. The problem after injury is one of stiffness and this is due to a relative shortening of the ligaments due either to oedema or direct injury. This stiffness may cause great disability to the sportsman if it persists. When there is pain, or in the early stages of an injury, passive movements must *not* be encouraged. Rest in the early stages leads to absorption of the oedema and repair of the damaged ligament. This period of rest is followed by gentle active movements as soon as the pain and swelling have subsided. The exercises are gradually increased until a full range of movements has been obtained. Vigorous exercises may well lead to stiffening of the joint rather than increasing the range of movements. Accurate reduction of fractures involving the joint surfaces is essential to obtain a full range of movements after an injury. Failure to obtain this by manipulative treatment necessitates internal fixation of the fragments.

CHAPTER 28

Injuries to the wrist in sports

J. N. RIMMER MChOrth, FRCS

The wrist joint is commonly injured in those sporting activities where falls are numerous on to hard surfaces as in rugby, football, ice-skating and so on. However, repetitive injuries to surrounding tendonous structures may be sustained by high levels of repetitive activity in tennis or badminton: usually the precipitating stresses are chronic and are exacerbated by the relative avascularity of the tendon structure which has a low metabolic rate.

ANATOMY

The radio-carpal or wrist joint is a condyloid or bi-axial joint. The parts forming it are the distal end of the radius and lower surface of the articular disc which stretches from the ulnar margin of the radius to the notch at the base of the styloid process of the ulna above, and the lunate, scaphoid and triquetral bones below. The former constitute a transverse elliptical concave surface, the 'receiving cavity' and the latter form a smooth convex surface received into that cavity.

The line of the joint corresponds to a line convex upwards joining the styloid process of the radius and ulna (Fig. 28/1).

The joint is surrounded by an articular capsule strengthened by anterior and posterior ligaments together with medial and lateral ligaments. The 'articular disc' is triangular in shape and binds the lower ends of the radius and ulna together. It is attached, by its apex, to a depression between the ulnar styloid and the inferior surface of the head of the ulna and, by its base, to the proximal edge between the ulnar notch of the radius and its carpal surface (Fig. 28/2). When the hand is adducted, it articulates with the triquetral bone and when the hand is neutral, with the lunate. As hand movements on the forearm are not solely confined to the radio-carpal joint it is necessary to consider the mid-carpal joint (Fig. 28/1) in the context of wrist injuries. This consists of the joints between the proximal and distal row of carpal bones and between the carpal bones themselves in the proximal row.

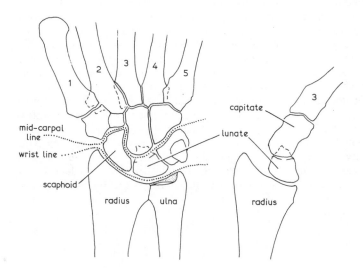

Fig. 28/1 The wrist joint showing the wrist and mid-carpal lines

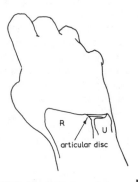

Fig. 28/2 The location of the articular disc binding the lower ends of the radius and ulna

The joints of the proximal row of carpal bones

The joints between the scaphoid, lunate and triquetral bones are of the plane variety and are connected by dorsal, palmar and interosseous ligaments. The dorsal and palmar ligaments are weaker than the dorsal (Chaubal, 1959). The interosseous ligaments are two narrow bundles, one connecting the lunate and scaphoid bones, the other the lunate and triquetral bones.

The joints of the two rows of carpal bones with each other

The joint between the scaphoid, lunate and triquetral bones on the one hand and the second row of carpal bones on the other is named the mid-carpal joint (Fig. 28/1) and is made up of two portions: on the medial side is the head of the capitate bone and the hamate bone which articulate with the concavity formed by the scaphoid, lunate and triquetral bones and constitute a modified condyloid joint; on the lateral side the trapezium and trapezoid articulate with the scaphoid and constitute a plane joint. The ligaments are the dorsal, palmar, medial and lateral. The lateral and medial ligaments are short: the one is placed on the radial and the other on the ulnar side of the carpus. The former, the stronger and more distinct, connects the scaphoid and trapezium, the latter the triquetral and hamate.

Movements of hand and forearm

These movements involve both radio-carpal and mid-carpal joints. They are flexion, extension, radial deviation and ulnar deviation.

PALMAR FLEXION

About 65 to 75 per cent of flexion occurs at the radio-carpal (wrist) articulation, the rest at the mid-carpal joint. The lunate is almost horizontal, so that most of its proximal articular surface is dorsal instead of being in contact with the articular surface of the radius.

EXTENSION

Most movement takes place at the mid-carpal joint. In extension and hyperextension, the lunate turns its distal articular surface dorsally; the capitate turns and becomes vertical with its base orientated dorsally and its neck abuts against the posterior lip of the radius. The proximal end of the scaphoid follows the lunate and the distal part of the scaphoid follows the capitate only partially. A large part of the proximal articular surface of the lunate remains unsupported anteriorly by any bony socket.

RADIAL DEVIATION

About 60 to 65 per cent takes place at the mid-carpal joint. The entire proximal surface of the scaphoid is in contact with the radius, the styloid process of which touches the trapezium. The lunate moves under the triangular cartilage.

ULNAR DEVIATION

About 50 per cent of ulnar deviation takes place at the mid-carpal joint. The line of transmission of forces passes through the capitate and the proximal half of the scaphoid and the radial styloid.

The tendons around the wrist

At the level of the lower radius and ulna a transverse section shows the tendons in distinct groupings, flexor tendons anteriorly, extensors dorsally and thumb tendons on the outer side of the radius (Fig. 28/3). Two

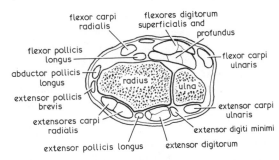

Fig. 28/3 The tendons passing over the lower radius and ulna

synovial sheaths envelop the flexors, one for the superficial and deep flexors of the fingers, the other for the flexor pollicis longus. On the back of the wrist, beneath the fibrous extensor retinaculum, lie the six tunnels for the passage of the extensor tendons. One tunnel on the lateral side is for the abductor pollicis longus and extensor brevis; next, behind the styloid process are the tendons of the extensor brevis and the longus of the wrist, on the medial side of the dorsal tubercle of the radius the extensor longus of the thumb, then the extensor digitorum and extensor indices. Between the radius and the ulna is the extensor digiti minimis and lastly, between the head styloid process of the ulna is the extensor carpi ulnaris.

INJURIES TO THE SOFT TISSUES

Sprains of the wrist

It is true that falls on the hand may sometimes cause a synovitis of the synovial membrane (lining the joint) and an effusion into the joint ensues concomitant to sprains of the volar wrist ligament. These injuries are far rarer than bone injuries but nevertheless one does see them without bone damage. The injury may be treated by a simple elastic bandage for ten to fourteen days.

Traumatic tendinitis

In such sports as tennis, squash, badminton and rowing which require repetitious movement of the wrist tendons and owing to their relative avascularity, the wrist tendons become the site of swelling (tendinitis) or the investing synovium and fibrous sheaths become irritated (peritendinitis). The commonest site is certainly in the thumb extensor pollicis brevis and abductor pollicis longus on the radial side of the wrist. There is aching pain with slight swelling over the lower quarter of the radius and thumb movements are accompanied by 'wash-leather creaking'. Temporary rest from sport is necessary. It is usually wise to apply a dorsal plaster of Paris slab to include the thumb, wrist and forearm or a local injection of anaesthetic and hyaluronidase prior to this helps relieve symptoms. Similar attacks in the flexor carpi radialis and extensor carpi ulnaris are occasionally seen with acute local tenderness or swelling over the area just prior to the insertions into bone: they are treated in a similar fashion to the thumb tendons.

Tendo-vaginitis stenosans

Pain over the radial side of the wrist associated with thickening of the fibrous sheath (De Quervain's disease, 1895) is a well-known entity. Careful palpation may reveal a small hard fibrous nodule about the size of half a pea. Pain is produced by adducting the thumb across the palm of the hand. Provided the condition is not chronic, hydrocortisone injections may give relief; however, if it is chronic, then division with removal of a segment cures the condition. Care has to be taken not to injure the filaments of the radial nerve which pass over this area as a divided nerve may leave a painful neuroma, which in itself is vulnerable to repeated trauma.

Acute peritendinitis crepitans

This is an inflammatory condition of acute onset which appears to involve a large area of tendon sheaths; it is commonly seen in athletes in the extensor longus tendon and its muscle. The swelling extends usually from the wrist across the lower forearm, and on thumb movements creaking is felt underneath the examining fingers. A similar condition is mainly seen in the extensor tendons crossing the dorsum of the wrist beneath the extensor retinaculum. The condition is best treated

by splintage, resting the part for at least two weeks.

Injuries to the triangular cartilage of the wrist

This rare injury usually occurs on falls on the outstretched hand with an added rotational element. It involves detachment of the apex of the triangular cartilage from the ligamentous attachment to the fossa on the lower ulnar head (Fig. 28/4). On rotation of the

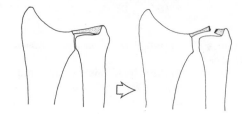

Fig. 28/4 A tear of the triangular cartilage

forearm, it gives rise to a disturbing 'click' which may be painful. If acute and diagnosed early, it is best treated by repair of the ligamentous attachment. If chronic, it is usually treated by excision of the whole cartilaginous structure.

FRACTURES AND DISLOCATIONS AROUND THE WRIST

The scaphoid fractures

The scaphoid may be fractured at any of three levels – the distal pole, the waist or the proximal pole. The most common level is the 'waist' fracture, the others being comparatively rare. The blood supply variations of the scaphoid may account for the occasional 'death' of the proximal segment. One of the most common fractures seen in sports is the 'waist' fracture of the scaphoid (Fig. 28/5), caused by falls on the outstretched hand or 'hand-off' injury in rugby. There is swelling of the wrist in the region of the 'anatomical snuff-box', with tenderness in the same area; there may initially be a negative x-ray but this should not put one

Fig. 28/5 'Waist' fracture of the scaphoid

off doing a further x-ray examination between the tenth and fourteenth day, when the fracture line may become evident.

The fracture should be immobilised by plaster which includes the thumb up to the distal joint and the forearm up to below the flexor elbow crease. The position of immobilisation should be in the ball-holding position of the hand with the wrist in dorsiflexion (Fig. 28/6). This fixation should be maintained for six to

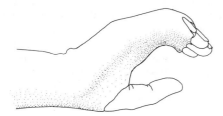

Fig. 28/6 Position of immobilisation after a scaphoid fracture

twelve weeks. If, at the end of this period, healing is not evident on x-ray then the freedom of the hand should be allowed; however, if pain is encountered on activity then internal fixation by screws should be done (Maudsley and Chen, 1972). London (1961) has shown that the majority of fractures given this freedom will unite but the percentage of non-union in the experience of this author has been up to 25 per cent and screw fixation has been so successful that he has adopted this procedure.

Established non-union of the scaphoid

The inevitable result of non-union of the scaphoid is the establishment of degenerative arthritis of the mid-carpal and radio-carpal joints. Although this may be painless it always results in limitation of wrist movement, and in the athlete where wrist trauma is apt to occur injury causes further pain. In these instances the scaphoid should be curetted, packed with bone and internally fixed by screwing, with, perhaps, excision of the radial styloid.

Established painful arthritis

Painful arthritis is probably best treated by excision of the proximal carpus or wrist arthrodesis.

Rupture of the inter-osseous ligaments between scaphoid and lunate

This results often and is not recognised; a gap occurs between the scaphoid and the lunate which can be painful. It is diagnosed by x-ray and the gap noted. The injury is best treated by operative re-position and internal fixation.

Dislocation of the lunate

The lunate is a wedge-shaped bone with its broad base forward. A fall on the outstretched wrist may displace it forward by rupture of its dorsal attachment to the capitate (Fig. 28/7a and b). The anterior proximity of the median nerve within the confines of the carpal tunnel often causes numbness or tingling in the thumb and radial three fingers. The diagnosis is confirmed by x-ray examination and in new cases re-position may be afforded by traction and a direct push from in front of the wrist. Old unreduced cases are best treated by operative removal of the lunate as are cases where the lunate dies from loss of blood supply even though successfully reduced.

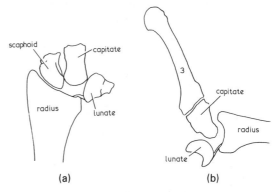

Fig. 28/7a&b Forward dislocation of the lunate

Injury to the lower radius

Fractures of the lower radius are classified as forearm fractures but it is best to include them in wrist injuries. The usual cause in sports is a fall on the outstretched hand. In the young athlete before growth is complete the injury results in a backward displacement of the lower radial epiphysis (Fig. 28/8). If displaced greater than one third of the way across the radius it is best treated by manipulation and fixation on a dorsal plaster slab.

In the adult, sporting injury may result in a vertical splitting of the lower radius with widening of the breadth of the articular surface of the radius in both

Fig. 28/8 Fracture-displacement of the lower radial epiphysis (lateral view)

Fig. 28/9 'Male-type' fractures of the lower radius

planes (Fig. 28/9). Although this often results in broadening of the radial articular surface the late results are good, often with, perhaps, some loss of dorsiflexion movement.

Falls on the wrist with the hand in palmar flexion may result in a fracture of the lower radius with varying degrees of obliquity of the fracture line (Fig. 28/10).

Fig. 28/10 'Smith' fracture

This is known as a Smith fracture. If the fracture extends into the articular surface and displaces, the eponymous name of Barton is applied to it! The usual treatment is by manipulation and immobilisation of the forearm in full supination with plaster including the elbow and wrist.

FIRST AID TREATMENT

It is important in all spheres of sports that facilities be made available for adequate initial care to be afforded to all participants, and to spectators. This means that splints, slings and bandages should be available for mild or severe injuries around the wrist and personnel able to apply them adequately. Comfort by pain relief and elevation to reduce swelling often means that later treatment can be made much more easy.

REFERENCES

Chaubal, K. V. (1959). *Dislocations of lunate*. Dissertation for MCh(Orth) thesis, Liverpool University.

De Quervain, F. (1895). Uber eine form von chronischer tendovaginitis. *Korrespondenz-Blatt fur Sweitzer Arzte*, **25**, 389.

London, P. S. (1961). The broken scaphoid – the case against pessimism. *Journal of Bone and Joint Surgery*, **43-B**, 237–244.

Maudsley R. H. and Chen, S. C. (1972). Screw fixation in the management of the fractured carpal scaphoid. *Journal of Bone and Joint Surgery*, **54-B**, 432–441.

CHAPTER 29

Injuries to the hand in sports

J. N. RIMMER MChOrth, FRCS

The use of the hand in sports is widespread. Whether in direct handling by the protected or unprotected hand its vulnerability to direct or indirect trauma can be estimated by the numbers of injuries which present at specialised sports or hand injuries clinics. Even in those sports in which the hand is protected by the use of gloves, as in cricket or boxing, there still remains a large number of injuries presenting at hospitals.

The hand may be used without protection for ball handling, catching, throwing or through its constant grasping and power function with various forms of bats, rackets and weights or even as an organ of communication in gesturing or signalling to other participants or spectators.

THE ANATOMY OF THE HAND

Connected to a large area of the sensori-motor cortex, the nerve supply to the hand comes mainly through the median, ulnar and radial nerves; the former two deliver both a sensory supply to the skin and a motor supply to the intrinsic muscles. The radial nerve limits itself to a sensory supply only. In addition, a rich complex supply is afforded by all three nerves to the sweat glands and blood vessels making the hand an important regulator of temperature of the body as a whole. On the front of the hand a marginal contribution to grip is made by the sweat gland secretion.

Basically, the bony skeleton of the hand consists of a platform made up of small carpal bones proximally and a radiating quadumvirate of metacarpal bones, the thumb metacarpal being placed laterally and almost in a plane at right angles to the other metacarpals. From the medial four metacarpals the three phalanges to each finger arise and from the thumb the shorter phalangeal chain of two phalanges. The fine movements of the digits are controlled by intrinsic muscles and the grosser movements by extrinsic tendons, i.e. the flexors on the front and the extensors behind.

Movements

The basic pattern of power, pinch and hook grips are applied to fingers and thumb. Additionally, the hand may be used in sports in the 'paddling' position or as a 'platform' with the wrist hyperextended in swimming and floor gymnastics respectively.

LIGAMENTOUS INJURIES OF THE FINGERS AND THUMB

Anatomy

The metacarpo-phalangeal joints are of the condyloid variety, each having a palmar and two collateral ligaments (Fig. 29/1). In the fingers, side-to-side movements of the thumb metacarpo-phalangeal joint are much more restricted. The palmar ligaments are of thick, dense fibrocartilage attached on either side to the collateral ligaments, loosely to the metacarpal and firmly to the phalangeal bases. In addition they blend on either side to the deep transverse ligaments of the palm and their sides give attachments to the fibrous flexor tendon sheaths.

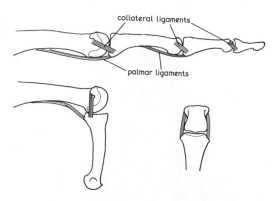

collateral ligaments

palmar ligaments

Fig. 29/1 The collateral and palmar ligaments of the metacarpo-phalangeal joints

Sprain of the collateral ligaments of the metacarpo-phalangeal joints

Sprains of the collateral ligaments are common in the thumb, but less common in the finger metacarpal joints. The former lead to continued pain and swelling which constitutes a severe handicap to thumb usage in gripping and untoward sudden sideways strains. Patients should be warned of these continued effects. In the initial stages it is often better to protect the ligaments by a small splint made from three to four sheets of plaster of Paris moulded directly on to the thumb, maintained for two to three weeks; later, continued pain can be lessened by an injection of hydrocortisone around the joint. With metacarpo-phalangeal joint sprains, again they should be immobilised initially by a metal well-padded splint extending from the butt of the palm up to the distal joints of the finger for two to three weeks. These injuries seem not to have continued pain, as in the thumb collateral ligament joint sprains, and can be protected by immobilising with strapping to adjacent fingers.

Sprains of the proximal interphalangeal joint ligaments
The collateral ligaments of the proximal finger joints appear especially vulnerable to sprains sustained mostly during body contact sports. The immediate swelling and pain may be more pronounced unilaterally and the finger joint should be tested for instability and x-rayed. During the painful initial stages it is wise to immobilise the joint for up to ten days, then mobilise the finger by gartering to the adjacent fingers. The patient should be warned of persistent swelling in the joint with some discomfort on movement (Fig. 29/2).

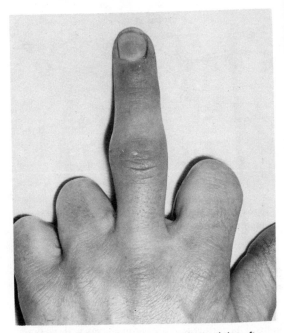

Fig. 29/2 Swelling in the proximal finger joint after collateral ligament injury

Collateral ligament rupture at metacarpo-phalangeal level
With greater violence the collateral ligaments are prone to complete division. They usually rupture at joint line level but may be avulsed with bone fragments at either end; instability ensues and it is detected clinically by stressing laterally the affected joints.

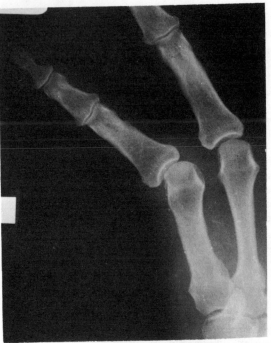

Fig. 29/3 X-ray appearance after rupture of radial collateral injury

Figure 29/3 shows the x-ray appearance of stress films where ruptures of the radial collateral ligaments are demonstrated. The small and ring fingers would appear to be the most common fingers to be affected. Treatment for certainty should be operative, as conservative treatment cannot guarantee as good a result. In the author's experience the resultant disability of instability where treatment was expectant weighs heavily towards operative treatment. Repair of the ligaments should be afforded by interrupted white silk and the fingers maintained at 60° flexion for three weeks. In the thumb, similar operative treatment is necessary where the most common injury is to the collateral ligament on the ulnar side. Non-operative treatment often leads to instability, an extremely disabling condition.

In those undetected ruptures and in long-term disability an attempt should be made to construct new collateral ligaments by free fascia lata grafts, although no absolute guarantee can be given to completely cure the instability. The only absolute cure, but which is difficult to obtain, is by metacarpo-phalangeal fusion in a position of function; thumb mobility being ensured by the basal carpo-metacarpal and terminal interphalangeal joints.

Collateral ligament rupture at interphalangeal joint level

Radial-sided collateral ligament rupture at the proximal interphalangeal joint of the small finger is illustrated by the stress film in Figure 29/4.

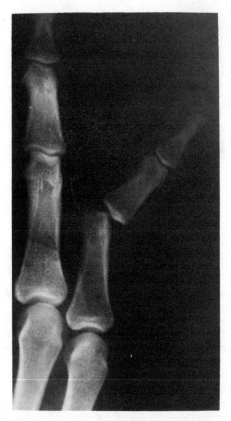

Fig. 29/4 Stress x-ray film after collateral ligament rupture at the proximal interphalangeal joint

Operative repair is needed for fresh injuries. It is necessary to maintain the finger in the mid-range position postoperatively at about 45° of flexion for three weeks, with some 'lively' splintage following for a further three to four weeks. Long-term results have shown the success of this aggressive treatment with only a minimal loss of flexibility in a few instances.

CLOSED TENDON INJURIES IN THE HAND

Extensor mechanism

Direct finger-tip injury from ball-game pursuits often results in 'attritional' lengthening of the extensor tendon insertion; the flexion deformity resulting at the terminal interphalangeal joint is known colloquially as a 'mallet' finger (Fig. 29/5). The deformity is corrected by application of one of the plastic splints of which many are on the market and maintained for five weeks. If the deformity is of the magnitude of 90°, it is considered better to operate and overcome the tendon lengthening by 'darning' the tendon over the joint with white silk, afterwards maintaining the joint in extension for three weeks. Slight loss of flexion range may result in the long term.

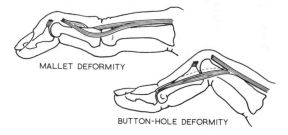

MALLET DEFORMITY

BUTTON-HOLE DEFORMITY

Fig. 29/5 Results of injury to the extensor tendon mechanism

Occasionally indirect trauma to the extensor tendon 'middle slip' insertion over the proximal phalanx occurs again with attritional lengthening of the insertion. The resultant deformity is the 'boutonniere' finger where the terminal interphalangeal joint remains in extension and the proximal interphalangeal joint adopts an attitude of flexion (Fig. 29/5). The lateral slips of the extensor mechanism move away from their anatomical axis and cause the deformity. Fresh injuries are treatable by splintage in an attempt to reverse the deformity. The splint should be close fitting and maintain the proximal joint in extension and the terminal joint in flexion. Late deformities should undergo operative treatment whereby the extensor is restored as best as possible to its anatomical position.

Flexor tendon injury

The rare avulsion of the long profundus tendon is depicted in Figure 29/6a, b, and c. A frequent cause is grabbing an opponent's jersey or shorts in rugby. The resultant immobility of the terminal joint is diagnostic and often the bone fragment avulsed from the terminal

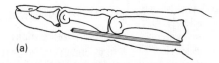

(a)

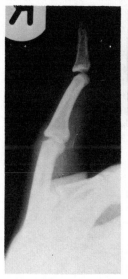

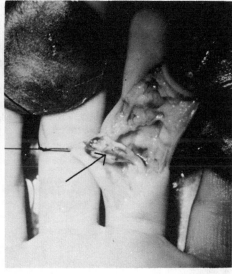

Fig 29/6
(a) The mechanism of avulsion
of the long flexor profundus tendon
(b) X-ray appearance of a rupture
avulsion of the long flexor
profundus tendon
(c) Operative findings: the arrow
indicates the tendon end

(b)   (c)

phalanx can be demonstrated (Fig. 29/6b). The treatment is operative with the re-position of the fragment with wire fixation (Fig. 29/6c). The finger should be immobilised in flexion for three weeks.

FINGER AND THUMB DISLOCATIONS

Most finger joint dislocations occur at the proximal interphalangeal joints with body contact sports. The middle phalanx is displaced backwards and results in the clinical 'step-off' which is so easily recognised: on the spot diagnosis is easy and often the joint is restored by a single sharp traction on the finger. As the joint capsule is not breached this manoeuvre is, in the majority of cases, successful. Simple gartering to adjacent fingers is all that is necessary but it is imperative to check reduction by x-ray. In the thumb, the common displacement is at the terminal joint and re-position is done in the same way. Occasionally both interphalangeal joints can be concomitantly displaced in a 'stairway' fashion.

The rare metacarpo-phalangeal dislocation where the proximal phalanx is displaced backwards on the metacarpal head demands care, as the volar capsule often 'buttonholes' and renders closed manipulation impossible. It is in such cases that open reduction and re-position is necessary because of the trapping effect on the metacarpal head.

PERI-ARTICULAR AND INTRA-ARTICULAR FRACTURES

Intra-articular fractures without significant joint surface deformation
These fractures are treated by gartering the injured digit to the neighbouring digit from which it tends to deviate. Finger movements are encouraged immediately.

Condylar fractures
Fractures without significant displacement usually only involve one condyle of the proximal phalanx and are treated by gartering. Fractures with displacement are usually unstable, rotation resulting in effacement. Treatment is operative with Kirschner wire fixation. Even after restoration, occasionally the fragment may die but its buttressing effect can have a fair outcome.

Bennett's fracture-dislocation
This injury commonly occurs in body contact sports and from falls. The outcome is an intra-articular fracture through the base of the thumb metacarpal with a

variably sized triangular fragment of bone remaining articulated while the main shaft carrying the larger articular surface is displaced. The resultant pain and swelling at the thumb base is easily detected and the fracture confirmed by x-ray.

Treatment is by operative reduction of the fracture and screw fixation through the fragment which allows anatomical re-position of the metacarpo-carpal relationship. The consequent stability ensures restoration of movement and delays possible later degenerative osteoarthritis.

Chip or flake fractures around joints

Without displacement, chip or flake fractures are commonly seen at the bases of the middle phalanges. If the joint is stable then simple splintage is all that is necessary for three weeks.

Where the fracture occurs with displacement and the joint is unstable then open fixation should be done. However, late diagnosis often leads to a fair result as depicted in Figures 29/7a and b. The initial x-ray on the left shows the displaced fracture with subluxation and the result at two years on the right shows a fairly respectable joint surface without any operating being performed.

Fractures of the head or necks of metacarpals

These fractures are common sporting injuries particularly in boxing. Those through the metacarpal head can be left alone and healed by elevation and early movement. With fractures through the metacarpal neck significant displacement can occur. The head moves into the palm of the hand and the fracture angulates backwards. Moderate angulation can be left alone but significant displacement should be reduced by manipulation: if this is unsuccessful then open operation should be performed.

It is important to realise that hand injuries in sports require adequate first and second treatment. First aid requires the services of an adequately trained first aider, physiotherapist or doctor on site at the time of the injury. Simple immobilisation and, above all, elevation of the hand is all that is necessary. Second aid, which should always follow, should be afforded at a special hand clinic at hospital run by a *specialist* in hand surgery. Too often hospital care is left to a junior doctor without supervision and poor results follow. Within the same confines physiotherapists and occupational therapists should work within the hand service team, for it is only by team work that the very best results are achieved.

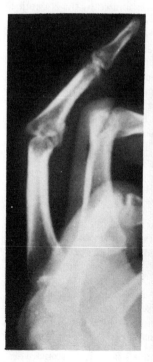 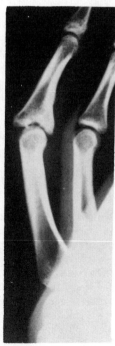

(a) (b)

Fig. 29/7a&b X-ray appearance of chip or flake fracture at the base of the middle phalanx
 (a) displaced fracture with subluxation
 (b) the result, two years later

CHAPTER 30

Pelvic and thigh injuries

LISLE THOMPSON TD, MChOrth, FRCS

ANATOMY

The hip bone is formed by the fusion of the ischium, pubis and iliac bones which meet at the acetabulum. Anteriorly, the pubic bones articulate at the symphysis pubis. Posteriorly the iliac bones articulate with the lateral surface of the sacrum. The sacro-iliac joint is a synovial joint of the plane type and its strength depends on the posterior and anterior sacro-iliac ligaments.

The hip joint is a ball and socket type of joint. Its strength is dependent on the deep acetabulum and on muscle action rather than ligaments. The most important is the Y-shaped ligament of Bigalow which lies anteriorly and is the strongest ligament in the body (Fig. 30/1).

The important anatomical landmarks are:

1. The head of the femur which can be felt in the ilium with the femoral artery lying in front of it just below the middle of Poupart's ligament
2. The greater trochanter
3. The anterior superior iliac spine
4. The tuberosity of the ischium.

Nelaton's line is drawn from the tuberosity of the ischium to the anterior superior iliac spine. The tip of the greater trochanter just touches this line in the normal limb. Bryant's triangle is drawn by dropping a perpendicular from the anterior superior iliac spine onto the bed on which the patient rests. The distance from this line to the tip of the greater trochanter is compared with the other side.

An oblique plane passing through the promontory of the sacrum behind, and the arcuate line in front divides the pelvis into true and false parts. The false pelvis is an expanded part of the cavity lying above and in front, the true pelvis lying below and behind the pelvic inlet.

Flexion of the hip joint is limited by the abdominal wall when the knee is flexed. Tension in the hamstring limits flexion of the hip to about 90 to 100° when the knee is extended. Hyperextension of the hip is limited by the strong iliofemoral ligament of Bigalow. Abduction is limited by the pubofemoral ligament and by tension of the adductor muscles. Adduction is limited by contact with the other limb. Tension of the lateral rotator muscles and the ischiofemoral ligament limit medial rotation while lateral rotation is limited by the medial rotators and the iliofemoral ligament.

SOFT TISSUE INJURIES OF PELVIS AND HIP

Bruising in the gluteal region

Superficial bruising occurs with pain and tenderness at the site of the injury and the contusion can be seen.

TREATMENT

This consists of ice packs in the initial stage followed by local massage and exercise to promote the absorption of the haematoma. Injection of local anaesthetic (1% plain) plus lignocaine may help the absorption.

Deep bruising may produce a large haematoma which can be seen and felt very quickly due to the looseness of the connective tissue of the buttock.

TREATMENT

In minor cases ice, and contrast baths later, may be

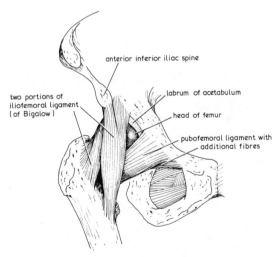

anterior inferior iliac spine

two portions of iliofemoral ligament (of Bigalow)

labrum of acetabulum

head of femur

pubofemoral ligament with additional fibres

Fig. 30/1 Anterior aspect of the right hip joint

satisfactory. If the swelling is large it may have to be aspirated either with a needle or through a small incision under a local anaesthetic. This limits the pain and stiffness which often follows such an injury and enables active treatment and exercise to be carried out finally.

Muscle injuries

There may be a strain or tear of muscle origin from the iliac crest, the ischial tuberosity or the adductor region. A flake of bone may be avulsed from the muscle origin at the time of the injury which can be seen on x-ray examination. Examination of the site shows tenderness and swelling.

TREATMENT

In the early stages cold and pressure should be applied to the painful area and later, as the swelling and tenderness subside, heat and graduated exercises. Ultrasound may help the painful area, and injections of hydrocortisone also help relieve pain.

These injuries tend to recur, but they can be prevented by careful 'limbering up' exercises before taking part in sporting activity. Some cases can become chronic with calcification in the muscle origin. Treatment with an injection of hydrocortisone and physiotherapy in the form of short wave diathermy and gentle stretching exercises, may help the pain and stiffness.

Pain from injury to the hamstring origin at the ischial tuberosity may be similar to the sciatica from a disc lesion of the lower lumbar spine. Examination of the spine and a negative Lasègue's test with no neurological signs will help in the diagnosis.

FRACTURES OF THE PELVIS

These may occur in rugby football, or from falls at speed from motor cars, cycles or horses.

Fractures of the false pelvis along the pelvic ring

These fractures may be due to a direct injury of the ilium or an indirect injury when the trunk muscles are avulsed from the iliac crest. In the same way the sartorius may pull off the anterior superior iliac spine and the straight head of rectus may pull off the anterior inferior iliac spine. There may be an avulsion from the ischial tuberosity due to a pull of the hamstring muscles causing ischial apophysitis. This is possible, for example, in the lead leg of high jumpers using the straddle technique.

There is tenderness and swelling at the site of injury which is painful and swollen. Later, bruising will occur. An x-ray will confirm this fracture.

TREATMENT

In the early stages cold and pressure with rest will limit the bruising and swelling. Later, heat with gentle exercises as soon as possible should be started. Operative treatment is rarely indicated. Ultrasound and an injection of hydrocortisone may be needed for any local painful area.

Fractures of the true pelvis

There are three main types:

1. Solitary fracture of a pelvic bone
2. Intra-articular fracture
3. Disruption of the pelvic ring.

Solitary fracture of a pelvic bone

This may affect the pubis, ischium, sacrum or coccyx. Symptoms include pain and tenderness at the site of injury; the patient can walk. The injury is characterised by tenderness at the fracture site with some swelling; the limbs are equal in length; shock is minimal. X-rays confirm the fracture.

TREATMENT

Bed rest for a few days is advised until the pain has lessened. This is followed by heat and gentle exercises.

Intra-articular fractures

Here the posterior wall of the acetabulum may be fractured with a dislocation of the head of the femur as well. There may be a central dislocation of the head of the femur. The patient complains of pain about the hip joint. There may be some stiffness at the joint but no shortening of the leg. The sciatic nerve may be damaged in the posterior wall fractures of the acetabulum with weakness of dorsiflexion of the foot. X-rays confirm the fracture.

TREATMENT

Reduction of the dislocation and internal fixation of the posterior fragment of the acetabulum may be necessary. Rest in bed until the fracture is healed will be required, followed by partial weight-bearing with crutches. Fractures of the side wall of the acetabulum require traction for about six weeks; no weight-bearing is allowed for three months and this is followed by gentle weight-bearing for a further three months. Aseptic necrosis of the head of the femur may occur in one year and osteoarthritis may develop in some cases after five years.

Disruption of the pelvic ring

In this type of fracture there may be damage to the urethra, the sciatic nerve or a major blood vessel in the pelvis. There are three types of fracture which have one thing in common, both sides of the pelvic ring being broken causing an unstable pelvis.

The crush injury: The patient complains of pain in the pelvis. He is shocked and cannot stand. There is pain over the front of the pelvis which is tender. The legs show no shortening and there is no excessive rotation in either leg. X-rays show a fracture of the pubic and ischial rami on both sides.

There may be damage to the urethra in this type of fracture and this is suspected if blood is seen at the external urinary meatus.

TREATMENT
The urethral damage may have to be repaired. The fracture of the pelvis requires no special treatment except rest in bed till the patient can raise his legs from the bed. This takes about three weeks: he then can get up using sticks and will become more mobile as the pain becomes less.

Hinge separation of the symphysis: This is caused by a rolling type of injury, the force pushing the ilium on one side, downwards and outwards. One sacro-iliac joint is hinged open and the symphysis separates like an oyster. The patient complains of pain in the pelvis and cannot stand up on his feet. The gap can be felt in the symphysis and the leg on the damaged side lies in external rotation with no shortening. X-rays confirm the damaged pelvis.

Complications include severe intra-pelvic bleeding, but damage to the sciatic nerve or urethra is rare.

TREATMENT
The disruption of the pelvis is controlled by a firm binder. The patient remains in bed for about six weeks after which walking exercises can begin.

The vertical fracture of the pelvis: This is caused by a fall from a height landing on one leg. This could happen, for example, in rock climbing or in some imperfectly executed gymnastic routines. The patient complains of pain in the pelvis and cannot stand on his feet. There is pain and tenderness on the symphysis and sacro-iliac joint on the same side. The leg on that side is shorter due to the pelvic bone being pushed up on that side. X-rays confirm the injury.

Complications include possible intra-pelvic bleeding and often damage to the sciatic plexus.

TREATMENT
Strong skeletal traction on the leg reduces the upward displacement of the ilium, and traction on the leg is maintained for six weeks. Weight-bearing is not allowed for about three months.

FRACTURES OF THE NECK OF THE FEMUR

These are rare in young people, though the possibility must be borne in mind in hip injuries. This fracture can result from cycling falls at high speed. The possibility of a slipped upper femoral epiphysis must be remembered.

DISLOCATIONS OF THE HIP JOINT

Anterior dislocation
This occurs when the leg is forced into abduction and external rotation. The main sign is that the leg lies in external rotation, flexion and abduction. The head of the femur can be felt in the obturator foramen. X-rays confirm the diagnosis and whether a fracture is present as well.

Complications may include avascular necrosis of the head of the femur. There may be damage to the sciatic nerve and stiffness due to myositis ossificans.

TREATMENT
Under a general anaesthetic the hip is manipulated into position. Sometimes the head of the femur may be button-holed in the capsule or caught in the tendon of the psoas muscle and an open operation is required to reduce the dislocation. The leg is then immobilised on traction for six to eight weeks.

Posterior dislocation
This occurs when the femur is forced backwards with internal rotation and adduction. There may be a fracture of the posterior wall of the acetabulum as well. The leg lies in adduction and internal rotation with flexion of the hip joint.

There is sometimes damage to the sciatic nerve, avascular necrosis of the head of the femur or myositis ossificans.

TREATMENT
The hip joint is reduced under a general anaesthetic. If there is a fracture of the posterior wall of the acetabulum, the reduction may be unstable and the bony fragment may have to be replaced and fixed by means of a screw. Traction is applied as for an anterior dislocation.

OSTEITIS PUBIS

This is a painful inflammation of the symphysis pubis due to chronic inflammation. It is more common in footballers but may occur in runners and walkers.

The patient complains of pain in the groin which may spread to the adductors, hip or external genitalia. The pain is relieved by rest and made worse by hip movements especially rotation and leg strains on the pelvis by contraction of the rectus abdominus. There may be a history of slight fever. An erythrocyte sedimentation rate (ESR) and white blood cell (WBC) count may sometimes be raised though not always. X-rays may show a widening of the pubic symphysis with calcification in the later stages.

TREATMENT

This is symptomatic and consists of limiting physical activity until the symptoms are better. Phenylbutazone (200mg) three times daily with meals may also help and short wave diathermy may relieve pain. When the pain has subsided, gradual resumption of physical exercises will be required or the pain will return.

Chronic rheumatic diseases such as ankylosing spondylitis and Reiters disease must be excluded. Chronic adductor strains may also cause symptoms which are somewhat similar.

SPRAIN OF THE HIP JOINT

This occurs after a twisting injury to the hip. The patient develops a painful limp soon after the injury and complains of pain over the front and inner side of the hip. The pain may be referred to the inner side of the knee and thigh. There is tenderness over the front of the hip joint which is held in flexion and abduction; movements are painful. An aspiration of the joint may be carried out to exclude infection. X-rays are taken to exclude a fracture or other disease such as infection or tuberculosis.

TREATMENT

Rest from weight-bearing is essential in the early stages with the patient walking with crutches. A firm supporting spica bandage of crêpe will help relieve the pain and non-weight-bearing exercises are begun as soon as possible. As the pain and muscle spasm subside, weight-bearing may then be resumed.

TROCHANTERIC BURSITIS

This bursa lies between the deep surface of the fascia lata and the superficial surface of the greater trochanter with the gluteal muscle insertion. It may be inflamed by a direct blow on the trochanter or by the fascia lata slipping over the trochanter in vigorous exercises.

The patient complains of pain over the greater trochanter which has a deep aching character. It is more common in women than men, and the condition is aggravated by a trick movement which can make the tensor fascia lata slip over the trochanter by flexing the hip at the same time as the gluteus maximus is contracting. There is tenderness over the greater trochanter and pain when the fascia lata moves over the trochanter in flexion and extension of the hip. X-rays exclude any underlying bone damage or disease.

TREATMENT

Rest from training; short wave diathermy helps resolution of the early acute cases. Hydrocortisone may be given by injection into the bursa. In some cases surgical division of a tight band of fascia lata may be required.

AVULSION FRACTURES OF THE GREATER AND LESSER TROCHANTER

Avulsion fractures of the tip of the greater trochanter are caused by a sudden contracture of the gluteus medius. The patient complains of sudden pain over the tip of the greater trochanter, and walks with a limp. Signs include tenderness over the tip of the greater trochanter. There is a loss of power of abduction of the hip which causes a positive Trendelenburg's test, i.e. when weight is put on the injured leg in standing the opposite hip drops rather than rises. X-rays confirm the fracture.

TREATMENT

Mild cases of strain may settle quite quickly but the unstable fractures require internal fixation by figure-of-eight wiring.

Avulsion fractures of the lesser trochanter are caused by a sudden contracture of the psoas muscle. The patient complains of sudden pain while running or kicking; the pain being felt in the adductor region of the thigh. Bruising follows quite soon after the injury. There is painful tenderness over the lesser trochanter region with pain on adducting the leg at the hip joint. X-rays confirm the injury.

TREATMENT

As soon as the pain allows, non-weight-bearing with gentle exercises is the best treatment. As the pain diminishes more vigorous exercises are commenced. Surgery is not required.

SOFT TISSUE INJURIES OF THE THIGH

Bruising

This occurs after a direct injury to the thigh and causes bleeding in and around the thigh muscles (Fig. 30/2).

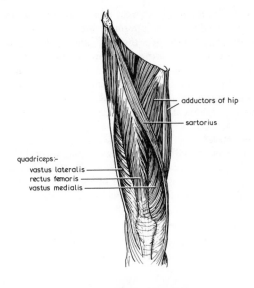

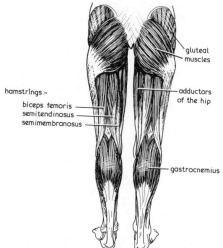

Fig. 30/2 The muscles of the thigh, anterior and posterior views

The patient stops playing and complains of severe pain which is caused by pressure in the muscle due to bleeding. The pain is at the site of the injury and the patient also complains of stiffness in the thigh with difficulty in walking. There may be a superficial abrasion of the overlying skin with swelling and tenderness over the injured muscle.

TREATMENT
Immediate application of a cold compression bandage helps to limit the bleeding. In severe cases the patient is put to bed for a day or so, to limit bleeding. Large collections of blood may have to be drained surgically. In less severe cases limitation of activity is immediately enforced with no attempt to help the pain by gentle exercise. In this way the onset of myositis ossificans, i.e. calcification of the haematoma by osteoblasts spreading from the injured periosteum, is less likely. As the condition settles, gentle graduated exercise is begun; short wave diathermy will help to encourage absorption of the haematoma and relieve muscle spasm.

Muscle ruptures
This commonly occurs in the rectus femoris muscle but may also be found in the adductor muscles or in the hamstrings. It is interesting to note that the muscles which develop these injuries, act on two joints, flexing one and extending the other. As the muscle is relaxing a sudden strain is put upon it causing the tear before the muscle has properly relaxed. The strain may be either an indirect injury or the result of a direct blow over the site of the injury when the muscle is contracting.

The patient complains of pain at the site of the injury which is severe at first and later becomes more dull in nature. There is tenderness at the site of the injury where a gap may be felt. Later, swelling occurs which may be quite marked and may cause bruising at a considerable distance from the injury. There is pain when the muscle is tensed which limits activity.

TREATMENT
Cold pressure bandaging helps to limit the bleeding; gentle exercises as soon as possible after the injury are advised. Injections of hydrocortisone with local anaesthetic and hyaluronidase (Hyalase) will limit adhesion formation later. Muscle spasm is helped by short wave diathermy. Late cases of adhesion formation and stiffness may require gentle manipulation under a general anaesthetic to relieve the pain and stiffness of the injured hamstring. In some cases the damage to the fascia lata may cause a muscle hernia which, if it becomes a nuisance, may have to be repaired surgically. Hamstring injuries, where the tendon is pulled a little out of the muscle belly, require care in rehabilitation to prevent recurrence. A careful examination of the patient's running technique is required.

Hamstring tendinitis
This commonly affects the biceps femoris tendon at its insertion into the head of the fibula rather than the other hamstrings where the injury is where the tendon leaves the muscle belly. In injuries to the biceps tendon the usual symptom is a complaint of pain at the outer

side of the knee, which is made worse by running, or felt on getting up from squatting. The medial hamstrings produce pain at the level of the junction of the middle and lower thirds of the thigh along the postero-medial border.

In injuries to the biceps tendon there is tenderness at the insertion of the biceps into the head of the fibula. Flexion of the knee allows the injured biceps tendon to be removed away from the lateral joint line, thus differentiating it from an injury to structures on the outer side of the knee. X-rays show no bone damage. In late cases there may be a little calcification over the head of the fibula where the biceps tendon is attached.

TREATMENT

This is on similar lines to a tennis elbow with ultrasound treatment and hydrocortisone injections into the painful muscle (see Chapter 27).

FRACTURES OF THE SHAFT OF THE FEMUR

These occur in the course of various sporting activities and treatment is on the accepted orthopaedic lines for such fractures. It is important to remember that these fractures can cause extensive bleeding which leads to shock. A litre or more of blood may be lost into the soft tissue. The bleeding and shock can be limited considerably by careful handling of the patient and early splinting of the fracture before transporting the patient to hospital.

Careful examination of the pelvis and hip joint will help to localise the site of the injury. Gentle movements which do not put tension on a damaged ligament do not cause pain. Stretching a damaged ligament does cause pain and the movement is restricted. Careful palpation of the site of injury will help in identifying the injury.

Pain due to bruising of the articular cartilage of the joint may not appear for a week or so after the injury due to vascularisation of the injured cartilage. As the vascularisation becomes less with healing, so the pain lessens and exercises can be encouraged. Gentle movements, as the pain becomes less, will help limit the formation of adhesions.

Adhesion formation causing stiffness is treated by manipulation under a general anaesthetic when the pain has resolved. Such a manipulation is carried out firmly and steadily, taking care to break adhesions in all directions. If the manipulation is carried out too early or inefficiently, irritation of the joint and its musculature and more adhesion formation will follow.

CHAPTER 31

Injuries to the knee joint

I. D. ADAMS MD

ANATOMY

The knee joint is very vulnerable because of its basic structure, which is a hinge with long levers on either side (Fig. 31/1). The knee is really two joints, one between the femur and the tibia, the other between the patella and the anterior surface of the lower femur. The rounded end of the femur contacts the flat upper part of the tibia, and the two menisci or cartilages lie between them. The menisci are deeper around the edge and so provide a slight depression on the flat tibia for the rounded femur but even then the basic stability of the joint is almost nil. Its strength depends upon its capsule and ligaments together with the muscles acting across the joint.

The knee has always been considered a simple joint but over the last decade the whole concept of the functional anatomy of the knee has changed and the exact functions of each ligament are still open to argument. The joint is surrounded by a capsule, the posterior part of which is only taut in full extension of the knee and provides some stability even in medial and lateral directions. The anterior part of the capsule is only taut in full

flexion and is extended as a pouch above and behind the patella. The only structures within the capsule are one small tendon and two menisci.

The medial ligament of the knee passes from the femoral condyle to the upper margin of the tibia. It is composed of a superficial layer which is attached to the tibia several inches below the joint line and a deep layer which is attached to the medial meniscus and the upper margin of the tibia. The whole ligament forms a wide fan-like structure.

The lateral ligament of the knee is a narrow band passing from the femoral condyle to the head of the fibula and should not be considered the major support on the lateral aspect; this function is performed by the ilio-tibial tract. There are also thickened areas in the capsule which are sometimes described as ligaments.

There are also two major ligaments which are situated centrally, deep within the joint and because of a fold in the capsule are actually outside the joint capsule. These are (1) the anterior cruciate ligament which runs upwards and backwards from its origin on the anterior lip in the mid-line of the upper tibia to the femur and (2) the posterior cruciate ligament, the key

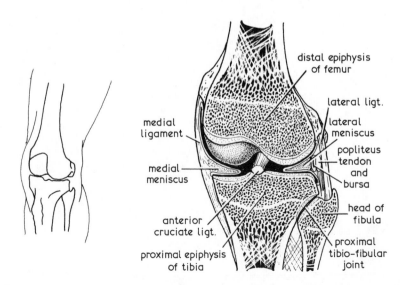

distal epiphysis
of femur

lateral ligt.

lateral
meniscus

popliteus
tendon
and
bursa

head of
fibula

proximal
tibio–fibular
joint

medial
ligament

medial
meniscus

anterior
cruciate ligt.

proximal epiphysis
of tibia

Fig. 31/1 Oblique view of the left knee joint

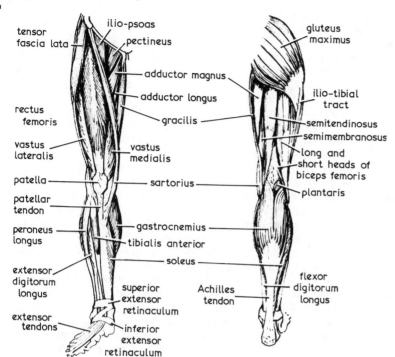

tensor
fascia lata
ilio-psoas
pectineus
adductor magnus
adductor longus
rectus
femoris
gracilis
vastus
lateralis
vastus
medialis
patella
sartorius
patellar
tendon
peroneus
longus
gastrocnemius
tibialis anterior
soleus
extensor
digitorum
longus
superior
extensor
retinaculum
Achilles
tendon
extensor
tendons
inferior
extensor
retinaculum

gluteus
maximus
ilio-tibial
tract
semitendinosus
semimembranosus
long and
short heads of
biceps femoris
plantaris
flexor
digitorum
longus

Fig. 31/2 The muscles that
move the leg and foot
(anterior and posterior views)

to stability of the joint, which arises just medial to the mid-line of the femur and runs downwards and backwards to the tibia. These ligaments are important in the antero-posterior plane.

A major stabilising factor for the knee joint are the muscles (Fig. 31/2). Anteriorly, the powerful quadriceps muscle is inserted into the patella and then through the patellar tendon into the upper part of the tibia. Posteriorly, there are not only the hamstring muscles from the thigh but also the gastrocnemius muscle from the calf. This stabilising factor is important in sport because we can only strengthen the ligaments in a minor way but we can ensure maximum help from the muscles.

A previously unreported series of 8 899 sports injuries seen in the sports medicine clinic of St James' Hospital, Leeds over a four year period and in an accident and emergency department over a three year period show that ligamentous injuries of the knee comprised nine per cent (803 patients) and of the ankle 11.4 per cent (1 014 patients), these being the two most frequent diagnoses.

EXAMINATION

Injury to the knee may damage skin and subcutaneous tissue, muscle, tendon, ligament, capsule, cartilage or bone. Initial examination of an injured player has to decide only three things.

1. Is there a possibility of a fracture?
2. Is there severe ligamentous injury?
3. Is there a torn cartilage?

These are the three serious problems which have to be considered at first.

It is important to have some idea of what happened to the athlete or player at the time of injury as well as any history of previous trouble with the knee joint before proceeding to an examination. The mechanism of injury is important in diagnosis and this is best recalled immediately. Did the patient have the weight on the leg? Was the leg bent or straight when injured? Was the patient turning and if so, in what direction? When laid on the ground could the patient bend and straighten the leg? If unable to straighten the leg, what position was the best he could manage? Was the patient aware of any snapping or tearing sensation? How soon after injury did any swelling occur? If there was contact with an opponent where was the patient struck and from which direction? In many cases it is a precise history of the mechanics of injury and of the symptoms upon which a diagnosis is made.

Examination should start with observation for the presence of any deformity or swelling. Obvious deformity, severe pain, tenderness over bone and loss of power raise the possibility of fracture and the patient should be moved as carefully as possible to hospital. Can the patient fully flex the knee and, more particularly, can he fully extend the joint? If there is any loss of movement this must be recorded. Carefully palpate the joint for swelling and localised tenderness. It is important to localise accurately any tenderness and in particular to say whether this tenderness was over bone or over the joint line.

Examine the knee for stability, testing in full extension when instability implies damage to the posterior cruciate, the posterior capsule and the medial ligament. Also check for stability in approximately 30° of flexion when the posterior capsule and the posterior cruciate ligament are relaxed; instability in this position implies a possible rupture of the medial or lateral ligament which will not show when the joint is in full extension if the posterior cruciate ligament is intact. Considerable swelling developing within 30 minutes of injury means there has been bleeding into the joint, i.e. haemarthrosis, and this implies serious injury. On some occasions, however, the absence of this sign may be misleading in that if the injury is sufficiently severe then the capsule itself will be torn and the blood will leak into the subcutaneous tissues, particularly at the back of the knee. Similarly, it is important to remember that a complete tear of the ligament may be less painful than a partial tear but this type of injury can almost always be differentiated from the minor injury by the fact that there has been significant violence, the patient is usually aware that something has torn or given way and, in the more serious injury, there is gross instability when the patient attempts to bear weight.

Effusion which is due to damage or irritation of the synovial lining of the capsule will show several hours later. This might be caused by a direct blow or in response to an internal injury of the knee.

When there is a possibility of serious injury to the knee joint then this must be adequately examined in proper surroundings and examination may include x-rays, arthrography (when dye is injected into the joint) or arthroscopy (when a small telescope is placed into the joint for direct vision). All methods of examination have advantages and disadvantages.

Routine x-rays do not show soft tissue such as the menisci so a radio-opaque dye may be injected into the joint in an attempt to show these tissues. However, there is a risk of infection; the x-rays may still not show the area of interest; and the interpretation of the films requires considerable skill. Arthroscopy allows a direct view of the majority, but not all, of the articular surfaces of the knee joint and the menisci but carries the risk of a general anaesthetic and of infection.

PRINCIPLES OF TREATMENT

The basic principles in the treatment of knee injuries are those applicable to other injuries. Initially, check for possible fracture or severe ligament injury both of which should be seen at hospital. Other injuries should be treated by *ice* followed by compression for 36 hours after which definitive treatment usually begins. Contrast bathing is most helpful in reducing swelling with more complicated forms of electrotherapy being only marginally better.

For the athlete it is essential that exercises be carried out from an early stage but these must be exactly performed and their severity frequently adjusted to the capability of the injured limb. Speed of rehabilitation is important in the athlete but the maximal rate of progress through an exercise routine is very close to that which will exacerbate the condition or cause another injury so great skill is required.

Initially, simply lifting the leg with the knee fully extended may be carried out and then with increasing weight strapped to the ankle or using a lead boot, progressing to at least 20lb (9kg) in the adult. When flexion of the knee to 90° is pain-free, extension from this position may be started, using a De Lorme boot for increasing resistance. An adult must be able to fully extend 30lb (13.5kg) ten times in 45 seconds before starting to run. This is necessary to provide joint stability. The adult should similarly lift 40lb (18kg) before returning to sports other than rugby when the weight should be 45lb (20kg). This may appear a lot but it is required to protect the joint against body contact forces.

It is important to ensure that there is muscular balance between the two legs, a difference of greater than five per cent statistically increases the chance of further injury. This balance should be between the strength of the two quadriceps muscle groups and also between the hamstrings and the quadriceps of the same limb when the hamstrings should have at least 60 per cent of the strength of the quadriceps (Klein and Allman, 1969).

In order to protect a joint it is essential to have strength applied very quickly to counteract potentially damaging forces so 'power' is required. Power or explosive strength may be improved by activities such as hopping which should only be attempted late in the rehabilitation phase. Hopping may be carried out for distance or height or up a slope, all methods being useful.

Fitness testing should be carried out before the player returns to competition and this must be related to the requirements of the athlete's own sport. Can he sprint, check, twist, jump, stretch as required? If there is any discomfort it is better to have a further week of rehabilitation rather than have a possible recurrence or endure the remainder of the season performing below par with a minor chronic injury.

Contusions of the knee

Contusion of the knee is common in many sports but particularly football. There is a history of a direct blow and on examination there may be localised swelling, tenderness, possibly bruising and slight limitation of movement. Initial treatment is ice, that is to say, ice, compression and elevation. An ice pack is applied to the injured area and held in place for at least 30 minutes by an elasticated bandage, the leg being elevated. The player has a quick shower, not a leisurely bath, and a compression dressing is applied. This may consist of a layer of cotton wool over which is a crêpe or elastic bandage and the compression should extend for a hand's breadth above and below the joint. This should stay in place for 36 hours after which the patient should be encouraged to move the joint. The player usually returns to full activity within the week.

Ligamentous injuries

Ligamentous injury, usually known as a sprain, of the knee is less common than the similar injury to the ankle joint but is often more serious. The injury may range from the trivial to the most severe and could keep the athlete permanently from competition. The severe injuries typically occur when the whole bodyweight of the opponent is against the joint when the leg itself is carrying weight and therefore fixed to the ground, for example, in a rugby tackle.

Minor ligamentous injury with tenderness over the attachment of the ligament to bone, pain on stressing the ligament and without effusion, may be treated as a contusion but with a definite rehabilitation phase in which increasingly severe turning movements are incorporated.

Moderate sprains show considerable pain, swelling which is localised at first but may become generalised, tenderness, pain and some apprehension on movement, pain and possibly some laxity on stressing the ligament. In this injury a variable proportion of the ligament has been torn and the important aspect of treatment is to prevent the patient accidentally stressing the ligament, thereby converting a partial into a complete tear. The initial treatment with ice must be followed by a firm bandage which gives great support to the joint and prevents movement but allows the initial swelling to take place. A Robert Jones bandage, which consists of three alternating layers of cotton wool and domette bandage, is the most usual form of firm bandage. Three or four days later this should be removed for re-examination of the knee in case the initial examination, obscured by pain and muscle spasm, led to the wrong diagnosis. Depending upon the severity of the condition a decision is then made regarding further treatment. This will vary from some support with periodic exercise to immobilisation in a plaster cast.

Complete tear of the ligament constitutes a severe injury. The history is one of severe violence, the patient usually being aware of a tearing sensation and instability of the joint. Pain may be variable. Swelling within the joint or in the subcutaneous tissues rapidly appears. Laxity in full extension implies rupture of the posterior cruciate ligament. Laxity of more than 10° greater than in the uninjured knee, when the joint is examined in part flexion, implies damage to the medial or lateral ligament. Antero-posterior instability of the tibia in relation to the femur may be misleading; examination of this with the foot in a neutral position may be positive but in the minor injury this should be abolished when the foot is internally rotated. A posterior sag of the tibia in relation to the femur is always significant.

The presence of a ruptured knee ligament in an athlete requires surgical repair to all the torn structures. This should be carried out within ten days of injury and this is why moderate sprains should be re-assessed after three or four days in case the initial diagnosis is wrong. Care must also be taken in this type of injury to look for the presence of 'O'Donoghue's triad' – tears of the medial ligament, the anterior cruciate ligament and the medial meniscus (O'Donoghue, 1970). This is also called the 'unhappy triad' because unhappily the full extent of the injury is often not appreciated.

Cartilage injuries

'You have a torn cartilage' are words of impending doom to the athlete which are not inevitable; troubles arise not from surgical technique but through inadequate rehabilitation. There is a covering of articular cartilage over the weight-bearing surfaces of the bones within the joint and there are also two C-shaped menisci – it is these latter structures which the athlete calls cartilages. They are avascular and may develop, within their substance, cysts or tears which do not heal. Once torn, there is the choice of leading an inactive life with possible occasional trouble or having the cartilage removed surgically. After removal, the space occupied by the meniscus is filled by a replacement but not of the same material or quality so the joint is marginally worse than previously. Therefore, the operation should not be undertaken lightly and also, it may be very difficult to decide whether the symptoms are truly from a torn meniscus or from which of the two menisci.

A meniscus usually tears when the knee joint is carrying bodyweight, the foot being fixed as may happen with a studded shoe and the body is rotated in relation to the foot. The patient usually complains of pain on one side of the joint and often of inability to fully extend the knee, so called 'locking'. This occurs about 30° short of full extension and typically, full extension suddenly returns minutes or days later. Momentary difficulty in extension with the knee more fully flexed is not locking and not due to a torn cartilage. Generalised swelling of the joint may occur later that day or next morning. An athlete with this type of history requires a medical opinion and the initial treatment of simply ice.

Other knee injuries
Less common causes of knee pain include patellar tendinitis known as 'jumper's knee' because it is often associated with sports such as basketball which demand take-off and landing on hard surfaces (Blazina et al, 1973). It is characterised by pain in front of the knee, below the patella and precipitated by forceful knee extension. There is localised tenderness in or around the patellar tendon, usually near its proximal attachment. The condition comes on gradually over several matches and may be very persistent. Treatment is, initially, rest – a dreadful word to the athlete! – for about two weeks. The condition is helped by ultrasound, anti-inflammatory drugs, injection of hydrocortisone and more rarely, operation.

A condition peculiar to the early teenage, enthusiastic athlete is Osgood Schlatter's disease. This affects the tibial tuberosity – the prominence on the upper part of the anterior surface of the tibia into which is attached the patellar tendon. Comparative overstrain of the quadriceps muscle acting upon a delicate area of growing bone can produce a painful reaction. It usually involves boys aged 12 to 16 years; there is an aching pain over the tuberosity which is worse during or commonly after exercise, and there is local swelling and tenderness. The condition may be diagnosed clinically, although the x-ray has a characteristic appearance of fragmentation. Treatment is very definitely rest until the bone settles down. I merely prohibit organised physical activity for several months but some orthopaedic surgeons place the joint in a full leg plaster for six to eight weeks followed by a gradual return to full activity. Usually the condition settles satisfactorily but may recur during the growth phase of adolescence.

Injury to the knee joint is common and may be very difficult to manage. The most important single factor is to ensure that the athlete does not cause further damage by returning to sport without adequate, balanced strength. It is neglectful to allow an athlete to participate with a weak leg or swollen knee.

REFERENCES

Blazina, M. E., Kerlin, R. K., Jobe, F. W., Carter, V. S. and Carlson, G. J. (1973). *Orthopaedic Clinics of North America*, **4**, 665–678.

Klein, K. K. and Allman, F. L. (1969). *The knee in sports*. Pemberton Press, New York.

O'Donoghue, D. H. (1970). *Treatment of injuries to athletes*. W. B. Saunders, Philadelphia.

CHAPTER 32

Injuries to the ankle

I. D. ADAMS MD

Injury to the ankle joint is the most common sports injury, comprising about 12 per cent of the total number of injuries. Eighty-five per cent of the ankle injuries are sprains, that is ligamentous, and four out of every five of these involve the lateral ligament. The problem with these injuries is that they are so common, familiarity breeds contempt, and the result is frequently unsatisfactory treatment. In the general public, one-third of patients with ankle sprains still have symptoms after 12 months.

ANATOMY

The true ankle joint is of the hinge type with movements limited to dorsiflexion and plantar flexion; many of the movements we associate with the ankle joint actually occur at the subtalar and other joints of the mid-foot.

The ankle joint is formed superiorly by the concave articular surface of the tibia, a downward projection of the tibia to form the medial malleolus, and a downward projection of the fibula to form the lateral malleolus; the convex articular surface of the talus is partially held in their grip (Fig. 32/1). At the ankle joint, the tibia and fibula provide a narrower mortice posteriorly and the talus itself is broader anteriorly so that in plantar flexion the joint is at its most unstable and in dorsiflexion at its most stable.

The medial and lateral ligaments of the ankle run downwards and backwards from the malleoli and prevent forward displacement of the leg in relation to the foot. The medial ligament is triangular in shape with its

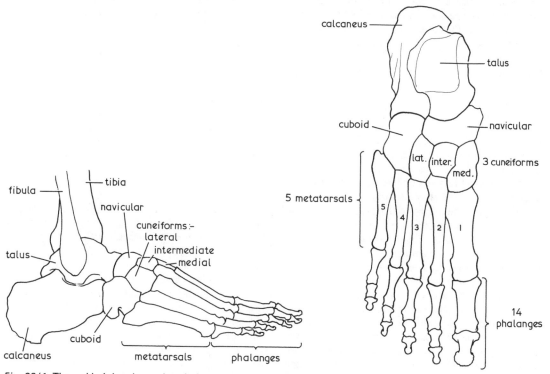

Fig. 32/1 The ankle joint shown in relation to the bones of the shin and feet

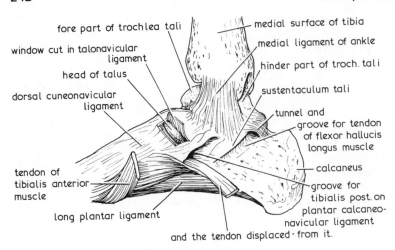

fore part of trochlea tali
medial surface of tibia
window cut in talonavicular ligament
medial ligament of ankle
head of talus
hinder part of troch. tali
dorsal cuneonavicular ligament
sustentaculum tali
tunnel and groove for tendon of flexor hallucis longus muscle
tendon of tibialis anterior muscle
calcaneus
long plantar ligament
groove for tibialis post. on plantar calcaneo-navicular ligament and the tendon displaced · from it.

Fig. 32/2 The medial aspect of the ankle joint

apex attached to the medial malleolus, its base attached to the posterior part of the talus, the calcaneus, the neck of the talus and slightly to the navicular. The lateral ligament is in three parts and is attached above to the lateral malleolus; the anterior band runs downwards and forwards to be attached to the talus and is taut in plantar flexion; the middle cord-like part is attached to the calcaneus and is taut in dorsiflexion and inversion; the posterior band is attached to the posterior tubercle of the talus and is taut on dorsiflexion. There is also a ligament between the tibia and fibula; although not in the ankle joint itself, it is often involved in injuries to the ankle (Fig. 32/2).

ASSESSMENT

The immediate assessment of an ankle injury on the playing area or in the dressing room is an appropriate starting point. The immediate decision to be made is whether there is likely to be a fracture and this is most easily decided immediately after injury. At this time, it is possible to examine an unswollen ankle which is ideal for inspection and palpation on all but its posterior aspect. An hour later this advantage may be lost through swelling, and examination becomes difficult.

A history of an acute tearing or snapping sensation with severe pain and disability requires that the athlete should be seen by a doctor as this is likely to be a fracture or a complete tear of the ligament. In other cases, the injured joint should have all bones palpated as far as possible, at first very gently but then with increasing pressure, to be certain there is no tenderness of the bone itself which could be an undisplaced fracture. Ligamentous tenderness is usually anterior and/

or inferior to the prominence of the malleolus on either side of the joint.

The athlete should then be encouraged to move the ankle joint through a full range of movement, initially while sitting on the floor, then with partial weight-bearing and finally with full weight-bearing. The athlete should be asked to stand on tip-toe, jog, run, turn and if he manages this, he may then continue with the activity. If the athlete is unable to complete this procedure he should be removed from the activity area to a more suitable place for examination.

At this time, the areas of maximal tenderness should be reassessed and the initial area of swelling noted. Some injuries of the ankle develop considerable swelling within a very short time – this is often unrelated to the severity of injury but does itself cause considerable tenderness and disability. Swelling must be prevented as far as possible and the ice, compression and elevation routine started immediately. All the swelling has to be removed during the recovery phase and the more there is to remove, the more delayed will be the return to sport.

The most common injury is to the lateral ligament and is caused by a plantar flexion and inversion strain. There is tenderness below and usually in front of the lateral malleolus. There may also be some tenderness on the opposite side of the joint because the stretch to the lateral side of the ankle is associated with compression on the medial side of the joint and the capsule or ligament may be nipped between the bones.

A complete tear of the ligament must be excluded. This may be checked by assessing talar tilt, that is, considerably increased inversion of the heel in relation to the lower leg when the heel is manually inverted or everted. Care must be taken to compare this finding with that in the uninjured ankle because there is considerable individual variation. The test may be difficult to perform owing to pain and if there is serious doubt about the possibility of a rupture then examination under anaesthetic may be required.

A further test for stability is the anterior 'drawer' test which is carried out by having the foot in 20° of plantar flexion, applying the flat of one hand against the anterior surface of the tibia to push backwards and the cupped fingers of the other hand behind the talus gently pulling forwards. Significant forward movement of the talus in relation to the tibia indicates a rupture and when this is a possibility, the ankle must be assessed by an orthopaedic surgeon.

Injury to the lateral ligament is the most common but damage to the medial ligament does occur and is caused by eversion of the foot. There is also the possibility of damage to the tibio-fibular ligament due to a forced dorsiflexion strain and this injury heals extremely slowly. On examination there would be general tenderness and swelling on both sides of the joint with pain made worse by dorsiflexion of the foot.

TREATMENT

Treatment of all these ligamentous injuries is basically the same. The first object must be the control of bleeding and swelling. The usual routine of ice, compression and elevation should be applied from the moment the injury is reported. There must be some form of strapping for 24 to 36 hours and then a re-evaluation.

An active process of rehabilitation is favoured but there are some cases which do better with a short period in plaster of Paris. Infilling of the two hollows at the back of the ankle joint, on either side of the Achilles tendon, usually implies an effusion within the joint and this should be treated in plaster for one week. There are also some players who cannot be guaranteed to follow advice and therefore require effective immobilisation in plaster for two or three days to prevent them causing further damage to the joint. There are considerable problems with the long-term use of plaster in an athletic situation; microscopically it has been possible to show that the ligamentous attachment to bone remains abnormal for 24 weeks after six weeks in plaster, consequently prolonged periods in plaster for an athlete require a considerable period of rehabilitation.

Thirty-six hours after the initial injury the stage of definitive treatment and rehabilitation begins. Initially, this may only consist of attempting to regain the full range of movement non-weight-bearing, gradually progressing to weight-bearing, strengthening and rotation exercises with particular emphasis on all those activities requiring coordination. This active programme must not be forced too quickly and any evidence of increased swelling or pain requires an immediate re-adjustment of the exercise. Care must be taken to correct abnormal gait as soon as possible because false patterns of movement rapidly become habit. The exercises are time consuming and laborious but appear to produce satisfactory results. Strapping is no substitute for strength and coordination around the joint; for in order to be effective in reducing the force of bodyweight and providing stability to the joint, strapping has to be so strong that normal movement is abolished.

The ankle injury which persists for several weeks also requires great care to be taken in re-establishing the strength of inversion and eversion of the foot. It must also be remembered that there will be some wasting of the involved calf and thigh musculature which has to be corrected.

There has to be a check on the extensibility of the gastrocnemius and soleus muscle group, because limited dorsiflexion appears to be an important factor in the causation of a sprained ankle. This is thought to be due to the tightness of the Achilles tendon which tends to naturally invert the foot thereby making further inversion and sprain likely.

Full functional testing must be carried out before the player or athlete resumes activity. Attention to these apparently minor injuries is important to ensure that the individual does not develop a chronic or recurrent ankle problem.

OTHER SOFT TISSUE INJURIES

An ankle complaint which is not always directly related to injury is discomfort around the joint due to tendinitis. Tenderness may be localised along the course of the posterior tibial tendon running behind the medial malleolus or along the peroneal tendons running behind the lateral malleolus. Palpation may reveal a fusiform swelling, acute tenderness and crepitation on movement of the involved tendon. This condition is most often seen in runners and there does not appear to be any local treatment with a significant advantage. Some people favour the use of ultrasound, others apply ice directly to the area, or prescribe anti-inflammatory tablets or an injection of hydrocortisone alongside the tendon.

The most important factor is to restrict markedly the athlete's activities until symptoms and signs subside after which there has to be a graduated return to activity. Adhesive strapping to limit the movement of the joint is of some value but it must be carefully applied because any direct pressure over the involved tendons will aggravate the condition.

There are various lesions of the Achilles tendon which may be extremely disabling. The most spectacular is a rupture of the tendon which classically occurred in the older, heavier athlete but is now more common in the younger group. There is usually a very definite history of sudden, acute pain over the tendon with remarks from the patient such as 'I thought I had been shot'. Examination two or three hours later may be confused by the considerable swelling which occurs but there is usually a palpable gap in the Achilles tendon about 5cm from its distal attachment. Function of the Achilles tendon must be checked and many doctors or coaches merely ask the patient to plantar flex the foot against slight resistance but the athlete can do this by using the accessory muscles and considerable resistance should be provided to check the functional capacity of the Achilles tendon.

The treatment of an acute rupture is open to argument in terms of the usual conservative versus radical approach. Plaster of Paris with the foot in slight plantar flexion for six weeks produces reasonable results but with a rehabilitation period lasting several months. Surgery with end-to-end suture may produce an excellent result but still involves six weeks in plaster, a long rehabilitation period and the associated risks of anaesthesia, infection and delayed healing in a relatively avascular area. It would appear to me that surgery is the treatment of choice in the younger, athletic patient.

In the runner, particularly, there are various less dramatic Achilles tendon pains which are, none the less, disabling. The common condition is a peritendinitis where the athlete develops swelling, usually along the medial border of the tendon, and associated with considerable tenderness. This typically occurs in runners with a large training mileage and is usually associated with some minor abnormality of gait or flat foot which affects the alignment of the Achilles tendon in relation to the calcaneus. The initial treatment of this condition is to stop training, elevate the heel with a pad of chiropody felt or Plastazote and use ultrasound. Peritendinitis sometimes shows a good response to an injection of hydrocortisone alongside but not into the tendon. Occasionally the condition persists and surgery is required; then there has to be a gradual return to activity in a condition which has a great tendency towards chronicity. It is essential to look for minor biomechanical abnormalities and attempt to correct these during the rehabilitation phase.

There is a superficial bursa over the attachment of the Achilles tendon and this may become an acute problem as the result either of direct blows or by friction from the so-called 'Achilles protector'. Usually this bursitis settles with control of the footwear and judicious padding. There is also a deep bursa which is less frequently a cause of trouble. Inflammation of both these bursae may be helped by a direct injection of hydrocortisone; sometimes surgery is necessary.

Considerations after injury: treatment

CHAPTER 33

Immediate post-injury considerations in games

LEON WALKDEN MRCS, LRCP

All mobile collision sports have a quota of injuries. Specific injuries are not confined to any particular sport, but regular injury patterns do occur among players in their chosen pastime.

The circumstances, diagnostic assay, treatment and management of injuries both on the field of play and immediately afterwards vary considerably, particularly in personnel and facilities available. Ideally, a team is covered by a doctor and physiotherapist, both skilled in medicine in sport, and an enlightened coach; the playing area is regularly inspected while first aid facilities at hand include a stretcher, inflatable splints and a treatment room, easily accessible from the field of play, which is equipped with good lighting, running water, couch, steriliser and ice, and so on. In practice, facilities at most matches seldom extend beyond the proverbial bucket and sponge and an elementary first aid box, possibly locked with the key unavailable! This happens despite encouragement and prompting from the concerned sporting organisation.

GENERAL CONSIDERATIONS

At all times medicine in sport should be advisory rather than authoritative, similar to its role in the community, and it is as well for the attendant to remember this. He should, ideally, have a working knowledge of the prevailing laws of the sport, be situated close to the field, undisturbed and able to watch the game closely, so allowing maximum opportunity to recognise cause and site of injury.

When summoned on to the field of play (solely by the referee) it is most important to remember what *not* to do and as far as possible no treatment should occur before a shrewd idea of the diagnosis has emerged. It should be appreciated that the attendant has arrived at a situation which every casualty officer envies – within a minute of the incident and before effects such as exudate, swelling, bruising, painful muscle spasm can cloud the diagnosis.

Well before the player is touched important aspects can be elicited such as; Who saw the incident? What happened? Where is the site of the injury? Observation and inspection are paramount necessities by which the presence of vital normal function such as consciousness, breathing, limb movements, source of haemorrhage is established without necessarily touching the injured player. Removal of a mouthguard, if worn, reassurance in approach to the casualty, and quiet authoritativeness to the other participants are fundamental.

Palpation and establishment of movement range must be with the player's cooperation rather than despite him. Passive movements may rarely be employed as a primary diagnostic or therapeutic aid. Fortunately, the human anatomy, with one or two notable areas of exception, has been duplicated thus allowing comparative examination of the uninjured side. The attendant should be ever mindful of the possible pitfalls, such as the artificial eye, the slight long-standing squint, the 'normally' deformed nose of an earlier injury, long-standing calcification and hard swelling of an old quadriceps muscle injury, the permanent lump over an old costal cartilage injury or deformity of the acromio-clavicular joint from former damage.

The attendant is there to give advice and assistance and must have control of the situation. No one should attempt to drag the injured player to his feet without the agreement of the attendant, or medical or paramedical supervision.

Within one minute or thereabouts basic decisions of likely diagnosis and playability should be made or, if not possible in such a short time, decided off the pitch after unhurried removal of the player. Where the particular sport permits replacements or substitutes, the casualty should be taken directly to the main facilities.

Always before the match, the attendant must be acquainted with the location of a stretcher and the address, location and telephone number of the ground. In major injury an unnecessarily long delay can occur with the ambulance careering around the countryside vainly following inadequate instructions as to the whereabouts of, say, the Tolpuddle Martyrs fifth eleven pitch. The appropriate official should also be notified of the hospital to which the injured player has been taken.

Specific areas of injury may be considered from surface anatomical situations, being ever mindful that there are areas of increased vulnerability in particular sports.

REGIONAL INJURIES

Head, neck and face

Difficult diagnostic and management decisions arise with these areas. Applied forces causing injury to the head and neck are mechanically similar to those applied to a heavy ball on the end of a chain. The forces are sudden acceleration and deceleration, hyperextension, flexion, rotation and compression – the last mentioned commonly with the vertex of the skull fixed as in a rugby front row player when the scrum collapses, or in a badly executed tackle with the head anterior to the hip or thigh or an acute frontal approach to the tackle. These forces can result in the rare but terrible injury of fracture-dislocation of the cervical spine with consequent paralysis.

Tangential blows can produce serious brain damage, apart from lacerations and facial bone fractures, by shock waves passing through the skull into the loosely suspended brain covered by three membranous layers or meninges. These are namely the tough outer fibrous tissue or dura mater (the inner lining of the skull), the middle layer or arachnoid and the inner membrane closely applied to the surface of the brain, the pia mater (Fig. 33/1). The resultant spaces are traversed by blood vessels and the space between the inner two membranes contains the cerebrospinal fluid. Hence the importance of the awareness of the possibility of structural damage to the brain which can be fatal in a matter of hours. There were eight fatal accidents in rugby in England from October 1971 to November 1978, a fatality in soccer in 1978 and a fractured skull in hockey in the same year.

Momentary insensibility, confusion, unsteadiness, incoordination and retrograde amnesia, are all symptoms which make the removal of the injured player from the field of play mandatory.

An unconscious player represents an emergency and immediate attention should be given to fundamental principles – if he is not breathing, then resuscitation is vital whether or not there is a suggested broken neck. Remove the mouthguard if present, check deeply with a probing index finger that there are no loose avulsed teeth, dentures, chewing gum or anything else in the mouth and throat preventing maintenance of a good airway. Concurrently, start emergency resuscitation with the neck extended and chin well forward. After establishment of normal respiration and if there is no suspected neck injury, the injured player should be placed on his side with the knee of the uppermost leg bent at a right angle.

If mouth-to-mouth resuscitation is not causing movement of the chest, or lividity, foaming at the mouth and extreme restlessness are occurring, the player may be asphyxiating because of airway obstruction from a foreign body. Sit him up and at the same time apply sharp pressure with the heel of one hand

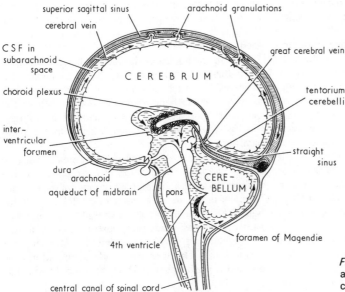

Fig. 33/1 The meninges of the brain and the circulation of the cerebrospinal fluid

from behind placed over the spine just below the ribs to attempt expulsion of the foreign body. This can be carried out very quickly; if unsuccessful, while inverting the player, give sharp blows between the shoulder blades; there are enough strong men around to make this a rapid manoeuvre which in practice has proved life-saving. In every case the player must be taken to hospital without delay.

The classical example of only transient alteration in brain function without any structural damage, is concussion. On the field, diagnosis and decision can be difficult and misleading in the two following phases of concussion and symptoms.

Firstly, the mildest degree of concussion occurs with doubtful loss of consciousness, very transient memory loss and the player appearing mentally alert at the time of examination. If he is able to rise promptly to his feet without assistance, to stand firmly with eyes closed, to perform heel-toe and 'tandem' walking, followed by a shuttle run to a mark then he may continue to compete but he should be watched carefully for the rest of the game for any further signs developing. His fellow players should also be told to watch him.

Secondly, difficulty arises with moderate degrees of concussion where the player may not necessarily go down but be 'out on his feet' – a situation analogous to the boxer stopped on a 'technical knock-out': he is dazed, amnesic, unsteady, possibly aggressive and unreasonable, and repeating the same phrases. For example, to the question 'What is the score?' he may reply 'Has the game begun yet?' In all sports, such casualties must be withdrawn from the game with firmness, and the captain and referee must assist if necessary. Remember, there is no sophisticated method on the field of play or, for that matter, in a neurosurgical unit to determine whether or not a player at the moment of injury has suffered a simple concussion or is going to develop secondary brain damage necessitating urgent surgical interference.

Neck injuries can vary from a simple muscle sprain with the neck held in flexion, or an acute wry neck caused by subluxation of one of the pars articularis facets with the chin rotated to the opposite side and pointing upwards, to fracture-dislocation and resultant paralysis. The utmost vigilance is required.

The player may, on questioning while down on the ground, be able to manage full limb movements, but, for example, if he complains of a sensation of numbness or tingling, heat running into the arms or hands, no matter how transient, he must be removed on a stretcher and referred to hospital. Persistent high interscapular pain requires similar firm management and the game suspended until ambulance facilities have been arranged. These signs indicate suspicion of cervical nerve root damage or developing cord involvement at C7 level and require strict immobilisation before removal. At Twickenham Rugby Football Union ground a Ferney-Washington 'scoop' stretcher is always present for such an eventuality. In the period October 1973 to April 1978, there were ten reported cases of neck injuries involving paralysis (quadriplegia) in rugby in England, estimated by the writer from insurance claim reports.

Cuts and lacerations predominate in this area in rugby and to a much lesser extent in soccer and hockey. Seventy-five per cent of lacerations occur in the front five forwards in rugby with usually over half requiring suture. All lacerations should be adequately cleaned: a dilute solution of cetrimide and chlorhexidine is preferred for this purpose, though in the absence of anything else, soap and water is excellent for debridement. A protective dressing should be applied before returning to play. If there are facilities available to suture a wound this should be carried out forthwith; if not, the casualty should be referred for suturing within four hours. (The numbing effect of the injury makes local infiltrative anaesthesia unnecessary for immediate suture: there is no swelling of the tissues, there is more accurate alignment of the skin edges and as a result a more acceptable scar. In preparation, never shave any segment of the eyebrows before suture – re-growth is uncertain in timing and the resultant appearance might result in litigation.) Prevention of such injuries or at least reduction of their incidence would be assisted considerably by firmer application and review of existing laws, increased club and player cooperative responsibility and equipment modification.

A plastic/rubber composite stud is feasible for those sports. There is no room for complacency: the incidence of disfiguring lacerations is not falling and the elimination of the nylon stud and sharp-edged sole is not the answer. Sports authorities must maintain regular contact with the Shoe and Allied Trades Research Association. Finally, it is a foolhardy player who has not had a full course of tetanus immunisation plus regular booster injections.

In any collision sport eye injuries can be disastrous. In the middle of the furious scrambles of forwards and centres for the ball rebounding at eye level in basketball, the eyes are very vulnerable. Eye injuries may also arise from fingers, thumb, or collision of heads in any sport. Mistiness of more than a brief duration or partial loss of vision require examination off the pitch; where there is contusion the application of ice and prompt hospital referral is advised. Apart from the pain of a corneal abrasion which resolves fairly rapidly after 48 hours or so depending on dimension, discomfort may not always be a prominent symptom of eye injury despite obvious haemorrhage into the interior or posterior chamber of the eye. (Proxymetacaine hydrochloride (Ophthaine) drops plus an eye pad will relieve the abrasion pain: the possession of an ophthalmoscope is invaluable to eliminate more serious injury and avoid hospital referral.)

Dislocation and fracture of the teeth occur in the unguarded mouth. If this occurs, retrieve the tooth, wash it gently in normal saline or under the tap and apply sustained gentle pressure until the blood and tissue fluids are expelled. Gentle pressure will maintain position until specialist dental advice is sought. Latex mouthguards, dentally moulded and fitted, drastically reduce facial and dental injuries, and concussion. The type available 'off the peg' in sports shops should be avoided as it is loose, ill-fitting, and can and has caused asphyxia. Examination for a fracture of the lower jaw includes a full inspection and palpation via the mouth: a swab plus probing finger may reveal bleeding from a tooth at the gum margin; biting on a folded handkerchief can produce localised pain even as posteriorly as the tempero-mandibular joint. With such signs present, a fracture is likely. The player who is tackling is usually the victim, frequently through incorrect technique or the faulty coaching of smother tackling in rugby.

Injuries to the nose primarily require arrest of haemorrhage. This is best effected on the field of play by firm pressure on the distal one inch (2.5cm) of the nose using ice, adrenaline gauze or ribbon gauze packing. Any displacement of the nasal septum can often be corrected painlessly on the spot by pressure with the handle of a scalpel or straight forceps inserted into the nasal vestibule. No further investigation or treatment is rewarding for approximately four days due to oedema, and bruising.

The shoulder and arm

Any injury to the shoulder joint and girdle is not adequately examined until comparison with the surface anatomy of the normal side has been made. The angular 'step down' of the acromio-clavicular joint injury, the absence of the normal gentle rounded curve of the shoulder in gleno-humeral dislocation, especially when viewed from behind, the forward displacement of the humerus in dislocation of the elbow joint (no rarity in schoolboys) will all be readily established.

Fractures, particularly of the ulna or head of radius, may not be accompanied by a complaint of pain. Quite frequently only loss of power is apparent until later, when exudate and haematoma formation promote discomfort. Fractures of the metacarpal bones can result from a misguided punch providing a salutary lesson to the offender. Whether or not reduction of dislocation of the phalangeal joints is promptly attempted by skilled attendants, a subsequent x-ray is essential. A Bradford support or Kirschner malleable padded metal splint should be applied to injured fingers post-match.

Thorax and abdomen

Direct forces as in tackling, kicking and crushing, cause injuries to the thorax in team games, though surprisingly, rib fractures are not so common as those of other bones. A reasonable opinion should be possible 'on site' as to whether or not the ribs are broken (Fig. 33/2). Naturally, the exertional dyspnoea caused

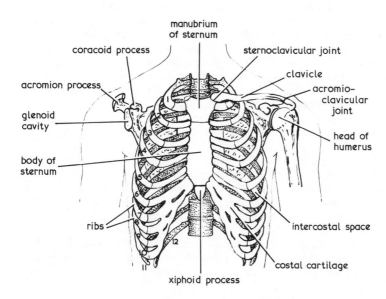

Fig. 33/2 The position of the bones of the thorax and the costal cartilages

by the game will increase the pain. Sudden but slight pressure with the heel of one hand over the lower end of the sternum and the heel of the other hand over the back bone will produce confirmatory pain at the site of the fracture. If the diagnosis is still uncertain and discomfort persists, further decision should be taken on the touch line; a hasty, ill-advised return to competition may produce the alarming sign of blood stained spit on the pitch thus showing there is lung involvement. An x-ray is essential.

At the costal margin, in the lower part of the front of the chest, the ribs join the costal cartilages and this is the area of maximum chest movement. Costal cartilage injuries are generally due to a crush injury: they are characterised by a sore area, possibly a palpable click on inspiration and the development within half an hour or so of a hard swelling which to some extent will be permanent. An x-ray frequently reveals no fracture. Strapping is inadvisable and the player is match fit when totally pain free. This usually takes five to six weeks.

Serious abdominal injuries are fortunately rare: this is surprising when one considers the blunt trauma to which the area is exposed, e.g. a high velocity boot over the ball, a football weighing approximately 450g and reaching speeds of up to 100km per hour, or a 200g hockey ball at approximately the same speed, from 10 to 15 metres in a penalty corner. A winded player left alone will recover completely after a minute or two. Intelligent awareness and suspicion on the part of the attendant on the field of play are important; if the winded player shows delayed recovery, vomits, looks pale or shocked, prompt hospital referral is required. Unfortunately, the three main internal organs – the spleen, liver and intestines – do not show early bleeding externally; internal bleeding can be rapid and catastrophic.

Be advised: get the player to the hospital in time. Similarly, blunt trauma in the loin may fracture one or more transverse processes or damage the kidney. If a player is injured in this way, even apparently slightly, a routine urine test for the presence of blood, using Haemostix, should be performed after the match; if the test is positive, hospital referral is necessary.

The pelvis and lower limbs

Success in team sports basically depends on running ability. In consequence, more ill-advised decisions to continue playing in the match are made for injuries to this vulnerable region than anywhere else. Objective examination is essential: try to decide whether it is a direct or indirect injury: question the possibility of previous injury at the site, e.g. wasting of the vastus medialis in a former knee injury and look for signs of deformity by comparison with the other limb.

Again, initial pain may be misleading; whereas a superficial type of soft tissue lesion or ligamentous stretch may produce intense transient discomfort which rapidly disappears with an equally rapid recovery, a condition such as an oblique fracture of the fibula just above the lateral malleolus may initially produce a complaint of loss of power and inability to support the body, even though there is a palpable click at the fracture site.

Injury to the quadriceps muscle mass whether due to strain, boot, ball, stick or knee drastically reduces in-match mobility. The 'charley-horse' of a central trauma, or the 'dead-leg' of the laterally placed lesion need to be treated properly; such injury should be treated early and off the field of play, rather than rubbing with liniment and attempting to 'run it off' with reckless endeavour. The injury site should be first covered with olive oil or Vaseline petroleum jelly to reduce ice burn risk, then crushed ice applied for at least twenty minutes with compression and elevation. A hot bath should not be taken, only a quick shower, followed by replacement of the compression dressing and elevation; ice application should be repeated three times daily for the 48 hour 'treatment vacuum period' until review. A player who cannot flex his knee to a right angle 48 hours after the quadriceps injury is most likely suffering from an intramuscular haematoma. This will necessitate careful management, patience, rest, ice contrast treatments, ultrasound, and static quadriceps contractions, otherwise calcification at the site or myositis ossificans may appear insidiously within six weeks.

The sudden jumping when in full stride, or the slide tackling manoeuvre of soccer, may produce avulsion injuries of muscular attachments to the pelvic rami and chronic adductor muscle strain in the thigh, with instability of the symphysis pubis. These injuries also occur in other sports but are much less common. Hamstring injuries, including partial tears, will also drastically reduce coordination and mobility. Avulsion of the biceps femoris tendon of origin has been known to occur. Examination should be full and include the prone position to accurately define the lesion. Frequently it is a recurrence of an injury due to inadequate preparation after the previous one. It should be emphasised that recurrent thigh and adductor lesions require orthopaedic and radiological investigation rather than expectantly persisting with physiotherapy.

The knee, probably the most publicised joint with reference to injuries in sport, is examined initially with the player sitting, not standing. Gently locate the site of pain or tenderness; encourage the player to carry out a few static quadriceps contractions for promoting confidence thus facilitating assessment of the range of active movements; locate the joint line – at the inferior end of the patella with the knee extended. The degree of any injury to the collateral ligaments can be assessed roughly by the range of abduction or adduction, and the presence of ability to draw the tibia forwards in relation to the femur indicates damage to the anterior cruciate ligament. Any suspicion of the presence of these abnormal signs in a previously normal knee joint demands that weight-bearing be avoided and the player carried off for an early orthopaedic opinion: ice should be applied. An effusion into the knee joint may only appear by the time the player has reached hospital. If in doubt, any player with a full movement range who cannot hop on the afflicted leg should come off. (Note: in the case of a minor collateral ligament tear, ice followed by four-hourly treatments with ice and ultrasound preferably for 48 hours often rapidly assist recovery.) With such precautions much recurrent knee joint pathology could be considerably reduced.

Ankle injuries may well be by the type of sports footwear which gives no support to the ankle joint and increases forefoot running instability. A stirrup of extension plaster or the Louisiana Wrap technique are useful measures to augment support.

The traction force of extreme plantar flexion from the prolonged kicking of a soccer ball with the strain of the blow borne by the dorsal capsule of the ankle joint, has long been suspected of exacting a toll on the kicker's foot with periosteal roughening and bony outgrowths developing laterally. Basketball perhaps shares the running with abrupt changes of direction as in soccer with resultant chronic troublesome stresses. On the field, the decision simply demands absence of full painless movement for the player to be advised to leave the field of play. Likewise, competitors with acute inversion sprains, or injury to the inferior tibio-fibular joint should leave the field. The ice technique already mentioned should be used routinely. To some, it would seem reasonable that, after injury, immobilisation of the ankle joint with plaster of Paris, for up to a week as an initial measure, would reduce the incidence of recurrence.

Although the team attendant's main preoccupation is with primary treatment, he should envisage other responsibilities. He should feel that he has a moral duty to bring to the notice of club officials and the referee after the match any injuries caused in his opinion by dangerous or violent play or improper playing equipment. Furthermore, he should be prepared to discuss with them any player who is predisposed to repetitive injuries particularly concussional incidents. Where injuries are concerned on the field of play, there is no place for heroes!

CHAPTER 34

First aid in sport

J. A. FOWLER BA, MCSP, DipTP, SRP, MBIM

First aid, immediately following injury, is the start of rehabilitation. Much of the advice offered is not new; it is the first treatment in a continuing plan, rather than first aid. The more severe type of injury is dealt with because many of the knocks or damage sustained during sporting activity are of a minor nature and, though causing excruciating pain for a short while, can be treated effectively by 'cold sponge, reassurance and a rub'.

The importance of fitness in preventing sports injuries is well documented and many authors have shown that consideration must also be given to clothing and equipment (Williams, 1965; O'Donoghue, 1970).

PRINCIPLES OF TREATMENT

Pitfalls are many and can best be avoided by experience; basically one must not be over-enthusiastic or too timid in approach. Often a rigorous attitude will achieve results but so also can a more conservative approach. A tremendous responsibility is placed upon the first person to treat an injury. The pressures can be enormous in assessing when to allow a player to restart; what are the economics and the match importance; what to do at the moment which will bring about a perfect result later; and there are many others. In gaining experience what does one consider? The following recommendations are offered as guidance and not intended to be absolute.

Functional anatomy and kinesiology

It is a distinct advantage to have a sound basis of functional anatomy and the study of movement in injury and in health. Study of movement is reinforced largely by experience and one needs to understand the movement that will cause injury (Browning, 1976).

Diagnosis

This is the province of the doctor but those who are seeing the injury first should be able to diagnose the average sports injury. Many of the treatments recommended are only first aid, subsequent treatment has to be carried out under the supervision of a doctor who will make his own diagnosis.

Correct diagnosis is important, otherwise essential immediate treatment is directed towards the wrong aims and valuable time is lost. The work of Cyriax (1978) is a valuable aid.

Speed of treatment

Action must be taken at once and the injured person must be made to do something in return. In most sports injuries the length of the disability period depends upon the speed with which the initial treatment is made. This refers only to acute recent trauma which has a more pressing need for instant response. Stress injuries usually have a chronic cause but often they have an acute end or result which may require first aid treatment. Overuse injuries of ligaments or tendons are usually chronic conditions unless the overuse produces attenuation and then rupture.

Prevention of further injury

The steps taken during the first aid period should always consider prevention of further injury. For this reason, returning to competition supported by strapping or bandage is not favoured unless the latter is to cover a mild or moderate graze. Application of strapping or bandaging may mask a worsening situation or may serve to shift stress to some other area and cause injury.

No one who has had a local anaesthetic injection into a lower limb ligament or joint should be allowed to restart match play (Williams, 1965). A tennis or table tennis player may get away with it if it is the arm not being used to hold the bat or racket.

Know when to call a doctor

Recognise when you are out of your depth. The list provided by Williams (1965) gives some precise advice in this area. It includes, for example, all cases of head injury involving unconsciousness for more than ten seconds; all cases of minor injury where there is no marked improvement after 48 hours; and any or all cases of doubt.

SEVERE INJURIES

The majority of sports injuries are slight, but severe and very severe injuries can be sustained and the first aider should be prepared for them. Here are some rules to follow.

AMBULANCE

Send for an ambulance without delay. Procrastination is pointless.

BLEEDING

Bleeding should *not* be stopped by applying a tourniquet. If a tourniquet is forgotten or left on for too long, gangrene can follow devitalisation of tissue. The bleeding can usually be controlled by either digital pressure over a pressure point, or by dressings over the site of the injury. The technique is to soak up the blood by applying sufficient pads. A shell dressing of the type issued to HM Forces is ideal.

UNCONSCIOUSNESS

The unconscious person should not be moved until fully recovered. Concussion is an ever present danger. Loosen tight clothing and cover the person with a coat or blanket if conditions warrant it. Immobilise the injured person. If consciousness is regained quickly, allow the person to stay until his mental faculties are recovered. An escort must be provided to the dressing room or car where a period of rest should be encouraged.

In no circumstances should the injured person be allowed to resume play after prolonged unconsciousness.

In unconsciousness, steps must be taken to prevent the tongue falling back and the airway being blocked. This is achieved by:

(a) Turning the head to one side with the person lying semi-prone. The tongue can be fixed by inserting an airway (if one is available).

(b) Removing dentures.

(c) Allowing ample fresh air.

(d) Allowing nothing to be given by mouth while semi-conscious. This is particularly important after recovery of consciousness if there is any likelihood of an operation being necessary. Food or liquid contents of the stomach may delay anaesthesia because of the danger of vomiting.

(e) It may be necessary to commence artificial resuscitation; 'mouth-to-mouth' or 'mouth-to-nose' breathing is the method of choice unless there are facial injuries (Figs. 34/1 and 34/2). External cardiac massage may be required if it is thought that breathing has ceased (Fig. 34/3). Anoxia will lead to cardiac arrest.

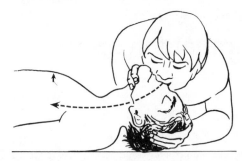

Fig. 34/1 Mouth-to-nose respiration. The chest of the casualty rises as it fills with air

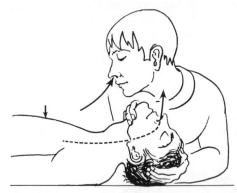

Fig. 34/2 The operator removes his mouth and breathes in himself. The chest wall of the casualty falls on expiration

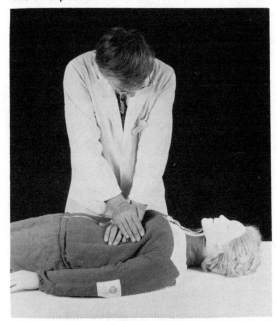

Fig. 34/3 External cardiac massage

(f) If the person is pale, the head should be lowered if possible; and if the person is flushed, the head should be raised. The former indicates a drop in blood pressure and the latter a rise.

EPILEPSY

This is a disorder of the nervous system causing sudden complete loss of consciousness often with convulsions and coma. Some sufferers may have warning of an attack and can take the necessary steps to be in a position of safety.

First aid is relatively simple if the condition is recognised. There must be protection from injury at the two crucial periods – onset and convulsions. If possible, a gag consisting of a folded handkerchief should be inserted between the teeth to prevent the tongue being bitten. In the absence of a proper mouth gag, a well-padded dessertspoon is an asset in a first aid kit. It is not always possible to put in a gag as the rigidity is almost immediate.

All tight clothing must be loosened to prevent constriction and when recovery is effected the patient should be encouraged to sleep.

Most epilepsy sufferers are aware of their condition except in the case of the initial attack due to an injury. It is wise to remain nearby until medical assistance is obtained. With increasingly better treatment more epilepsy sufferers will participate in sport and thus present a possible risk to themselves and others.

BACK INJURY

This may occur for a variety of reasons – a car or bicycle crash, a rugby tackle, or an awkward fall on rough ground. The person should not be moved unless absolutely necessary and, unless removal is from a burning vehicle or a similar awkward situation, the following technique is adopted.

At least three or four persons are needed. One person should time or control the lift and should be stationed at the head. The head should be in the neutral position with slight traction in the long axis.

Two or three persons are then deployed both sides of the body and legs so that the lift can occur evenly and just sufficiently to put a stretcher underneath. Body alignment must be maintained during the lift and the stretcher padded to maintain alignment. Flexion *must* be prevented.

FRACTURES

If a fracture is suspected, the part should be immobilised with no other interference except to control any bleeding. To immobilise the part, a sling, the other limb, or any rigid object such as a tree branch or a broom handle may be used. Await medical assistance

and arrange transfer to hospital.

At the time of the injury keep the treatment to a minimum, help the patient to bear the pain, offer reassurance and give *no* drinks. Do not offer a cigarette unless asked for one.

COMMON INJURIES AND TREATMENT

Skill in treatment comes by experience. All persons, medically and non-medically trained, who are responsible for sports teams or individual athletes, should enrol on first aid courses. The local branch of the St John Ambulance Brigade is always very willing to help in this respect.

Contusions or bruises

These are usually caused by direct blunt violence or crush or direct contact with another performer and/or playing surface. Often the skin is unbroken although there may be extravasation because of damage to blood vessels. There may be some occlusion of capillaries and normal nutrition is impeded. The affected part stiffens because of pain, swelling and muscle spasm.

The aim of first aid is to limit bleeding by the application of a dispersant such as a solution of heparinoid and hyaluronidase (Lasonil) or a heparinoid gel (Hirudoid) (Quiles, 1965; Bass, 1969), cold compresses and pressure bandaging. If the haematoma is not too severe, or the sport is non-contact or the bruise is in a part of the body not vitally important to the performance, then the player may be allowed to continue. If strapping or bandaging is necessary then it is preferable not to allow the individual to restart.

Judgement needs to be exercised in restricting, for example, soccer and basketball players with upper limb injury, or racket/bat players with opposite arm injury.

Cuts and abrasions

These may be trivial superficial cuts, grazes or scratches, or may be deeper. They can be caused by sharp or blunt pressure on the body acting obliquely or tangentially.

A superficial bruise is red with excoriation of the skin. Scratches may be patterned if left by finger nails, studs or spikes. An abrasion may present with streaking or directional markings if the person is dragged along the playing surface. It is helpful to remember these markings in cases of inquiry into violence or breaking of the rules.

Superficial cuts are best cleaned with an antiseptic such as chlorhexidine (Hibitane) or chlorhexidine and cetrimide (Savlon) and collodion, or a dry dressing may be applied after using an iodine spray. An alternative is to apply sterile paraffin gauze underneath the dry dressing. To allow a player to continue to play it may only be necessary to spray the area with iodine or collodion or allow sterile talcum powder to 'cake' on the area.

Deeper cuts may require suturing. A gaping wound can be overcome by using thin strips of Elastoplast and placing them under tension at right angles to the wound and then bandaging over them. A puncture wound may hide a deeper more serious damage with internal bleeding.

Concussion

The skull is a closed box and if knocked, the brain and blood vessels will absorb the shock. If the force is great enough a skull fracture or ruptured blood vessels may result; this can lead to pressure and brain damage. Any blow will also directly damage brain cells.

Loss of consciousness must be regarded seriously and anyone knocked out for more than ten seconds should not be allowed to restart and should be kept under observation for 48 hours, preferably in hospital.

Cramp

This is a sustained painful spasm of muscle. One cause is the disturbance of electrolyte and fluid balance which affects the level of excitability of motor units. As yet, the phenomenon has not been completely explained.

To overcome cramp it is best to put the muscles on physiological stretch by working the antagonist strongly, e.g. if the calf muscles cramp, then extension by flexion of the knee and dorsiflexion of the foot is needed (De Vries, 1961; 1962). A passive stretch may be added to supplement the action of the non-affected muscle group. A frequent sufferer from cramp should be clinically investigated or at least advised as to the maintenance of a good fluid intake (Norris et al, 1957; Denny-Brown, 1953). Massage and heat are helpful in alleviating the condition.

Strains

This term is used to describe damage to muscle tissue. There are two types (chronic and acute) and four categories of strain (Ryan, 1969).

Chronic strain describes the overuse syndrome leading to fatigue and muscle spasm; specialist treatment is required. Acute strain is the result of a single violent force, usually to those muscles passing over two joints, and occurs by forcing contracting muscle to lengthen, for example by a blow.

In *Grade 1* strains, damage is to very few fibres and the sheath is intact. They are treated by immediate application of ice lasting 10 to 15 minutes (Wooton-

Whitling, 1977), then compression bandage for 30 minutes to one hour, followed by gentle active stretching. Normal weight-bearing is allowed. Ultrasound may be given immediately.

In *Grade 2* strains, more cells are crushed or torn, the sheath is still intact but bleeding is considerable. They are treated immediately with ice for 10 to 20 minutes and a pressure bandage is then applied. No active movement, stretching or weight-bearing is allowed for 24 hours but rhythmic static contractions may be possible if the pain is tolerable.

In *Grade 3* strains a very large area of muscle is involved and the sheath is at least partially torn. Damage may be found in more than one area. Bleeding is considerable but it is more diffuse because of the torn fascia. The treatment is as for Grade 2 strains but arrangements are made for admission to hospital.

A *Grade 4* strain involves a complete rupture of the muscle with an obvious gap between the ends of the muscle. Hospital treatment is required but immobilisation, ice and compression are needed immediately.

Sprains

A sprain is an overstretch injury of a ligament at the extremes of range. It can be chronic or acute with three categories, Grade 1, 2 or 3, i.e. minor strain, severe strain and total rupture (Colson and Armour, 1961; Featherstone, 1957). In all these injuries there is pain, swelling, tenderness at the site and some loss of function.

Movement will cause pain and thus the site may be either muscle or ligament, i.e. a contractile or non-contractile structure. To differentiate, the muscle is contracted strongly isometrically (static). If this causes no pain it is non-contractile tissue which is affected; conversely, if pain results contractile tissue is involved (Cyriax, 1978).

If damage is negligible, an aerosol refrigerant (Coolspray) may be applied and the player allowed to continue when the pain subsides.

If the injury is minor (*Grade 1*) although a few fibres are damaged then apply ice for 10 to 15 minutes, with cold compresses and a pressure bandage to the affected joint in the neutral position. If the injury is to the lower limb the patient is allowed to walk but is not allowed to do anything else for 24 hours. Rhythmic isometric contractions of the major muscle groups should be encouraged at once.

A *Grade 2* sprain requires a greater force for the injury to occur and unless the therapist is experienced then the patient should see a doctor. Again, ice and a cold compress under a pressure bandage are essential, with the joint placed in the neutral or shortened position. Rest and elevation are required for at least 24 hours, and no weight-bearing is allowed. If the subject is well-motivated then isometric rhythmic contractions should be encouraged. The doctor may give a local anaesthetic but on no account should the patient be allowed to continue or restart playing, as a relatively minor injury may become a more serious one.

In *Grade 3* sprains or a complete tear there may be rapid effusion with exquisite pain and tenderness; there is instability and complete loss of function. The injury must be seen by a doctor. The first aid treatment is splinting and rest in an elevated position to allow for reduction of swelling by gravity. The part can be treated with ice, or cold compresses; a pressure bandage should be applied with the ligament in the shortened position.

Rib injuries

If rib fractures are suspected then the patient should not restart unless in a non-contact sport and even this may be a doubtful procedure. At the very least the exertion will cause more pain and at most, further damage to the rib cage may puncture the pleura and lead to a pneumothorax developing.

It is essential that the patient sees a doctor but the immediate treatment is rest in a sitting position. Strapping, though providing some relief by splinting the ribs, is not recommended as it tends to restrict breathing even more. It is prudent to restrict any strapping to the area overlapping the fracture but not all round the chest, and this only in respect of the lower more mobile ribs. The patient can usually be taught to fix the affected area with muscular effort and use the unaffected parts. If there is bruising only, the decision to allow a restart will depend upon the distress felt by the patient when breathing and upon the importance of the event.

Injuries to the testes and scrotum

Bruising of the testes and scrotum occurs by direct body contact or a blow from apparatus or sports equipment. The injury is extremely painful and incapacitating for a short while though at times it may be more prolonged. In the latter instances the player is removed from the playing area and a sponge or towel soaked in hot water is applied to the scrotum. When the pain subsides the patient is encouraged to micturate. If the urine contains any blood, the patient must see a doctor.

Locking of the knee

Locking of a joint can be caused by extreme pain due to muscle spasm or by the interposition of a foreign body or torn cartilage. The knee joint is particularly prone and care must be exercised as this joint may become locked either by spasm of the biceps femoris due to injury at its lower insertion to the head of the fibula, or it may be caused by a tear in the lateral meniscus (Williams, 1971).

The patient with a locked knee due to a meniscus tear should not be allowed to restart. If it is caused by muscle spasm, this may be relieved by the use of an aerosol refrigerant (Coolspray) but otherwise the treatment outlined previously applies.

'Winded' players

A blow to the solar plexus produces a momentary paralysis of the diaphragm with spasm of the abdominal muscles. Consequently, respiration is impaired and the player may feel nauseated; he is said to be 'winded'.

Treatment consists of reassurance and allowing the person to adopt a comfortable position. Recovery is usually rapid and a cold sponge at the nape of the neck can help. If recovery is slow with signs of shock and restlessness, the player should be taken out of play and medical advice sought.

Dislocations; subluxations

The most usual joints to dislocate are the shoulder and the fingers, especially in rugby players. Fingers are also commonly dislocated in basketball and volleyball. Reduction of the shoulder should not be attempted by the inexperienced because of the possibility of damage to the axillary nerve; very often reduction can be effected by the person himself with a little help. More precise information may be found in textbooks on fractures or orthopaedics, e.g. Colson and Armour, 1961; Featherstone, 1957; Adams, 1978. It is not advisable to allow the player to restart play and there should be at least two to three days rest of the arm in a sling if it is the first dislocation, and longer if the condition occurs frequently.

With finger dislocations or partial dislocations it is possible, after using Coolspray, to apply force along the axis and so reduce the joint. The affected finger is then immobilised by strapping it to adjoining fingers. The player may be allowed to restart but must seek medical help later.

First aid is the start of rehabilitation and is the first treatment in a continuing plan. Everyone dealing with sports people should have some knowledge of first aid and the principles of treatment will assume knowledge of anatomy, movement, simple diagnosis, speed in treatment and prevention of further injury. It is essential that personal limitations be recognised so that more specialist treatment can be instituted. Finally, it is important that therapists involved with sports people should gain skill in treatment which can only come by experience gained in the 'park'.

REFERENCES

Adams, J. O. (1978). *Outline of fractures including joint injuries*. 7th edition, Churchill Livingstone, Edinburgh.

Bass, A. L. (1969). Treatment of muscle, tendon and minor joint injuries in sport. *Proceedings of the Royal Society of Medicine*. **62**, 925–928.

Browning, G. G. (1976). Sports medicine and the physiotherapist. *Physiotherapy*, **621**, 246–250.

Colson, J. H. C. and Armour, W. J. (1961). *Sports injuries and their treatment*, Stanley Paul, London.

Cyriax, J. (1978). *Textbook of orthopaedic medicine*. Volume I. *Diagnosis of soft tissue lesions*. 7th edition, Baillière Tindall, London.

Denny-Brown, D. (1953). Clinical problems in neuromuscular physiology. *American Journal of Physiology*, **15**, 368.

De Vries, H. A. (1961). Electromyographic observations of the effects of static stretching upon muscular distress. *Research Quarterly*, **32**, 468–479.

De Vries, H. A. (1962). Evaluation of static stretching procedures for improvement of flexibility. *Research Quarterly*, **33**, 222–229.

Featherstone, D. F. (1957). *Sports injuries: their prevention and treatment*. John Wright, Bristol.

Norris, F. H. Jr., Gastiger, E. L. and Chatfield, P. O. (1957). An electromyographic study of induced and spontaneous muscle cramps. *Electroencephalography and Clinical Neurophysiology*, **9**, 139–147.

O'Donoghue, D. H. (1970). *Treatment of injuries to athletes*. W. B. Saunders Co., Philadelphia.

Quiles, J. (1965). Enzymes in the treatment of acute sports injuries. *Proceedings of the 5th Latin Congress Physical and Sports Medicine*.

Ryan, A. J. (1969). Quadriceps strains, rupture and charley-horse. *Medicine and Science in Sports*, **1**, 106–111.

Williams, J. G. P. (1965). *Medical aspects of sport and physical fitness*. Pergamon Press, Oxford.

Williams, J. G. P. (1971). Diagnostic pitfalls in the sportsman's knee. *Proceedings of the Royal Society of Medicine*, **64**, 640–641.

Wooton-Whitling, Y. (1977). Ice in the treatment of sports injuries. *British Journal of Sports Medicine*, **11**, 146.

CHAPTER 35

Physiotherapy for sports injuries

VALERIE STEELE MCSP, SRP

AIMS OF TREATMENT

Physiotherapists involved in the treatment of sports injuries require a clear picture of the aims of treatment. These may be summarised as follows:

1. To enable the injured athlete to return to his or her sport quickly and safely.
2. To regain the strength, mobility and coordination of the muscles of the affected area so that the healing or healed tissues are sufficiently protected.
3. To maintain and if necessary increase the general strength and cardiovascular endurance of the patient.
4. To influence any biomechanical abnormalities such as muscle imbalance, limb imbalance and inflexibility.
5. To gain the cooperation, not only of the athlete, but of the coach or any other influential person to ensure that the patient is discouraged from returning to sport too soon and that the faulty technique precipitating tissue damage is corrected.
6. To make a positive contribution towards the prevention of another injury by advising on further rehabilitation exercises.
7. To provide a psychological 'prop'.
8. To try to prevent the subsequent development of degenerative disease due to the unavailability of treatment.
9. To provide a prophylactic service.

The injured sportsman should only return to sport when the doctor and physiotherapist are satisfied that adequate strength and mobility in the affected area have been regained. He should persevere with rehabilitation, even if it is lengthy for some conditions. In top class competition, particularly, a minimal loss of function is not only the difference between winning and losing, it can lead to re-injury or tissue breakdown in a previously uninvolved area of the body because of compensation and resultant unnatural movement.

Exercises to maintain general body strength and cardiovascular fitness should be included in the treatment because they will keep the person as fit as possible until he is ready to resume training. Too many athletes sustain further injury in attempting to regain general fitness too quickly following an enforced lay off. An active physiotherapy approach should enable the person to be concerned with more specific fitness when training is resumed.

Bender et al (1964) investigated strength levels in relation to injuries in new military cadets. They found that athletes with average or above normal strength levels were less susceptible to injury than those with below average strength or with imbalance in excess of 10 per cent between the lower limbs. This must be considered during rehabilitation.

Balance between the agonists and antagonists is also thought to be important both in the prevention and treatment of sports injuries, although more work needs to be done to advise on the pre-requisite strength values for different sports. It is believed that the strength value of the hamstrings should be 60 to 70 per cent of the quadriceps for most running sports.

It appears that weakness in one area of the body can lead to involvement elsewhere. Nicholas et al (1976) have shown a strong correlation between ankle and foot injuries on the one hand and ipsilateral weakness of the hip abductors and adductors. This type of relationship must be accounted for during rehabilitation.

Inflexibility is a prevalent problem among many athletes. Poor flexibility appears to lead to a high incidence of muscle injuries, joint lesions and non-specific aches and pains. The naturally inflexible are helped by carefully performed stretching exercises and they should be encouraged to persevere with these throughout their competitive careers.

Some athletes are excessively prone to injury because of musculo-skeletal abnormalities which render them inappropriately equipped for withstanding the demands of certain sports. The physiotherapist should be aware of this: the following two examples may help to explain this.

1. A boy with marked hyperextension of his knees has naturally lax ligaments and therefore contact sports expose him to an unacceptably high risk of serious injury to these joints.
2. A child with several degrees of hyperextension of the elbow is more prone to elbow dislocation than his

'normal' contemporaries. He should be discouraged from participating in such sports as rugby, judo and wrestling.

Ideally, a child with an unsuitable physique for safe involvement in a particular sport should be recognised early in school life so that he can be encouraged to adopt a more suitable sport.

The physiotherapist should have a basic understanding of sport so that the mechanics of injury and the stresses to which the performer is subjected can be understood. Coaches have a far greater knowledge of the finer points of technique and the physiotherapist can gain much by liaising with them. If the physiotherapist suspects that an injury was caused by poor technique or biomechanical abnormality, this should be discussed with the coach so that the style can be altered.

Prophylaxis will probably play an increasingly important role in the field of sports medicine as further research is carried out and it is shown that adequate training can prepare the tissues more effectively for the demands of sport. Physiotherapists are ideally trained for this type of work which should enable future generations of sportsmen to avoid many of the lesions that are commonly seen in sport today.

INITIAL EXAMINATION AND ASSESSMENT

When the doctor has examined the patient and, hopefully, been able to make a definitive diagnosis, the physiotherapist should carry out an examination and assessment. This must be done meticulously so that the most suitable treatment can be given. Each injured person should be treated according to individual needs; the physiotherapist should adapt the treatment to the person, not vice versa.

The physiotherapist must acquire information from the patient before carrying out a physical examination; this should include what is his sport, the actual event and level of competition. The mechanics of the injury should be clearly understood as this aids the rehabilitation as well as the diagnosis. The physiotherapist should enquire about past injuries; if a similar injury has occurred previously, it is helpful to discover the patient's opinion of the value of previous treatment because this may point towards a particular course of treatment.

The equipment used by the player/athlete merits attention because ill-fitting or unsuitable footwear, for example, may be a contributory factor which, if ignored, will precipitate further problems.

A thorough physical examination can then take place. The damaged structure should be carefully investigated; where there is a limb injury the opposite side should be used for comparison. The joints proximal and distal to the injury should be examined, particularly if the injury is a chronic or an overuse lesion because adaptive changes may have taken place; failure to include this aspect can mean that the player returns to sport ill-prepared and further breakdown almost inevitably ensues. The spine should always be included in the examination because poor strength and/or mobility in the trunk seem to contribute to some sports injuries.

The general strength and flexibility of the patient should be assessed; exercises may be required to influence either or both of these. Cardiovascular fitness should also be tested, provided that in so doing the patient does not impose stress on the lesion.

TREATMENT

Continual assessment enables the physiotherapist to provide effective treatment. Sophisticated electrical equipment can be used but more than adequate treatment can be provided by a competent physiotherapist used to handling soft tissue injuries.

Full range of efficient muscular and joint motion, including accessory movements, must be regained before the patient can be considered to be rehabilitated for sport. Controlled exercises are introduced 24 to 48 hours post-injury for most conditions. In the first instance, the activities are selected so that the damaged tissues are not subjected to any pressure which could lead to further inflammation, increased scar tissue and adhesions. Initially, the movements are performed to enhance drainage and gently mobilise the tissues. The severity of the exercise is increased as healing advances and this enhances resolution provided that the player avoids excessive stress by never pushing the movement through pain. Pain is a warning signal that must not be ignored.

The physiotherapist must adapt the treatment to the stresses of the patient's sport. A prop forward and a full back will require subtly different exercises if both sustain similar ankle sprains, because of their dissimilar roles on the rugby pitch; a female gymnast with a similar lesion would require the emphasis to be placed much more on fine balance and coordination.

The physiotherapist may employ many techniques. Familiarity with the feel of injured tissues is essential as this guides the treatment. Massage and transverse frictions certainly have a place; vertebral and peripheral mobilisation and manipulation techniques as described by Maitland (1977a, and b) and Cyriax (1977; 1978) are useful methods of treatment. Connective tissue massage (Ebner, 1977) is also useful in the management of many of the soft tissue lesions seen in sport. Proprioceptive neuromuscular facilitation techniques (Knott and Voss, 1968) and other means of applying manual resistance have a major part to play because they enable the therapist to guide the movement and adjust the resistance according to the 'feel' of the tissues.

Muscular atrophy occurs quickly as a result of injury; the resulting weakness means that the patient cannot safely participate in sport. During rehabilitation, a wide variety of exercises are used aimed at improving (a) strength, (b) endurance, (c) power and, (d) flexibility.

Modified circuit training should be used whenever possible to maintain a degree of cardiovascular endurance. The exercises must be selected carefully to ensure that they do not affect the damaged structures, for example, an arm and trunk circuit may be given to a patient with a leg injury. Work on a static bicycle may be possible when the pounding effect of running is contra-indicated. There are many injuries that benefit from work in a swimming pool – an athlete may even be able to run in water when it would be injurious to do so on dry land.

A suitable warm-up should be performed at every level of rehabilitation to ensure that the muscles are ready for work.

The physiotherapist should be familiar with the injuries where exercise may be contra-indicated. The list includes Achilles tendinitis, patellar tendinitis, intramuscular haematoma of the quadriceps femoris and tenosynovitis.

TREATMENTS AVAILABLE

The use of ice for the initial management of injuries has already been mentioned in Chapter 34. It must be stressed that the following methods of treatment are used usually in conjunction with exercises or some other form of therapy, and not as a treatment on their own.

Contrast bathing

Contrast bathing is an effective method of reducing swelling and it may be introduced 24 to 48 hours post-injury. Heat, in the form of a hot pack or hot water bottle, is applied to the tissues for one minute to cause vasodilatation and so increase the circulation; this is followed by an ice-pack towel or iced water bath for two to five minutes to induce vasoconstriction and thus encourage drainage. The process is repeated five times. The advantage of contrast bathing over more sophisticated electrical treatments is that it is both effective and cheap, as well as being something which the patient can easily do at home several times during the day.

Ultrasound

This is a popular piece of equipment for treating soft tissue injuries, whether they are acute, due to overuse or chronic. The mechanical effect of the sound waves is thought to encourage re-absorption of extravasation at cellular level and to reduce sensory stimulation, consequently affording pain relief.

The two frequencies of sound that are commonly available in Great Britain are three and one megacycles, penetration being greater with the lower frequency. The choice of frequency and intensity is very much according to the preference of the physiotherapist. The ultrasound may be given as a continuous or pulsed beam. The pulsed beam is favoured by some operators because it ensures the dissipation of any heat which is desirable in the presence of acute inflammation.

Interferential

This medium frequency electrical equipment has been used for some time in Europe to manage many soft tissue lesions and is now becoming popular in Great Britain. It is used in the treatment of acute injuries to produce an analgesic effect. The patient must be warned that it may only afford temporary relief which will permit natural movement; it must *not* be used to allow immediate participation in sport.

The currents can be adjusted to cause an increase in circulation which is valuable for sub-acute and chronic lesions. Interferential can also be used to stimulate muscle and this is useful for the management of chronic muscle injuries such as groin strains which sometimes prove resistant to other forms of therapy.

Hot pack and infra-red

The main effect of these modes is to raise the temperature in the superficial structures; the thermal effect in the deeper tissues is minimal. An infra-red lamp or hot pack can be used as a prelude to exercise to ease the pain, relieve muscle spasm and increase the superficial circulation. From the psychological aspect, the patient may benefit from heat because most people associate warmth with a feeling of well-being.

Short wave diathermy and microwave

Physiologists have shown that the most effective way to elevate joint temperature is to exercise the area. Both short wave diathermy and microwave cause an increase in temperature of those body tissues that are positioned within their electric fields. The heating effect is produced in the deep as well as the superficial structures and this can be made use of for treating some sub-acute and chronic lesions, particularly in circumstances where full range exercise is temporarily undesirable, for example, chondromalacia patellae.

Diapulse

This machine, which emits pulsed electro-magnetic waves, is said to shorten the time taken for tissue to heal. It was developed in the United States of America and now European firms have introduced equipment following similar principles. Healing is said to be enhanced by the pulsed electro-magnetic waves which can be used immediately after injury because a thermal effect, which is undesirable in the early stages of inflammation, is not produced.

Faradism

Faradism may have an occasional place in the treatment of sports injuries. It can be used to overcome muscle inhibition which is sometimes present following an injury or operation. For example, it can be applied to the quadriceps femoris if adequate contraction cannot be gained actively. Some physiotherapists also use faradism during the early treatment of muscle strains; the affected muscle is supported in a shortened position and the current used to produce alternate contraction and relaxation so that the formation of adhesions is discouraged and the drainage of exudate encouraged.

SPECIFIC INJURIES

It is not practicable to mention the specific physiotherapy for many sports injuries, but four injuries involving different structures will be discussed.

Ligamentous injuries

Klein and Allman (1969) have shown that ligamentous weakness in the knee leads to joint instability. This applies to other joints as well and it is therefore important that ligamentous injuries are diagnosed and treated early so that chronic disability is avoided. Adequate muscle function must be ensured to protect the damaged ligament and encourage resolution; proprioception must be re-educated as it is so vital in the avoidance of further sprains.

Sprain of the lateral collateral ligament of the ankle (inversion sprain) is one of the most common sports injuries. Minor sprains involve one or more bands of the lateral ligament. More serious sprains can be associated with capsular damage, interference with the inferior tibio-fibular syndesmosis, the calcaneo-cuboid joint or the base of the fifth metatarsal. Intracapsular injuries inevitably require more treatment than extracapsular injuries. The muscles traversing the joint may be implicated in ankle sprains. The physiotherapist must examine all the joints of the foot to eliminate the presence of any unrecognised lesion elsewhere which could have contributed to the injury and

may adversely affect rehabilitation. The strength of the muscles of the hip and knee should be assessed and suitable exercises prescribed if weakness is proven.

TREATMENT

Contrast bathing is used 24 to 48 hours after injury; ultrasound, diapulse or interferential may be chosen by the physiotherapist to encourage re-absorption of inflammatory exudate and relieve pain. Foot and ankle movements are then carried out with the leg supported in elevation to further encourage drainage; inversion and eversion must be performed gently within the limit of pain. Intrinsic foot exercises must be included because the integrity of the arches is essential for the normal functioning of the foot. A strapping, holding the ligament is a shortened position, may be indicated between treatments.

As the swelling and discomfort subside, weight-bearing exercises are performed within the limit of pain. A correct walking pattern must be encouraged from the first because bad habits become established rapidly and are difficult to correct. When the patient can perform a good range of active inversion and eversion, resistance is applied to the invertors and evertors; particular emphasis is placed on the peronei which are inevitably involved in the injury and must be strengthened to protect the healing ligament. Repeated balance and coordination exercises are essential to re-educate effective proprioception; without these activities, a sprain could re-occur at the slightest provocation. A Jonas board (Fig. 35/1) or other balance

Fig. 35/1 A Jonas board used for retraining balance (reproduced by courtesy of Jonas Woodhead and Sons, Leeds)

boards are useful pieces of apparatus for retraining balance. Running, jumping and hopping activities are only introduced when the patient can demonstrate controlled balance during single leg exercises; poor landings due to insufficient muscle control will otherwise lead to further injury and ligamentous laxity. Rotational and side-stepping activities are included in final rehabilitation.

Muscle strain

A small or large number of muscle fibres may be damaged in the injury and the number will dictate the speed of recovery. Rest is inadvisable because the inevitable muscular atrophy as a result of injury is further enhanced by total inactivity. The muscle should be gently encouraged to work as soon as pain permits.

The injury may involve the upper or lower attachments or the mid-belly; the latter usually resolves more rapidly because of the greater blood supply. The physiotherapist is asked to treat acute and chronic lesions. Chronic lesions are often long established – they may be due to repeated minor pulls which the athlete has considered too trivial to warrant attention. By the time that help is sought the muscle has shortened, and adhesions, excessive scarring and fibrosis may be present. These lesions are inevitably difficult to treat and progress is often slow; graduated stretching and strengthening exercises must be done until maximal function is regained.

TREATMENT

With an acute injury, after the first 48 hours contrast bathing, ultrasound, interferential or faradism may be used for the reasons mentioned previously. Ice may be required to relieve associated muscle spasm.

Management is dictated by the physiotherapist's assessment of the severity of the lesion. Early treatment is directed towards the re-absorption of inflammatory exudate, relieving pain and muscle spasm and encouraging pain-free muscular activity, albeit in a limited range. It may be desirable to carry out active assisted exercises to ensure that the damaged muscle is not subjected to excessive stress.

Resistance techniques – designed to encourage relaxation by working the antagonists then contracting the affected muscle – are valuable because they help to relieve muscle spasm, overcome inhibition and regain extensibility. The severity of the exercises is gradually intensified but again it must be stressed to the patient that the activities must be done properly and they should not be painful. Manual techniques are very useful because the operator can regulate the effort demanded of the muscles, while a weak arc of movement can be appreciated and rectified. Stretching and resistance exercises which provide for all the needs of the muscle, endurance, strength and power, must be performed. The movements must be accomplished slowly at first, but later increased speed of motion and rapid alteration of pace are included in the rehabilitation programme.

Exercises can usefully be carried out in water a few days after incurring a muscle strain but the athlete may need to avoid certain movements. For example, it is undesirable for a patient suffering from a groin strain to attempt breaststroke for the first two to three weeks.

Tendon injuries

Exercise is often contra-indicated in the initial management of these lesions be they acute, chronic or through overuse. They can be slow to resolve because of the inherent poor blood supply of the tendon.

Injury to the Achilles tendon or the paratenon is common in sport. A definitive diagnosis is required but ultrasound is often the treatment of choice: when swelling exists, contrast bathing is also useful. The tendon should be maintained in a shortened position because repeated stretching will lead to further irritation. A heel pad should therefore be incorporated into the patient's shoes or one inch (2.5cm) heels may be worn. A strapping is occasionally necessary. As healing progresses and the pain and swelling diminish, the tendon can be subjected to manual stretches which should not elicit pain. Later, a strengthening and flexibility programme is introduced. Balance and coordination exercises for the ankle and foot are included in the regime.

Chronic lesions often require transverse frictions and firm mobilisation techniques as well as electrical treatment to soften the scar tissue and enhance the circulation.

Recurrent lesions of the Achilles tendon and surrounding structures are common and it is important that the physiotherapist ensures that the patient has adequate strength, flexibility and muscle balance in the region to reduce the chances of re-injury. All the joints of the foot must be checked, as should the more proximal joints, to ensure that possible contributory factors are not overlooked. The patient's footwear, both sports and every-day shoes, should be inspected for signs of excessive or uneven wear. Training and competition surfaces must be considered and the patient should be encouraged to do a large proportion of his training on grass rather than road or composition flooring. The physiotherapist should watch the patient's running to ensure that a fault in style has not precipitated the lesion.

Meniscus lesions

PRE-OPERATIVE CARE

Many athletes who require a meniscectomy do not present with symptoms and signs that necessitate an immediate operation, although the indications are such that the surgeon can make a definitive diagnosis. A pre-operative strengthening regime is advisable for these athletes, firstly because many have experienced repeated insult to the knee with ensuing muscle weakness and second, because adequate strength before the operation should reduce to a minimum the resultant muscular atrophy. This means that in normal circumstances, rehabilitation can progress more rapidly. All the muscles surrounding the knee should be considered by the physiotherapist when preparing an exercise programme. The quadriceps, hamstrings, gastrocnemius, ilio-tibial tract, gracilis and sartorius require special attention as all play a part in stabilising the joint.

POSTOPERATIVE TREATMENT

Adequate rehabilitation is important following any surgical procedure if a patient is to return to sport without exposure to an unacceptably high risk of further injury.

Most surgeons advocate immediate postoperative isometric quadriceps contractions for their meniscectomy patients. There is a variance of orthopaedic opinion regarding the duration of the patient's stay in hospital, the type of support used, the time at which weight-bearing is introduced and so on. However, the patient usually commences outpatient physiotherapy following removal of the stitches.

Ideally, outpatient physiotherapy should be provided daily. After a careful examination of the knee and associated structures, the early treatment in the department is aimed at reduction of any swelling and contrast bathing can be useful. Effective quadriceps contractions must be achieved with particular attention being paid to the vastus medialis for it is most important that final extension of the knee is gained at this stage. General hip and foot exercises are also performed, both legs being worked. The knee should be bandaged between treatments, and between home contrast bathing and exercise sessions, until the effusion has cleared. The patient should be instructed to keep weight-bearing to a minimum as it can increase the swelling and retard progress.

Knee flexion and weight-bearing exercises begin as soon as the swelling has subsided but the knee must be carefully observed for any signs of irritability. Resistance exercises may be given either manually or by using weights, pulleys or springs. These exercises must be performed correctly.

The strength of the uninvolved leg must be considered when assessing the weight requirements for the operated knee; if a footballer can straight leg raise 30lb (13.5kg) with his unaffected leg, then ultimately, he should be expected to perform similarly with the involved knee. Obviously, a 120kg rugby forward needs to use far greater resistance to adequately rebuild his quadriceps as compared with a marathon runner or a young footballer.

Table 1 shows the rough guide which is used in the Sports Clinic at St James' Hospital at Leeds, to assess whether a patient's quadriceps are considered strong enough to attempt running.

These values are adjusted according to each patient's physique. At all times the lifts are performed slowly and extension is held for three to five seconds. Lighter weights with higher repetitions are used to build up endurance.

Exercises must also be carried out to strengthen the hamstrings, gastrocnemius and the hip muscles. Klein

Table 1 Minimum schedules of weighted boot exercises to be performed before return to running and to contact or rotary sports

Sport	Exercise	Repetitions	Load
Running	Straight leg raising.	3 × 10	15–20lb (6.8–9kg)
	Flexion/extension: returning the boot to a support between each lift.	3 × 10	30–35lb (13.6–15.9kg)
Contact or Rotary	Flexion/extension: returning the boot to a support between each lift.	10	50lb (22.7kg)

and Allman (1969) described hip adductor exercises which appear to favourably influence the medial ligament of the knee and these would seem advisable following a medial meniscectomy. Similarly, hip abductor exercises seem to be of some benefit to the lateral ligament and should be included following a lateral meniscectomy.

Before the patient returns to sport, the physiotherapist must ensure that his muscles have been re-educated to cope with twisting and turning, as well as sprinting or jumping. Further injury seems very likely if this vital stage is omitted because the various structures need training to work efficiently; this appears to be the phase that is often forgotten, yet it is a vital stage to rehabilitation.

The physiotherapist, working in conjunction with a doctor, has much to offer the field of sports injuries. There is much to be gained from meeting the coaches, trainers and athletes to discuss certain aspects of sport and a great deal can be learned from their opinions. A considerable amount is yet to be discovered about the management of many of the lesions that are commonly seen. This is a challenging field of physiotherapy because, generally, the patients are very well motivated and are willing to cooperate in endeavours to find a more scientific and effective approach to treatment. This should be to the benefit, not only of the sporting fraternity, but of all patients with a similar injury.

REFERENCES

Bender, J. A., Pierson, J. K., Kaplan, H. N. and Johnson, A. J. (1964). Factors affecting the occurrence of knee injuries. *Journal of the Association of Physical and Mental Rehabilitation*, **18**, 130–134.

Cyriax, J. (1978). *Textbook of orthopaedic medicine*, Volume 1, 7th edition. Baillière Tindall, London.

Cyriax, J. and Russell, G. (1977). *Textbook of orthopaedic medicine*, Volume 2, 9th edition. Baillière Tindall, London.

Ebner, M. (1975). *Connective tissue massage*. Robert E. Krieger, Huntingdon, New York.

Klein, K. K. and Allman, F. (1969). *The knee in sports*. Pemberton Press, New York.

Knott, M. and Voss, D. E. (1968). *Proprioceptive neuromuscular facilitation patterns and techniques*. Harper and Row, New York.

Maitland, G. D. (1977a). *Vertebral manipulation*, 4th edition. Butterworths, London.

Maitland, G. D. (1977b). *Peripheral manipulation*, 2nd edition. Butterworths, London.

Nicholas, J. A., Strizak, A. M. and Veras, G. (1976). A study of thigh muscle weakness in different pathological states of the lower extremity. *American Journal of Sports Medicine*, **4**, 241–248.

CHAPTER 36

Fitness testing after injury

DENNIS WRIGHT MCSP, DipTP, SRP

This chapter is concerned with the problems of fitness following injury in order to prevent or reduce the danger of recurrence when participation is resumed.

The essence of sports injury management is bound up with the problems of 'fitness to participate', whether this refers to a resumption in training or to a return to competition. The greater the degree of involvement whether it be with the athlete, the team, the club, or a sport generally, the more difficult it becomes to be completely objective and the greater the tendency to become empirical in reaching decisions. As one's interest develops the more danger there is of being influenced by the athlete's changing moods or the team's needs and demands.

Keen observation and experience will always have a place in the satisfactory outcome of any fitness assessment but these qualities must be integrated with an objective and scientific approach which embodies fundamental anatomical, physiological, pathological and psychological considerations. Experience provides an approximate time schedule for the recovery from any injury, but it also creates sufficient opportunity to realise the individuality of each one and to understand the folly of forecasting the outcome.

The ideal programme of recovery in any injury is one of steady, uneventful progress. Minor deviations from the ideal are frequently encountered and in the field of sports injury these still remain within the limits of normality. Serious set-backs, as presented by recurrence or complete breakdown, represents either a lack of organisation, a lack of patience or a lack of discipline.

GENERAL CONSIDERATIONS IN TESTING FOR FITNESS

The nature of the injury

This means that the site, the tissues involved, and the severity of injury will obviously determine the overall time schedule of recovery and will determine the need for more careful testing at every stage.

The stage of pathological improvement

Sight must never be lost of the fact that, following injury, the body's natural reaction is to attempt to repair the damage. Consequently it is of paramount importance that we are familiar with the subtle changes which occur as recovery progresses through its acute, subacute and chronic stages of inflammation. Failure to observe these stages leads to a singular lack of success.

The sport involved

This factor will determine the emphasis of the tests employed. Tests used will to an extent mirror the specificity of the sport.

Competition role

The playing position or role of the participant in the sport must be considered. The skills demanded frequently vary within the same team. This applies particularly in field invasive games.

The level of involvement

Generally speaking, the need for higher standards of fitness run parallel with higher levels of involvement, even though motivation, dedication and experience can often disguise the fact.

SPECIFIC CONSIDERATIONS

The validity of the result of any fitness test depends on many factors. Generally speaking we are only concerned with physical fitness because significant mental involvement tends to be confined to the higher levels of sport.

Physical fitness is a relative quality and the standard of this quality can vary from the once-a-week squash player to the Olympic Games decathlete. Regardless of the standard, there are certain basic components of fitness which contribute to the whole. These are mobility, endurance, strength (power) and coordination. In any test of physical ability whether it be general or local, it is these components which should be assessed. It may well be that only one, or perhaps a combination of them, is of particular interest at any one stage in the recovery programme. However, in the final analysis all these individual qualities must be tested before the verdict of 'fit to play' can be issued. It must be remembered that to the professional athlete 'fit to play' means 'fit to work' and the thoroughness of the tests employed must be correspondingly searching. This is not to say that the sprained ankle joint is any different in a member of the 'Extra B' team to that sustained by the international team player. One often has to be realistic and accept that the opportunities to avoid potentially dangerous situations are available far more frequently in the 'Extra B' game and that the consequences of failing to avoid them are not quite so devastating in their implications.

FITNESS TESTING

Fitness testing must be an on-going routine throughout the recovery period in order to detect improvement and chart progress. The psychological effect of being able to demonstrate a measure of improvement by tangible recording is of inestimable value to all concerned. Progress which is seen to be made has a strong motivating effect.

The testing for fitness, or the lack of it, generally takes place in three main areas:

1. the treatment room
2. the gymnasium
3. the field of play.

The significance of an immediate post-injury assessment is minimised by many considerations, not the least of which is the athlete's own acceptance of pain. Pain is a complex phenomenon and the measurement of it, along with that of pain tolerance, remains the greatest obstacle to the evaluation of treatment methods. It is the difficulty in measuring these factors which prevents the treatment of sports injuries from becoming truly scientific.

Mobility (flexibility)

As a quality of physical fitness mobility deserves the greatest consideration. Recovery of mobility is the most important yardstick of improvement while a lack of it remains the biggest obstacle to full recovery. A failure to achieve the normal range of movement is the most common cause of injury recurrence because of the limitation in full function which it inevitably creates. The ideal situation for which we should aim is one where active mobility, accomplished by the athlete's own effort, equals passive mobility (the range achieved by an external force during relaxation of the part), whether we are referring to the stretch of a muscle or the movement of a joint.

Strength

It would be irresponsible to produce mobility without the support and protection of muscle strength. In any re-education programme mobility and strength should progress in unison. An important stabilising factor in most of the freely moveable joints of the body is the strength of the approximating effect on opposing articular surfaces by muscle contraction.

The product of time and distance gives a measure of power and is the characteristic of complete fitness to be finally restored in a rehabilitation programme following injury. Power is exhibited in propulsive actions involving either propulsion of the body itself or of sporting implements. Apart from the fact that it is measurable by virtue of performance, power also bestows a certain quality to movement.

Coordination

If there is normal mobility and strength it is highly probable that coordination is reasonably efficient. Coordination in sport is tied up with the skills of a particular sport, and the level of involvement will determine the standard of these skills. Skills have to be practised in order to establish neuromuscular patterns. In considering the long-term injury, it is vital that we should consider the effects which immobilisation and disuse have on these important mechanisms. In some sports, e.g. weightlifting, slight lapses in coordination often result in serious injury.

The principles advocated in the text are illustrated by referring to the tests which can be employed in assessing the fitness of three common sites of injury in three different major sports. These include a hamstring injury in a sprinter, a shoulder injury in a rugby football player and a knee injury in a soccer player.

HAMSTRING INJURY IN A SPRINTER

A typical injury of this kind tends to follow a time schedule of three to four weeks before full activity is resumed. Full participation should not be allowed until the muscle is pain free on:

1. deep digital pressure on the specific site of injury
2. full stretch application
3. strong contraction against heavy resistance
4. performing all the skills of the sport.

EARLY STRETCH TESTS FOR INJURED HAMSTRINGS

1. This involves sitting with one leg extended out in front and the other fully flexed (Fig. 36/1a). An attempt is made to touch the toes of the extended leg with both hands. The distance from the finger-tips to the toes is measured and the result compared with that recorded when the leg positions are reversed.

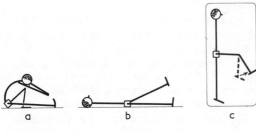

Fig. 36/1

2. This test involves lying on the floor and raising a straight leg while the other leg remains perfectly flat (Fig. 36/1b). The angle between the raised leg and the horizontal is measured at the point where either the knee begins to flex or the position of the other leg is unable to be maintained.

3. This method is to lie on the unaffected side and flex the knee and hip of the injured leg to 90° while the trunk and the other leg remain in the same alignment (Fig. 36/1c). While the thigh is retained in the same position, the lower leg is passively stretched and the degree of movement measured.

LATE STRETCH TESTS FOR INJURED HAMSTRINGS

1. With the heel of one foot resting on a chair seat, an attempt is made to touch the toes with both hands while retaining a fully extended knee. The distance from finger-tips to toes is recorded and compared with the other leg when their positions are reversed (Fig. 36/2a).

2. A slightly more exacting test is that of repeating (1) but with the leg raised to a higher level as on a table top (Fig. 36/2b).

3. A very demanding test of the hamstring group of muscles to withstand stretch is that of crossing the legs and retaining the feet close together while stooping forwards and downwards in an attempt to touch the toes of the rear leg (Fig. 36/2c). Measure from finger-tips to toes and compare both legs. The leg which crosses behind is the leg under stress.

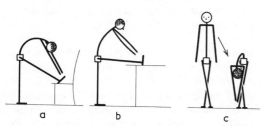

Fig. 36/2

STRENGTH TESTS FOR INJURED HAMSTRINGS

1. The simplest test and one which allows safe progression to be made is that of lying face downwards and with an initial weight of 2kg fixed to the ankle or foot of the injured leg. Bend the knee to 90° and then slowly lower it back to the starting position. Progress is made by increasing the weight by 1kg and repeating the exercise (Fig. 36/3a).

2. Another specific test of hamstring integrity is that of assuming a kneel-standing position with the feet anchored firmly under a wallbar, or even held manually. The athlete leans forwards from the knees beyond the vertical and then pulls back to recover his position (Fig. 36/3b).

Fig. 36/3

FUNCTIONAL TESTING FOR INJURED HAMSTRINGS

1. Stand sideways to a support which can be grasped. Swing the injured leg forwards and backwards progressing to a gradually increasing level. In this initial test bend the knee on the forward swing (Fig. 36/4a).

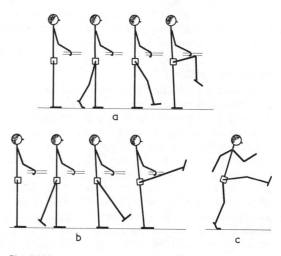

Fig. 36/4

2. This is a variation on (1), but is a much more demanding test. The injured leg in this test is maintained in a fully extended position throughout the swing. To avoid recurrence of injury the height of the swing forwards must be increased gradually. The trunk must be kept in an upright posture throughout (Fig. 36/4b).

3. The athlete performs a high-kicking action by stepping forwards for two paces and on the third step swings the leg forwards and upwards to successively higher levels (Fig. 36/4c).

Running on the spot should initially be at a slow pace with a low knee action, progressing to a quicker pace with a high knee action. It is essential in practice to acquire even timing by virtue of symmetrical leg action.

The actual running stage is a vital one because it is now that recurrence most frequently occurs. There should be a progressive schedule over a period of at least one week which should be discounted if there is any semblance of pain. A sharp stabbing sensation is an untoward sign of recurrence, while a dull heavy feeling suggests that progress should be halted at that stage and previous tests of mobility repeated and compared with earlier recordings. Efficient running entails considerable reflex coordination. This is shown by the innate ability to take perfectly even strides with each leg. Consequently, uneven pacing suggests an interruption of this ability by virtue of pain resulting from the demands made when full bilateral mobility is lacking. Uneven pacing can develop into a running habit which, if established, becomes difficult to eradicate.

The re-education of running begins with jogging and finishes with all out sprinting. In this gradual process three variables need to be considered – speed, footwear and surface. Initially, the athlete jogs at a slow pace in flat ridged-soled training shoes on a dry yielding surface and builds up by increasing the pace until he is running in spiked shoes on a firm surface. This is the only safe way of reaching maximum sprinting ability. The only other factor to be considered is the ability to make an explosive start; hitherto the speed running being executed from a gradual build up of speed in a 'rolling-start'.

A conclusive test to convince one of the ability to withstand the stretch involved in the push-off and the strong contraction in the pick-up action is to attempt some progressively faster shuttle-runs. Starting from blocks in an explosive start would be an important final test to convince one of the injury's full recovery.

To give the injury, as well as the athlete, every consideration, each running session should be preceded by a sensible preparatory warm-up period of progressive mobility and strengthening exercises.

SHOULDER INJURY IN A RUGBY PLAYER

EARLY MOBILITY TESTS FOR SHOULDER INJURY

1. Grasp a pole or brush handle with the arm stretched sideways. While the elbow is maintained in a fully extended position, the stick is rotated forwards and backwards (Fig. 36/5a).

2. A second test is similar to (1) but with the arm stretched upwards above the head (Fig. 36/5b).

3. A third test is another variation of (1) but with the arm stretched forwards (Fig. 36/5c).

These three exercises with a pole can also be used as early strengthening activities, particularly if the hand is moved towards one end of the pole, or if the pole is replaced by a brush so that one end is weighted.

A useful test of progress in the early stages of recovery is to attempt to touch the finger-tips of both hands behind the shoulder blades using the injured arm alternately above and below (Fig. 36/5d). The distance between the finger-tips is measured.

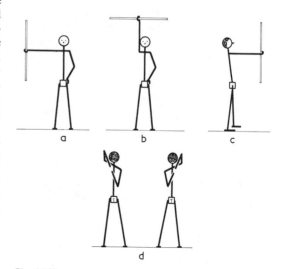

Fig. 36/5

LATER MOBILITY TESTS FOR SHOULDER INJURY

1. Hold a light barbell (5kg) at arm's length above the head then lower it behind the neck (Fig. 36/6a).

2. Grasp the ends of a rope which pass over a pulley, hook, or bar and move each arm alternately up and down to full stretch (Fig. 36/6b).

3. Hold a light barbell at arm's length overhead while lying astride a bench. Lower the barbell beyond the head while retaining straight arms (Fig. 36/6c).

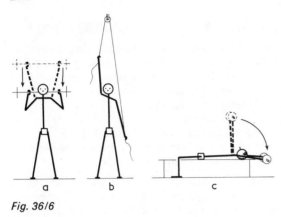

Fig. 36/6

EARLY STRENGTH TESTS FOR SHOULDER INJURY
Any progressive system of dumb-bell or barbell exercises for the arm beginning with light weights would be a satisfactory measurable test.

LATER STRENGTH TESTS FOR SHOULDER INJURY
1. A useful test is that of raising bodyweight in a modification of the press-up exercise. The feet are placed at a higher level than the arms on the seat of a chair. The shoulders are raised to full arm's length (Fig. 36/7a).

2. A more strenuous modification is that of dipping between two benches. The feet and the arms are placed on each bench and the body is lowered between them (Fig. 36/7b).

3. Another test using bodyweight as resistance is by sitting between two benches with legs outstretched and the hands flat on each bench. The buttocks are then raised from the floor by extending the elbows (Fig. 36/7c).

4. A similar exercise test is that of raising the buttocks and pulling backwards to sit on a stool or chair (Fig. 36/7d).

In all these examples of strength tests, it should be realised that either the starting position or the eventual finishing position are also making demands on mobility.

FUNCTIONAL TESTING FOR SHOULDER INJURY
Progressive weight transference to the arms is a necessary inclusion, not only because of the demands on mobility and strength but also as a test of the athlete's confidence.

1. Initially the hands are retained in contact with the floor while the legs are simply kicked upwards into the air (Fig. 36/8a).

2. As a progression the player is asked to drop on to the hands and kicks into the air simultaneously from a crouched position (Fig. 36/8b).

3. The natural sequence from this is a straightforward handstand from the standing position (Fig. 36/8c).

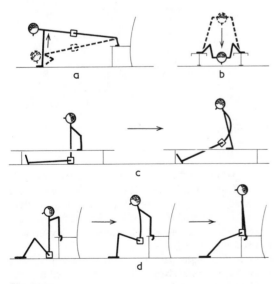

Fig. 36/7

Fig. 36/8

4. Wheel-barrow walking in various directions is a searching test to employ (Fig. 36/8d).

5. In a similar manner, crab-walking in all directions is also a severe test of shoulder integrity (Fig. 36/8e).

6. A gymnastic forward roll is a necessary functional skill to be tested both from a standing and a running start.

The basic skills of the sport itself must now be practised. Rugby skills consist of passing and catching a ball, tackling, being tackled and avoiding tackles, scrummaging and scoring points by kicking goals and scoring tries. These skills are performed by players in all positions. However, there are certain positional skills which make particular demands. An example of this is the hooking position which has relevant demands so far as the shoulders are concerned. Therefore, the hooker with a doubt about his recovery from shoulder injury must be tested thoroughly in his particular skills, no less than his ability to suspend his body mass from the adjacent supporting prop forward.

KNEE INJURY IN A SOCCER PLAYER

Injuries affecting the knee joint require application of a deeper knowledge of anatomy than most others. The testing of knee joint integrity centres on both its mobility and stability under varying conditions.

EARLY MOBILITY TESTS FOLLOWING A KNEE INJURY

1. In a prone lying position, attempt to bend the affected knee (Fig. 36/9a). Either the angle between upper and lower legs is measured or the distance between the heel and the buttock.

2. In a high sitting position on a table, bend the knee and simply measure the angle attained (Fig. 36/9b).

3. A third test is employed to assess the ability to fully extend the knee by either relaxation or active contraction of the quadriceps muscles. The gap between the back of the knee and the table is measured (Fig. 36/9c).

4. Sit on the front edge of a stool with the toes of both feet against a wall. Raise the buttocks and thrust the knees forward towards the wall. The heels must be maintained in contact with the floor (Fig. 36/9d). The distance between the knees and the wall is measured.

LATER MOBILITY TESTS FOLLOWING KNEE INJURY

1. While kneeling on a firm surface attempt to sit on the heels (Fig. 36/10a). Measure progress by recording the distance between buttock and the heel of the affected leg.

2. Place the foot of the injured leg on the seat of a dining chair. The heel should be level with the front edge of the seat and must be retained in contact with the seat. The knee is now thrust forwards towards the back of the chair (Fig. 36/10b). The distance between the knee and the back of the chair is measured. This should be compared with the other leg and progress charted.

3. The simple squat position and its variations are the ultimate in knee mobility tests. The ability to progress forwards while squatting, either by moving alternate legs or by hopping on both feet together is a severe test of full flexion (Fig. 36/10c).

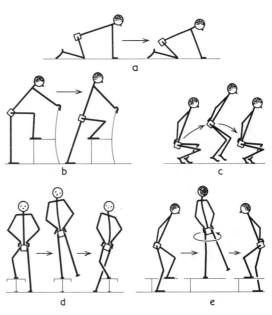

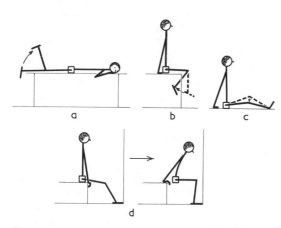

Fig. 36/9

Fig. 36/10

4. Stand alongside a bench with the foot of the injured leg flat on top of the bench. While this foot remains stationary step to the opposite side of the bench with the other foot and then return (Fig. 36/10d).

5. Stand alongside a bench as before, but while extending the injured knee twist around quickly to finish facing the opposite direction and with the sound leg on the opposite side of the bench (Fig. 36/10e). Then reverse the procedure.

EARLY STABILITY TESTS FOLLOWING KNEE INJURY

Any sensation of instability or the actual evidence of it by locking or giving way is the warning sign that further testing should be halted.

1. Long sitting on the floor with the knee fully extended. Initially a plastic ball is kicked with the inside of the foot and ankle (Fig. 36/11a). Progress using a football and then a medicine ball. The routine is repeated with the outside of the foot.

2. The previous test is repeated but with the knee flexed to varying degrees (Fig. 36/11b).

3. These two tests should be repeated in the more functional position of standing but still progressing from straight leg to flexed, and from plastic ball to medicine ball (Fig. 36/11c).

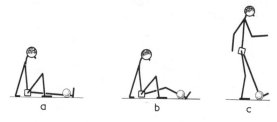

Fig. 36/11

4. Hopping exercises are particularly useful in testing knee stability because of the strain placed upon the joint by making it support the weight of the body. Hop in a circular direction around an object. The specificity of the test is increased by reducing the diameter of the circle or by reversing the direction.

5. A variation on (4) is hopping around a square but making sure that the foot is pointing forwards throughout and that the direction is changed at 90°. Another variation is by describing a figure-of-eight around two objects. Progression is made by decreasing the distance between the objects.

LATER STABILITY TESTS FOLLOWING KNEE INJURY

1. Jumping from heights is another excellent method of testing stability as well as restoring confidence. The three variables to be considered in making the test progressive are the height, the landing surface and the method of landing. Initially, a gymnasium bench may be of sufficient height and the landing made on a rubber mat. The ultimate requirement would be to jump from a height of 3 feet (1m) on to a firm surface and in a crouched position. The important aspect of jumping tests is to ensure that the landing is made with equal weight on both feet. An understandable reluctance and apprehension can be overcome by reducing the height to a minimum and by making the landing surface as reasonably soft as possible to encourage the taking of bodyweight on the affected leg only.

2. An invaluable test of lower limb fitness is that of 'bounding' over a series of benches. If the benches are so placed as to allow only one footstep between them, there is no escape from using the affected leg (Fig. 36/12). The test is a modified hurdling exercise and can

Fig. 36/12

be performed at an increasing speed. Power and coordination are essential qualities in executing a flowing rhythm.

The essential skills of soccer are passing, dribbling, trapping, shooting and tackling. These are useful individual tests in themselves and form a necessary preliminary before progression into the training modifications of the game itself.

Reaction to these tests may be a recurrence of pain, swelling and an increased temperature of the joint area; these are indications of negligence either in observation during the tests or in too rapid a progression.

Testing for fitness is a fascinating challenge which requires careful organisation. Athletes should be made to feel that, in the physiotherapist, they have an ally who is concerned only for their interests and welfare. They must not be made to feel that every test is a personal battle where every deficiency is to be used as evidence to support a pre-determined decision to prevent them from participating. Varying degrees of elation and disappointment are the inevitable companions of fitness testing. Experience is the only tutor in learning to recognise whether a situation demands support and encouragement or guarded optimism and a restraining influence.

The attitude towards injury of athletes varies considerably. The acceptance of pain and physical deficiency with the consequent limitations on skill and ability is often exhibited to remarkable levels. However, experience will also teach one to realise that the decision on fitness which will benefit the athlete in the long-term will be the best decision to make for the short-term.

CHAPTER 37

Rehabilitation in sport

BARRY T. MADDOX BA, MCSP, SRP

PRINCIPLES OF REHABILITATION

The principle aim of rehabilitation is to restore full function after an injury or a disease. The differences between rehabilitation of the average patient and a sportsman are of degree and specificity. While rehabilitation of the average patient ceases when he can walk without a limp and manage stairs, the rehabilitation of the sportsman must continue not only to a much more advanced level of activity, but it must also be designed to meet the specific demands of his sport. It is for this reason that physiotherapists working in the field of sports medicine must be knowledgeable about the sports with which they are involved, not only about individual techniques such as the different types of strokes in racket games, but also about the tactics of the games. Ideally, the physiotherapist should have participated in the sport in order to more fully appreciate it from a player's point of view. There should be a close liaison between physiotherapist and coach, in order to have a direct and logical continuation from treatment to early training. Similarly, the coach should know something about the principles of physical treatment so that communication will not be complicated by misinterpretation of jargon.

Rehabilitation should start at the moment of injury, although perhaps the most important thing at that stage is knowing what not to do. Early treatment is dependent upon the nature and severity of the injury and not initially on the type of sport. The essentials of such first aid are simply to ease pain, limit swelling and encourage early movement without over-stressing the injured part. However, when the acute reaction to the injury is diminishing and early repair has started, the rehabilitation programme becomes more specific to the sport. This programme must have the optimum balance of exercises to promote strength, endurance, flexibility, speed and coordination. This balance should not only fit the sport, but in team games should fit each position on the field. Obviously, forwards in soccer or hockey will need running speed and endurance, while a goalkeeper will need more general bodily speed and agility. Similarly, weightlifters will aim mainly to develop power, sprinters will aim for speed, and marathon runners will want to develop endurance.

Whatever programme is designed for an injured sportsman, he must be absolutely clear about what to do, how to do it, when to do it and how many repetitions to do. The programme must be carefully progressed from day to day, always responding to the 'feedback' from the previous day's work, so that the injured part is allowed to take a little more strain at each stage without ever being suddenly overloaded. This type of regime not only builds up muscle, but actively stimulates the repair process, much in the same way as more callus formation is stimulated if the opposing fragments of a fracture are allowed a little movement rather than complete immobility.

Treating the actual injury is only a part of rehabilitation in sport for it is essential to give exercises to all the unaffected parts of the body, so long as the exercises do not jeopardise the injured part. Such collateral exercises should be strenuous enough to make the patient breathless in order to maintain cardiovascular fitness. With a fairly severe knee injury, for example, exercises to the unaffected parts of the body could include bench press, sit-ups, chinning, curls, press-ups, step-ups with the good leg, etc. The ultimate example of this principle is seen in the Paraplegic Olympic Games.

Although active exercises are the essence of rehabilitation, the physiotherapist in sports medicine requires also the use of other techniques, including electrotherapy and massage. The choice of such supplementary techniques is usually determined not so much by the sport as by the local problems associated with the injury of which the most common are pain, swelling and restricted movement.

LOCAL PROBLEMS

Pain

It must not be forgotten that while, initially, pain is nature's warning that damage is occurring, after an injury the pain is often out of proportion to the force producing it. Its effect then is to over-protect an injured part and so prevent the movements which are vital to normal physiological function.

This does not justify the total ablation of pain by local anaesthesia, but it does mean that pain should be reduced sufficiently to allow the player to move the injured part more easily. In most cases, the degree of pain relief afforded by such physical agents as locally applied ice packs and ultrasound is sufficient, although sometimes analgesic medication is necessary. In such cases soluble aspirin is useful because of its additional anti-inflammatory effect, but equally it must be remembered that aspirin is not a trivial drug and it should always be used with great care. Supportive strapping is also useful in the early stages to protect injuries from unnecessary pain or damage.

Swelling

Ideally, swelling should be prevented by early ice cold compression, elevation and temporary local rest. One of the great skills of the physiotherapist in sports medicine is the recognition on the field or track side of those injuries which are severe enough to develop a swelling. In this context it is helpful to know the individual players, for some players make a fuss over the most minor injuries while others are loathe to admit injury. Similarly, it is useful to feel the 'pulse of the game', for an extended interval created by an injury can allow a losing team to sort out its mistakes. When joint injuries are involved it is important to distinguish between a haemarthrosis, which is usually quite severe and swells within minutes, and a synovitis, which may appear initially as a very trivial injury but takes many hours to swell so that the full extent of this injury is evident only the following morning. Clearly there is little or no real structural damage in many so-called injuries which stop football matches, especially in the professional game. It would be pointless to treat every one of these, especially if it meant taking each player off the field, either temporarily or even for the rest of the game.

When swelling has occurred, its dispersal may be aided mechanically by the following methods:

1. The pumping action of isometric exercises.
2. Ultrasound to the periphery of the swelling.
3. Positioning of a limb so that gravity will assist the drainage of swelling away from the distal parts of the body.
4. At a later stage by effleurage massage and heat, especially if an injury has passed into the chronic stage.

The resolution of large swellings may also be aided by the use of proteolytic enzymes, e.g. trypsin and chymotrypsin (Chymoral Forte). It is advisable not to use any form of heat until after about 48 hours, since the reflex vasodilatation may cause further haemor-

rhage as blood clots are dislodged. It is safer, therefore, not to prescribe the useful home treatment of contrast bathing until at least the third day.

Restricted movements

This problem may be caused by various types of internal joint derangement, but the main causes affecting rehabilitation are protective muscle spasm and joint swelling. Protective muscle spasm is not always accompanied by pain, although it is the patient's conscious or unconscious attempt to avoid pain. If the patient is helped to move the joint without producing too much discomfort, he will start to get his confidence back. This is obviously achieved by pain relieving methods, particularly cryotherapy, and carefully graded movements. Sometimes this means moving in only a limited part of the joint's range, or moving in only one plane, in order to get the patient started.

Intra-articular swelling is a special category of swelling, for most cases of synovitis diminish only with rest, and cannot be dispersed with electrotherapy. The classical treatment for a grossly swollen knee is a Robert Jones bandage, the main effect of which is probably simply to splint the joint, although the pressure may help to prevent further swelling of the joint. With such cases the only definitive rehabilitation is a programme of isometric exercises to maintain the tone in those muscles which pass over the affected joint.

Chronic extra-articular swelling can be a stubborn problem, particularly following a fracture of the lower end of the tibia. While this can be dispersed with elevation, massage and electrotherapy, the swelling can sometimes recur over five or six months. It is important in such cases to support the skin with firm bandaging, otherwise the foot and ankle simulates an elastic bag which readily fills up with fluid. The Coban bandage has been found to be ideal for this purpose, and patients may be instructed to wear it whenever the leg cannot be raised, but not to wear it all the time. Usually the problem is overcome when the calf muscles reach their normal strength and there is a full range of ankle movement.

NON-ACUTE CASES

Not all rehabilitation problems begin with an acute injury. Sometimes a sportsman has had an illness and seeks professional advice about early training, or, perhaps, during a tournament, a player develops a mild febrile condition. While always keeping in mind the fact that strenuous activity can be dangerous following acute febrile conditions, especially those of viral origin, the two main parameters to guide rehabilitation are the pulse and temperature. It is advisable also to check respiratory ventilation and blood pressure. Rehabilitation should not begin until the heart rate and body temperature have both returned to their normal resting levels. The resting heart rate of a top athlete is rarely anywhere as high as the average 72 beats per minute. Once it has returned to normal, the player is tested with a little light activity, aimed at not increasing the pulse rate to more than double its resting level. If the heart rate does not return to normal during a period of rest within the two minutes immediately following the activity, or if there is a resultant increase in body temperature within two hours, the patient is not tested again until the next day, and then with proportionately less activity. If the patient passes these tests, he may be tested two or even three times more the same day, with an increase in activity each time, and then even more the following day. It should be emphasised that this system is very much a 'rule of thumb' and there is a case for not exercising athletes so soon after febrile conditions because of the danger of myocarditis. Ideally, such athletes should be given an electrocardiograph (ECG) before commencing training. Obviously, if the patient feels worse after such exercise, or does not feel ready to begin rehabilitation, it is probably safer to wait a day or so longer. Patients undergoing this regime are advised to drink large quantities of fluid and to rest in well aerated rooms between exercise sessions, at least during the early stages of the programme.

Another type of problem with no history of injury, is the athlete who develops pain only at high levels of performance, for example during a 100m sprint, or after 10 miles (16km) of cross-country running. It is very difficult to locate any abnormality with the usual repertoire of clinical examination and therefore it may be necessary to accompany the athlete to the gymnasium, track or field in order to let him properly demonstrate the problem. Sometimes electrotherapy is indicated but the really critical treatment is to prescribe the optimum ratio between rest and activity. Basically, the principle is to work the athlete hard at the level just below that which evokes pain, occasionally almost producing the pain for a few seconds. Ice packs may be applied immediately after the work-out in order to diminish any inflammatory response which may occur.

A special category of injury, which fortunately is rare, is that which befalls the sportsman who suffers damage to the skull, brain or spinal cord (Fig. 37/1). Initially these patients require emergency medical and surgical treatment which is almost always followed by time in hospital. Such cases may not reach the sports physiotherapist until several weeks or even months after the injury; even then there is much to be done.

One of the main effects of a serious head injury is the extra-dural haemorrhage which can cause pressure on

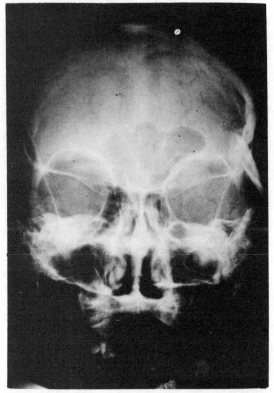

Fig. 37/1 Radiograph of skull showing a depressed fracture of the left temporal bone, caused by a cricket ball striking the side of the skull. The blood vessels which line the inside of the temporal bone are invariably damaged in this type of injury, resulting in an accumulation of blood between the brain and the skull in an extra-dural haemorrhage

the brain and result in a hemiplegia (Fig. 37/2). The introduction of computerised axial tomography has enabled surgeons to localise cerebral haematomata and thus aid the speed and accuracy of decompression surgery. Even then some patients are left with a hemiparesis and varying degrees of spasticity. Treatment is initially by proprioceptive neuromuscular facilitation techniques (PNF), although patients will be started in the gymnasium as soon as possible. It is surprising how soon they can manage simple manoeuvres from sports activities such as stopping, then hitting a hockey ball, or hitting a shuttlecock. This is usually the most enjoyable part of their treatment and often makes demands on the skills of the physiotherapist who should try to extend the patient further every day, while keeping good control.

Injuries to the spinal cord may result in bilateral

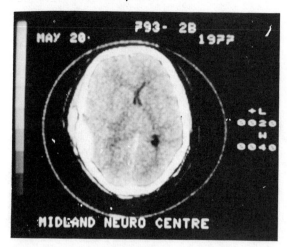

Fig. 37/2 The brain from above, showing an extra-dural haemorrhage beneath the left temporal bone: this view obtained by the use of an EMI scanner. Such scans allow an extra dimension to diagnosis since they are able to localise accurately most accumulations of blood which are not visible on ordinary radiographs. This information allows accurate decompression surgery to be carried out. This patient has since passed academic examinations and leads an active sporting life

paralysis with segmental loss of sensation below the level of the injury. Cervical spine lesions result in tetraplegia while cord lesions at lower levels may result in paraplegia of varying severity. The ultimate achievement by patients with spinal cord injuries will depend on the level of the injury, but like most injuries the personal motivation and the design of the rehabilitation programme will play important roles. The basic principle of the rehabilitation is to make those parts of the body above the lesion as strong as possible and often this will be stronger than a healthy person. The latissimus dorsi muscles with their high level nerve supply and attachment on the iliac crests, are very important and require much attention. This is particularly so with those patients who can be taught to walk with the use of crutches and bracing with calipers. Many paraplegics have achieved world class status in sports such as archery and swimming, as well as becoming competitive in wheelchair basketball and table tennis. Every four years, paraplegics from all over the world meet to take part in the Paralympic Games, which include athletics, lawn bowling, weightlifting, fencing and shooting as well as those sports already mentioned. Many people do not realise that these games are also open to those with cerebral palsy, amputations and who are blind.

TESTING

Whatever the onset of the problem, whether a sudden acute injury or gradual overuse, or some infectious condition, at some point after treatment and rehabilitation has begun, the fitness of the patient will have to be tested. This is usually done at two levels:
1. between treatment and early training, and
2. between advanced training and competitive play.

The first level

In order to make this first step and commence early training, the injured limb should fulfil the following criteria:

1. It must have at least 50 per cent of its normal power measured with 10RM (according to De Lorme, 1945).
2. It must have at least 80 per cent of its full range of movement.
3. It must have less than 20 per cent of its full potential swelling.
4. It must have virtually normal stability, although this may be supported slightly by strapping at this stage.
5. There should be no pain at rest, nor gradual increase in pain as the work-load increases, although slight pain during or immediately after exercise is acceptable.

The patient continues to have physiotherapy during the period of training, so it is at this point that there must be close liaison between the therapist and the trainer; in addition the therapist must understand what the coach or trainer is trying to achieve and what is demanded not only from the sport but also from the level at which the player will ultimately compete.

The second level

This second stage of fitness testing has to be very demanding, otherwise the player returning to the game will be vulnerable to further injury. The more advanced general criteria are:
1. Absence of pain.
2. No swelling.
3. Full power.
4. Full range of joint movement.
5. Full extensibility of muscles, particularly those which pass over two joints, e.g. the hamstrings.
6. Endurance, e.g. minimum jog of 20 minutes or 2km.
7. Speed, e.g. 100m sprint and shuttle runs.

In addition to these general criteria, there are specific tests depending on the types of skills and situations demanded by the sport. These include, for example, block tackle in soccer, two leg jump in hockey, scrummaging in rugby and lunging in badminton. It is only when a player has passed all these tests that the aim of rehabilitation has been achieved, that is, the attainment of match fitness.

The objectives and methods of rehabilitation in sport have been discussed. What must be emphasised is that the physiotherapist working in this field must have total commitment. His effort should equal that of the sportsman as he fights to achieve physical and mental perfection. Each stage of rehabilitation must be carefully observed and analysed, always making sure that there is a sound reason for every variation in treatment and advice. It is only then that sportsmen can achieve the necessary fitness to overcome the apparent limitations imposed by time, space and gravity. It is only then that physiotherapists may claim a small part in the establishing of new world records or the winning of gold medals.

REFERENCE

De Lorme, T. L. (1945). Restoration of muscle power by heavy resistance exercises. *Journal of Bone and Joint Surgery*, **27**, 645–667.

Addresses of some useful sports associations

UNITED KINGDOM

Alpine Club
74 South Audley Street
London W1Y 5FF

Amateur Boxing Association
Francis House, Francis Street
London SW1P 1DE

Amateur Rowing Association
6 Lower Mall
Hammersmith
London W6 9DT

Amateur Swimming Association
Hon Sec: N W Sarsfield MC
Harold Fern House
Derby Square
Loughborough LE11 0AL

Association of Chartered Physiotherapists in Sports Medicine
Mrs Paula Wilcox
45 Uxbridge Road
Stanmore
Middlesex HA7 3LH

The Back Pain Association
Grundy House
Somerset Road
Teddington TW11 7TD

British Association of Sport and Medicine
Hon Sec: D P Chapman MCSP
Half Moon House
Burwash Road, Heathfield
East Sussex

British Canoe Union
Flexel House
45/47 High Street
Addlestone, Weybridge
Surrey KT15 1JV

British Olympic Association
1/2 John Princes Street
London W1M 0DH

The British Psychological Society
St Andrews House
48 Princess Road East
Leicester LE1 7DR

British Sub-Aqua Club
16 Upper Woburn Place
London WC1H 0QW

British Society of Sports Psychology
Hon Sec: Ms P Crisfield, Division of
 Sport and Science
Crewe and Alsager College of Higher
 Education
Alsager, Stoke-on-Trent ST7 2HL

British Surf Association
16/18 Bournemouth Road
Poole, Dorset
BH14 0ES

British Universities Sports Federation
28 Woburn Square
London WC1H 0AD

British Water Ski Federation
16 Upper Woburn Place
London WC1H 0QL

Central Council for Physical Recreation
Francis House, Francis Street
London SW1P 1DE

Chartered Society of Physiotherapy
14 Bedford Row
London WC1R 4ED

English Basketball Association
Calomax House, Lupton Avenue
Leeds LS9 7DD

Ergonomics Society
Department of Human Sciences
Loughborough University of Technology
Loughborough
Leicestershire

Federation Internationale de Medecine Sportive
Secretary General: Farnham Park Rehabilitation
  Centre
Farnham Royal, Slough
Buckinghamshire SL2 3LR

The Football Association
16 Lancaster Gate
London W2 3LW

The Golf Society of Great Britain
Mrs E J Drummond
Gleneagles, Maddox Park
Little Bookham
Surrey KT23 3BW

Institute of Biology
41 Queen's Gate
London SW7 5HU

Institute of Sport Medicine
Ling House, 10 Nottingham Place
London W1M 4AX

International Trauma Foundation
Battle Bridge House
300 Gray's Inn Road
London WC1 8DU

Keep Fit Association
16 Upper Woburn Place
London WC1H 0QW

The Lawn Tennis Association
Barons Court
London W14 NEG

Martial Arts Commission
Secretary, D Mitchell
4–16 Deptford Bridge
London SE8 4JS

National Documentation Centre for Sport, Physical
  Education and Recreation
The University of Birmingham
PO Box 363
Birmingham B15 2TT

National Ski Federation of Great Britain
118 Eaton Square
London SW1W 9AF

Organisation of Physiotherapists in Private Practice
% Miss J M Botteley
90 High Street, Henley in Arden
Solihull, West Midlands

Physical Education Association of Great Britain and
  Northern Ireland
Ling House
10 Nottingham Place
London W1M 4AX

Remedial Gymnasts Association
Public Relations Officer
Mrs S Harwood, 1 Johns Villas
Sivell Place, Heavitree
Exeter

Road Runners Club
Secretary: Judith Goodsell
10 Honywood Road
Colchester
Essex
CO3 3AS

Robert Menzies Foundation
6 St James's Square
London SW1Y 4LD

Royal Ballet Company
155 Talgarth Road
London W14 9DE

Royal Life Saving Society
Dexborough House
14 Devonshire Street
London W1N 2AT

Royal Society of Health
13 Grosvenor Place
London SW1X 7EN

Rugby Football Union
Whitton Road
Twickenham
Middlesex

Society of Orthopaedic Medicine
201 Albany Street
London NW1

Society of Sports Sciences
Hon Sec: Mr D Kellett
Didsbury School of Education
Manchester Polytechnic
Manchester M20 8RR

The Sports Council
16 Upper Woburn Place
London WC1H 0QP

UNITED STATES OF AMERICA

American Alliance for Health, Physical Education,
Recreation and Dance
1201 Sixteenth Street NW
Washington DC 20036
USA

The American College of Sports Medicine
1440 Monroe Street
Madison, Wisconsin 53706
USA

American Medical Association
535 Dearborn Street
Chicago, Illinois 60610
USA

The Human Factors Society
Box 1369, Santa Monica
California 90406
USA

International Council of Health, Physical Education
and Recreation
1201 Sixteenth Street NW
Washington DC 20036
USA

International Recreation Association
345 East 46 Street
New York
NY 10017
USA

President's Council on Physical Fitness and Sport
Washington DC 20201
USA

United States Track Coaches Association
745 State Circle
Ann Arbor
Michigan 48104
USA

CANADA

Canadian Association of Health, Physical Education
and Recreation
333 River Road
Ottawa, Ontario
Canada KIL 8B9

Canadian Medical Association
1867 Atta Vista Drive
Ottawa
Ontario
Canada K1G 3Y6

INDIA

Netaji Subhas National Institute of Sports
Patiala
India

NEW ZEALAND

New Zealand Federation of Sports Medicine
PO Box 26–179
Auckland 3
New Zealand

BELGIUM

Association of Sports Medicine of Belgium
Secretary, Dr J J S'Jongers HILOLabMensPhysiol
Vrije Universiteit Brussel
Campus Oefenplein
Brussels
Belgium

FISU (Student Sport)
Boulevard de Tervuren 101
Leuven
Belgium

International Council of Military Sport
119 Avenue Franklin Roosevelt, Brussels 5
Belgium

BRAZIL

Federacao Brasileira de Medicine Desportiva
De E H de Rose
Sede Associacao de Medicina Desportiva
AMRIGS Av Sen Salgado Filho 135
Porto Allegre
Brasil

BULGARIA

Bulgarian Academy of Sciences
Acad G Bontchev str 61 1
1113 Sofia
Bulgaria

CHINA

Research Institute of Sport Science
Tiyiguon Road
Beiijung (Peking)
China

EAST GERMANY

Zentraalinstitut fur Arbeitsmedizin der DDR
1134 Berlin
Noldnerstr 40–42

EIRE

Irish Association of Sport and Medicine
Dr Moira O'Brien
Department of Anatomy, Royal College of Surgeons
St Stevens Green
Dublin 2
Eire

FRANCE

French Olympic Preparation Centre
88800 Vittel
France

International Council of Sport and Physical Education
UNESCO House
Place de Fontenoy
Paris 7e
France

WEST GERMANY

IAKS (Sports Facilities)
D–5000 Koln 40
Kolner Strasse 68
Koln
West Germany

Institute fur Sportstattenbau
Sportochschule
Carl Diem, Weg
Koln-Mungersdorf
West Germany

ISRAEL

The IRA Memorial Foundation for Development of
*   Human Engineering*
5 Shderot Haoranim
Ramat Efal 52960
Tel-Aviv
Israel

ITALY

Instituto Medicina Sport
Via Campi Sportivi 46
1–00197 Roma
Italy

International Society of Sports Psychology
Edizioni Luigi Pozzi
Via Panama 68
Roma 00198
Italy

JAPAN

The Human Ergology Research Association
Business Centre for Academic Societies Japan
4–16 Yayoi 2 – chome
Bunkyo – ku
Tokyo 113
Japan

Japan Amateur Sports Association
Kishi Memorial Hall
1–1–1 Jinnan, Shibuya – ku
Tokyo
Japan

Japanese Society of Physical Education
% Department of Physical Education
Faculty of Education, University of Tokyo
Hongo 7–3–1
Bunkyo – ku
Tokyo 113
Japan

Japan Olympic Committee
Kishi Memorial Hall
1–1–1 Jinnan, Shibuya – ku
Tokyo
Japan

Meiji Life Foundation of Health and Welfare
1–1–18 Shiroganedai
Minato-ku
Tokyo
Japan

POLAND

Institute of Sport (Poland)
Ceglowska Str 68/70
01–890 Warsaw
Poland

*Polish Institute of Biocybernetics and Biomedical
    Engineering*
KRV Street 55
00–818 Warsaw
Poland

PORTUGAL

International Physical Education Association (FIEP)
Ave 5 do Outubro
50 r/c – D to Lisbon
Portugal

Index